MW01141284

Courage and Innovation

The Story of the Men and Women Who Created Canada's Airport Authorities

David J. Langlois

Sans Souci Publishing

12 rue Somerset, Hudson, QC, J0P 1H0,
CANADA

Courage and Innovation -

The Story of the Men and Women Who
Created Canada's Airport Authorities

Copyright © David John Langlois 2019

David John Langlois has asserted his right
to be identified as the Author of this Work.

All rights reserved. No part of this
publication may be reproduced, storied in
a retrieval system or transmitted in any
form or by any means, electronic,
mechanical, photocopying, recording or
otherwise without prior written permission
of the author.

The author has researched material and
interpreted facts from that research.
Whilst every effort has been made to
validate research material the author
cannot held responsible for the statements
contained in the cited material.

ISBN 978-0-9809730-3-7 (Hardcover Edition)

ISBN 978-0-9809730-1-3 (Paperback Edition)

ISBN 978-0-9809730-2-0 (Digital Edition)

For Patricia.

Friend, soulmate, & believer.

"Everyone has a story.
The least we can do is make sure it's told."

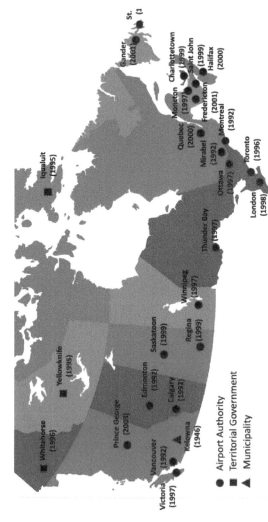

The National Airports System: Locations and Dates of Transfer

Legend:
- Airport Authority
- Territorial Government
- Municipality

Whitehorse (1996)
Yellowknife (1995)
Iqaluit (1995)
Prince George (2003)
Edmonton (1992)
Saskatoon (1999)
Calgary (1992)
Vancouver (1992)
Kelowna (1946)
Regina (1999)
Winnipeg (1997)
Victoria (1997)
Thunder Bay (1997)
Gander (2001)
St. (1
Charlottetown (1999)
Moncton (1997)
Saint John (1999)
Halifax (2000)
Fredericton (2001)
Quebec (2000)
Montreal (1992)
Mirabel (1992)
Ottawa (1997)
Toronto (1996)
London (1998)

Source: Pathways: Connecting Canada's Transportation System to the W

Table of Contents

Acknowledgements

It is an effort fraught with danger to acknowledge the help of the many individuals who spoke with me, sent me documents, allowed me to mine their memories, and generally suffered through my many questions. If I have left anyone out the error is mine.

For their invaluable assistance I give thanks to Steve Baker, Muir Barber, Robert Basque, Paul Benoit, Chrisie Berry, Jim Blake, Randy Bogle, Jean-Jacques Bourgeault, Bill Bredt, Drew Britz, Mary Brooks, Wayne Brownlee, Richard Bureau, Derek Burney, Nick Careen, Joyce Carter, Lino Celeste, Leila Chaibi, Sylvain Choinière, Terry Chou, Graham Clarke, John Cloutier, David Collenette, Keith Collins, Meg Comiskey, Skip Cormier, Jim Cowan, Bob Creamer, Darren Dalton, Vince Dancho, Deana De Roche, Mark Duncan. Doug Eyford, Michael Farquhar, Jocelyne Ferland, Gaëtan Gagné, Gerry Gallant, Joanne Gallant, John Gibson, Ron Gilbertson, Daniel-Robert Gooch, John Hansen, Michael Hayward, Nancy Healey, Charlene Hewitt, Jeremy Hill, Wilson Hoffe, Lynn Holwell, Lisa Dwyer Hurteau, David Innes, Jack Jamieson, Richard Jasieniuk, Otto Lang, Bernie LeBlanc, Rex LeDrew, Lee (Leafy) Lindsay, Don Mazankowski, Tyler MacAfee, Wayne McAllister, Scott McFadden, Andrew McGillivray, Nick Mulder, Doug Newson, Ronald Odynski, Romano Pagliari, Pierre Payette, Wayne Pidskalny, Jacques Pigeon, Nick Purich, Philippe Rainville, David Reble, Darcy Rezak, Graham Ross, Edgar Rouleau, Rich Roy, Mike Seabrook, Michael Senzilet, Steve Shaw, Gerry St. Germain, Derrick Stanford, Robert Stromberg, Kay Tenn, Mike Tretheway, Derrick Thue, John Watson and Bill Whalen. Without their help and insight my task would have been far harder.

For the histories of airports prior to 1988 I have relied extensively on the *History of Canadian Airports*, written by T. M. McGrath in 1983, and revised for a second edition in 1988. His contribution to my understanding of Canadian airports prior to 1988 was invaluable.

For the chapter on the British Commonwealth Air Training Plan (BCATP) I relied heavily on the *Aerodrome of Democracy: Canada and the British Commonwealth Air Training Plan 1939-1945* by F. J. Hatch. Written in 1983 the book is a unique resource for anyone interested in a compete history of the BCATP.

I am indebted to Michael Farquhar for allowing me access to his personal files. The speeches he gave in the 1980's and 1990's are a mine of information and I have used them liberally.

Thanks to Mike Hayward for lending me the interview notes made in 1995 by Shirlee Matheson for her book *A Western Welcome to the World – Calgary International Airport*. Also her updated notes from 2015-16. The notes allowed me to write the Calgary chapter with a degree of assurance that otherwise I would not have had.

Mike Tretheway deserves much credit not only for explaining the economics of aeronautical services but also for a much detail about how YVR got to be where it is today. He is a gold-mine of information.

Rich Roy deserves mention for his editing of the manuscript and his comments on circular logic, parallel construction, incomplete thoughts, repetition, grammar and general content. Any faults remain mine.

I relied upon the oral histories of many folk who graciously allowed me to interview them. Without their time and assistance these stories would not be told. I am just the historian, the vehicle. They are the ones who put their time, effort, energy and creative abilities into creating these community assets.

Most of all, to my wife, Patricia Halford, for her support, patience and understanding over the years as I researched, interviewed, read and wrote. This book is dedicated to her.

Acronyms

The following acronyms are used in this history:

AA	Airport Authority
ACAA	Atlantic Canada Airports Association
ADAP	Airport Development Aid Program
ADM	Aeroports de Montréal (Dorval and Mirabel)
ADM	Assistant Deputy Minister
AIF	Airport Improvement Fee
AG	Auditor General for Canada
AIP	Airport Improvement Program
ASP	Airport Security Program
ATB	Air Terminal Building
ATAB	Airport Transfer Advisory Board
ATTF	Airport Transfer Task Force
BAA	British Airports Authority
BAA Plc	The private sector company created out of the BAA
BCATP	British Commonwealth Air Training Plan
BTACP	Board of Trade Airport Planning Committee
CAA	Canadian Airport Authority
CAB	Canadian Air Board
CAC	Canadian Aviation Corps
CAC	Canadian Airports Council
CAD	Canadian Dollar
CATSA	Canadian Air Transport Security Agency
CEO	Chief Executive Officer
CFO	Chief Financial Officer
CGAO	Civil Government Air Operations
CGTAS	Canadian Government Trans-Atlantic Air Service
CNR	Canadian National Railway
COS	Chief of Staff
CPI	Consumer Price Index
CPR	Canadian Pacific Railway
CSCE	Canadian Society of Civil Engineers
DFC	Distinguished Flying Cross
DG	Director General
DHist	Directorate of History, Department of National Defence
DM	Deputy Minister
DOT	Department of Transport
DSC	Distinguished Service Cross
DSO	Distinguished Service Order
EASA	Edmonton Air Services Authority
EFT	Elementary Flying Training

EFTS	Elementary Flying Training School
ERAA	Edmonton Regional Airports Authority
GTAA	Greater Toronto Airport Authority
ICAO	International Civil Aviation Organization
LAA	Local Airport Authority
MP	Member of Parliament (Federal)
NAS	National Airports System
PFC	Passenger Facility Charge
plc	public limited company
PMO	Prime Minister's Office
PPP	Public Private Partnership
RAF	Royal Air Force
RAFTA	Regional Airports Task Force Association
RCAF	Royal Canadian Air Force
RBC	Royal Bank of Canada
RFC	Royal Flying Corps
RJ	Regional Jet
RNAS	Royal Naval Air Service
SeMS	Security Management System
SMS	Safety Management System
TC	Transport Canada
TCA	Trans-Canada Air Lines
WW1	World War 1
WW2	World War 2
YEG	Edmonton, AB aerodrome
YFC	Fredericton, PE aerodrome
YHZ	Halifax, NS aerodrome
YMX	Montréal Mirabel, QC aerodrome
YOW	Ottawa, ON aerodrome
YQB	Québec City, QC aerodrome
YQM	Moncton, NB aerodrome
YQR	Regina, SK aerodrome
YQT	Thunder Bay, ON aerodrome
YQX	Gander, NL aerodrome
YSJ	Saint John, NB aerodrome
YUL	Montréal Dorval, QC aerodrome
YVR	Vancouver, BC aerodrome
YWG	Winnipeg, MN aerodrome
YXE	Saskatoon, SK aerodrome
YXS	Prince George, BC aerodrome
YYT	St. John's, NL aerodrome
YXU	London, ON aerodrome
YYC	Calgary, AB aerodrome
YYG	Charlottetown, PE aerodrome

Chapter 1: Introduction

*"Sometimes it's the people who no one imagines
anything of who do the very thing that no one can
imagine."*[1]

In the 1980's some quite unassuming people, who no one imagined anything of, as the above quote so aptly puts it, put into motion a sequence of events that ultimately created the Airport Authorities. They did the very thing that no one could imagine.

This is the story of those people and the Airport Authorities they created. It tells how the Airport Authorities came to be governed and managed; how the Airport Authorities have shown that a locally managed airport can be far more responsive to the needs of its community than was possible when Transport Canada ran the airports; and how the Airport Authority may contribute to that community's economic health to a far greater extent than anyone could have imagined. The success of the Airport Authorities has shown that the faith imparted to those women and men who accepted the responsibility of creating them was well placed.

The Department of Transport (DOT) airport model worked fairly well during the late 1940's and early-to-mid 1950's. But by the late 1950's air travel was becoming more competitive, especially over the lucrative North Atlantic air routes, and the volume of passengers carried by airlines began to grow dramatically. The DOT's plans for development and re-development of airports under its control never seemed to get ahead of the curve, and throughout the 1960's the DOT found itself reacting to events instead of being ahead of them.

By the early 1970's it was readily apparent that a large and burgeoning bill for increased aerodrome services was waiting in the

---

[1] As said by Alan Turing (played by Benedict Cumberbatch) in the movie *The Imitation Game*, written by Graham Moore. Black Bear Pictures, 2104.

wings for the Canadian federal government if it was to respond to this increased demand. Given that the Canadian economy had gone through strained times in the 1970's and 1980's, and the national debt was so very large, such a bill was politically unacceptable to the federal government.

Other countries (such as the United States, Great Britain and Australia) had begun to investigate the possibility of using Public Private Partnerships (PPP's) in the development and administration of areas which formerly had been the sole domain of the public sector. Roads, railways, electrical generating stations, dams, hydro networks, and telecommunications networks were all candidates for a PPP since these were all capital-intensive projects which served a public good. England had privatized its major airports in the 1960's with the creation of the British Airports Authority. The United States had a well-developed airport industry that went hand-in-fist with the airlines. It was not a great leap to apply these principles to the air transport industry and, in Canada at least, to the worry of finding a solution to the cost of repairing, maintaining, and re-building the country's major aerodromes.

This book attempts to put in perspective the issue of Canadian airport PPPs. Why did aviation so quickly become such an important part of the country's transportation fabric in the 1930's? What was the impetus for the creation of the British Commonwealth Air Training Plan (BCATP) wherein Canada trained more than 131,000 aircrew from Canada, England, South Africa, Australia, and New Zealand (and the United States, prior to its entry into WW2 in 1941)? Why did the 190 aerodromes built for the BCATP become the core of Canada's air transport system? How did the governance of such a large number of aerodromes, dispersed over a vast country, become the responsibility of the DOT (eventually renamed Transport Canada)? Who developed a "one-size fits all" approach to the aerodromes? Why were the Airport Authorities created? Who were the (sometimes outsized) personalities involved? When, and how, was the policy surrounding the privatization of aerodromes developed? And why was the process called "devolution"?

I have attempted to answer these questions. The book is a modest addition to the outstanding work undertaken in the 1970's by T.

M. McGrath when he published his comprehensive *History of Canadian Airports* in 1983. A second edition of the book was published in 1988, however the creation of the Airports Authorities in Canada was still an idea at that time, and McGrath mentions them only in passing.

In forming the Airports Authorities, Canada has created something unique. It is not like the British Airports Authority which although it is privatized has a degree of economic regulation, nor is it like the American airports, in which the U.S. federal and municipal governments have direct political control over them. Often the operators of an American airport are essentially an extension of the municipal administration, and operators are subject to the whims of a political arena and of the airlines which use the airport. In Canada the Airport Authority Boards of Directors are nominated by municipal, regional, provincial and federal governments, by local socio-economic groups such as the Board of Trade or the Chamber of Commerce, by various labour or professional organizations, or by the Airport Authority Boards themselves. When a vacancy occurs, the Boards write a statement of competencies, give that statement to the nominator, and ask for the names of two or three nominees. The Board then decides who of the nominees would be the best "fit" with the existing Board. The Board is the Airport Authority's governor, with a single link to staff through the CEO.

As you read this book you will notice two distinct and sometimes contradictory themes.

The first theme is that the public servants responsible for the creation of the Airport Authorities had the courage to keep the public interest at heart. The lands the airports sat on were in almost all cases strategic assets of Canada and they believed the lands should not be alienated. They believed that it was their responsibility to gain for the Canadian taxpayer the best return on the previous 60 years of investment into the national airports system[2]. In order to gain that "best return" they worked

---

[2] The actual investment is difficult to determine with any precision because the financial records no longer exist. From my research it would seem that the total amount invested over a period of 60 years by Canada into the 22 airports which are managed by 21 Airport Authorities, from their creation in the 1920's and

innovatively, faithfully and professionally to implement government and ministerial policy. They constantly had to keep in mind that what they were doing had to bear public scrutiny. They were stewards of public property and were responsible for husbanding these resources.

The second theme is that in many instances the desire of the public servants to get the best deal for Canadians was seen by the private sector as hard-headed, unreasonable and difficult. You will read that point-of-view in the individual accounts of the creation of the airport authorities. The private sector teams who were trying to create their airport authority quite often could not understand why things took so long, and needed to be done in so much detail. All they could see were the legal bills piling up. They had little or no understanding of the restraints under which the public sector worked and they frequently got frustrated at the slow pace of things.

But in the end you will read that most of the negotiating team members for the Authorities expressed respect for their public sector counterparts. At the end, once the lease was signed, they appreciated the hard work and effort put into arriving at an equitable solution.

Another item you may notice when reading this book is the change that came over the airport staff when they went from being members of the public service to private sector employees. In the first days of transfer a great number of the employees thought of themselves still as members of the public service and, depending on the acumen of the managers, it took a little, or a lot, of time for the staff to realize that they were now private sector employees. Eventually, however, they came to realize that their job was primarily customer service. I think that the following vision statement[3] from the Saskatoon Airport Authority exemplifies this change in attitude:

_____

1930's to when they became Airport Authorities in the 1990's and 2000's, is anywhere from $8 to $10 billion (actual dollars, not accounting for inflation).

[3] *Where the SKY meets YXE*, Saskatoon Airport Authority 2016 Annual Report.

Introduction

To continuously advance the growth of our region as a centre for commercial aviation excellence by:

- *Ensuring excellence in safety and security*

- *Surpassing expectations through a culture of superior customer service*

- *Seamlessly connecting Saskatchewan's communities to the world*

- *Operating efficiently with care to the environment*

- *Successfully partnering with our stakeholders*

- *Developing and empowering our people*

At the core of everything we do, we are accountable for our actions, always being honest, ethical and respectful of resources, the treatment of our customers and each other.

Being the best in our business

Primary to our business is minimizing all risks to provide a safe, secure, and healthy environment. As good corporate citizens, we value innovation, operational excellence and continuous improvement. We responsibly manage our assets to deliver environmental stewardship, corporate citizenship and regional prosperity.

Our people and partners

Our people grow our business. We work together as a team to foster a cooperative environment that values our accomplishments and exceptional performance. We succeed when our partners do, and we proactively seek opportunities to collaborate with them to advance the success of all.

Our customers

We provide facilities and services that are driven by customer expectation and strive to provide an airport experience that is genuinely valued by our guests.

In 2003 I conducted my first Performance Review of a Canadian Airport Authority. The Reviews are a requirement of the Ground Lease between the Airport Authority and Transport Canada, and must be done at least once every five years. Since then I have conducted more than 45 such reviews at 16 airports across Canada.

Over the years there has been a substantial maturing of the work conducted by the Airport Authorities and at one point I began to think that a record of that work would be worthwhile. History tends to happen to us when we aren't looking, and we sometimes need to make a conscious effort to record what we have seen.

As I worked with the Airport Authorities I began to understand what a success they have been. Since 1992 they have invested more than $26 billion[4] in infrastructure, almost all of that in their local communities, and paid more than $6 billion[5] in rent to the federal government. An amount that no one in government or the private sector would have thought possible in 1992. And they have done that at no cost to the Canadian taxpayer.

This book addresses in a very small way some of the issues that were not addressed by the original leases, or have arisen over time, such as staff training, inequitable rent, what to do when the lease expires, or the safety and security requirements placed on the airports after 9/11.

Finally, there is analysis of the costs involved in running the airports, and how that relates to the airlines. As of 2018 an airport authority could expect to see the following as a percent of total revenue:

- Air operations - 30%;
- Airport Improvement Fee – 30%;
- Non-aeronautical operations (concessions, parking, commercial leasing) – 40%.

In other words, in today's world the airlines' contribution to the airport's revenue through landing fees and terminal fees is about 30% of the airport authority's total revenue, whereas 30 years ago it was 60%, or even 70%, of total revenue. The Airport Authorities were very quick to realize that such reliance upon a single revenue source was an economic danger and they put in place strategic plans to diversify revenue sources. Consequently, as more and

---

[4] $31.6 billion in 2018 dollars. All references to money throughout are to Canadian dollars – CAD.

[5] $7.8 billion in 2018 dollars.

more of the airport's revenue is derived from non-aeronautical sources the impact of the airline becomes less and less. Which leads us to a paradox: an airport is the only place from where an airplane may operate, but its contribution to the airport may, eventually, be quite small.

One key thing for the reader to remember is that the overall costs of the airport system in 1992 went from a $750 million drain to the Canadian taxpayer (which in inflation adjusted terms is $1.2 billion in 2018) to a rent income to the federal government of $400 million a year, which means the Canadian taxpayer is $1.8 billion a year better off. That is an effect really worth highlighting as one of the consequences of the devolution policy.

The book is in large part based on the memories of those who were there at the beginning. As an historian, access to primary sources is paramount. It is those who were there at the time who are the best source of information, even though their memory and point-of-view is their own, and sometimes memory fades. But if you take that bias into consideration, and you are able to cross-check with several other sources for the same issue, then maybe, just maybe, you can arrive at the best version of what happened. That is what I hope I have done here.

Unfortunately, many of the founding members of the Airport Authorities, and the public servants who worked at Transport Canada, have died over the intervening years. They were the custodian of the memory of those times, and from the comments I heard from others about them I wished I had had the opportunity to speak with some of them.

All of those who formed the organizing committees that eventually morphed into the airport authorities were the movers and shakers of their communities, and they put heart and soul into ensuring that "their" local airport got what it deserved. They had a passion for the job that went far beyond just wanting to ensure their airport survived. So too were the federal public servants who fought for the Queen. They had intellect, and energy, and foresight, and an endurance that would not let them fail. They were tough negotiators, looking to get the best for the Canadian public. They wanted the devolution to succeed, and to succeed far beyond what anyone thought that it would. Both groups did the very thing that no one could imagine.

I hope that this book serves as a memento of their foresight and commitment. They paved the way with hard work.

Perhaps Ben Franklin said it best "Human felicity is produced not so much by great pieces of good fortune …, as by little advantages that occur every day."[6]

David J. Langlois
Hudson, Québec, April 2019

---

[6] *The Autobiography of Benjamin Franklin*, Amazon Classics, Seattle, WA, USA, p. 136.

Chapter 2: Historical Context

Early Days

Aviation in Canada began in August 1840 at Saint John, New Brunswick, when Louis Anselm Lauriat became the first person to complete a balloon ascent in Canada, which he did in his hot-air balloon *Star of the East*. He survived the experience but never again went up into the air.

The first passenger flight occurred 16 years later, on September 8, 1856, when Eugène Godard, operating a balloon called Canada (the first lighter-than-air device constructed in Canada), carried three passengers from Montréal to Pointe-Olivier, Québec, a distance of about 20km almost due East of Montréal. The balloon landed safely.

The first powered heavier-than-air flight in Canada occurred on Bras d'Or Lake at Baddeck, Nova Scotia on February 23, 1909, when John Alexander Douglas McCurdy piloted the Silver Dart over a flight of less than 1 kilometer.

Later that same year, in August, McCurdy and F.W. Baldwin, both graduates of the University of Toronto School of Practical Science, demonstrated the Silver Dart and the Baddeck No.1, a second aircraft built in Canada, to Canadian military authorities at Camp Petawawa. Both aircraft were damaged during the demonstrations and so McCurdy and Baldwin did not impress the military authorities. McCurdy later flew a record-setting over-water flight from Florida to Cuba in 1910. Although a record for an over-the-water flight, he didn't quite make it and landed in the water a few miles off-shore. He survived.

In 1910 two large aviation exhibitions were held at Montréal[7] and Toronto[8], where several Canadian aviation records were set.

---

[7] In Pointe-Claire, just behind the current City Hall on Blvd. St. Jean. At the time the area was known as Lakeside.

[8] Tretheway Farm, Weston, at the corner of Jane Street and Tretheway Drive, later known as De Lesseps Field. Used by De Havilland and Canadian Airways, it closed in 1940. Although the hangar was still in existence in 1965 the site is now occupied by 20 storey apartment buildings.

In October 1910, at an air exhibition near Belmont, New York, Grace Mackenzie[9] and her sisters became the first Canadian women to fly.

The first aviation fatality in Canada, and the only one before WW1, was John Bryant who was killed in a crash in Victoria, British Columbia on 6 August 1913. Bryant was visiting British Columbia from the US with his wife Alys McKey Bryant, who was also a pilot, and their Curtiss biplane. Earlier in the trip Alys had become the first woman to pilot a plane in Canada.

More than 23,000 Canadians served in the British air services during WW1 (Royal Flying Corps, Royal Naval Air Service, and, after April 1918, the Royal Air Force (RAF)), with more than 1,500 killed. Billy Bishop, William George Barker and Alan Arnett McLeod were awarded the Victoria Cross. More than 180 Canadian pilots achieved the designation "ace", with five or more credited victories. Canadian aircrew served in every operational theatre during WW1, and in roles including air-to-air combat, bombing, air photography and artillery spotting.

In 1915 the Curtiss Aeroplane and Motor Company of New York set up a small plant in Toronto for manufacture of the JN-4 training aircraft. The Curtiss factory built 20 aircraft, with pontoon float landing gear, which were exported to Spain. This was the first export of Canadian-built aircraft. The company was soon purchased by the Canadian government and operated as Canadian Aeroplanes Ltd. By the end of WW1 the factory had built 2,900 aircraft, including an order of 1,000 JN-4s, completed in three months and shipped to the United States for pilot training on their entry into the war. Canadian Aeroplanes Ltd. stopped aircraft construction at the end of the war.

In spite of the many Canadians in military aviation, the Canadian government had shown little interest in organizing its own air force. Canadian politicians made no attempt to fund flight training, aircraft purchase, or construction of airfields. The Canadian Aviation Corps (CAC), with only three members, was

---

[9] Daughter of Sir William Mackenzie. Sir William was known for the erection of a huge trestle bridge across the Mountain Creek gorge in the Beaver River valley in British Columbia. Designed by W. A. Doans, the bridge rose 150 feet and was 1,070 feet in length, reputedly one of the largest wooden trestles ever built.

founded in 1914 by Sir Sam Hughes.[10] The CAC had an ineffective false start, never flying in combat, and the only aircraft in its possession was abandoned after a few months. Canadians seeking flight training, aside from a few who entered schools at Toronto and Vancouver, either had to travel to enlist in French or British air forces, or received training when the British Royal Air Force (RAF) set up schools in Canada in 1917. A Canadian Air Force was established in early 1918, but it was disbanded shortly after the end of the war. Not until 1920 was a permanent Canadian Air Force established.

Many Canadians had aviation training due to the war, and by 1919 surplus aircraft were plentiful. The first paying passenger flight in Canada occurred in 1920, between Winnipeg and The Pas. Although the total number of aviation companies, registered aircraft, and registered pilots then declined between 1920 and 1924, the freight carriage had increased greatly. Canadian aviation was slowly transforming from the experimental era to the commercial era.

At the end of the war the United States abandoned to Canada several surplus Curtiss HS flying boats that had been used for antisubmarine patrols. These aircraft were donated to the Canadian government and were heavily used in the immediate post-war period. Seaplanes could use lakes and rivers instead of airstrips, making them ideal for exploring remote regions (of which in Canada there is much – even today). The flying boats were used both by the nascent Royal Canadian Air Force (RCAF), and by forestry companies seeking to patrol their logging areas for forest fires.

---

[10] The idea of a Canadian Aviation Corps was conceived by Colonel Sam Hughes, Canada's Minister of Militia and Defence. Hughes had asked British authorities how Canada could help the war effort in the field of military aviation. Britain suggested that Canada could help by supplying military aviators. Hughes appointed Ernest Lloyd Janney as provisional commander and authorized him to spend up to $5,000 on an aircraft. A Burgess-Dunne floatplane was purchased in the United States, shipped to Vermont and then flown to Valcartier, Quebec where it was taken apart, crated, and shipped to England. Janney and the two other CAC members, Lieutenant W. F. Sharpe, a pilot, and Staff Sergeant H. A. Farr, a mechanic, accompanied the aircraft. The aircraft was left abandoned and damaged on Salisbury Plain, having never flown any combat operations. By May 1915, the CAC had dissolved.

Aircraft manufacturing in Canada restarted in 1923 in Montréal. The Canadian Vickers company took on a contract to build eight flying boats for the new RCAF and the Noorduyn company began producing the Noorduyn Norseman which was used in bush flying operations throughout Canada. The Norseman was adopted by the US Army Air Force during WW2 and many units were produced. War surplus aircraft gave way to types specifically designed for civilian service. By the 1930s enclosed cabins greatly improved pilot and passenger comfort.

Although mail had been carried by air in various demonstrations throughout the early 1920s, it was not until 1927 that the Post Office started regular use of air mail.

The Canadian Air Board (CAB) was founded 1919 and had regulatory control over all civil and military aviation. It was merged into the Department of National Defence in 1923. The Aeronautics Act of 1919 established Federal control over aviation and gave the legislative authority for air regulations. All aviation, civil and military, was under Canadian Air Force (later the Royal Canadian Air Force - RCAF) control until 1926. In that year, the Directorate of Civil Government Air Operations (CGAO) took over responsibility for all non-military aviation regulations.

By 1927, a system of airways crossing the country had been proposed: the Trans-Canada Airway[11]. The plan was to provide a major airport every 100 miles, with emergency landing strips every thirty miles, across the country. Airfields were to be equipped with navigational and runway lighting. Navigation beacons were to be provided. For the first five years, from 1927 to 1932, there were only two civil airports in the country, both in the Province of Québec, one located at St. Hubert and the other at Rimouski. Starting in 1932 many unemployed men were put to work clearing air strips with hand tools and horse-drawn machinery as a method of providing some employment. This was one of the very first instances of Corporate Social Responsibility. By 1937, the airway system stretched from Vancouver to Sydney, a distance of 3,108 miles (5 001 km).

In 1928, the Dominion Meteorological Service began providing aviation weather forecasts, but this was suspended in 1932 due to

---

[11] A map of the Airway is given in at the end of this book.

government austerity during the Depression. On the creation by the government of Trans-Canada Air Lines (TCA) in 1936, aviation weather forecasts were once again provided, with forecasting stations at Moncton, Toronto, Kapuskasing, Winnipeg, Lethbridge and Vancouver, and also at intermediate weather stations. Later in the 1930s, surveying and planning took place for an airway system to reach from Edmonton into the far north.

The Canadian Pacific Railway (CPR) petitioned the federal government to start an air service in 1919 but the government refused the request as it did not want to get involved in aviation. By 1930, Canada was one of the few countries without a national airline.

In Western Canada, Western Canadian Airways was founded in 1926 by James Richardson. The airline specialized in northern operations and was particularly noted for an airlift of materials and men for surveying associated with the port of Churchill in 1927. Following acquisition of some competitors, in 1930 the airline was renamed Canadian Airways. In 1928 Cherry Red Airline was founded in Prince Albert, Saskatchewan for similar purposes.

The effect of the Great Depression was severe on the Canadian civil aviation industry. The Federal government did not wish to spend money on aviation while the economy was in poor condition. R.B. Bennett, the Prime Minister from 1930 to 1935, was famously quoted as saying he didn't want government-funded aircraft flying over farmers whose fields were blowing away around them. Government air mail contracts were cancelled, putting small aviation companies reliant on flying the air mail into financial difficulty. However, to make it politically acceptable to continue funding them, air photography, transportation of police to northern posts, air mail, and other civil operations were taken up by the RCAF.

In 1936, the government created the Department of Transport (DOT), responsible for civil aviation, railways, canals and marine. The Department of National Defence no longer played a role in the administration or regulation of civil aviation.

Also in 1936 a gentleman named C. D. Howe[12] played a critical rôle in the founding of Trans-Canada Air Lines (TCA). Rather like the railways of the preceding century, TCA was founded as the national cross-Canada carrier to keep out foreign competitors.

CPR had been a part shareholder in Richardson's Canadian Airways from the beginning, and by 1941 it had purchased the remaining shares in Canadian Airways, and other regional airline operations, to form Canadian Pacific Air Lines in 1942.

From 1943 to 1947 TCA operated the Canadian Government Trans-Atlantic Air Service (CGTAS) to provide trans-Atlantic military passenger and postal delivery service. In 1943 the federal Mackenzie King government made TCA the country's official trans-continental airline.

For more than 50 years afterward, TCA (which became Air Canada in 1965) and Canadian Pacific Air Lines[13] benefitted from government regulation of air routes, fares, and standards of service. Government regulation was thought to be essential to prevent destructive competition between TCA and Canadian Pacific Air Lines. The two airlines would remain commercial and political rivals for the rest of the 20th century until they merged in 2001.

Aerial photography was an urgent task for mapping remote regions of the country. War-surplus aircraft donated to Canada by the British and United States governments, or purchased by new private aviation companies, were the foundation of aerial survey and air photography in Canada. During the interwar period extensive air mapping was carried out by the RCAF. Mapping of remote regions from the air was valuable in developing forestry

---

[12] Clarence Decatur "C. D." Howe, PC (15 January 1886 – 31 December 1960) was a powerful Canadian Cabinet minister, representing the Liberal Party. Howe served in the governments of Prime Ministers William Lyon Mackenzie King and Louis St. Laurent continuously from 1935 to 1957. He is credited with transforming the Canadian economy from agriculture-based to industrial. During WW2, his involvement in the war effort was so extensive that he was nicknamed the "Minister of Everything".

[13] Canadian Pacific Air Lines was rebranded to CP Air in 1968. In 1986 it went back to its old name of Canadian Pacific Air Lines but this was short-lived, as in 1987 it and Nordair merged with Pacific Western Airlines, who renamed the merged fleet Canadian Airlines, which in turn merged with Air Canada on January 1, 2001.

and mining resources in Canada's North. The operational experience gained during this time was a foundation of the BCATP during WW2.

Worldwide commercial civil aviation expanded greatly after the WW1. Many European countries founded subsidized national airlines (Sabena, KLM, Lufthansa, Air France and others) for reasons of national prestige, security and commerce. The United Kingdom founded Imperial Airways with the mandate of tying together the far-flung regions of the British Empire, providing air mail and passenger services for overseas British and allied territories. In the United States, the conditions of a large land mass, uniform language and culture, large and growing population, and good flying conditions, favoured rapid growth of private airlines. Many regional airlines grew and looked to expand traffic to Canada and Latin America. In the United States, Pan American World Airways (Pan Am) became the unofficial national flag carrier, being given preferential support by the American government in its negotiations with other governments.

Conditions in Canada were different from those in Europe. Inter-city airline operations were important for although there was an extensive railroad network covering much of Canada, that network was fundamentally east-west. Float aircraft, operating on northern lakes and rivers, had become the basis of much commercial aviation for mining, paper industry, medical, police and mail carriage, so many private carriers formed regional airlines to serve this business. Little investment in fixed air strips was required for floatplane operations. About the only government subsidy available was the contract to carry air mail; however, with the onset of the Great Depression, even these contracts were cancelled.

In the mid-1930's Britain's Imperial Airways began negotiating with Pan Am on the potentially lucrative and prestigious trans-Atlantic route. Canadian interests were at risk since a trans-Atlantic route that bypassed Canadian territory would greatly impede commercial aviation development in Canada. No national airline existed, and none of the regional airlines were able to negotiate with Imperial Airways for trans-Atlantic routes. One route, feasible with the aircraft of the time, would run from New

York to Newfoundland to Ireland to London, bypassing Canadian territory completely.[14]

During the 1920's and 1930's international aviation treaties were negotiated, mostly among European countries. The Air Navigation Convention signed by European countries in 1920 was an attempt to provide international rules for air traffic. Canada's representations at the negotiations were not well received, but Canada was able to obtain an amendment to one article of the convention that permitted Canada and the United States to make their own agreements on cross-boundary air regulations.

Although John Alcock and Arthur Brown[15] had flown over the North Atlantic in 1919, the first non-stop trans-Canada flight from Halifax to Vancouver was only in 1949. A cross-Canada air mail demonstration by the Canadian Air Force was staged in 1920, but this was a relay of a half-dozen aircraft. American aviator James Dalzell McKee and RCAF Squadron Leader Earl Godfrey[16] took nine days in September 1926 to fly from Montréal to Vancouver. During the course of the flight it was decided a "Trans-Canada Trophy"[17] would be created to commemorate the flight. In appreciation of the RCAF and the Ontario Provincial Air Services, McKee presented the trophy, requesting it be awarded each year to the person who best advanced aviation in Canada. McKee also provided an endowment for a replica of the trophy to be given to each winner. McKee was killed in a floatplane crash later that same year.

It was not long before people began to pay attention to an airplane's capabilities. An aircraft could traverse and photograph in hours rugged undeveloped country that would take weeks to cross by canoe, dog team, horseback, or on foot. Resource companies

---

[14] Newfoundland was British territory until 1949, when Newfoundland and Labrador joined the Canadian confederation.

[15] Both were British airmen, who had flown for the RFC during WW1.

[16] Who ended his career in the RCAF as an Air Vice-Marshall.

[17] The Trans-Canada Trophy, also known as the McKee Trophy, is awarded by the Canadian Aeronautics and Space Institute to a Canadian citizen who has made an outstanding, contemporary achievement in aerospace operations, whether a single act within the year prior to the award or a sustained level of performance over a period of several years.

thrived with the ability to move personnel and material year-round. Particularly important was winter flying, in conditions so cold that oil had to be drained from engines and kept indoors overnight, then preheated and poured back in. Engines were kept (not very) warm by means of a tent erected around them, with a kerosene heater providing the heat. For northern fliers skis and floats were quite often more useful than wheels. These flights were made under the most primitive of conditions, in planes with open cockpits, often with no prepared airfields, no reliable weather forecasts, no radio or visual navigation aids, poor maps, and often no indoor facilities for repairs.

The bush pilot era produced such notable pilots as Wop May and Punch Dickins. In January 1929 Wop May's flight from Edmonton to Fort Vermilion,[18] Alberta carrying diphtheria vaccine became a headline news story. Both May and Dickins, along with many other bushplane aviators, became founders of Canadian aviation businesses.

Fred Stevenson barnstormed after the war and flew in Manitoba and Northern Ontario. In 1927 he joined Richardson's Western Canada Airways and airlifted 14 men and 17,000 pounds (7,700 kg) of material in support of exploration at Fort Churchill. These flights were proof of the utility of aircraft in the North. He was killed in an air crash on 5 January 1928 while testing repairs to his Fokker Universal.

And then in September 1939 the war intervened and everything changed. The wide-open spaces and clear skies of Canada provided an ideal place in which to train budding fliers, bombardiers, navigators and gunners. Far away from the war in Europe (and eventually the war in the Pacific) the opportunity presented itself for Canada to make the one invaluable contribution to the war effort: the British Commonwealth Air Training Plan.

---

[18] Fort Vermilion, established in 1788, is a hamlet on the Peace River in northern Alberta. It is 350 miles (570 km) northwest of Edmonton.

The BCATP

During the WW1 the RAF had built in Ontario and operated training bases at Long Branch, Armour Heights, Camp Borden, Leaside, Beamsville, Deseronto, Rathbun and Mohawk.[19] The bases were operated under British military control, wholly independent of Canadian military command. By November 1918 the program had graduated about 3,000 pilots and observers, and more than 7,000 mechanics and aircraftsmen.

In May 1938 concerns about the outbreak of war with Germany caused the British Air Ministry to consider Canada again for air training purposes and an Air Mission was duly organized and sent off to Canada.[20] The Mission met with Prime Minister William Lyon Mackenzie King and explained what they wanted to do, with an expectation that Canada would agree. However the political and practical relationship between Canada and England had changed over the intervening 20 years, and King was having nothing to do with a British organization operating independently within Canada. Canada would *cooperate* with British authorities, but Canada would remain *in control*.[21]

"we … are prepared to have our own establishments here and to give in those establishments facilities to British pilots to come and train here. But they must come and train in establishments which are under the control of the government of Canada and for which the Minister of National Defence will be able to answer in this parliament with respect to everything concerning them."[22]

Sir Kingsley Wood, British Secretary of State for Air, reported to the Foreign Office in London that an offer had been sent "to

---

[19] At a cost of more than £4 million GBP, about $475 million in 2018.

[20] Work on proposing Canada as a training site for British aircrew had begun two years earlier due to the efforts of Group Captain Robert Leckie, DSO, DSC, DFC. In 1936 he had written a memorandum to Group Captain Arthur Tedder (later Marshall of the RAF, Lord Tedder) reminding him of the role Canada had played in WW1 in training aircrew.

[21] F.J. Hatch, *Aerodrome of Democracy: Canada and the British Commonwealth Air Training Plan 1939-1945*, Minister of Supply and Services Canada, 1983, p. 10.

[22] Canada, Parliament, The Senate, *Debates*, 14 June 1938, 521, and House of Commons, *Debates*, 1 July 1938, 4523-4532.

Canada to explore … the possibilities of working out such a scheme for training facilities in Canada."[23] The British were concerned about the need to provide aircraft, airfields, and ancillary facilities to train pilots who would be urgently required at the start of WW2. Existing training facilities in Europe were likely to be subjected to enemy attack, rendering them unsuitable for a large-scale training program, and Canada had large, open skies, well removed from hostilities.

Work continued throughout the remainder of 1938 and through to August 1939 on the details of the new training scheme. There was much to settle as initially the British thought that any recruits supplied by Canada would be considered part of the RAF establishment. King was having none of that and remained adamant that any Canadians trained in the program would enter the RCAF. By January 1939 it had been decided that 50 British and 75 Canadian pilots would be trained in a trial program. Elementary Flying Training (EFT) was outsourced to eight civilian flying clubs, located at Vancouver, Calgary, Regina, Winnipeg, Hamilton, Toronto, Montréal, and Halifax:[24] a major innovation.

In June 1939 thirty-three student pilots were sent to the eight flying clubs, and thirty to Camp Borden. Fifty-seven received their pilots wings on 30 October 1939. Due to the increasing possibility of war the fifty British trainees who were to have taken part in the training never arrived, and the initial training agreement between Britain and Canada was never fully implemented.

However, the discussions and work throughout 1938 and 1939 had brought the RAF and RCAF to a much better and informed place as to the practicalities of training large numbers of aircrew in Canada.

When war did break out on 3 September 1939 Canada aligned herself with England in the coming battle. The RAF wasted no time in asking the RCAF to put in place a training program for 2,000 pilots a year and as many air gunners, bombers, navigators,

---

[23] The United Kingdom, Parliament, House of Commons, *Debates*, 7 July 1938, 595.

[24] *Aerodrome*, p. 11.

and observers as possible. By the end of September the number requested by the RAF had increased fourfold, to 8,000 pilots a year and others, for a total of 50,000 aircrew a year.

This caused King to consider his political position. He was a cautious man and saw that the British would expect to enrol large numbers of Canadians in the RAF. This had happened in WW1. He was also concerned about the cost, and the political impact on his government. The Canadian Chiefs of Staff had estimated that the first year of the war might cost Canada $492 million,[25] of which $150 million was needed for air defence.[26]

These numbers would pale in comparison with what the British would propose the next time the RAF and RCAF met, just a few weeks later.

The British arrived in Ottawa on 14 October 1939 and met with the RCAF two days later. Initial requests were for training 850 pilots, 510 air navigators, and 870 wireless operator / air gunners every four weeks, about 29,000 air crew a year. Twelve elementary flying schools, 25 advanced flying schools, 15 air observer schools, 15 bombing and air gunnery schools, three air navigation schools, and one radio training school were asked for. Manning was estimated at 54,000 personnel. It was estimated that 5,000 aircraft of various types would be needed.[27]

The cost was estimated at $889 million for capital and maintenance over three years. The British would supply $140 million worth of aircraft, spare parts and accessories leaving $749 million to be divided amongst Canada (one-half), Australia and New Zealand (one quarter each).[28]

King was astounded. He maintained that this was "a scheme suggested by the British government and for which the British

---

[25] $1.6 Billion in 2018.

[26] *Aerodrome*. p. 16

[27] Ibid. p. 18

[28] Ibid. p. 19

must be mainly responsible."[29] For him to go to Parliament and ask for funding would have been political suicide.

Negotiations continued until an agreement was finally signed just after midnight on 16 December 1939. That evening, a small group

Figure 1. Rt. Hon. W.L. Mackenzie King and Dr. O.D. Skelton at the signing of the British Commonwealth Air Training Plan agreement.

of men gathered in the office of Prime Minister Mackenzie King for the signing of an "Agreement Relating to the Training of Pilots and Aircraft Crews in Canada and Their Subsequent Service." There was a brief discussion as to whether the document should be dated the 16th or the 17th. It was to have been signed on the 16th but Mackenzie King pointed out that as it was now actually the 17th he preferred that date to be used and the others agreed. The 17th also happened to be the Prime Minister's birthday and for him this would indicate an auspicious beginning to the British Commonwealth Air Training Plan, for anniversaries, like certain numbers, and the hands of the clock when they were in a straight line, held special messages for King.[30]

---

[29] *United Kingdom Air Mission, Notes of a meeting on 31ˢᵗ October with members of the Canadian War Cabinet,* DHist 181.009 (D786).

[30] *Aerodrome,* p. 25.

After a pause for a round of birthday greetings the Agreement was signed by Lord Riverdale for the United Kingdom and by King for Canada. The delegates from Australia and New Zealand, also party to the negotiations, had left for home before all the details were settled and their signatures were added later.[31]

The benefits that came with the implementation of the BCATP were evident, particularly in the creation of building and employment opportunities. Assistance was needed for the construction and administration of the Plan, and work suddenly became available for a range of trades including electricians, plumbers, clerks and stenographers, and of course for flight instructors and aircraft service staff. In total, the BCATP employed 6,000 civilian employees and over 35,000 military personnel across Canada for most of the war's duration.

Historian Patricia Myers notes that a large portion of paycheques received from BCATP job creation stayed within their communities, indicating that the increase of employment activity was of local benefit.[32] It could be argued that this was the initiative that pulled Canada out of the Great Depression.

The scope of the plan required the construction of facilities to train up to 1,500 aircrew from the signatory countries every month. Originally, 58 training airfields were to be provided, with the first to be operational by 1940. Thirty-seven more had to be completed by 1941 and the remainder by April 1942. Not only did the BCATP succeed in carrying out its original objectives, it exceeded them considerably as additional pressure was applied to construct more facilities than originally envisioned and to complete them more rapidly than originally scheduled.

In the event, 33 airfields were completed by 1940, 69 were completed by 1941, and 81 by 1942. Six more were built in 1943 and one final airfield was completed in 1944.[33] It should be remembered that for each of these airfields a "satellite" landing

---

[31] Ibid. *p. 25.*

[32] Patricia Myers. *Sky Riders: An Illustrated History of Aviation in Alberta, 1906–1945*, 1995. We see the same effect with the AAs today. Their contributions to the local economies amount to hundreds of millions of dollars per year.

[33] *Aerodrome*, p. 207.

field was also constructed. Each of these satellites required many of the same facilities that were provided on the main bases. In total, 190 new airfields were constructed between 1940 and 1944 for the BCATP.

Under the original agreement to establish the BCATP, Britain was to pay $218 million, Canada $313 million, Australia $97 million and New Zealand $21 million – a total of $649 million.[34] Costs, however, escalated far beyond the 1939 estimates. In the end, Canada paid $1.617 billion[35] of the total cost of $2.231 billion.[36] That meant that each taxpayer living in Canada during the war ended up contributing about $200 just to pay for the BCATP.[37]

An excellent project management organization, standardized designs and extensive use of prefabricated components meant that once the plan had gotten properly underway, the time from green field site to operational facility was progressively reduced, and in at least one case took only six weeks. Runway layouts were standardized in an equilateral triangular pattern, so that there was always a runway available within 30° of the wind direction and cross-wind landings minimized. Thirty-five million square yards of runway, taxiway, and other paving had been laid by the end of the Project.

Support facilities required many different types of building to be designed: hangars, workshops, machine shops, boiler rooms, administration offices, classrooms, barrack blocks, mess blocks, hospitals, motor pools, recreation halls and club rooms.[38] From the outset, standard designs with prefabricated components were used whenever and wherever possible. In total, some 8,300 hundred buildings were constructed in a little over two years. Included in

---

[34] In 2018 this was equivalent to $11.4 billion!

[35] $28.2 billion in 2018.

[36] *Aerodrome*, Table A-3 Summary of BCATP cost and contribution, p. 200.

[37] About $3,500 in 2018.

[38] Alistair MacKenzie, *A CSCE National Historic Civil Engineering Project lays the groundwork for Canada's present air transportation infrastructure*. CSCE National History Committee. History Notes, Canadian Civil Engineer, October 2001.

this number were some 700 of the largest buildings on the project: the aircraft hangars.[39]

When the plan was finally completed in 1945, Canada was left with a large number of airfields in every province for which the Air Force had no further need. This unexpected legacy from WW2 was to provide Canada with the basis of a valuable post-war air transportation infrastructure.

The legacy of airfields from the BCATP gave Canada a jump-start to the new air transportation age that was to follow WW2. Modifications and additions to the original designs were required to almost all the airfields built for the BCATP in order to adapt them to their new civilian functions. The original site selection criteria for the airfields carefully considered topographical and infrastructure requirements, and also required that they be located as near as possible to established settlements which could provide commercial and social services. Therefore, the siting of the great majority of the BCATP fields resulted in their being admirably suited to enable them to be adapted to a civilian role.

Post WW2

In 1936 the government decided to remove civil aviation, air navigation (radio) and meteorological services from the remit of National Defence and in turn give them to the newly formed Department of Transport (DOT). C.D. Howe was the first Minister of Transport and by 1940 he had seen the completion of the Trans-Canada Airway, and the creation of Trans-Canada Air Lines, the Air Transport Board, the organization of air services, and the general development of an indigenous Canadian air industry. Moreover, at the end of WW2, the government wanted to control the air industry and ensure its development, avoiding the problems the railway industry had suffered at the hands of private enterprise.[40]

Howe became Minister of Reconstruction and Supply in 1947 and by 1948 had ensured that all airports surplus to the needs of

---

[39] Ibid.

[40] https://www.otc-cta.gc.ca/eng/publication/at-heart-transportation-a-moving-history, accessed 4 March 2019.

National Defence had been handed over to the DOT, who in turn selected those it needed for civilian use. The remainder were sold off by the War Assets Disposal Corporation, mainly to municipalities.

In 1946 commercial and private aircraft flew 28.2 million passenger miles. By 1949 307.9 million passenger miles were flown. Civil aviation was off to a good start.[41]

When TCA introduced the DC-3 in 1945 runways were upgraded to provide 4,500 feet (1 372 m) of landing space at sea level. The North Stars required 6,000 feet (1 829 m), and in 1946 the International Civil Aviation Organization (ICAO) recommended 8,000 foot (2 438 m) runways for first-class international airports, with pavement strength for 150,000 lbs (68 040 kg) gross weight aircraft.[42]

In the immediate post-war period (1945-1955) the DOT devoted its efforts and financial resources to the improvement of airports to accommodate four-engine aircraft and to update safety and navigational aids (lighting, Instrument Landing Systems, radar). Super Constellations, introduced by TCA in 1954, required 7,500 feet (2 286 m) of runway.

During those ten years passenger traffic quadrupled and air terminal buildings (ATB) at the major airports were seriously overcrowded. Consequently a massive program of re-construction was begun in the mid-1950's with ATBs being erected at Gander, Halifax, Montréal, Ottawa, Toronto, Winnipeg and Edmonton. These were large buildings, modelled on the most modern international designs, and incorporating features from airports around the world. They attracted much attention in the airport world and established a high reputation for Canadian airports.[43]

Although operating subsidies were improved from time-to-time to meet increased costs, many municipalities still found the costs too high, gave up running their own municipal airport, and handed their airport back to the DOT. One of the main costs was the need to improve the ATB and the municipalities were unwilling to

---

[41] T.M. McGrath, *History of Canadian Airports*, Transport Canada, 1984. p. 26.

[42] *History*, p. 27.

[43] Ibid. p. 28.

commit to that level of expenditure. Over the period 1959 to 1972 municipalities handed back seven major airports: Fredericton, 1959; Timmins, 1961; Kamloops, 1961; Vancouver, 1962; Calgary, 1967; Saint John, 1968; and Regina, 1972.[44]

Leases of Crown land for the creation of an airfield had been in existence since the 1920's, but ownership of any improvements to the land (runways, taxiways, aprons, ATBs, hangars, access roads) remained with the Crown upon the lease expiration, without any recompense to the lessee for their expense. Because of this, investments by private individuals on airport lands were scarce. However, in 1955 the policy for land leases changed to allow land lease for long periods of time, and to compensate a lessee for their capital investment (less depreciation) in the event of lease cancellation. This was the first instance of the DOT's philosophy of the capital cost of leasing aerodromes.[45]

When TCA began using its first jet aircraft (the DC-8) the impact on the airports was enormous: the principal runway lengths in use at an airport now had to increase to at least 9,000 feet (2 743 m). By 1961 Dorval's three runways were 7,000 feet (2 134 m), 9,600 feet (2 926 m) and 11,000 feet (2 353 m).[46]

---

[44] Ibid.

[45] Ibid. p. 29.

[46] An 11,000 foot runway 200' wide and 24" thick uses 162,962 cubic yards of concrete, about 16,300 truckloads, at a cost of approximately $15 million.

Chapter 3: Development of Devolution

In 1974, eighteen years before the first Airport Authorities (AAs) came into being, the Airport Enquiry Commission[47] under Mr. Justice Gibson reported on its findings of the proposal to build a new airport at Pickering, 30 miles (48 km) northeast of Toronto. Although the Commission recommended against a new airport at Pickering, they made some prescient observations on what was necessary for there to be an effective AA:[48]

> *It appears to the Commission that there are many advantages to be gained by the separation of the planning, management and operation of airports from the other important responsibilities of the Ministry of Transport, Canada, in the air transportation system.*
>
> *[If there were Airport Authorities, the] Ministry of Transport, Canada, would be freed from the day to day problems associated with the development and operation of airports. ... The Ministry would continue its vital functions of establishing standards for aerodromes and certificating aerodromes. ...*
>
> *The Airport Authority should be vested with authority for the planning, development, and management of ... air transportation ... it would be responsible, subject to Ministry of Transport, Canada, certification standards, for the establishment of terminals, runways, taxi-ways, aprons, freight warehouses, parking areas, internal roadways and rapid transit lines, and all non-airport related activities conducted on the airport lands.*
>
> *It would construct the passenger terminal, lease terminal space to the airlines and maintain control over the leasehold improvements effected to the leased space. While the Authority should cooperate with the airlines as much as possible, it must discharge its ultimate responsibility which should be convenience and consideration of passengers.*

---

[47] *REPORT OF THE AIRPORT INQUIRY COMMISSION*, Information Canada, Ottawa, 1974.

[48] Ibid. *Ch. 20 An Airport Authority*, pp. 241-245.

The Authority would be responsible to ensure that there is sufficient variety of quality restaurants and refreshment facilities to meet the varying tastes and financial situations of the passengers. It would be the responsibility of the Authority to ensure that no advantage is taken of the fact that a passenger is a captive customer. The Authority would be responsible for determining the other types of services that should be provided for the convenience of passengers and the variety of retail shops that should be established. The Authority would assume responsibility for establishing standards of furnishing of all leased space and standards of performance to be observed by all leaseholders.

The Authority would have responsibility for architectural control in the design of structures that would be erected on site by others, such as hangars of airlines, so that there is an architectural harmony in all structures erected on the airport land.

The Airport Authority must have authority over the control of public motor vehicle modes of transport to the airports. This will entail the granting of exclusive franchise to operators.

The Authority should also have power to grant an exclusive franchise to a bus operator. In this manner, the Authority can set standards for the type of vehicle in order to provide a comfortable and convenient ride to and from the airport which should encourage a greater use of bus transportation over that of present experience.

The decision as to the type of rapid transit system that will be chosen to provide access to the airport will have to be made by a cooperative effort on the part of the Airport Authority and the Rapid Transit Authority, if public acceptance of the rapid transit system is to be achieved. ...

In sum, the Airport Authority should have power to do anything which is calculated to facilitate the discharge of its duty, ... which will meet all reasonable demands for the transport of passengers and goods.

The skill in directing any great enterprise requires the blending of the talent of part-time outsiders ... and full-

28

time insiders who do the actual management of the business. The part-time outsiders are represented by the Board of Directors [who] should be responsible for establishing policy and broad guidelines. The Board of Directors should be composed of interested citizens who can bring an outward looking ... viewpoint to the resolution of the problems which will confront the Authority. The full-time insiders are represented by an Executive Management Board who can bring a practical inward looking ... expertise to the execution of the policy and guidelines established by the Board of Directors. The respective roles of the two ... should be harmonized but not confused.

...

There is a tendency on the part of all governments to overlook the fact that they all derive their authority from the same source, that they all exist primarily to serve the public interest and all obtain their financial resources from the same source. ... If we are to avail ourselves of the present opportunity to preserve and expand the ... transportation system, so that it may make its important contribution to the well-being of the nation, all governments will have to surrender some of their jurisdiction to the Airport Authority.

As you will have noticed, every single important responsibility that is currently undertaken by the Canadian Airport Authorities was named by the Commissioners in their report.

Early days of an airport devolution policy

The section in Mr. Justice Gibson's report about airport authorities struck a nerve with some of the folk at TC who thought it the right thing to do, but the staff both in the Government and within TC wanted nothing to do with it. The situation needed a change at the head, and that change was Otto Lang, who became Minister of Transport in 1974.

Right from the beginning, one of the things that struck him most about the department was the strength of the staff: they had a superb knowledge of, and expertise in, the Canadian transportation system.[49] They demonstrated to him a striking concern about the alienation of land, always an issue for that owned by the federal government. Before a federal department could alienate federal land it had to ensure that the land would be available anytime, for any need.

As an example, when Lang arrived as Minister the staff in the department were concerned about how long it took to get a solution to the question about whether or not certain activities could, or even should, be conducted on airport lands. Their concern was based on what are fully legitimate federal rules: making sure that before TC alienated any Crown owned land for a long period of time there was a fuller consideration of whether there was, or would be in the future, any need for that land in any way, at any time. So, if a company wanted to suddenly set up a major freight handling facility in, say, Winnipeg, close to the airport, this quite often meant the company's operation being on airport land, and, obviously, the company would want some security for the time that it leased land. The TC officials realized that by the time that the question of alienation was examined by Ottawa there were too many opportunities for that transport handler to decide that he should look at Fargo or Grand Forks, just south of Winnipeg, and the United States border, where the issue might be handled a lot more quickly.[50]

So that led the staff at TC to the thought "what could we do about having more airport control locally over the situation?" and one of the ideas which emerged was, in effect, the one that was eventually pursued. "Could we have a local airport authority which by and large would be in charge of the way everything was handled but with a broad federal oversight and control of the land?"[51]

And with that idea in mind, which Lang thought was a delightful one, in 1978 TC chose an Assistant Deputy Minister to travel to Canada's major airports to determine how they would react to the move of the airport management to a local authority. That local authority would be carefully chosen for its independence and a lot

---

[49] Otto Lang, interview with the author, 12 December 2018.

[50] Ibid.

[51] Ibid.

of decisions could then be made locally rather than involving Ottawa.

That trip got a favourable reaction from the airports and caused TC to conduct its first major review of how airports were managed in Canada, specifically with a mandate to propose possible options for change. The review was carried out by TC's *Task Force on Airport Management*. The Task Force reported in July 1979 *(The Haglund Report)*.

The report noted that TC's air administration was responsible for the ownership and operation of 169 airports (90 directly, the rest through municipalities and other agencies). In an effort to be self-sustaining, revenues generated from these 169 airports were consolidated in TC's Revolving Fund, and then monies from the Fund were allocated for airport operations. It was, in effect, a means of cross-subsidization whereby surplus revenues generated at the large, busy airports could be transferred to smaller airports with inadequate revenues. The Fund was also used for airport maintenance, but there was never enough money to do all the maintenance necessary, so it became a game of the squeaky wheel got the grease.

Haglund recommended autonomous airport commissions at each of the principal airports in the country (virtually identical to the 26 airports in the present National Airports System). In addition, there was to be a central co-ordinating Canadian Airports Authority modelled on the Canada Ports Corporation[52], which was being legislated at that time under the *Canada Ports Act*.

Because of the difficulty of making a significant institutional change, little action was taken on the recommendations of the *Haglund Report*. The idea of divestiture had been presented, but there was no audience for it. At the same time, in the early-1980's, a group at the University of British Columbia[53] was addressing the issue of airport financing. The group didn't come to the model of an AA but did work on a governance model. Bill Stanbury, David Emerson and Mike Tretheway were commissioned by the

---

[52] During my interview with her, Mary Brooks expressed many thanks that the Airports Authorities did not end up looking like the Ports Authorities.

[53] Of which Bill Stanbury and Michael Tretheway were members.

Vancouver International Airport Transition Advisory Group (VIATAG) to do this pro bono as they were already writing papers[54] concerning the role of aviation connectivity in economic development.

A year or so later divestiture as envisaged by *Haglund* was raised again in the political environment, this time by Jean-Luc Pepin (Minister of Transport), but the proposal died again.

In 1984 a Conservative government under Prime Minister Mulroney was elected on a platform of reducing the federal debt. A principal plank of that platform was economic regulatory reform. This time the issue of divestiture of the airports was in line with the deregulatory agenda. By that time the cost of running the airports was $750 million a year. Mulroney made Don Mazankowski[55] (Maz) the Minister of Transport.

Maz lost no time in furthering the Government's deregulatory agenda for in July 1985 he introduced a position paper[56] on transportation in the House of Commons. Called *Freedom to Move — A Framework for Transportation Reform,* the paper outlined sweeping revisions to transportation policy that involved reduced economic regulation and greater reliance on market forces. A "lighter" regulatory framework was believed to be more conducive to industry, would allow more competition, and result in lower costs to consumers. However, reduced regulation did not mean reduced oversight and inspection. The intent was to implement "economic" regulation of transport.

Maz was determined that TC would undergo some changes as he found it subject to great political interference and, certainly in the case of the airports, bogged down in the details of airport operations. There were no clear-cut policies as to how airports were to be run, with myriad differences between the TC Regions across the country. For example, after the House had retired for the day he would find himself still at his Ottawa ministerial office

---

[54] David Emerson and Mike Tretheway, *The Role of Airports in Economic Development,* 1984.

[55] Don Mazankowski, Minister of Transport, 1978-1979; 1984-1986.

[56] *Freedom to move: a framework for transportation reform.* Transport Canada, Ottawa, 1985.

"signing everything":[57] leases for cigarette and Coke vending machines, leases for concessions and parking, leases for buildings on airport lands, and for a host of other minor and insignificant things, and he thought to himself "this has got to change."[58]

The Mulroney government had been elected on a platform of economic regulatory reform and of setting clear policy direction. The mantra was: User pay, user say. In order to set clear policy direction in 1984 Maz appointed a study group to determine what to do with the airports. The study group reported one year later and recommended the establishment of AAs wherever possible.

At the same time as the study group was conducting its review, on behalf of the Government Erik Nielsen's *Ministerial Task Force on Program Review*[59] issued a *Report on Real Property*[60] which recommended that "the government should also consider instituting a fundamental change in policy for airport operations from ownership and centralized public service operations to managed and owned airports". The government followed up this recommendation by stating that "the government will pursue the development of a new management structure for the federal airport system in Canada." [61]

In 1986 the Government reported the need for a fundamental change in airport policy with a new approach of non-federal ownership and operation. The Nielsen Report recommended that airports be transferred to local authorities, while responsibility for safety and security remained with Transport Canada. Air navigation was to be handled separately, and air regulation and certification of airports were to be separated from airport management.

At the time, the *Report on Real Property* thought that legislation would be necessary in order to implement the policy and noted that "to successfully establish airport authorities it will be necessary

---

[57] Mazankowski. Interview with the Author, 19 November 2018.

[58] Ibid.

[59] *New management initiatives: initial results from the Ministerial Task Force on Program Review*. 1985.

[60] *Real property : a study team report to the Task Force on Program Review*. 1985.

[61] Ibid. p. 28-29.

to proceed with the preparation of federal legislation for approving the creation of authorities. This will ensure that this major policy change is addressed by Parliament..."

Such a new policy[62] concerning a future management framework for airports in Canada was announced by Benoît Bouchard, the Minister of Transport, in April 1987. This policy was based on the view that local management (rather than a central administration) would be more efficient and responsive to the community that it served. The policy stated in essence that: (1) the government would be prepared to receive proposals for transfer of ownership and/or operation of federal airports (organizations accepting a transfer could include provinces, municipalities, local authorities or the private sector); and (2) the government envisaged a new business-like approach to airport management for those airports not transferred.

The Minister's announcement in April 1987 presented the decision to move forward on two parallel yet distinct thrusts:

1. discussions regarding ownership by "others", where there was a local interest, i.e. the Local Airport Authority option; and,

2. a new approach to managing airports retained by TC that would emphasize commercial orientation, potential contribution to local economic development and responsiveness to local interests and concerns, i.e. the TC AA model.

This intent resulted in the National Transportation Act of 1987 which re-wrote the ways and means that Transport Canada used to regulate the four "modes" of transport: rail, roads, marine, and air. It was a major policy change for Transport Canada which was now responsible for a safe, economic, efficient, and adequate network of viable and effective transportation services. TC was now to ensure that the highest practicable safety standards were met; to let competition and market forces determine the service provided; and, to incur economic regulation only in regions and for services where it was necessary. Transportation was recognized as a key to regional economic development.

---

[62] *A future framework for the management of airports in Canada : a new policy.*

A major principle of the new Act was the devolution[63] of the airports to the private sector. There was a desperate need for the investment of capital into airport terminals but the Government had other priorities for financing, and investment in airport infrastructure was only going to happen in the most direst of need. What was needed was something different, and that something different was the airport authority model.

By January 1987 an Airports Transfer Task Force (ATTF) had been created and extensive studies completed to determine whether a self-sustaining system of airports could be provided which would allow for independent operation of local airports. Four options had emerged from those studies: private sector operation; local airport authorities; TC airport authority model; and Crown corporations. Under any of these options TC would retain responsibility for safety and security, air navigation, air regulations and airport certification.[64]

In April 1987 the evolutionary policy advanced a step further when the Government announced that AAs would be allowed to assume direct management of airports. The policy, developed by the ATTF, had eight Guiding Principles:[65]

- Safety and security regulation would remain under federal government control and the new operator would have to adhere to the conditions of issue of the aerodrome certificate;
- An equitable benefits package for the transfer of federal government employees would have to be negotiated;
- All federal taxation revenues, including the Air Transportation Tax (which brought in $435 million in 1987/88) would be retained by the federal government;
- No long-term funding increases would be undertaken by the federal government;
- Reasonable compensation for the airport transfer, whether by sale or by lease, would be required;

---

[63] "privatization" was seen to be too strong and forceful a word, so "devolution" became the phrase of the day.

[64] *History*, p. 22.

[65] Farquhar, 3 October 1989.

- Existing leases, licenses and commercial contracts would have to be honoured;
- Special federal programs such as for official languages and the transportation of the disabled would have to be maintained; and,
- The new operator would be subject to the Competition Act and the new National Transportation Act.

Recognizing that the public may have concerns over "privatization" the Government emphasized that it would continue to be directly responsible for safety and security regulation and to provide all route navigation and air traffic control.[66]

But progress towards the creation of AAs stalled, and the Secretary of State for Airport Transfers began to express his own frustration.[67]

Within TC the policy branch was wedded to divestiture, but the operational side had reservations because it was change. They saw their jobs threatened. They didn't know if their jobs would be transferred and so there never was an enthusiastic basis of support amongst the TC airports operational and management staff. However, the Secretary of State for Airport Transfers was fully committed. His marching orders were "the bureaucracy will do this or we, the politicians, will find some other way to do it."[68]

The TC Team

After some discussion with Gerry St. Germain (who was Secretary of State for Airport Transfers), Glen Shortliffe, TC's Deputy Minister, decided he was not going to leave the task of devolution with the airports group. The issue had sat for a long time and nothing had happened. He had created the Airports Transfer Task Force (ATTF), now he also recommended the government create the Airports Transfer Advisory Board (ATAB) as an independent group, outside the government realm, reporting directly to the Minister of Transport.

---

[66] Ibid. p. 8.

[67] St. Germain, interview with the author, 20 September 2018.

[68] Farquhar and Cloutier, interview with the author. 23 October 2018.

The ATAB, created in July 1988, had eight private sector members[69] from across Canada who had broad experience in the air industry.[70]The Board's mandate was to provide the Minister with advice and recommendations concerning the evaluation of submissions related to the transfer of airports to local airport authorities (LAAs). The ATAB anticipated that once it recommended a not-for-profit model, which could not raise equity capital, the airport was going to need cash up-front to finance construction because the banks and the bond market would never give 100% financing for major capital projects. There had to be some kind of equity, and equity came from what in the U.S. is called a Passenger Facility Charge (PFC). There could also be grants, but grants were out of the question in the devolution policy. It was anticipated that eventually every airport would have the freedom to levy a PFC, or an equivalent. The timing of that would be around when the capital projects would have to be built as determined by the AA.

The ATTF reported directly to the DM and was under the direction of Victor Barbeau, the ADM Airports Group. Its mandate was the day-to-day conduct of analysis, negotiations and policy development.[71] The ATTF was comprised of five persons: Michael Farquhar as Executive Director, and Yvon Souci, Peter Williams, Frank Siba, and John Cloutier as members. Jacques Pigeon (Senior General Counsel) and Michael Senzilet (Counsel), both Justice Canada lawyers assigned to Transport Canada, provided legal advice. There were also a few TC support staff. The ATTF met with the DM about every two weeks to update him on progress and issues.

---

[69] Chaired by Glen Shortliffe, Transport Canada DM.

[70] Lawyers, accountant, academic, real estate developer, pilot, airline executive, etc.

[71] "policy development" as part of the mandate was to prove extremely important. Unlike other Transport Canada initiatives in which policy _had_ to be developed by the Policy Group and which might take _months, or even years,_ to develop, the ATTF was able to develop its own policy in a timely manner. (italics mine)

Options for devolution

The ATTF had little to go on apart from a directive that said "get rid of the airports". The only other models at that time were the British Airports Authority (BAA), and the airports in the United States. A generic table of these ownership models is seen here:

Item	Level of Airport Ownership (public to fully private – left to right)			
Ownership	Public	Public	Public/ Private	Private
Investment	Public	Public/Private	Private	Private
Management	Public	Private	Private	Private
Types of Private Sector Involvement	• Concessions • Leases	• Management contract • Leases • Project Finance • Build-Operate-Transfer	• Concessions • Leases • Build-Operate-Transfer	• Leases • Bonds • IPO

Figure 2: Options for Airport Ownership

The BAA was a creation of Roy Jenkins, who as Minister of Aviation introduced the British government's Airport Authority Act in 1965. Under that Act BAA was to take responsibility for four state-owned airports from the Ministry of Aviation: Heathrow Airport, Gatwick Airport, Prestwick Airport and Stansted Airport, in an attempt to take airports out of direct government control and make them run better and more profitably. This was in response to an unclear and indecisive government airport policy over the preceding 20 years.

For the duration of WW2 civil aviation had been banned in Great Britain, but in 1945 the newly elected Labour Government allowed civil aviation to commence again. In alignment with Labour policy, direct governmental control of airports and the air system was deemed the best way to proceed since it was believed that the airports would never be able to "pay their way".[72] A government white paper described an airport plan that would oversee and coordinate airport development. No plan emerged and by the 1950's anarchy had set in between and amongst the many airports competing for passengers and airline services. In 1961 the Conservative Government issued a second white paper which abandoned the objectives set out in 1945 and stated "that

---

[72] Rigas Doganis, "A National Airport Plan", Fabian Tract 377, 1967, p. 1.

henceforth airports should be run as business enterprises without state assistance or responsibility".[73] The white paper proposed that the control of the Heathrow, Gatwick, Stanstead and Prestwick airports be assumed by a newly-formed corporation, The British Airports Authority.

In the following few years, the BAA acquired Edinburgh Airport (1971), Glasgow Airport (1975) and Aberdeen Airport (1975). The BAA was a for-profit company, able to distribute its profits as it saw fit: to shareholders as dividends or to re-invest in the company.

As part of Margaret Thatcher's moves to privatize government-owned assets, the Airports Act 1986 was passed which mandated the creation of BAA Plc as a vehicle by which stock market funds could be raised with an initial capitalization of £1,225 million GBP.[74]

The ATTF was not convinced that the BAA model was one to follow in Canada. Under the Airports Act the British government had sold the property, rights and liabilities to BAA, retaining licensing and oversight under the Civil Aviation Authority. But the expected profitability for BAA had not occurred, for although the BAA as a whole was profitable, that profit was generated solely by Heathrow, with Gatwick and Stanstead operating at huge losses.

The ATTF did not favour a BAA solution where the profit was given out to the shareholders as dividends and not re-invested in the airports. It wanted the profits to stay within the financial framework of the AA for its use as capital.

The other side of the coin was the American system where the airport had two major revenue streams to fund capital projects. The first was the U.S. Federal Airport Improvement Program (AIP). The second was that a municipally-owned airport could issue bonds with tax benefits for funding capital projects.[75] The ATTF didn't want to create either of these scenarios in Canada. It wanted to get the federal government out of any direct funding

---

[73] Ibid. p. 3.

[74] About $3.4 billion in 1986.

[75] *Senzilet*. Email 15 January 2019.

(through grants) or indirect funding (through tax benefits) for capital expenses at the airports.

The United States Airport Development Aid Program (ADAP), funded with user fees earmarked for the Airport and Airway Trust Fund, was established in 1970 as a response to the congestion and delay problems that plagued airports in the late 1960s.[76] ADAP provided U.S. Federal matching grants to airports to pay for certain types of capital improvements, principally construction of new runways, taxiways, and aprons to relieve airside congestion. ADAP expired after 10 years, however U.S. Federal assistance for capital improvements continued through the AIP, created by the Airport and Airway Improvement Act of 1982[77] because FAA projections of future traffic demand indicated that there could be severe airside congestion at a number of major airports over the next 20 years. Although some of the delays might have been eased by improved air traffic control technology, the FAA view was that the primary constraint on the growth of the system would be "a lack of concrete" and that there would be a need for more runways, taxiways, and ramps.[78]

This basic strategy was challenged on the grounds that it biased the outcome toward capital intensive solutions, Critics argued that U.S. Federal development grants encouraged airport operators to overbuild. In other cases, the facilities built with U.S. Federal support were substantially different in form and more expensive than needed to accomplish their intended function. But more fundamentally, the existence of a U.S. Federal program providing aid for only certain types of capital improvements at airports distorted investment decisions and led airport operators to build not necessarily what they needed but what the Government was willing to help pay for. By accommodating demand wherever and whenever it occurred through increasingly large and complex new

---

[76] *Airport System Development*, Office of Technology Assessment, Washington, 1984.

[77] Ibid, p. 21.

[78] Ibid, p. 21.

capital facilities, more growth was encouraged at precisely those locations where it was most difficult and expensive to absorb.[79]

Before WW2 the U.S. Federal Government was inclined to the view that airports, like ocean and river ports, were a local responsibility, and the U.S. Federal role was confined to maintaining the navigable airways and waterways connecting those ports. At the onset of WW2, the U.S. Federal Government began to develop airports on land leased from municipalities. U.S. Federal investment was justified on the grounds that a strong system of airports was vital to national defense. After the war, many of these improved airports were declared surplus and turned over to municipalities. U.S. Federal assistance to airports continued throughout the 1950s and 1960s at a low level and was aimed primarily at improving surplus airports and adapting them to civil use. Major U.S. Federal support of airport development resumed in 1970 with the passage of the Airport and Airway Development Act, which was in large part a response to the congestion and delay then being experienced at major airports. This act established the user-supported Airport and Airway Trust Fund and ADAP.[80]

U.S. Federal assistance to airports under ADAP was distributed as matching grants for capital improvement projects. There were several formulas for allocation—entitlement (calculated from the number of passengers enplaned at the airport), block grant (based on State area and population), and need (discretionary funds). Over the 10-year life of ADAP outlays from the Trust Fund amounted to approximately $4 billion.[81] ADAP expired in 1980, but a similar program of airport development assistance, AIP, was established in 1982. Before AIP was enacted there was extensive debate about the future direction of U.S. Federal airport aid, sparked by proposals to withdraw assistance for ("to defederalize") major air carrier airports.[82]

---

[79] Ibid, p. 22.

[80] Ibid, p. 22.

[81] About $26 billion in 2018.

[82] *Airport*, p. 22.

Supporters of defederalization advanced two arguments: that the U.S. Federal Government was overinvolved in financing airport development and that U.S. Federal assistance was not necessary for large airports because they were capable of financing their own capital development. By excluding large airports from eligibility for U.S. Federal grants, the Government could reduce the overall cost of the aid program and at the same time provide more aid to small air carrier and general aviation airports. Under various proposals, the top 40 to 69 airports (in terms of enplaned passengers) would have lost eligibility for U.S. Federal aid. The advantage to large airports, as pointed out by supporters of defederalization, would be freedom from many legal and administrative requirements involved in accepting U.S. Federal assistance.[83]

Opponents of defederalization contended that the proposal was unwise for several reasons. First, it would have eliminated U.S. Federal assistance for the very airports that provided the bulk of passenger service and had the greatest problems of congestion and delay. It was at these airports, the backbone of the national system, where a U.S. Federal presence was most easily be justified. Further, passengers using large airports paid about three-quarters of the taxes supporting the Airport and Airway Trust Fund. Thus, defederalization would have lead to subsidy of smaller airports by larger ones. Some observers also questioned the ability of many airports to carry out necessary capital improvements without U.S. Federal participation. While agreeing that U.S. Federal grants form only a small percentage of total capital budgets at large airports, they argued that it was a needed revenue source for all but the very largest 5 or 10 airports.[84]

Some proponents held that defederalized airports should be allowed to charge a "passenger facility charge" or "head tax" to make up for the loss of U.S. Federal funds, but U.S. Federal law prohibited airports from taxing passengers. Others objected to the PFC while supporting the concept of defederalization, holding that airports could raise sufficient funds through retained earnings or through the private bond market to cover their capital needs. One major objection to the PFC was that passengers would have

---

[83] Ibid, p. 23.

[84] Ibid.

to bear a double tax when using a defederalized airport. They would have had to pay both a ticket tax supporting the Airport and Airway Trust Fund and a PFC at the arrival or departure airport.[85]

The major airlines, as represented by the Air Transport Association, were indifferent on the question of defederalization but opposed to the PFC. They held that a PFC would impose unnecessary administrative burdens on them and would be unfair to passengers. Other observers noted that the underlying reason for the air carriers' objection was that a PFC would give airports an independent source of revenue and weaken the voice that airlines had in airport investment decisions.[86]

Airport operators were divided. Some very large airports, such as Chicago O'Hare, supported defederalization on the condition that it was accompanied by the freedom to impose a PFC. The Airport Operators Council International, an organization representing airports of all sizes, expressed qualified support of the concept of "optional defederalization" where airports could choose whether or not they wished to receive U.S. Federal aid, rather than having the decision made for them on the basis of size and passenger volume. Many airports opposed both defederalization and the PFC.[87]

Another approach to airport financing was also raised during the debate over AIP, although it was not introduced into legislation. Under the general concept of "new federalism" it was proposed to turn increased responsibility for decisions on airport funding and programming over to State aviation agencies and departments of transportation.[88]

Supporters contended that State agencies were in a better position to determine the needs of local airports and could distribute grants with less red tape than the U.S. Federal Government. They pointed out that some States already had active aviation agencies that evaluated airport improvement projects and approved all applications for U.S. Federal assistance. In these cases, the needs of the airports and the State might have been better served by

---

[85] Ibid. p. 24.

[86] Ibid.

[87] Ibid.

[88] Ibid.

allowing State agencies more latitude in distributing airport grants.[89]

A stronger role for State agencies could have reduced the U.S. Federal role to basically that of a tax collector. Because of the interstate nature of air transportation, it would probably have been more efficient to continue to collect ticket taxes, fuel taxes, or other aviation taxes at the national level. However, the funds could have been passed through to the States on a formula basis, and the actual decisions on how funds were spent could have been made at the State level.[90]

There were several objections to the concept of new federalism. First, State agencies varied in strength. Many did not have the staff or the expertise to take on the responsibilities of evaluating airport development projects or administering grants. A period of transition would have been necessary while these States prepared to accept new responsibilities. Others argued that setting up 50 separate agencies to do the work of FAA would have added an additional layer of bureaucracy, since FAA involvement could not be completely eliminated. Still others saw interstate or multistate cooperation as a major stumbling block. For example, a State government, perhaps lacking perspective of the airport system as a whole, might find little incentive to aid development of an airport outside its borders or to enter into regional compacts to compensate citizens of adjacent States for airport noise impacts.[91]

In summary, the three "pillars" of airport funding in the U.S. are:

1. Airport Improvement Program (AIP)—The federal government contributes significant federal funding for airport planning and development through the AIP, which provides grants to public agencies—and, in some cases, to private owners and entities—for the planning and development of public use airports that are included in the National Plan of Integrated Airport Systems (NPIAS).

2. Passenger Facility Charges (PFCs)—PFCs are a source of local capital independent of use and lease agreements and are seen as

---

[89] Ibid.

[90] Ibid.

[91] Ibid.

a key instrument to promote competition and capacity. PFCs are an important source of funding for airport infrastructure and a frequent vehicle used to leverage capital. If the airport operator imposes a PFC, that PFC must be separately identified on the passenger ticket.

3. Tax-Exempt Debt—The availability of tax-exempt debt provides public airports a cost of capital advantage over private entities. Instruments such as governmental bonds, private activity bonds, and Build America Bonds have been the major financing mechanism for capital improvements at large, medium, and some small hub airports and as a result promote capital investment by state and local governments.

Neither the British nor the American systems in use at that time appealed to the ATTF. The ATTF did not want to go as far as total privatization, realizing that selling all the airports and their assets was not in the public interest of Canadians. Over the previous 60 years the government had invested billions of dollars[92] in the airports and to transfer all that to the private sector would not be good public policy. Neither was the government in a position to subsidize the airports to the extent that the American government was doing in the United States. Virtually all commercial service airports in the United States are publicly owned and/or operated either by a state, county, city, single-purpose airport authority, or multi-purpose authority with various forms of private sector participation in their operation and investment. Some U.S. airports are owned by a government entity (state, county, or city) but are operated by a single- or multi-purpose authority under a long-term lease.

Lease or retain ownership? The policy framework.

The ATTF was in a quandary. If neither privatization not subsidization were the answer, what, then, was to be the option? The issue was that the airports are the intersection of the public and private interests, and how best to preserve those interests?

---

[92] Estimated at $8 to $10 billion.

One of the first things the ATTF developed was a policy and framework for undertaking the divestiture. That work was presented to the Minister of Transport and the TC DM, both of whom were supportive of the proposed policy and framework.

Michael Farquhar was one of the few in TC who had worked in all the central agencies of the federal government, and he along with his deputy John Cloutier, knew their workings, and knew what it took to get a project of this magnitude and complexity through to the finish line. A lot of governmental projects start out and often never progress very far because those doing the work are unable to cross the goal line with them. Scoring a goal is the thing that the ATTF did well. It developed the Guiding Principles, went to Cabinet with its Framework, and understood that to prevent the possibility of end runs it had to have Cabinet approval. Once it had Cabinet approval it was going to be difficult for others to undo that approval.

During 1988 negotiating principles for divestiture were developed, feasibility studies for takeover were undertaken, and discussions between TC and the organizing bodies in Vancouver, Edmonton, Calgary and Montréal began regarding those four major airports. Organizing bodies were also at work in Victoria, Winnipeg and Halifax but for various and sundry reasons the early efforts by those three bodies came to naught.[93]

The ATTF looked at airports as three separate business operations: airside, concessions and land development (there was a lot of land available for businesses that needed to be close to the airport). Once the ATTF took airport operations apart into those three business operations then it became easier to come up with the process and the approach and to document all the functions conducted by an airport.

The policy making was done within the ATTF. Normally policy making was done by the Policy Group but the ATTF vision (or foresight) had been "if you want this done in a hurry, and you want it to succeed, then you have to give us the mandate to do what needs to be done without being delayed by the traditional

---

[93] The chapters on those three airports have greater detail on why the transition teams were not able to form an AA by 1992.

bureaucratic processes."[94] At the time TC had 20,000 staff, but the ATTF (with just five staff) had total freedom from them. It could deal with the media, meet with the Transition Groups, meet with the DM and the Minister, meet with staff, anything it thought necessary. The ATTF did newspaper interviews, radio spots, TV interviews, met with city councillors to explain the policy and processes, and with opposition MPs to let them know what was happening. The outreach undertaken by the ATTF "just became normal for us as part of our modus operandi. The operational freedom was both rewarding and productive."[95]

The ATTF discovered that one quite difficult issue to communicate to others in government when discussing the divestiture was the asset value of the airports. Value is not defined solely in terms of finance, there was the inherent strategic, military and commercial value of the lands. The ATTF knew the lands were incredibly valuable but also looked upon the lands from the perspective of 18th and 19th century history. Land is important to a nation: for military purposes, for industrial purposes, for strategic purposes; and the people of Canada owned this vast asset of incredibly well-situated land. There was this non-monetary value of the land that people had to appreciate. Primarily for national security reasons, the government, in the face of turmoil of any kind, political, military, from either inside the country or without, had to be able to put their hands on these assets if they had to.

The Department of Finance officials at the time wanted to sell all the airports because the increased revenue could offset the large deficit and national debt and they thought that at the time of divestiture there would be a large cheque coming into the federal government. But once the ATTF met with Finance and made them realize that these airports were costing the federal government $750 million a year, it became quite clear that government was not going to get a cheque. As the ATTF explained it to Finance, "you're never going to convince a buyer to ante up the money for a money-losing proposition"[96] because the

---

[94] Farquhar and Cloutier, interview.

[95] Ibid.

[96] Ibid.

buyer's question would be "Why would we pay you money to buy something that's losing money?"[97]

That was the final weight that tilted the discussion in favour of a lease. Once the decision was made that the government was going to rent, and the ATTF was given the mandate to say "the government is going to rent, it's going to continue to own the land"[98], there was a whole myriad of other options and variables that had to be considered. If the government was going to rent, how would it set the rent? The ATTF had to remember that the collection of assets that it was trying to transfer ranged from Toronto Pearson to Charlottetown, and so it had to come up with something that would work, which is how it developed policy on the different components. A key guiding principle was that the policy would apply equitably to any airport, whether it was Pearson or Charlottetown. The ATTF had to treat them equitably because they would talk to each other.

Many times the ATTF counselled the Minister or the DM that if they caved in to this demand from that AA, within days they would have a line-up outside the Minister's door. All the others were going to want the same thing. The airports talked to each other. There was a jungle telegraph out there so, if they gave this dollar to this AA, could they afford to give 20 other dollars to the other AAs?[99]

At the same time the ATTF found characteristics unique to each airport it could use to tweak the deal for that particular airport.

The key underlying principle for everything was that the government was to be financially "no worse off than it otherwise would have been had it continued to operate the airport". Unfortunately this principle sometimes got lost in the space of time. When the Auditor General (AG) did his review in 2000 and said the process was flawed, the fact that the airports no longer cost the government $750 million annually was not fully considered. The thing the auditors reported on was the fact that

---

[97] Ibid.

[98] Ibid.

[99] Ibid.

the rent payments weren't what the AG thought they should be due to "significant weaknesses in management practice."[100]

The ATTF decided it had two roles to play. First, it was working for the taxpayer, so it had to do what was right for the taxpayer. Second, the transfer initiative was not about money, it was a transportation initiative – economic regulatory reform. The reason for airport transfers was because TC, as the operator, was not responding to the demands of the day: financially or operationally. So if the system was taken apart and broken down into each airport, it would reflect the needs at the local level. It was a transportation initiative, not deficit reduction.

Naysayers and challenges

However there were many in government who did not share that opinion about it not being deficit reduction. For many months the transfer proceeds were part of the ongoing discussions with Finance.

Very few people understood what the rent formula produced. There was a strong point-of-view within the bureaucracy that somehow, not only could it not happen, would not happen, or should not happen, it was wrong that the government should make a "profit" on a public asset. The ATTF felt strongly that in principle there was nothing wrong with Canada making a return on its investment because Canada had invested billions of dollars into the development of the airports over the course of 60 years. Certainly it was the opinion of the ATTF that the AG never grasped that point of view.

The ATTF met with the AG several times to examine critically and in great detail the policy principles, with the ATTF light heartedly suggesting to the AG that "We're more worried that you're going to find the deal was too good"[101] rather than finding it wanting. Indeed, many in TC agreed with the AG's skepticism about the upside benefits of the transfer policy. If the ATTF hadn't had the political support that it had, it would never have

---

[100] *Report of the Auditor General of Canada, October 2000*, Chapter 10, p. 5.

[101] Farquhar and Cloutier, interview.

gotten the policy principles, let alone the airport transfer agreements, through the governmental processes.

TC's own finance group had difficulty understanding let alone agreeing with the financial aspects of the lease.

The ATTF did not favour a BAA solution (profit) nor did it favour an American style system (municipal government). It rejected those two systems and decided that the AAs would be incorporated provincially or federally as not-for-profit corporations. So the ATTF created a lease arrangement in which the AAs could operate independently by sustaining themselves as a not-for-profit business operation, which was the whole unique aspect of the deal. A non-share distributing corporation.

The question the ATTF asked the financial markets (Smith Barney, Standard & Poor, Canadian Bond Agency, Dominion Bond Rating Agency) was "How does this thing need to be structured so that the bank will lend the AA money?"[102] To test that question the ATTF went to the syndicate bankers and the rating agencies in New York and Toronto, and said "OK, this is the kind of formula we're thinking about. We want to have a structure that will allow these entities to self-finance. Does that mean we should regulate them financially, not regulate them, what kind of controls should we, or should we not, have?"[103] And that's where the ATTF realized that the AAs had to have complete freedom in terms of what they could charge. The government therefore imposed no financial regulation. That gave the AAs the imprimatur of the rating institutions so that when the airport was transferred the AA could immediately go to the banks, ask for cash to build, and the banks would agree (this resulted in a half billion dollar investment in Vancouver within a year of transfer).

The ATTF gave the financial market the background and the structure and explained where it was heading. One of the key criteria was that there would be absolutely no recourse to suborn any of the debt of the AAs to the federal government. Once the AA took over their airport they could borrow any amount they wanted to, but it was the financial institution's responsibility to

---

[102] Ibid.

[103] Farquhar and Cloutier, interview.

never think that the federal government was going to step in and fix it.

The ATTF wanted to know from the financial institutions what should, or should not, be done? If the AA follows that advice, will it be able to raise money? That was crucial so the ATTF made sure that it adjusted and fine-tuned the formula and policy based on the answers that it received.

The ATTF was a very small team, just a handful of people. As legal advisors it had initially Jacques Pigeon and then Michael Senzilet and an excellent lawyer out of TC's Toronto region as well. It had the best legal minds, from a government perspective. The lawyers would say "no, you can't do that, you can't say that."[104] And then the ATTF would say "so how can we do this?"[105] It was the best testing ground. It was important that the legal advice the ATTF received could stand up to every private sector lawyer the AAs hired. (As proof of their legal integrity, the leases and associated transfer documents have stood the test of time, with not a single challenge, legally, on the substance of the documents.)

The ATTF took legal counsel with them when they went to consult the rating agencies and investment bankers. Which was important because their legal counsel had to get his mind around the industry, the financing, and other issues as they arose. Legal counsel was involved in those discussions from the very beginning so that he could draft the text of the leases in the best possible way.,

Although the task force, reconstituted as the Airport Transfers Directorate, was only five principal officials, and two or three support staff, it did everything. There was a team lead. One person handled the financial end, and the other three were project managers assigned to each airport transfer file. The project manager's job was not as a negotiator. It was as a liaison and a coordinator, a facilitator, because the team lead realized that some of those discussions could get a little heated with the AAs, and what he wanted to do was to have one person on the task force not

---

[104] Ibid.

[105] Ibid.

involved in the negotiations. He always had someone who could liaise with the AAs and who was not involved in the negotiations.

The integrity of the ATTF seemingly was never questioned. It was their strong personal commitment to tell it the way it was, factually and honestly, and not to lie. They felt they were respected for being honest. The ATTF might say something to the AA, and if the AA disagreed it might appeal to the Minister, but when the ATTF indicated it was reflecting the Minister's view, the AA eventually learned that that was government policy.

When the ATTF went to negotiate with an AA it would do a lot of analysis and brain-storming before going on the trip to establish its basic position, its fall-back position, and its bottom-line position. It had various degrees of flexibility that it worked out beforehand where it could go and what it could do. There were issues where it could not compromise. Such as precedence, uniformity of treatment, and so on. These issues were inviolable. And on occasion the ATTF found itself in the position of being able to assist the AA in finding a mutually acceptable solution to a specific problem issue it was attempting to address.

There were things that were thought out as they occurred. Such as how employees were going to be treated. That was a major policy piece. The ATTF hired experts to advise them on the HR issues, pensions, etc., and came up with the policy that the AA had to accept all of the TC employees working at the airport, and the employees had to have a compensation package equal to or better than what they were getting from the public service.

Then there was the matter of selling it to the employees. The ATTF dealt with the unions and the employees and met with many of them one-on-one and said "these are the two guiding principles: you're not going to lose your job, and you're not going to lose any money, as a matter of fact you might stand to gain."[106]

So when the AA came up with a proposed compensation package in their HR policy, the ATTF would hire an expert to review it. And the ATTF expert would then contact the AA's expert and the two of them would do the adjustments and tweaking. Eventually,

---

[106] Ibid.

when it got down to the 6th or 7th AA waiting to transfer, they had all essentially shared each other's information and knowledge.

Two–stage transfer process

The transfer took place in two stages.

First, the local organizing committee had to form and incorporate an Airport Authority. This Authority had to be a not-for-profit company incorporated under federal or provincial laws. Once the Authority was in existence, TC would sign with the Authority an Agreement to Transfer.

Second, once an Agreement to Transfer was in place, negotiations would then begin. The Agreement actually consisted of several documents, the most complex of which contained the rent formula. Once the negotiations were at a point where both TC and the Authority were in agreement, then a transfer date would be determined and at that time all the legal documents would be signed.

As I write this, it all seems so very simple. But the devil is in the details, as it is said, and there are many who will tell you that many devils were involved.

The LAA Rent Formula – 1992

The base rent formula was allocated amongst three broad sources of revenue: airside and general terminal; concessions and commercial; and, industrial and real estate. From each of these three revenue sources the government would receive a base payment plus participation in any additional revenue resulting from value-added initiatives of the AA. The formula was sensitive to inflation and traffic fluctuations. The ATTF was concerned that the rent formula provide a fair and equitable balance between the financial interests of the government and those of the AA. The long-term financial viability of the AA was just as important as a fair return to the government. [107]

Airside was considered on a cost recovery basis. The AA couldn't make a "profit" on airside revenues. The rent formula started off

---

[107] Ibid. p. 8.

with base costs, which included operating costs, and capital costs, in terms of if TC had continued to operate the airport these are the costs TC would have had. For airside, base costs were quite important. The formula then said the AA could earn income, up to base costs. As long as the income did not exceed base costs the AA paid no rent for airside revenues. If the AA charged over and above its costs to the airlines then there was rent to be paid on the excess.

	Business Compenents	Base Revenues	-	Base Costs	=	Base Rent
	Airside/Terminal General (AGT)	Stated landing fees from airlines	-	Stated costs of operating the airport	=	Base AGT
Base Rent	Concessions	Rental fees from boutiques	-	Stated costs of maintaining the rental spaces	=	Base concession rent
	Real Estate (Base Rent)	Rental fees from existing land leases at date of trasnfer	-	Not applicable	=	Base real estate rent

Figure 3: LAA - Base Rent Formula

Revenues from concessions were considered like a shopping mall. Each individual concessionaire had base costs. However if the AA had commercial profits on the concessions it had to pay rent. Basically the bulk of the rent payable to the government came from concessions, and concession revenue was linked to passenger volume. Ergo rent was sensitive to passenger volume and rent received by the government would fluctuate up and down accordingly. For example, not long after transfer in 1992 across Canada there was a major drop in passenger volume and, therefore, revenue. The formula reflected that drop as a decrease in rent receipts.

All existing contracts were transferred over to the Airport Authority on the same rent basis as the concessions - base costs and then excess over costs would be subject to rent.

The ATTF believed the formula to be equitable, both to the taxpayer and to the AA, and would not endanger the Authority's financial viability.

At that time the ATTF did not have any idea, in terms of land development, just what would occur over time. It knew there were a lot of businesses that needed access to airside or where it would be advantageous to be on airport land, and it thought, it's only a matter of time before the AAs run out of land to rent, or lease. The ATTF knew that the land had significant value, particularly in some of the major airports, and it was an asset of Canada, so the government should share in a portion of the revenues from the development of that land.

Participation rent was the other major portion of the rent formula.

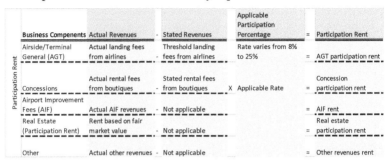

	Business Compenents	Actual Revenues		Stated Revenues	Applicable Participation Percentage		Participation Rent
Participation Rent	Airside/Terminal General (AGT)	Actual landing fees from airlines	-	Threshold landing fees from airlines	Rate varies from 8% to 25%	=	AGT participation rent
	Concessions	Actual rental fees from boutiques	-	Stated rental fees from boutiques	X Applicable Rate	=	Concession participation rent
	Airport Improvement Fees (AIF)	Actual AIF revenues	-	Not applicable		=	AIF rent
	Real Estate (Participation Rent)	Rent based on fair market value	-	Not applicable		=	Real estate participation rent
	Other	Actual other revenues	-	Not applicable		=	Other revenues rent

Figure 4: LAA – Participation Rent Formula

When the ATTF first began looking at airports and the lands on which they were located, the federal government and TC were not in a position to develop industrial and business operations on those lands. More importantly the federal government and TC had no idea at that time that those lands would be such large generators of cash as the lands eventually turned out to be. The ATTF knew that under existing policy TC was in effect stifling investment and land development and it had a hard time selling the first four deals within TC because the other bureaucrats could not believe that the existing land development policy was wrong.

Selling the deal

The ATTF also had to sell the deals to the Treasury Board Secretariat (TBS). They twice made formal proposals to TBS for approval of the transfer deals. Cloutier had very good relations with the Treasury Board analysts. He met with them twice a month and kept them informed of the kind of discussions the ATTF was having – "here's the philosophy, here's the reasoning; here's the direction; and here's why we can't do this, and why we can do that."[108] The ATTF knew that at some point it would have

---

[108] Ibid.

to go to TBS for approval of the leases and the transactions, and so, rather than wait until the end and risk having TBS say no, it did a continuous update with the TBS analyst so that when the request finally came, the analyst had already seen everything and trusted the information provided by the ATTF. The intent was that there be no surprises.

The ATTF did the same thing with Ministerial approvals by keeping Ministers informed on a continuing basis thereby avoiding major surprises. What allowed the ATTF to function, to be as successful as they were, was their relations with Ministerial staff and with the Minister of Transport. The Minister and his staff had to have the comfort that the ATTF knew what it was doing and was seeking Ministerial input and approval at the appropriate times.

In the negotiations the ATTF dealt with CEOs and local business owners and operators. Bright people who knew their businesses, and who knew how to relate to other businesses. But almost all of them did not have an appreciation for how the federal government bureaucracy functioned in practise. One clear advantage the ATTF believed it had in the negotiations was that the AAs often underestimated the capabilities of the bureaucrats ("the worst strategic thing you can do - underestimate your opponent"[109]). The ATTF had done its homework, and knew what it was doing. It was very quick to learn the legal side, and understood the basic business aspect of operating an airport. Some of the AAs thought of the ATTF as "just bureaucrats." And quite a few of the folk conducting the negotiations of behalf of their AA didn't fully understand government operations.

From the beginning of negotiations the ATTF dealt with the AA members who would almost always form the first Board. When the AA got to a certain point where they could see daylight at the end of the tunnel, even though a deal had not yet been made, they'd hire an executive director.

---

[109] Ibid.

Supplementary Principles

The ATTF developed 36 "Supplementary Principles" as to how the devolution of the airports was to proceed. These Supplementary Principles focused on general policy issues, personnel matters, safety, security and operational matters, commercial and financial matters and community relations. In addition the Supplementary Principles provided guidance on the creation of the LAAs.[110] Some of the 36 Supplementary Principles were:

- The LAA was intended to be a legally-created, financially-independent, business entity which would manage and operate the local airport system and associated business enterprises;
- Its Board of Directors would be appointed through a process acceptable to both the municipalities and the federal government;
- Board members must be Canadian citizens nominated by municipalities, provinces and the federal government;
- The Board would likely include representatives of local business and community interests, such as Boards of Trade, Chambers of Commerce and other representative socio-economic groups;
- Board members would have the requisite technical skills for operating an airport, such as engineering, law, business and finance;
- The Board members would probably not include elected officials nor government employees;
- The government's overall funding requirement for airports would not increase in the long term as a result of transfers;
- The valuation of the airports to be transferred would be on the basis of their fair market value, with proper consideration of their earning potential;
- Airports to be leased on a long-term basis;
- Airport authorities would be financially viable; and
- Airport authorities would operate at arm's length from government and without financial recourse to it.

---

[110] Michael Farquhar, *Privatization of Airports and Airport Operators, Airport Transfers, the Canadian Approach*. Speech to the American Transportation Research Board, Washington, D.C. 23 January 1989. Farquhar Personal Collection, p. 8.

It was an unusual way to develop policy.[111] Normally those in the policy group would be asked to solve a problem, write a "policy paper" outlining their thoughts, reasoning, and potential solutions, and then circulate their paper to many different groups for response. Eventually, perhaps, the paper became a regulation, or even law. But this was different. This was a "transactional" approach to making policy. First they made the Principles, then they made the Policy for Transfer. It was a good way to make policy. It has withstood the test of time. It has survived several governments and at least one attempt by a couple of the airports to pressure the government into complete privatization.[112]

The accountability of Board members provoked lively debate within both the ATAB and the ATTF. Some argued that Board members should be appointed by the municipalities and thus be directly accountable to the electorate. Others argued that this would make the AAs too responsive to local municipal concerns, i.e. should the resurfacing of an airport runway take precedence over a new library, or sports complex?[113] This discussion would not be wholly resolved until the issuance of the Public Accountability Principles in 1995.

Another concern was the form of transfer. Should it be an outright purchase, or a long-term lease? The lease was thought to be more acceptable to the public, and, in the event of an unlikely failure of the AA, would allow for the government to move quickly to reinstate control of all aspects of airport operations.[114]

Personnel matters were also considered. Federal government employees would be treated fairly at transfer ensuring that the AA offered comparable employment, pay and benefits packages (pension, medical, continuity of service, etc.) under the Canada

---

[111] See Annex "Policy Development in a Federal Government Department".

[112] Doug Young, the former Minister of Transport was in favour of complete privatization [Globe & Mail, 15 January 2014]. However, the remainder of the airports were not in favour of it.

[113] Farquhar, 23 January 1989, p. 9.

[114] Ibid.

Labour Code.[115] But "transfer" of public sector employees to an entirely unknown and untested private sector organization was a sensitive issue. Change (i.e. "transfer") breeds uncertainty, insecurity, frustration and rumour-mongering, and if not addressed will overcome the best-laid plans. This was change of a very high degree and without the acceptance of the employees the transfers would be difficult, if not impossible. To counter this the ATTF created airport site communications committees as a forum for the exchange of information on the status of the transfer negotiations. These fora allowed for discussions between the employees and the ATTF on such issues as job guarantees, surplus notices, salaries and job classifications, pension and health benefits, and collective agreements. [116]

Although protective policing, particularly relating to terrorism, was to remain the responsibility of the federal government, the provision of crash, fire and rescue services was to be the responsibility of the AA.[117]

Finally, the ATAB had determined that lease payments would be determined from fair market value of the airports, calculated on the basis of discounted forecast cash flow over the life of the lease. This included the impact of forecast traffic flows, anticipated capital expenditures for maintenance and improvements, projected landing fees, passenger facility charges, and other revenues and expenses.[118]

The ATAB also considered that the government should share a portion of gross revenues that were generated over and above the revenues initially calculated to determine the fair market value.[119] The "revenue sharing" approach would ease the pressure of being totally dependent on the accuracy of forecasts. The ATTF also

---

[115] Ibid. p. 10.

[116] Michael Farquhar, *An Executive Briefing on Partnership, Devolution and Power Sharing: Implications for Management.* Transport Canada. 3 December 1992, p. 9.

[117] Farquhar, 23 January 1989, p. 10.

[118] Ibid. p. 11.

[119] Ibid.

considered if a revenue sharing scheme without a parallel loss-sharing component could be negotiated.[120]

Another important consideration was that the government would not be subordinated to any other financial obligation of the LAA, and that the government would avoid any contingent liability for LAA undertakings[121] nor would it be a party to any joint venture.[122] The government's goal was to ensure that the financial lending institution, not the government, would bear the financial risk.[123]

The financial bottom line was quite clear in the minds of the ATTF. The net revenues, current and forecast, generated by the airport and flowing to the government had to be at least guaranteed and indeed increased under an LAA operation. The government had to be "no worse off" financially. As negotiators, the ATTF believed it was their task to ensure that delicate balance was maintained between the financial interests of the government on the one hand, and those of the LAA on the other. The ATTF members were not going to recommend to the Minister a transfer to an LAA unless they were satisfied on three counts: the financial terms were satisfactory to both parties; the airport site employees were fairly treated; and, the LAA had the competency and commitment to operate the airport in a responsible commercially-oriented manner. The LAAs would be free to establish their own fees and charges so as to facilitate their efforts to finance their operations on the open money market. [124]

On the date of transfer the LAAs would be required to purchase the airport chattels at net book value and provide assurances to the government that there would always be sufficient funds to attend

---

[120] Farquhar, 3 October 1989, p. 8.

[121] Ibid.

[122] Michael Farquhar, *The private sector's involvement in the development, funding and operations of airports and terminals*. Institute for International Research, New York, New York, 12 July 1990. Farquhar Personal Collection. p. 9.

[123] Ibid. p. 10.

[124] Farquhar, 3 October 1989, p. 9.

to the LAAs principal business: the management and operation of the airport.[125]

The ATTF had considered the issue of how the LAA was to raise funds from the financial markets prior to actually taking control of the airport. With no equity and no shareholders, why would the bank lend money to the LAA? The answer to that question was that there was no economic regulation of user charges set by the LAA. It was free to set its own site-specific user fees for landing, terminal usage, passenger facility fees, and other charges as it from time-to-time might impose.[126] The LAA would be able to issue airport revenue bonds for financing major capital undertakings.[127] The LAA would have great scope to develop the concessions in the ATB and to develop commercial operations on airport lands.[128] It would be the airport, not the airline, which would make the final decision on capacity expansions. Unlike the United States, where the airport has a very close relationship with the airline, and the airline can veto a decision by the airport, in Canada it is the AA which makes the final decision on infrastructure, albeit in consultation with the airlines[129] The ATTF was convinced that the ability to levy passenger charges would become an invaluable tool. Contrary to the system in the United States, where passenger charges were heavily regulated, the AAs would self-regulate on a cooperative, consultative partnership with the airlines. It was felt that this would remove pressure on terminal charges and place more responsibility directly and visibly on the key airport user: the passenger. Such passenger facility charges could be applied in a

---

[125] Farquhar, 12 July 1990. p. 10.

[126] Ibid.

[127] Ibid. p. 11.

[128] Ibid.

[129] Ronald Daniels and Michael Trebilcock, *Policy Instruments – Financing and Delivery of Infrastructure in the Public and Private Sector"* University of Toronto. Discussed by Michael Farquhar at a seminar on Infrastructure and Competitiveness, Investment Canada, 4 June 1993.

flexible manner and be directly linked to capital improvement projects at the AA.[130]

Discussion on the lease structure and how payments were to be made continued throughout this period and by mid-1991 the idea of "rent" was firmly established.

With the basics out of the way, now what? The first four – Local Airport Authorities

The Airport Authority approach was developed by Transport Canada in the 1980's and 1990's to replace an ill-defined and ad-hoc system of airport management. The government had exercised its responsibilities for more than 60 years with no statutory, regulatory or policy framework to define the role for the federal government in the operation of airports. Airport performance had historically been undermined by several factors, including a large centralized administration and restrictive public-sector labour agreements that increased airports' labour requirements. With local control, the expectation of the federal government was that airports would operate in a commercial and cost-effective manner and be more responsive to local needs. The transfer was also aimed at facilitating investment and relieving the airports of government financial constraints.

With the authority of the policy statement on the management of Canadian airports, Transport Canada officials undertook negotiations to transfer major airports, starting with those in the four cities that accounted for the majority of air traffic in the country (except for Toronto). Departmental officials negotiated with local representative corporations formed for that purpose.

In 1992, the government concluded negotiations with four private, not-for-profit local airport authorities (LAAs) in Vancouver (1 May), Calgary (1 July), Edmonton (1 August) and Montréal (comprising Dorval and Mirabel airports – 1 August). Each transfer was authorized by an Agreement to Transfer, a legal contract between the government and the local body that had been

---

[130] Michael Farquhar, *The Future of Airports in the U.S. and Canada.* Speech to the American Association of Airport Executives, 29 July 1991. Farquhar Personal Collection. p. 11.

formed, in accordance with federal guidelines, to manage the airport. The Agreement to Transfer set out the structure and rules to carry out the transfer, and it, along with the lease were the key documents.

The transfer process followed a set procedure. First the Agreement to Transfer was signed and about 3 months later, when all the preconditions had been met, the transfer documents (there were about 10 of them, one of which was the lease) were signed and the transfer took effect.

The transfer agreements were complex, lengthy documents. Key clauses for these first National Airport System (NAS) airports were:

1. the agreements were leases, meaning that ownership was to remain with the government; and,
2. the leases were to be in effect for a period of 60 years; with a 20 year extension if requested by the AA and approved by the minister.

Another key clause was the amount of rent (the "Canada Lease" agreement) to be paid to the government by the local authority; this amount varied by airport. The rent was determined under an approved formula, but was limited to a maximum base rent payable in any lease year.

In addition to rent, the Authorities had to make annual payments towards the amount owing as a result of the purchase of chattels and inventory from Transport Canada.

Throughout all the deliberations surrounding the creation of the AAs, the ATTF had no instructions to include governance. Even after the LAAs were formed in 1992, there were only the Accountability Principles, which in and of themselves were not directly about governance. Again, there were no instructions to the ATTF to add anything about governance. For although there was a desire on the part of the government to transfer these entities there was very little appetite to control them as entities. It was more to let the AAs do what they needed to do in order to operate effectively and efficiently as aerodromes. TC was concerned mainly with continuing to regulate the safe operation of aerodromes. The proposed Canada Airports Act was an attempt to instill governance but failed twice. The fact that it has not been pursued for at least the past 10 years may indicate that there is no real push on the part of TC to control the corporate entities that are the LAAs or CAAs.

What the ATTF accomplished by 1992

After a somewhat hesitant start to devolution, the transfer of the first four LAAs was completed by 1992. Actions to devolve the rest of the airports (now CAAs) were completed by 2003. At the end of 1992, the ATTF would report[131] that it had been able to transfer successfully operations to the four LAAs:

- The LAA is designed to be a not-for-profit organization, based on the assumption that all profits will be plowed back into the airport for future improvements. It has no shareholders.
- The initiative for creating a LAA must come from the local community, not from the government, and must have the endorsement of the local municipal governments and the Minister of Transport.
- The LAA must be incorporated under provincial enabling legislation or the Canada Corporations Act Part II.
- The ATTF received a specific negotiating mandate from Cabinet. It established a number of intra- and inter-departmental working groups, developed a relationship with Justice Canada lawyers both in Ottawa and the regions, established an open and on-going working relationship with the central agencies (which was essential to facilitate government approval of the deals), and drew heavily on expert independent consultants.
- The transfer of the five international airports to the four CAAs comprised more than 1,000 public servants and federal assets with a net book value of more than $600 million.
- The ATTF developed policies, rules, a rent formula, negotiated and drafted more than 1,000 pages of legal text, and developed and presented to Parliament two separate Bills addressing labour relationships, official languages, and commercial issues (including the income tax status of the LAAs).

---

[131] Michael Farquhar, 3 December 1992, p. 5.

- During the time of transfer there had been much change on the political front, but the original mandate held, despite extensive lobbying by the AAs.

- From a strategic negotiating perspective the ATTF had an advantage of negotiating separately, and sometimes together, with four different parties, who did not always agree on substantive financial, technical and legal issues.

- One of the most difficult, and at times frustrating, aspects of the negotiations, for both sides, was the fact that the private sector representatives did not always have a very good appreciation of how government and public servants worked. Especially with the pace at which things occurred, and the inability to control that pace, such as for legislation, and for Treasury Board and Cabinet approvals, plus the constant need for government to be publicly accountable for its own actions, both legally and financially.

- The ATTF had to explain to the AA that sometimes it would be good if the AA could wear a "taxpayers' hat" in order to appreciate the position the ATTF took a particular legal or financial issue. The basic objective of the ATTF, namely to transfer the airport to the private sector, was no different from that of the LAA, who wanted it transferred. It was important that the private sector recognized that the public servants were carrying out a policy mandate which may not have been easy to implement and that had been established by Ministers, not officials. The officials and the private sector were really participants in a common cause in the public interest, and one which ideally should have been devoid of adversarial conflict.

- The ATTF had to keep in mind that because it was engaged in a unique exercise it would be subject to very close scrutiny by Parliament, the Auditor General, central agencies, and the general public. Consequently it ensured that its files and records were complete, had independent reports on the validity and acceptability of the audit and insurance clauses, on an assessment of the LAA's employee's benefits plans, business plans and financial proposals, on the financial provisions of the ground lease through the eyes of insurance companies and financial institutions in Canada and the United States, and, finally, an independent review of all legal documentation by a major law firm.

Constraints

It is important to remember that there were three sides to everything that occurred during the years prior to, and also subsequently to, devolution and the transfer of the airports to the AAs. There was the political side, with the Governments of the day doing what their politicians do best: making speeches, taking a side, gaining advantage, posturing, explaining, equivocating. There was the AA side, doing their best to understand what it was that was being demanded of them to negotiate a "good" deal, and lobbying the Government like mad when they believed they were not getting their way.[132] And there was the bureaucratic side, with public servants trying their best to ensure that the Canadian taxpayer got the best return on more than 60 years' investment in airport infrastructure.

It is also important to note that during the period of devolution from 1984 to 2003 there were:

- eight Ministers of Transport from two very different political parties: Don Mazankowski (PC), John Crosbie (PC), Benoît Bouchard (PC), Doug Lewis (PC), Jean Corbeil (PC), Doug Young (Lib), David Anderson (Lib), and David Collenette (Lib);
- one Secretary of State for Airport Transfers: Gerry St. Germain (PC);
- seven Deputy Ministers at Transport Canada: Ramsay M. Withers, Glen Shortliffe, Huguette Labelle, Jocelyn Bourgon, Nick Mulder, Margaret Bloodworth, and Louis Ranger;
- and one federal election, in 1993 when the Government changed from Conservative to Liberal.

Year	Authority & Date of Transfer	Minister of Transport	Secretary of State for Transport	Deputy Minister, Transport Canada
1984		Don Mazankowski (PC)		Ramsay M. Withers
1985		Don Mazankowski (PC)		Ramsay M. Withers
1986		Don Mazankowski (PC) John Crosbie (PC)		Ramsay M. Withers
1987		John Crosbie (PC)		Ramsay M. Withers
1988		John Crosbie (PC) Benoît Bouchard (PC)	Gerry St. Germain (PC)	Glen Shortliffe
1989		Benoît Bouchard (PC)		Glen Shortliffe
1990		Benoît Bouchard (PC) Doug Lewis (PC)		Huguette Labelle

---

[132]Ibid. p. 6.

Year	Authority & Date of Transfer	Minister of Transport	Secretary of State for Transport	Deputy Minister, Transport Canada
1991		Doug Lewis (PC) Jean Corbeil (PC)		Huguette Labelle
1992	Vancouver, 1 May Calgary, 1 July Edmonton, 1 August Montréal, 1 Aug	Jean Corbeil (PC)		Huguette Labelle
1993		Jean Corbeil (PC) Doug Young (Lib)		Huguette Labelle Jocelyn Bourgon
1994		Doug Young (Lib)		Jocelyn Bourgon
1995		Doug Young (Lib)		Nick Mulder
1996	Toronto, 1 December	Doug Young (Lib) David Anderson (Lib)		Nick Mulder
1997	Ottawa, 1 February Victoria, 1 April Moncton, 1 September Thunder Bay, 1 September Winnipeg, 1 December	David Anderson (Lib) David Collenette (Lib)		Nick Mulder
1998	London, 1 August St. John's, 1 December	David Collenette (Lib)		Margaret Bloodworth
1999	Saskatoon, 1 January Charlottetown, 1 March Regina, 1 May Saint John, 1 June	David Collenette (Lib)		Margaret Bloodworth
2000	Halifax, 1 February Québec, 1 November	David Collenette (Lib)		Margaret Bloodworth
2001	Gander, 1 March Fredericton, 1 May	David Collenette (Lib)		Louis Ranger
2002		David Collenette (Lib)		Louis Ranger
2003	Prince George, 1 March	David Collenette (Lib)		Louis Ranger

Figure 5: Ministers of Transport, Secretary of State for Transport, and Deputy Ministers of Transport - 1984-2003

Notwithstanding these changes, and very active lobbying by the AAs, the political commitment remained constant throughout. There were three formal Cabinet reviews of the negotiations and the mandate for the ATTF remained the same "Do the best for Canadians."[133]

There was also the really inspirational and intellectual roles of Don Mazankowski and Ron Gilbertson. Those two were a team when Maz was the Transport Critic when in the Official Opposition because both realized that TC made a major mistake when it built Edmonton International without requiring the closure of Edmonton Municipal, similar to the Montréal mistake of not closing Dorval when Mirabel was built.[134] Maz and Gilbertson were passionate about the fact that their community, and also that of northern Alberta, was really being held back because of the lack of air-based connectivity. It was not uncommon to hear someone

[133] Ibid. p. 7.

[134] *Paul Benoit*, interview with the Author, 30 November 2018.

67

from the northern part of Alberta say "when you die in Edmonton or Northern Alberta you don't know if you're going to heaven or hell, but you can be damned sure you're going to have to make a connection through Calgary."[135] They felt that direct services would lead to greater prosperity, and from that came the idea that the airport would do much better under local control. And that is the beginnings of the idea of devolution, in September 1984 with Maz saying "we're gonna do this. Here we have a civil service that doesn't want to hear anything about this", but Maz got the ATTF in place, and then the ATAB, and that's a key lesson – to have a task force and an advisory board. "I'm not too sure that Crosbie was all behind this, but St. Germain was also key. But the leadership here really came from Maz and Gilbertson."[136]

But before we take a closer look at the first four AAs, let us hear the government's side of the story.

Politics

Well before Canada began to consider the possibility, other countries had decided to let entities other than the public sector operate airports. The United States had always had a large portion of its airport infrastructure operated by either municipalities or private sector entities with the provision of federal funding for infrastructure, and Great Britain had created the BAA, a totally private sector entity. Since the creation of the Canadian AAs, Australia now leases 22 airports to private sector corporations but within an economic regulatory environment which governs the fees an Australian airport may charge.

Commercialization of airports in Canada, as an operating principle, did not necessarily mean privatization, which implied a commercial sale to the highest private sector bidder.[137] As Michael Farquhar so eloquently put it "In Canada when it comes to the issue of airport transfers we are talking about privatization … sort of, perhaps, partially … but not quite."[138] The federal government's

---

[135] *Mazankowski*, 19 November 2018.

[136] Tretheway, Interview 28 November 2018.

[137] Farquhar, 3 October 1989, p. 3.

[138] Farquhar, 23 January 1989, p. 1.

philosophy was one of gradualism, and its point-of-view was that commercial interests would operate the infrastructure, but the government would retain ownership of the land. Private interests would neither own outright nor profit from the airport operations, unlike the BAA. Airport infrastructure could still be taken over and operated by the private sector, with revenues from landing fees and passenger charges offsetting operating costs and capital expenditures.

In 1989 the federal government owned 136 land-based airports and directly operated 76 of those. The cost to the government of airport operations that year was more than $750 million.

However, before anything could happen the political and bureaucratic wings had to get aligned.

Gerry St. Germain[139] was Caucus Chairman of the federal Conservative Party under Brian Mulroney[140] from 1985 to 1988. On a Thursday evening in 1988 he received a call from Derek Burney, the PM's Chief of Staff (COS), who asked him to come over to the Prime Minister's Office (PMO) as Mulroney wanted to speak with him.[141] St. Germain went over to the PMO and asked Burney "What's going on?". Burney replied he did not know but that the boss had asked to see St. Germain. A few minutes later Mulroney called St. Germain into his office. Almost immediately Mulroney said "I want you in Cabinet. You can have one of three Ministries: Fisheries, Indians, or Transport." St. Germain replied that he knew nothing about fish, was himself a métis, and, since he was a commercial pilot and had been in the RCAF, he'd like to go to Transport. Mulroney said "OK, we'll make you Minister of State for Transport. But's there's more. This devolution of the airports to airport authorities has stalled long enough. Crosby[142] and Mazankowski have set the stage. Now I want you to get this done."

---

[139] Secretary of State for Airport Transfers, Transport Canada, 1989 – 1992.

[140] Prime Minister from 1984 to 1993.

[141] Derek Burney. Interview with the author, 13 December 2018.

[142] John Crosby, PC OC ONL QC, Minister of Transport, 1986-1988.

A short phone call to Benoît (Benny) Bouchard, who was the Minister of Transport, informed him of Mulroney's decision to appoint St. Germain as Minister of State for Airport Authorities.

A second phone call from St. Germain to Glen Shortliffe, the Deputy Minister (DM) at TC, arranged for St. Germain to meet with Shortliffe the following Monday morning.

A third phone call was to Doug Eyford, who became St. Germain's COS and who (along with Victor Barbeau[143] and Michael Farquhar[144]) was to play a major role in ensuring the airport authorities came into existence.

When St. Germain arrived at Shortliffe's office on Monday morning, Shortliffe was not there. Instead all the TC ADMs were standing around the boardroom table to meet St. Germain. The discussion went something like this:[145]

- St. Germain "I want to get these airports privatized."

- The ADMs "So do we, Minister."

- St. Germain "So why hasn't it happened?"

- The ADMs "We'll brief you."

- St. Germain "I don't need to be 'briefed'. I want to get it done!"

- The ADMs "We're working on it."

- St. Germain "Well it not going quickly enough."

- The ADMs "We're doing our best."

- St. Germain "Your best isn't good enough."

At this point Shortliffe entered the room.

- Shortliffe "Good morning, Minister."

- St. Germain "I'm telling your people that I want to see the airports privatized, now!".

---

[143] Victor Barbeau, ADM, Head of Airports Group, Transport Canada.

[144] Michael Farquhar, Director General Airports Transfer, Transport Canada.

[145] When St. Germain recounted this to me I could not but help think of the BBC television program: *Yes, Minister.*

- Shortliffe "We're looking after it."

- St. Germain "That's not good enough. I want a point man. Someone who I can speak with at any time."

- Shortliffe "No, that's not going to happen. As I said, we will look after it."

- St. Germain "OK. So if you're not going to play ball with me, I'm resigning this job."

At that point St. Germain picks up the boardroom telephone and, in front of Shortliffe and all the ADMs, calls the PMO. The PM's secretary answers and he asks for Mulroney. She says she will put him through. While he's waiting Shortliffe signals him:

- Shortliffe "Wait, wait. We can give you someone."

St. Germain pauses, tells the PMO he'll call back, hangs up the phone and looks at Shortliffe.

- St. Germain "Who?"

And that was when Victor Barbeau, at that time Assistant Deputy Minister, Airports Group, was assigned as the point man to liaise with St. Germain on the devolution of the airports to the airport authorities. Barbeau had an excellent resource to call upon to assist him: Michael Farquhar, who from his experience in all the central agencies[146] of the government knew his way around, and who in 1983 had been part of the very successful team, under the leadership of the DM, Arthur Kroeger, in negotiating the new rates for the Crow's Nest Pass Freight Rates Agreement[147] as well as being involved in or managing a number of other significant national transportation policy initiatives.

St. Germain's opinion was that the bureaucracy at TC did not want their empire dismantled and the senior management was not excited about getting the devolution done. Although some TC

---

[146] Prime Minister's Office, Privy Council Office, Treasury Board Secretariat, and the Department of Finance.

[147] *The Crow's Nest Pass Agreement*, dated 6 September 1897, was an agreement between the CPR and the Canadian government to subsidize the movement of grain from western farmers to their markets. Its provisions were curtailed by the passing of the Western Grain Transportation Act on 17 November 1983 in an effort to reduce the national debt. The subsidy was removed entirely in 1993.

staff got on-side with the devolution, according to St. Germain there were a lot of folk who bided their time and dragged their feet, knowing that eventually an election would be called and in all possibility St. Germain would go away. He did not. He stayed, "snapping at their heels until the job was done".

But, as St. Germain said "The unsung heroes were Doug Eyford, Victor Barbeau and Michael Farquhar. They were the ones who actually made devolution a done deed. I was just the politician."

What would the ATTF have done differently?

I asked Mike Farquhar and John Cloutier, "it's now more than 25 years since the first AAs. With hindsight, if you had to do it all over again, what would you do differently?" Their answers are interesting:

1. We'd make it harder to amend the rent formula.

2. We would have regular financial audits by the AG. The existing audits are done by the AA's own auditors, but what is needed is an independent audit conducted by the AG, or by someone hired by the AG on the government's behalf.

3. We would have a process for better communications within government including central agencies, on the rent philosophy, so that we don't end up at the end with someone saying "Oh, we should sell these. Or, there's something wrong with the rent. Or, we shouldn't charge rent", or whatever. There should be an ongoing dialogue within government. There wasn't much interest in that kind of dialogue when we started because it was "how can you tax these airports when there's no money in it?" or "Don't bother me with that." It's hard to communicate when the other person doesn't want to listen. That was as far as we could go at the time, as was feasible. We knew what the issues were, and we pushed the boundaries as far as we could, but we got so much pushback. We could fight it, but we realized we'd lose time. And we wanted to get the job done.

4. We would set up a process for regular meetings between TC and the nominating entities. It doesn't happen today. We don't

think the governmental nominees necessarily fully appreciate what their unique role is as a Board member of the AA.

5. We would examine the existing structure in the nominating process to see if it reflects community interests in the broadest sense, because the nominating entities were thought of 30 years ago now, and do the nominating entities still represent the major interests of the local community?

6. We would re-examine the nominating process for an AA's Board of Directors. What is the role of the federal nominee? That has to be defined. Does he represent the government of the day? Does he represent the national interest? Is there a national interest in a local authority? What is his role. We never went through that. We just said, there's a federal government representative keeping an eye on stuff. It may be that you don't need the provincial and federal nominees. That is the question that should at least be asked. It would need study, and it is not something that one would think of, but why are they there? What is their purpose? Because if it is another body who is bringing their brain to the operations of the Board, that's fine. But if they still have a role in representing, in some way or other on that Board a federal government priority or defined perspective then you've got to make sure that whoever's nominated is doing that.

The appointment by the federal government of someone to the Board was done in the first place simply because it was felt that the federal government should keep an eye on the AA. But with experience it's worth re-examining the entire structure and process.

7. We would re-examine whether or not the level of accountability and transparency is adequate. If you are considering making changes you cannot sacrifice accountability. You cover accountability through the mandated independent audits. If I'm nominated to the Board, that's great and I bring whatever it is I bring to it, but I could be nominated by the local taxi company, is there any difference? We dealt with it superficially, because we wanted to ensure the local representation aspect of it, but the federal government sort of

felt it needed to have eyes on the ball and that was all it was. But I think a Board of Directors should be much more hands on and doing its fiduciary responsibility. A lot depended on the CEO. Some CEOs were very independent, some were very dominant and told their Boards what to do.

To these seven issues I add my own thoughts on what now could be done differently.

The Public Accountability Principles promulgated in 1995 require that "at least once every five years, the Authority shall cause a review of the Authority's management, operation and financial performance to be conducted by a qualified independent person ("the reviewer")".[148] At the time the Principles were written, the ATTF was concerned that formal oversight of the LAA's was missing from the Lease so it added this requirement for an independent review to offset, in some small measure, that oversight. I have conducted more than 45 such independent reviews and my experience shows me that they are a worthwhile endeavour for the Authority. The Authorities I have worked for have allowed me untrammeled access to anything and anybody in my process of establishing an opinion on safety, security, business practices, and governance. Not once in the 15 years I have conducted these Performance Reviews have I been asked by an Airport Authority to not look at something, or to not speak with someone, or to remove something from my report.[149] I believe that the Authorities for whom I have conducted the Reviews consider the review to have been worthwhile and that the Review presents an honest and complete appraisal of the Authority's activities.[150]

Later, in 2000, the Auditor General for Canada, in Chapter 10 of his October 2000 Report (Airport Transfers: National Airports System) reported that oversight was missing. He found TC to be

---

[148] *Public Accountability Principles for Canadian Airport Authorities*, s. 17.

[149] Although one time I was asked by TC to remove a statement from my report as they felt it was too critical. I refused. The statement was true.

[150] That is not the case for some of the Authorities. One Authority presented a three-page Performance Review – in effect, a whitewash. They are meeting the letter of the Agreement, not the intent.

"largely passive about monitoring and overseeing the NAS"[151] and recommended that TC "ensure that they [the AAs] comply with … leases, agreements to transfer, and by-laws".[152] In the formal reply to the AG, TC stated that it would implement "a more rigorous lease monitoring program" and establish "a national program to transfer critical knowledge and skills to all staff responsible for lease management."[153]

TC did, in fact, establish a Lease Monitoring Program and by 2005 was conducting annual lease reviews and writing Lease Monitoring Reports for each of the 21 AAs. This detailed level of oversight continued for about 10 years, but somewhere around 2015 the process got derailed, mostly, it would seem, to cuts in TC travel budgets which then precluded teams of inspectors from travelling to the airports to conduct the lease reviews. The inspectors now do not conduct site visits and instead rely upon "attestations" from the Authority that the Authority is following the rules. Since there does not seem to be any penalty specified in the Civil Aviation Regulations for misleading information to be given in an attestation or non-compliance with the rules, the Lease Monitoring Reports may not be as trustworthy as could be possible.

---

[151] Auditor General, October 2000, Chapter 10, p. 10-38.

[152] Ibid.

[153] Ibid. p. 10-42.

Chapter 4: National Airports Policy & Public Accountability Principles

By 1995 the four LAAs[154] had been a going concern for three years but the remaining 17 airports in the NAS that were going to go to an airport authority were still to be devolved.

It all happened in a bit of a rush (at least by a government bureaucrat's standards, it was a rush). From 1995 to 2003 seventeen Canadian Airport Authorities (CAAs) were created:

- 1996: Toronto Pearson
- 1997: Winnipeg, Ottawa, Moncton, Thunder Bay, Victoria
- 1998: London, St. John's
- 1999: Charlottetown, Regina, Saint John, Saskatoon
- 2000: Halifax, Québec
- 2001: Fredericton, Gander
- 2003: Prince George

But before all that happened there were several events that affected how the remaining airport authorities were to come about.

National Airports Policy

In 1993 the Liberal party was elected and formed the Government. Doug Young became Minister of Transport and immediately began to promote his ideas for the privatization of transport in Canada. A conservative-minded liberal, he was very much in favour of privatization[155] but his colleagues in Government did not all agree with him. There was robust debate, with Young on one side and Collenette on the other, as whether or not the airports should be privatized, or remain in public control but be operated in a more business-like fashion.[156]

---

[154] Four LAAs but five airports: Vancouver, Edmonton, Calgary, Montréal Dorval and Montréal Mirabel.

[155] David Collenette, interview with the author, 5 February 2019.

[156] Ibid.

On 13 July 1994 Young proposed the National Air Transportation Strategy. The Strategy defined what Canada's national airports should look like in the National Airports Policy (NAP).

The NAP signalled a fundamental change in the federal government's role in the management and operation of airports. It had three underlying principles:

- The federal airport system was to be commercialized;
- The federal government would withdraw from airport operations; and
- Transport Canada would retain its role as Regulator, with oversight and inspection responsibilities.

In 1994 there were 726 certified airports operating in Canada. 150 of these were owned, operated or subsidized by the federal government. These airports ranged from Toronto Pearson to small grass strips. 26 of the 150 were major international and domestic airports handling more than 200,000 passengers per year, representing 94% of all air passenger traffic in Canada.

The NAP divided the 150 airports in five groups.

- *National Airports System (NAS) airports*: 26 airports to be leased over a 60 year period to not-for-profit Canadian Airport Authorities.
- *Regional / Local airports*: 71 airports handling less than 200,000 passengers per year. These airports to be sold to local municipal governments no later than 31 March 2000.
- *Small airports*: 31 airports having no scheduled passengers.
- *Remote airports*: 13 airports where no alternative year-round transportation is available. These to continue to be operated by the federal government.
- *Arctic airports*: 11 airports (including 2 NAS airports at Yellowknife and Whitehorse[157]) to be transferred to the territorial governments.

---

[157] On 1 April 1999 the North West Territory was split into two, with the creation of the Nunavut Territory. At that point there were now three NAS airports in the North: Iqualuit, Yellowknife and Whitehorse.

The NAP contained some financial parameters for the new airports.

Regional and Local airports had to achieve financial self-sufficiency by 31 March 2000 primarily by cutting operating costs by a minimum of 20% and increasing revenues by increased use fees. After 31 March 2000 the government would no longer provide subsidies for operating costs. The airports would have access to a new Airport Capital Assistance Program (ACAP) of about $35 million annually, to be used for safety-related capital works, such as runways and taxiways, but not for air terminal buildings. If the federal government had not been able to sell the regional / local airport for a nominal amount to another level of government or the private sector, there was a strong likelihood the airport would be closed.

National Airports System airports had to achieve financial self-sufficiency for both operating and capital costs no later than 31 March 2000 to be achieved through a mix of cost reductions and enhanced revenue through increased user charges. This principle applied to airports operated by the federal government or an airport authority. After 31 March 2000 there were to be no further appropriations nor government assistance for the 26 NAS airports.

The essential financial principle that governed the transfer of NAS to not-for-profit airport authorities was that the government would be "no worse off" financially and indeed better off than if it had continued to operate the airport. Under the terms of the Airport Transfer Lease the amount of rent payable to the government would be based on the revenue per passenger. The large international airports, such as Toronto or Ottawa, would pay significant rent from the outset based on net cash flow the government would have generated under similar fiscal parameters and passenger volumes. The smaller domestic airports would likely pay little or no rent over the first 15 to 20 years of the lease. In addition to base rent, the federal government would share in participation rent derived from value-added initiatives of the airport authorities.

Expansionary infrastructure would be funded by the Authority and such infrastructure would revert to the federal government upon the termination of the lease.

The NAP took pains to highlight that any positive cash flow was to be derived from the commercial businesses of the airport such as concessions and real estate; it was not to be derived from the airlines (which at virtually every airport in Canada fell far short of paying for the full cost of the services and facilities provided by the airport operator. The lease rental formula was premised on a site-specific compensatory rate regime and not on a residual rate structure.

The NAP described a Canadian Airport Authority:

- It was unique;
- It was not a privatization in the normal sense as the airport was not sold or leased to the highest bidder;
- The land was transferred to the Authority on the basis of a 60-year lease with government retaining ownership of the land;
- The Authority is a not-for-profit business without shareholders;
- All net profits, after rent payments to the government, must be re-invested in airport-related activities;
- There would be no government economic regulation;
- The Authority would have total pricing freedom, consistent with international cost-recovery principles for airside services;
- The Board of Directors would be comprised of nominees from the three levels of government, business, labour and consumer interests;
- No government or elected officials could serve on the Board of Directors;
- The Board member's fiduciary duty is to the airport, not to their nominating entity;
- The Authority is entirely financially self-sufficient without any government appropriation;
- The Authorities' financial viability and financeability assured and clearly demonstrated by firm support from major financial institutions;
- Financing considerations reflect net cash flow or airport rather than asset value;
- The Authority would be subject to firm audit, insurance and default provisions;
- The Authority would be subject to comprehensive public accountability principles including a requirement for a code of conduct in its Bylaws for directors, officers and employees, a

transparent public tendering process, and independent review of its management, operation and financial performance every five years;

- All management and operational decisions were not to be taken by the government but by a Board of Directors composed of local private sector individuals drawn from the region served by the airport;
- It was expected that decision-making would be quick, decisive and responsive to changing economic circumstances and opportunities for economic development; and,
- The Authority would be more cost-efficient, commercially-oriented and innovative than under an institutionally constrained government operation.

The government's experience by 1996 was that there had been four highly successful years of operation by the four original Local Airport Authorities. Vancouver had financed a $375 million infrastructure investment in a new terminal building, runway and parkade. Edmonton was planning a major terminal redevelopment at a cost of $150 million, and Calgary and Montréal had major infrastructure improvements underway.

The principal source of financing infrastructure was an Airport Improvement Fee (AIF) over which the government had no control. The government did not approve the decision by an Authority to levy an AIF, the level of the AIF, nor the projects to be funded by the AIF. Also, the government was not a party to any joint venture, contingent liability, or subordination of rent payments.

Public Accountability Principles

At the same time as the NAP was coming into being, the ATTF was also developing the Public Accountability Principles for Canadian Airport Authorities (PAP). Since the four Local Airport Authorities were already in existence, the PAP would apply only to the new Canadian Airport Authorities.

The reason for the PAP was that soon after the creation of the LAAs it became apparent that TC had no means of oversight other than through its inspection programs. Moreover the rent formula was turning out to be costing a lot of money for the

LAAs.[158] The Department of Finance never wants to give up a source of revenue and even though there were some in Government who thought the rent was "outrageous"[159] the Privy Council Office and the Prime Minister's Office supported Finance. David Collenette thought it "incomprehensible" that the government had commercialized the airports in order to get them off the government's books from a direct expenditure and operations point-of-view and then the government comes along and taxes them: "It would have been better to use the GST"[160] [to replace the airport rent money].

In 1995 TC issued the PAP. In that document the government established guidelines for the Boards of Directors of the Airport Authorities:

a) *The Board shall be comprised of Canadian citizens nominated and appointed through a process acceptable to the local/regional municipal governments and the federal government;*

b) *The Board shall be representative of the community and, as far as practicable, shall consist of individuals who collectively have experience and have shown capacity in such disciplines as air transportation, industry, aviation, business, commerce, finance, administration, law, government, engineering, the organization of workers, or the representation of the interests of consumers, and who have the business acumen and experience to assist in the management of the affairs of the airport as an ongoing, viable, commercial enterprise;*

c) *The Board shall include at least one representative of the business community, one representative of organized labour and one*

---

[158] Although 10 years would pass before the federal government addressed this issue. In May of 2005, the federal government announced a new airport rent formula that was to simplify previously complex rental agreements. The formula was to provide large rent savings to airports over the terms of their leases via a common rental rule applied to all airports in the system. The rent formula was implemented as a stepped series of percentage shares of gross revenues. NAS airports paid rent in 2006 that amounted to 24% of their costs. The total amount of rent paid per passenger decreased steadily from $4.27 in 1992 to $2.49 in 2017 [source: Statistics Canada]. W.G. Morrison, *Dual-market airport operations and airport rent in Canada*, Laurier Centre for Economic Research and Policy Analysis, Wilfrid Laurier University, 2008.

[159] Collenette.

[160] Ibid.

representative of consumer interests, each of whom shall be identified as such;

d) *Directors shall not be elected officials nor government employees; and,*

e) *The Chair of the Board shall not have been an elected official or government employee at any time during the two years prior to election as Chair of the Board.*

f) *The Authority must hold an Annual General Meeting where it would present its annual financial report and business plan.*

g) *The Authority must conduct an independent performance review of its operations at least once every five years.*

Governance

Much to TC's chagrin, the issuance of the PAP document did not make an immediate change in how many of the AAs governed themselves. Even as late as 2003 the Board members of some AAs still thought of themselves as "managers" of "their" airport, not as governors.[161] It took several years, and quite a few reports from independent reviewers on the state of governance at the AAs, but by 2010 most, if not all, the AAs had adopted some form of Carver[162] as a model for governance, with the Board making policy, and the CEO executing that policy.

Notwithstanding the use of Carver or something similar, governance was still an issue for TC. Consequently most airport authorities in Canada modified their Bylaws and placed conditions, such as a skills matrix (gender, work experience or professional designation), that the Board wishes the nominator to comply with; that the Board may not necessarily accept any of the nominees; that the Board may determine the term length of the

---

[161] During one Performance Review I met with the CEO and he was almost in tears of frustration as he told about Board members leaving a Board meeting and then going airside to meet with their brother-in-law and contradicting a previous decision of the Board. When I returned for the next Performance Review five years later things had changed dramatically as the Board was by then following Carver (see next footnote).

[162] John Carver, *Boards That Make a Difference: A New Design for Leadership in Nonprofit and Public Organizations.* 1990. The book describes a model of governance designed to empower boards of directors to fulfill their obligation of accountability for the organizations they govern.

nominee; and that the Board may determine how many terms a member may serve.

By 2003 the Boards of the Vancouver, Edmonton and Calgary airport authorities (but not the ADM at Dorval) had also amended their Bylaws to include the PAP.

Another aspect of governance was the inclusion of airline representatives on the Boards of Directors. This was a normal occurrence in the United States but some Government members believed that having an airline with a seat on the AA's Board would allow too much influence on the AA's independence. Other members disagreed and wished that a Parliamentary Committee had been struck to examine the whole issue of governance.[163]

The CAA Rent Formula – 1995

By the mid-1990's it was apparent that the rent formula created for the LAAs had some issues. Consequently a revised formula was created for the CAAs. Although it too had two parts, a base rent and a participation rent, the basis upon which the rent was to be calculated was much simplified.

	Base Revenues	-	Base Revenues	=	Base Revenues
Base Rent	Stated $ amount per passenger multiplied by the actual number of passengers up to a cap level adjusted by CPI	-	Stated base costs adjusted for CPI	=	Base rent

Figure 6: CAA – Base Rent Formula

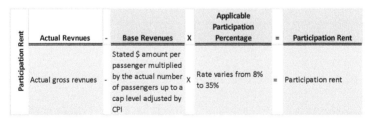

	Actual Revnues	-	Base Revenues	X	Applicable Participation Percentage	=	Participation Rent
Participation Rent	Actual gross revnues	-	Stated $ amount per passenger multiplied by the actual number of passengers up to a cap level adjusted by CPI	X	Rate varies from 8% to 35%	=	Participation rent

Figure 7: CAA – Participation Rent Formula

---

[163] Collenette.

Notwithstanding the attempt at simplification, the rent formula was again amended as a result of the National Airports Rent Policy Review conducted in 2005.

The Revised Rent Formula – 2005

In June 2001, Transport Canada began a review of the existing rent policy for the leased airports in the National Airports System. This review was initiated in response to demands by the airport and aviation communities and the comments of the Auditor General in October 2000 with respect to fair value of rent for Canadian taxpayers. Due to the significant impacts to the air industry resulting from the September 11, 2001, terrorist attacks, the rent policy review was delayed while the government worked to address the ensuing security and economic urgencies.

Focused work on the review began again in 2002, with analysis being completed in the summer of 2004. The intent of the policy review was to ensure that the Government of Canada's airport rent policy balanced the interests of all stakeholders, including the air industry and the Canadian taxpayer.

The scope of review covered the 21 airports with leases: Calgary, Charlottetown, Edmonton, Fredericton, Gander, Halifax, London, Moncton, Montréal (Trudeau and Mirabel), Ottawa, Prince George, Québec City, Regina, Saint John, St. John's, Saskatoon, Thunder Bay, Toronto (Pearson), Vancouver, Victoria and Winnipeg.

The four remaining airports not covered by the review were Whitehorse, Yellowknife, Iqaluit and Kelowna.

In 2005 nine airport authorities were paying rent: Calgary, Edmonton, Halifax, Montréal, Ottawa, Toronto, Vancouver, Victoria, and Winnipeg. Kelowna, which was transferred prior to 1992, paid $1 per year. In 2006, four more airport authorities, Regina, Saskatoon, St. John's, and Thunder Bay were scheduled to begin paying rent. Québec City was to begin paying rent in 2005 or 2006 depending on traffic volumes.[164]

---

[164] *Government of Canada Cuts Airport Rents*, Transport Canada, News Release, No. H098/05, May 9, 2005.

The key objective of the airport rent policy review was to determine a rent formula that struck a balance between the impacts on the air sector of rising rents, and a fair, ongoing return to Canadians as the owners of these valuable assets.

The original process of negotiating lease arrangements with the airport authorities yielded 21 separate deals, each with its own peculiarities. While each lease was negotiated in good faith and reflected the local conditions at the time, in looking at the leases as a whole, numerous anomalies and inconsistencies were identified.

The results of the review indicated that the Canadian airport model is unique. The government retained ownership of the airport lands although it transferred control of airport management, operation, development and financing to community-based, non-share, not-for-profit, self-financing corporate entities. Airports were transferred by way of a long-term lease rather than by placing them on the open market for bids. At the end of the 60-year leases, all assets revert back to the government unencumbered.

The review looked at airport rent payments to the government based on the existing formula and determined that they were excessive. Comparisons with public utilities, which have similar characteristics, and foreign airport transactions indicated that returns from the National Airports Systems airports would be more appropriately set in the order of $5 billion rather than the $13 billion under the current formula. The review also confirmed that existing formula anomalies distorted fairness among airports of similar size, and in some cases, created disincentives to normal commercial practices.

The issue of a fair return to Canadians was a concern raised by the report of the Office of the Auditor General released in October 2000, and was a key driver in the launch of the rent review. A subsequent OAG audit of the review in 2004-2005 looked at the approach taken and concluded that the work underway was satisfactory and that the department had put in place procedures for reviewing the rent policy that took into account its complexity.

Implementation of the new policy was phased in over the next four years, beginning January 2006, with the new formula achieving its full impact in January 2010. In 2006 alone, savings for the National Airports System were forecasted to exceed $48 million.

Some of the other highlights of the policy were summarized as follows:

- All airports were to be treated in an equitable manner.

- All airports benefited financially every year that they paid rent.

- Total rent to be paid was to drop by more than 60 per cent, from about $13 billion to $5 billion over the next 50 years or so of the leases.

- Toronto, as Canada's largest and busiest airport, was to see the largest long-term reduction in rent; the airport was to save $5 billion, going from $8 billion to $3 billion over the remaining life of the lease.

- Halifax, Montréal and Winnipeg were to have their rent reduced by half and Ottawa by two thirds.

- Others realized a substantial drop in the earlier years. Calgary avoided an increase in rent in 2006 and saved over $100 million in the next four years. Similarly, Edmonton saw a $40 million drop and Vancouver realized a $90 million reduction.

- Smaller airports benefited as well. Most saw a 70% reduction in rent, or more, over the long term. In the short term, the reductions were even more significant because of the immediate implementation of the new rent formula once each of the smaller airports began paying rent. For example, in 2006, Regina paid less than $50,000 instead of $680,000. Thunder Bay paid $12,000 instead of $330,000. In 2016, when Moncton began paying rent, it paid less than $200,000 instead of the $1.3 million under the 1995 formula.

In addition to the rent reduction, the government also forgave the remaining repayments owed from airport authorities for chattels (runway sweepers, snow blowers, computer equipment, and furniture that were sold by Transport Canada to the airport authorities at the time of the airport transfers). This amount was $21.9 million.

The new Airport Rent Formula was based on Gross Revenues, as follows:

- On the first $5 million 0%
- On the next $5 million 1%

- On the next $15 million 5%
- On the next $75 million 8%
- On the next $150 million 10%
- On any amount over $250 million 12%

For example, if the Gross Revenue of the AA was $50 million, the rent payable would be:

- First $5 million – 0%	$0
- Next $5 million – 1%	50,000
- Next $15 million – 5%	750,000
- Final $25 million – 8%	2,000,000
Total rent payable	$2,800,000

Notwithstanding the rent reductions, there were still issues with the rent formula that came to light quite quickly.

Rent & AIF

Not very long after the revised rent formula was introduced concerns about it were raised by AAs across Canada, TC had developed a set of "Guiding Principles" regarding the development of a new rent formula for airports and a major part of those guiding principles was a target dollar amount as income to the federal government's General Revenue Fund. This "target dollar amount" was based upon the total rent from all airports in the NAS, which in turn was based upon an airport-by-airport cash flow projection (completed in about 2004) done as part of the rent review process.

There were major faults with the rent review process, the cash flow projection, and the resulting rent formula. These faults arose from several factors:

1. Rent is driven by gross airport revenue. Gross airport revenue is a misleading indicator of the airport's financial health. In the absence of any recognition by TC of increasing operating and capital investment costs, which in turn drive the need for increases in revenue, the use of gross airport revenue as a basis for rent calculation is invalid.

2. Air traffic in the NAS grew significantly faster than TC used in its conservative projections for revenue. Therefore revenue and

rent grew faster than projected. Revenues are extremely unlikely to ever return to the levels used in the rent projections.

3. Significant construction cost inflation forced the AAs to increase their Airport Improvement Fee (AIF) rate to cover those costs. TC's projections did not anticipate any AIF rate increase in their revenue projections.

4. Passenger and air service growth in the NAS drove the AA's capital program faster than what was expected. To finance the expansion needs the AAs had to increase their AIF rate. TC's gross revenue projections and resulting rent did not anticipate the AIF rate increases.

5. AIF is a source of funds for capital investment and is not a source of operating earnings. Rent resulting from growth and increased operating earnings may be palatable, but paying rent on the AIF is poor public policy, and misleading to Canadian citizens. The AIF is used solely for financing capital investment, it is not a source of tax revenue. The increases in the AIF were necessitated by construction inflation and a need for more infrastructure maintenance and expansion to meet demand. Neither of these two fundamental costs improve bottom line profitability, yet the AAs pay rent on the AIF.

As a result some of the AAs began sending an annual letter to the Minister of Transport advising him of the huge discrepancy between what his staff's own projections called for and what the actual rent is for the year. Responses from TC were that revenue estimates used for the formula were developed during the turmoil following 9/11, and may have been conservative. TC also suggested that while recent years had been positive in terms of revenue growth, the economic climate can change quickly, and time was needed to determine if the new formula was reasonable over an extended period.

An AIF[165] causes an inefficiency to affect the AA. Since the AIF affects everyone and everything connected to it, the AIF will have unintended consequences. For example, if the AA begins to collect

---

[165] Scott McFadden, interview with the author, 7 December 2018.

an AIF all persons and companies associated with the AA will know pretty quickly that the AIF is now being collected. This knowledge affects their reasoning when it comes to fiscal decision-making because the AIF is seen as "free" money. If the AA engages with an airline to discuss future improvements to the terminal which will benefit the airline, the airline will normally have to either pay for those improvements outright, or contribute to the cost in some proportion. And this fiscal responsibility may, or may not, affect the airline's decision to approve the improvement. But if the improvement is to be funded through an AIF, the airline will, in all probability, say "because this improvement is AIF eligible, and will cost me nothing, then go for it!!".[166] This is "easy" money and may have made Canada less cost competitive compared to other countries since it (consciously or subconsciously) impacts every decision,[167] from art programs and runway length ("Calgary spent an enormous amount of money on a runway extension for which there is no legitimate business or even economic justification"[168]), to collective bargaining, board remuneration and salaries (and on top of all of these cost increases, "rent" is collected by the Federal Government as a percentage of gross revenues).

While the AAs would prefer to pay no rent, the rent that TC had established as a target would be bearable. At a minimum the removal of AIF revenue from the formula would make the formula logical in that it is based upon operating revenues and not financing for capital maintenance and expansion.

No worse off

The Auditor General for Canada, in Chapter 10 of his 2000 Report, was quite critical of TC's transfer of the first four airports to Local Airport Authorities. His report found "many significant weaknesses in management practices"[169] principally around the setting of "fair market value". He also was of the opinion that TC

---

[166] Ibid.

[167] Ibid.

[168] Ibid.

[169] Report of the Auditor General of Canada, Chapter 10 Transport Canada, Airport Transfers: National Airports System, October 2000, p. 10-5.

had lost revenues of approximately $474 million to the Crown due to renegotiations for the rent clause of the lease.

The Auditor General focussed on the period 1992 to 1999. We now have the luxury of looking at a greater period of time and I suggest that the numbers now present a very different scenario.

In 1991 it was reported that the airports system cost TC about $750 million to administer and operate. Over the previous 20 years (1971 to 1990) the amount spent by TC on airport infrastructure was estimated to have been less than $1 billion.

Let us compare that to the numbers since 1992, the date of first transfer.

Combined, over the period 1992 to 2018, the 21 Airport Authorities have spent approximately $26 billion on infrastructure[170], more than 26 times what the federal government had spent in the 20 years prior to devolution.

Over the same period, the AAs received revenues of approximately $28.8 billion. About $20.3 billion of that revenue was spent in the local cities, towns and hamlets in which the airports are located. From 1992 to 2017 the AAs have paid $6.4 billion[171] in rent to the federal government, and $5 billion in taxes to the municipal, provincial and federal governments. Approximately 192,000 people earn their living either at an airport authority or at a company located on airport land.[172]

Over the period 1992 to 2017 Transport Canada spent approximately $500 million on the 21 Airport Authorities, almost all of that (about $363 million) in the period 1992 to 1999.

Doing the math:

- TC has not spent $750 million a year for 26 years. Cost savings to the Crown: $31.6 billion (in 2018 $).
- The government has received rent for 26 years. Revenues to the Crown: $9.5 billion (in 2018 $).

---

[170] $31.6 billion in 2018 dollars.

[171] #9.5 billion in 2018 dollars.

[172] *Economic Impact: Canada's Airports in 2016.*

- TC spent about $0.5 billion supporting the AAs. Cost to the Crown: $0.5 billion.

So, it would seem that, as of 2018, the Crown is ahead by about $41 billion in revenues (not including the federal government's share of taxes) and that that amount will keep on growing.

Chapter 5: Issues that were never thought of in 1992

Airport performance under TC was historically undermined by several factors: large centralized administrations; restrictive public-sector labour agreements that increased airports' labour requirements; restricted ability to raise funds for capital expenditures; a requirement to treat each airport equally in order to minimize the perception of favoritism; and, and the realization that anything done would be done under the magnifying glass of public opinion. With local control, the expectation of the federal government was that airports would operate in a commercial and cost-effective manner that respected the environment and be more responsive to local needs. The transfer would facilitate investment and relieve the airports of government financial constraints. The transfer would decrease the government's spending by at least $750 million a year.

In the case of the AAs, the results of the transfer have been very effective. The AAs are safe, secure, responsible, not-for-profit operations that contribute substantially to the economic activities of their locale. The AAs model governance, fiscal probity, environmental awareness, and responsibility. The AAs are, when measured against any criteria, a formidable success.

There remain, however, several challenges.

Carriers

While TC needed to invest in infrastructure at many airports, the carriers really had to deal with only one entity or organization: TC itself. Moreover it was sometimes easier for the carriers to get infrastructure enhancements approved through political channels, although that could delay decisions on where the spend might be. From the carrier point-of-view the big concern was what would these "not for profit" organizations really cost the carriers? Where would the accountability lie? What disagreement protocol would be in place? Carriers would now have to deal with multiple authorities instead of one. How would their costs really stay the same or go down? It was not a happy time for the carriers. They were expected to fund most of the growth in the airports system through increased landing fees, and this at a time when they were losing money or just breaking even. Air Canada's airport fees at Toronto Pearson went up $350 million in a 5 year period, with very little ability to challenge or fight these costs. Although lawsuits were initiated against increased landing fees, increased passenger fees across the country became standard and the carriers were expected to collect them in their airfares, making Canadian carrier prices look excessive. This situation has not resolved itself, even today in 2019.[173]

Investment

Capital expenses and revenues are great indicators as they are reflective of what investment and income growth is present when government removes itself from trying to run a business. The 21 AAs have, since 1992, invested more than $26 billion in their airports, an amount far in excess of any that neither TC nor the government would have considered as politically feasible. That money has been raised without resort to taxes on Canadians. It was paid for by the users: the airlines through landing fees, the passengers through the airport improvement and parking fees, the concessions that pay rent, and the businesses that lease airport land. In other words, those that used the facility paid for the privilege, and those that don't, do not.

Economic engines to the local communities

As economic engines in their local communities the AAs have exceeded expectations. One measure of this is the level of employment generated by the airport, not only those employed directly by the airport, its operations, or by businesses located on airport land, but also those employed indirectly in other businesses located in the community. Direct employment at the 21 AAs is 192,000[174] persons. This is the total number of folk who run the airports and are employed by the businesses located on airport lands. Those 192,000 are paid more than 13 billion dollars

---

[173] Bill Bredt, email to the author, 23 November 2018.

[174] *Economic Impact: Canada's Airports in 2016*, Canadian Airports Council, http://www.cacairports.ca/sites/default/files/Economic%20Impact%20of%20Can ada%27s%20Airports%20-%20Final_0.pdf#overlay-context=, accessed 15 October 2018.

annually in salaries, almost all of which is spent in their local communities. That $13 billion in turn generates an economic output of more than $48 billion every year. In addition, the AAs alone pay in taxes annually $0.4 billion to the local communities, $1.7 billion to provincial governments, and $4.8 billion to the federal government.

Non-aeronautical revenue

Governments are not businesses, and are not in the "profit" frame of mind. And although the ATTF rent formula considered non-aeronautical revenue, it had no idea just how much that revenue stream would eventually mean to the AAs. However, non-aeronautical revenues do demonstrate the success of the business model that is the AAs.

Non-aeronautical revenue is any revenue not generated from airport operations. It generally, but not exclusively, comes from parking, concessions, and leases. By 2017 the AAs generated about $545 million annually in non-aeronautical revenue, about 38% of their total revenue. If AIF is included, the total non-aeronautical revenue rises to $1 billion a year, about 73% of total revenue.

Costs that TC never had

A sample of other costs that TC did not have to consider when they ran the airports but were downloaded to the AAs are shown below. These numbers are from Gander International Airport Authority.[175]

	2015	2016	2017
Advertising and Promotion	$304,562	$224,485	$229,359
Insurance	168,084	166,386	189,942
Other (travel, training, office, board fees)	516,289	483,073	411,013
Debt servicing costs	232,380	176,634	124,173
Security	242,313	301,682	283,917
Professional fees	134,523	67,207	82,915
Rent		72,600	48,891
Depreciation	1,568,830	1,661,145	1,721,914
Totals	$3,166,981	$3,153,212	$3,092,124

Figure 8: Costs never seen by TC

---

[175] Many thanks to Darren Dalton, CFO at Gander International Airport Authority.

Revenues at the Gander airport were $9.4 million in 2017, so more than 33% of revenue was spent in doing things that TC never had to consider when it ran the airport.

Training Airport Managers

Transport Canada had over the years instituted an excellent system of training for airport managers. This has changed. Training in Canada for airport managers no longer exists other than what an airport provides to its staff[176].

When TC operated the airports it was possible for an employee to gain experience from across the country because the TC Airports Group trained their managers, and trained line people and trades. It was a foregone conclusion at TC that people who showed promise would be moved around in the system to give them broader experience.

Consequently, because of this policy, at devolution the AAs inherited magnificently competent and trained staffs. Unfortunately since then the AAs have largely become silos, both in training and in exposure to how other airports are run. There are little bits of movement, for example the number two at one airport goes to be the CEO at another airport. But that is a problem because effectively the airports are cannibalizing their own. The U.S. airports, either city run or AAs, have a requirement that a certain percentage of their senior managers have airport training accreditation, such as from Ohio State, which provides airport management courses. The Association of American Airport Executives and IATA also have training programs, and ACI is about to get into that business as well. But the American airports are required to have a certain percentage of their managers with formal accreditation in airport management.

Formal accreditation is not the case in Canada. So far we have gotten away with this, but that is because to some extent the young generation, in the early 90's, were at the beginnings of their careers after having been trained by TC, and were able to then build on that training to become very good managers in their AA. But most

---

[176] Several persons interviewed by the author raised this as an issue.

of them have now, or soon will be, retired and there are very few folk left behind them with the appropriate airport or airline experience. They may know a lot about their own airport, but they have limited, or very likely none, experience in how things are done elsewhere.

Seeing things done differently from what you are used to is where a lot of innovation comes from. People have to see, and be a part of, how things may be done differently, and yet accomplish the same end.

At least two Canadian airports have implemented formal training programs for their managers.

At Pearson the GTAA has partnered with the Ivey Academy Education at Western University to deliver an executive leadership program for its 80 directors and associate directors. The GTAA also launched the GTAA Management Trainee Program, aimed at future managers who are currently in front-line roles. Participants in the 18-month program rotate through three consecutive six-month terms in three different operating units. In addition to training, the program gives them operational and leadership experience.

In Quebec City two senior managers enrolled in the IATA-Nanyang Advanced Management Program in Aviation and Air Transport (INAMP – AAT) program offered by Nanyang Technological University (NTU) in Singapore. NTU has partnered with the International Air Transport Authority (IATA) and International Civil Aviation Organization (ICAO) to design a curriculum specifically for aviation professionals with courses covering the spectrum from aviation law, airline business modelling, airport management, airline finance, and aviation data-driven decision making.

The BAA Plc is interesting because it has a formal exchange program and, in the BAA Plc, young mid-level managers can apply to go and work in an airport outside the BAA Plc world – for example a two-year secondment to Narita airport in Japan. In that secondment the person would not only see how Narita operates, but would also have exposure to the Asian markets, the Japanese way of doing business, financing, and other valuable things.

That process does not exist in Canada.

The U.S. has dealt with this through a formal training requirement for airport staff. There is also a limited amount of staff movement between the FAA and the airports, which both entities describe as beneficial. The public sector (the FAA) gets to see what the private sector is producing, and the private sector (the airports) get to see how the regulator sees the airport community. It is a "win-win" for both of them.

From the point-of-view of experience, there is much to be said for having practical experience in the field in which you work. If you have a pilot's license, you are much less likely to ask "why is that button there?" or "why must we follow that regulation?". If you are a construction engineer, and you have actually spent time building something with your own hands, you are far less likely to question good building standards. But when you have people with academic qualifications, and no practical experience, and you put them in charge, make them responsible for something that they may understand intellectually but have no practical experience in doing, then you must be prepared to put much effort into oversight and management.

It would be advantageous if TC and the airports could work out some kind of exchange, and also the airports amongst themselves, so that people could get experience. When you have people with talent, but have no opportunity for them to extend themselves, then both they and the airport lose out on an opportunity. When TC was running the show, if they had someone who showed talent they could say "OK, you're going to Sault St. Marie and if you are able to handle that, then we'll put you into a more demanding spot in Vancouver, and then maybe Toronto." There was a career progression that made sense.

Career development is good for future recruitment, but there are so many airports in Canada today that when they have to replace a manager they really struggle to find the right candidate, and the only way for them is to hire a search firm who purloins someone from another airport. That airport in turn then has to find someone with the transportation, aviation, political, and local knowledge necessary to function at that airport.

This is not a good, long-term solution. Canada's airports, as economic entities, need to find a permanent, long-term solution to this issue, and need to find it sooner rather than later.

Equitable Rent

With respect to ground rents the airports have two concerns:

- how the land rent due to the federal government ranks relative to the long-term lenders' security; and,
- how the risks of inflation are allocated between the players over the life cycle of the project.

The rent payable by the AAs may not be equitable and fair, when it is considered that the AIF is included as revenue in the formula used by TC to determine the amount of rent payable. Several aerodromes petitioned the Minister and obtained new rent formulas whereby they achieved equity with other airports in the NAS (Transport Canada estimated the rent payable by one aerodrome in 2010 was $400,000 instead of the $1,800,000, which would have been payable that year if the old rent provisions had continued to apply).

In spite of the important change in the federal rent formula, airlines and airports across Canada continue to question the dollars being taken from the aviation industry in this way. This hidden tax will continue to grow at a high rate year after year, as the AAs call for an even more fair and equitable rent structure in the future.

The issues are:

a. By indexing the land rent, the federal government is seeking a reward for a risk it is not taking, by building in an inflexible share of the airport revenues, which themselves are subject to fluctuation. Is the government entitled to do this? And, if so, is it entitled to be the only player who gets this rigid protection?

b. AAs as the tenant, and not the Federal Government as the Landlord, are responsible for maintaining and developing airports. Therefore rent should be based on the asset as it was transferred and not on the new and improved assets developed by the AA.

c. AA's should get a rent credit for any asset maintenance and/or development costs they incur.

d. The AIF is used exclusively for capital improvements to the airport property that is owned by the Federal Government. The AIF cannot be used to pay for rent. For both of these reasons the AIF should be excluded from Gross Revenue in the determination of rent.

Transport Canada established a target for the gross amount of rent it was seeking but AAs been paying many times that amount. The formula is flawed and it is failing to meet TC's own objective. The rent amount needs to be fixed at the amount that was established as TC's own target.

Revised Rent Formula - 2006

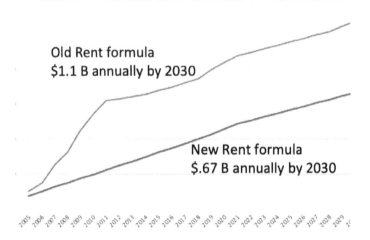

As may be seen from the chart, the difference in rent between TC's original target and the actual rent paid by the AAs is substantial. At the projections of revenue in 2006, the total excess in rent paid was to have been more than $400 million over the succeeding 15 years.

Double Taxation

The AIF is paid by passengers as a funding mechanism to the Authorities in order to allow the Authorities to budget for capital improvements to the aerodrome. It is not a revenue to the Authorities generated from operations – i.e. landings or take-offs of aircraft, or fuelling of aircraft. However, the federal government includes the AIF in its rent calculation:

$$rent\ payable = revenue\ from\ operations + AIF$$

The effect of this calculation is that the travelling public pays twice. This is an unfair benefit to the government.

Lease Expiry

For most of the AAs in Canada, if the Lease Renewal options are exercised there remains less than 35 years before the Ground Leases expire. The leases require that the land revert to the federal government unencumbered. That is, no debt may remain on the land and the infrastructure at the end of the lease. The lease also requires the Authorities to return the infrastructure to the federal government in a "first class" operating condition. These two requirements may create unfavourable, if not impossible, financial conditions for the Authorities as they endeavour to maintain the aerodrome, and not create any more debt.

When the federal government first created the lease structure for the Authorities in 1992 it had no appreciation of the value of investments in infrastructure that were going to be made by the Authorities. Throughout the 1980's the thinking of Transport Canada had been that approximately 500 million dollars was necessary to bring TC-managed aerodrome infrastructure up to international standards. Such an investment was politically unacceptable and in the middle 1980's the idea of transferring the ownership of the infrastructure to the Authorities (and the cost of updates) was born with the first four transfers (to Vancouver, Edmonton, Calgary and Montréal) taking place in 1992.

With more than 25 years of history now to hand, the total sum invested in infrastructure by the 21 Authorities in the NAS is more than 26 billion dollars, an amount no one could have foreseen in 1992. At the end of their lease the ownership of the investments made by the Authorities reverts to the federal government. If the Lease Renewal options are exercised, for all Authorities there remains only 35 to 50 years in their leases.

The experience with the creation of the Canadian Authorities is a success story *sans pareil* and the initial fears of Transport Canada that it would have to deal with failed Authorities, and their accumulated debt, have not been borne out by the facts.

Airport projects present special challenges as they are by nature very large, long term, expensive, highly-visible, quite often remote (at least in Canada they are remote), single-purpose structures designed to house a specific economic activity of vital interest to the community. They are also especially prone to significant political interventions e.g. Mirabel and Pickering.

The Authorities are no different. Near-term investment over the next five years will require billions for the parking, runways, lighting and approach systems, taxiways and aprons, and other infrastructure. And if the trend of the past 25 years hold true for the long-term, then it is not unreasonable to assume that $50 billion or more will be invested in infrastructure by the AAs over the next 45 years.

Projects are a capital challenge, and the Authorities manage them in a fiscally responsible manner. There is timely, orderly development which follows their Master Plans. Infrastructure has been upgraded in the past when costs were low but the future may be different.

There are several possible solutions to this quandary as to what to do at the end of the lease:

1. The land is sold to the Authorities and does not revert to the federal government at the lease expiry.

Selling the lands to the AAs would make a one-time payment available to Canada. An insignificant amount when compared to the annual federal budget or when compared to the National Debt.

Selling the lands to the AAs is not a good solution. The lands are highly valuable to Canada and Canadians. They are a strategic and a military asset both from their location near major cities and their size. They are a significant source of tax revenue and it would not be good public policy to sell such a valuable, and irreplaceable, asset.

2. The lease expires and all lands, buildings and chattels revert to the federal government.

The problem with this is the "no debt" and "first class condition" requirements of the lease. For the AA to be debt free at the end of the lease will require it to make no capital investments for the last 10 to 15 years of the lease, and that would be unrealistic. Airports are capital intensive – both for maintenance and new construction – if they are to be maintained in a "first class" condition. There is no way for this requirement of "no debt" at lease end to work if the requirement remains that the airport be returned in "first class" condition.

3. The lease is extended for a set period of time (say, 20 years) and the AA is told to pay off its mortgage so that is it debt free at the end of the extended period.

This is no different from scenario 2. Extending the lease just delays the pain.

4. The requirement that at lease end the airport is transferred back to the federal government debt free is removed.

This scenario would allow the AA to continue to maintain and develop the airport in a "first class" condition. However, the political reality of having to assume the responsibility for a large debt may be unacceptable to the government of the day.

5. The lease is bound to perpetuity or to a very long time, say 99 years.

This scenario would allow the AAs a measure of certitude in their business planning and their long-term strategic plan. It would essentially allow for business to continue "as is" and allow the AAs to continue to address capital funding issues with the banks and financial institutions as they do today.

Of the five scenarios listed here number five may be the best, as of all the five possibilities it alone allows for certitude and stability.

Increased Impacts of Security Requirements on the Authorities

The Federal government continues to be responsible for regulating all aspects of aviation safety and security. In addition, the National Airports Policy acknowledges the government's continued responsibility for the integrity and viability of the NAS as a whole.

Public confidence in safety and security is essential to maintaining an effective airport operation and while Transport Canada is addressing security concerns through regulation and the creation of separate agencies like CATSA, it is sometimes apparent that their focus is on the larger airports. Indeed some of the Government's regulatory changes appear to not have sufficiently taken into account the operational and financial burdens that this imposes on all airport operators.

These issues most certainly include:

- The effects of change on operational burdens and the downstream effect on human capital;
- The mandatory capital investment required to respond to changing human and air cargo security commitments;
- The gap between rising infrastructure costs and the prices charged to air carriers; and,
- Rising concern on the part of TC regarding the treatment of air cargo.

Safety Management System (SMS)

Under the Safety Management System (SMS) required of the AAs by TC, the management of risk is downloaded to the airport, with TC being responsible for the inspection/audit/evaluation role, and the airport being responsible for the design/development/administration role.

To ensure that it meets its responsibilities, the AAs have ensured that the design/development/administration of their SMS meets or exceeds the requirements of TC. They have done this by categorizing the risk areas, prioritizing those risks, establishing a probability of each risk occurring, and developing a risk mitigation/risk management strategy for each risk. However, TC continues to make rules, with a devolved responsibility to the AAs that they meet these rules. The cost of meeting the requirements of the rules may eventually be an issue.

In my experience, the AAs have a concept of "safety" which far exceeds that of an SMS. Although the Regulations require the Authority to have a robust SMS, the AAs for which I have conducted Performance Reviews have taken the idea of safety to a far higher level. They see safety as an economic driver that "good" companies do well. They believe that a good safety culture creates a truly safe environment. Their safety model is community based and includes improved tracking of security, occupational health and safety, public safety, and contractor safety programs. These five aspects of 'safety" are combined by the AAs into a single safety programme which is adhered to by all who work there. The AA's senior management "walks the talk" with respect to safety. Annual employee engagement surveys confirm this.

The following anecdote[177] may help to illustrate this culture:

A maintenance employee working at the Edmonton aerodrome related how he was concerned for his and for other worker safety when working alone or in isolated locations on the airport facilities and grounds. He and his buddies had developed a practice of maintaining communications with the office by phoning on a scheduled basis back to the office to "check in". Unfortunately, this was not always effective as sometimes the work they undertook preoccupied them to the point where they would forget to call.

The concern for worker safety persisted and he became aware of a tool/application used in the oilfields to support worker safety. A portable device worn by the worker which sends an electronic signal requiring acknowledgement was proposed and ultimately adopted by the AA.

What stands out in this story is that the focus was safety, the solution was proposed by an employee, validated by management and adopted because it made good business sense, supported worker safety and was consistent with the overall AA commitment to a safety culture. It also illustrates in concrete terms how the value of safety has penetrated to the most basic field operations

---

[177] Author's personal notes: *Performance Review of the Edmonton Regional Airports Authority*, 4 May 2017.

level and how management was willing to honour its commitment to safety. By validating and addressing legitimate employee concerns in an open and obvious manner the AA continued to advance its determination to be an effective organization.

This is the result of a long term, consistent, and well understood commitment to safety, the value of which is now part of how the AA does business and is a case study in mature safety culture implementation.

System safety is the application of engineering and management principles, criteria, and techniques to achieve an acceptable level of safety throughout all phases of a system. In simple terms, the safety management system (SMS) is a proactive business approach to managing and mitigating potential hazards within the organization to improve safety performance.

The AAs have implemented fully comprehensive SMSs at significant costs to themselves.[178] Their SMS regimes are in accordance with the applicable regulatory enactments and undergo close regulatory scrutiny from Transport Canada. The AAs have committed significant resources and efforts to maintaining a favourable rating from TC and enhancing their safety culture to the point where it has become the central strategic objective of the AAs, and is measured, monitored and improved.

Achieving this definition of system safety is the primary objective of the AA's SMS. A well-structured SMS provides the AA with a systematic, explicit, and comprehensive process for managing risks. This process includes goal setting, planning, documentation, and regular quality assurance and evaluation of performance to ensure that goals are being met.

The AAs have implemented the six basic SMS components: safety management plan, safety policy, safety risk management, safety assurance, quality assurance, and safety promotion, in accordance with all regulatory and limited policy guidance support from Transport Canada.[179]

---

[178] This is one of those costs "not foreseen by TC" at the time of devolution, but money which the AA must spend in order to maintain regulatory compliance.

[179] The SMS originally applied to air carriers. From 2005 to 2009, class 705 carriers implemented an SMS system mapped to a Regulatory Framework

The AAs find that their commitment to a safety culture sometimes outstrips the requirements of the TC Regulations and the experience of the TC inspectors. The Regulations sometimes do not reflect the use of latest technology nor best practices and are, consequently, may be out-of-date. This is sometimes an issue for the AAs as they endeavour to be the safest they can possibly be, but are constrained by the Regulations. Moreover, the technical knowledge of the inspectors is sometimes not at the same level as the AA's staff. The expertise of the AA's staff comes from their experience in running an airport, and sometimes the TC inspectors have had little, or no, experience in actually operating an aerodrome. Occasionally this lack of experience on the part of the inspector is sometimes an issue.

The CEOs are the Accountable Executive for the AA's SMS and have regular meetings with their Safety Officer to review incidents and progress against SMS goals.

All AAs have a Safety Policy which provides the foundation or framework for the SMS. It outlines the methods and tools for achieving desired safety outcomes. The Safety Policy also details management's responsibility and accountability for safety.

Safety risk management (SRM) is a core activity of SMS. SRM uses a set of standard processes to proactively identify hazards, analyze and assess potential risks, and design appropriate risk mitigation strategies. As a single example of safety risk management, a key part of an aerodrome's safety is the surface friction (skid resistance) of a runway, especially in inclement weather. The AAs monitor runway surface friction which feeds information directly to pilots.

Safety assurance is a set of processes that monitor the organization's performance in meeting its current safety standards

---

determined by TC. The implementation could not be mapped to a TC SMS model since none existed and so TC used Advisory Circular 107-001 as a guide. In 2007 TC required all NAS airports to implement an SMS, with no direction, no guidance, and no Key Performance Indicators. Several of the AA's were heard to say many "off-colour" words about TC and its requirements for the SMS at that time. Almost 10 years passed before the Authorities were able to implement an SMS that met the undefined expectations of TC, and it was not unusual for the individual responsible for the SMS at an airport to be more knowledgeable than their TC counterpart of how an SMS worked.

and objectives as well as contribute to continuous safety improvement. Some AAs use a computer-based system to monitor safety assurance.

Safety promotion includes processes and procedures used to create an environment where safety objectives can be achieved. Safety promotion is essential to create an organization's positive safety culture. Some AAs have an annual Safety Week as a key part of the safety promotion programme.

The AAs conduct emergency planning and full-scale safety exercises, usually every second year. A full-scale exercise involving multiple agencies tests the interoperability of agencies, airlines, AA staff, concession operators, operators of businesses located on airport lands, and the local police, fire and security organizations. On alternate years the AAs will conduct a table-top to determine if the standard operating procedures remain true.

The AAs oversee safety through a regular review with the CEO and staff. The review considers all safety incidents and accidents. Incidents and accidents are audited for continuous improvement.

The AAs have a safe disclosure program. Staff with safety concerns come directly to the managers/directors/senior management.

Airport Security Program (ASP)

As with the SMS, the responsibility for the design, development and administration of the Airport Security Program (ASP) will devolve to the AAs, with TC assuming the role of regulator and auditor.

Since 2003 the cost of CATSA has increased, but public perception is that service has gone down, especially when there are line-ups at the pre-board screening area and not all the screening lanes are open.

The concern is that the cost for the ASP is borne by the travelling public and the AAs, with TC deciding what functions will be within the ASP, with little or no input from the Authorities, and the Authorities having to fund those functions.

An ASP sets out an organization's security policies as an integral part of its business processes and is a part of the corporate management responsibility. The ASP is based on the same concepts used for the SMS.

Developed in conjunction with an efficient threat assessment mechanism and risk management program, the ASP is used to develop proactive, efficient and cost effective security measures.

An ASP allows an organization-wide approach to security through the development of a security culture as well as a system-wide security model encouraging - and dependent on - close co-operation between the AA and TC as the regulator.

An AA's ASP may use access control technologies (such as CCTV or ground radar for perimeter monitoring) allowing for better resource allocation to respond to human or wildlife incursion. This exceeds basic ASP standards.

The AAs conduct security planning and full-scale and desktop operations security exercises. Some AAs conduct an annual "Safety Week". Some AAs have an "Active Shooter" full-scale exercise. AAs conduct table-top and full-scale exercises on alternate years, and opposite to the Safety table-top and full-scale exercises. This means that each year there will be a full-scale exercise (alternating between safety and security).

Some AAs hold monthly active shooter lunchbox sessions which are designed to enhance personal awareness of what to do in the event of an active shooter incident. This presentation is delivered in partnership with the local police service provider and provides examples of recent events, shares statistical information in regards to active shooter incidents and talks extensively about what to do if faced with such an emergency. While staff cannot stop an active shooter situation, it is the AA's intent to ensure its staff and stakeholders have the knowledge and awareness should they ever be faced with such a terrifying situation.

In one AA the program has been received with enthusiasm, and has had direct participation from 904 airport employees (AA staff and tenants) over the 35 sessions held between March, 2015 and January 2017.

Policing at the AA may be conducted by a resident police detachment[180] or may be "on call" from the local municipal or provincial police. The policing conforms to the standard Canadian policing model for airports including general security and safety issues as well as those issues particular to the need to ensure the security of important transportation infrastructure.

Some AAs have a K9 Unit. The dogs reside in the police detachment and are trained to detect different scents.

Summary and Conclusions

The airport devolution policy achieved remarkable successes, but a surprising number of people do not appreciate how important airports are. Some academics have been critical of the AIF. And some will claim that the airports pay too little in rent, etc. but their major criticism is that the airport system is overbuilt and we should have fewer airports.

That is a valid criticism for an airport system developed in the 1930's when an airport was needed every one-hour flying time, and an emergency landing spot halfway between. As a result, going east from Vancouver, there was the airport in Vancouver, and then Langley, Hope, Princeton, Oliver, Rock Creek, Midway, Grand Forks, Trail, Salmo, Kitchener and Cranbrook, and the plane still hadn't left B.C.

The airport system of today would never have built that way from scratch. An example would be in New Brunswick, where an airport in Fredericton, Moncton and Saint John would not be as economic as one right in the middle of those three cities would be.

Looking elsewhere in the world where there is an airport serving multi-city markets the airport is usually in a rural area away from towns and cities. That reduces the noise component to urban residents, and makes it easier to access an airport. For example Dallas Forth Worth is not in Dallas, nor is it in Forth Worth. The same thing for Seattle Tacoma airport. The old Seattle downtown airport was inadequate for jet aircraft, and the air traffic volumes and the building heights just were not going to work. Tacoma had

---

[180] Resident police detachments are mandatory at "Tier 1" airports in Canada.

an airport, but when Seattle and Tacoma decided they were going to build a new airport they put it between the two cities.

Looking at the Canadian landscape, where there are pairs or tri's of airports today, if we were building new we would probably build a single airport in between. That has the advantage of lower cost, lower infrastructure cost, more economies of scale and operations, and economies in terms of market mass. So instead of communities being served by a turbo-prop four or five times a day, they would probably be served by a 737 or A320 and see 10-12 flights a day. But by diversifying the market base into different locations the economies and the critical mass for air services are lost.

The consolidation of Montréal's two airports into one, and Edmonton's two airports into one were dramatic developments, Edmonton in particular. There was Edmonton City airport, which was not part of the TC system, and Edmonton International airport. Neither airport had good air service to everywhere. Edmonton City had great service to Calgary and points north, but that was it. By not having that traffic, Edmonton International could never support flights such as non-stops to Ottawa, Montréal and Los Angeles. The market had to be consolidated in order to develop the set of connecting air services that the Edmonton community now enjoys. Without airport consolidation that never could have occurred. The consolidation freed up a huge section of land in downtown Edmonton for redevelopment. Moreover, the municipal airport created height restrictions in the city core. After the municipal airport closed it allowed developers to build higher than before, which allowed the Stantec Tower, at 63 stories, to be the 2nd highest building in Canada. That would not have been possible had Edmonton Municipal airport still been operating because the building is too tall and too close to where the downtown airport was located.

The consolidation of these two airports showed incredible leadership because this was not a popular decision. A lot of people supported the idea of two airports, and the issue had to go to referendum, twice, before it was decided. Ron Gilbertson gets a lot of credit for the consolidation of the Edmonton airports, and in hindsight it is absolutely clear that it has been a tremendous boon to Edmonton International. And at least now it is possible to envision the possibility of rail access to Edmonton International.

111

In Montréal, the decision to build Mirabel airport was ill-conceived to begin with. The original policy was to have the trans-border flights at Mirabel, in part to move the traffic out but also to feed the intercontinental flights, but at the last minute the decision was made to keep the trans-border flights at Dorval. As soon as that happened it killed the international flights to Mirabel. Dorval, before Mirabel, was the main connecting point for Canadians to get overseas to Europe and Africa, there wasn't much Asia service in those days. As soon as Mirabel opened Toronto became the main intercontinental gateway for Canada because a domestic customer could not connect to an international flight at Dorval. And there was no rail service to Mirabel. As a result Dorval's intercontinental flights started to fade away and never developed to what its potential was. L'Aeroports de Montréal (ADM, the old Dorval), after consolidation, is now becoming an interesting hub, and ADM is one of the busiest intercontinental airports in North America if you exclude trans-border traffic between Canada and the U.S. ADM has more intercontinental traffic than does Chicago. The consolidation of those two airports is something TC could never have achieved, and the devolution policy must take credit for that.

One of the objectives of the devolution policy was to get the airports off the back of the Canadian taxpayer. At one time the subsidies were about $750 million a year. Part of that subsidy reflects the costs of Air Traffic Control (ATC) (although ATC was largely financed by the Ticket Tax).

At the time the devolution policy was being developed TC represented the Ticket Tax to the Canadian public, and to the airport transfer groups in particular, as a tax to fund airports and air navigation. Then when the first four transfer groups began negotiating they said "Well we'd like a piece, our appropriate share, of the airline Ticket Tax." This caught TC by surprise. TC thought about it and came back and said "Sorry, but all of that tax actually is used to fund air navigation." Upon hearing that news the folk conducting the transfers on behalf of their local airport were not amused.

Then in 1995, when NavCanada was created, TC did agree that the airline ticket tax would disappear and be replaced by NavCanada putting fees on airlines (going from passenger paid to airline paid). It was also supposed to result in the cancellation of the federal fuel tax on general aviation (GA), but that cancellation never happened.

Overall I believe that the creation of the AAs was an inspired decision. If we go back 30 years the difference in Canadian airports between then and now is astounding, "like day and night".[181] Arguably I think we have one of the best airport infrastructures in the world.

The key thing is that the overall costs of the airport system in 1992 went from a $750 million drain to the Canadian taxpayer (which in inflation adjusted terms is $1.2 billion in 2018) to a rent income to the federal government of $400 million a year, which means the Canadian taxpayer is $1.8 billion a year better off.[182]. That is an effect really worth highlighting as one of the consequences of the devolution policy.

---

[181] Collenette.

[182] If the subsidies had continued from 1992 to 2018 at the same rate of $750 million annually, TC would have spent $20.25 billion on the airport system over that 27-year period ($25.8 billion in 2018 dollars). The rent stream over that same period to the federal government Consolidated Revenue Fund totals $6.5 billion, ($7.8 billion in 2018 dollars). So the net benefit to the Canadian taxpayer since the beginning of devolution is $32.3 billion (in 2018 dollars).

Chapter 6: the Airports Authorities

The following chapter provides details, characteristics and observations of the 21 Airport Authorities which form the most important part of the National Airports System.

In each case the author has written a history of the airport from its creation up to its handover to the Airport Authority, and then a recounting of the personal tales of the men and women who created their Airport Authority and the trials and tribulations they went through in order to succeed.

Birthing the Airport Authority was not an easy task and quite often those persons involved believed that notwithstanding the huge amount of labour they were investing their efforts would not result in handover. But they persevered and in many cases overcame tremendous logistical, financial, and political odds in order that their Airport Authority came into being.

You will also note in some of the personal histories that there was frustration on the parts of both the public and private sectors with the process. The public sector was committed to providing the best value to Canadians for the billions of dollars that had been invested by Canada in the airport infrastructure over the years. The private sector did its best to gain control over that infrastructure in the best possible way, from its point-of-view. This sometimes caused them to run up against the public servants negotiating the deal. Sometimes the results were not pretty when the private sector folk brought politics into the fray and tried to circumvent the public servants. But in the end it all worked out.

As an economic note, in a single year, 2017, the AA's contributed more than $2.6 billion dollars to the Canadian economy. They paid almost $153 million in property taxes to their local municipalities. Their employees earned more than $514 million. They purchased more than $857 million in goods and services from local businesses and spent more than $1.1 billion in capital investment in infrastructure. It is difficult to see how that level of economic investment could have happened if Transport Canada was still managing the airports.

	PILT	Salaries & Benefits	Goods & Services	Capital	Totals
All AA's - January to December 2017					
Calgary	14,958,000	33,721,000	116,740,000	130,799,000	296,218,000
Charlottetown	511,419	1,912,795	2,882,913	5,523,414	10,830,541
Edmonton	5,000,000	31,676,000	50,134,000	48,651,300	135,461,300
Fredericton	44,000	2,653,000	3,214,000	16,903,000	22,814,000
Gander	172,774	3,224,314	3,372,259	2,932,700	9,702,047
Halifax	1,500,000	22,160,000	25,743,000	30,131,000	79,534,000
London	803,000	3,642,000	2,823,000	1,283,000	8,551,000
Moncton	1,086,039	3,328,356	5,664,935	1,516,647	11,595,977
Montreal ADM	40,203,000	72,295,000	116,550,000	219,317,000	448,365,000
Ottawa	5,100,000	33,800,000	23,800,000	5,100,000	67,800,000
Prince George	274,311	2,711,862	3,650,953	4,611,381	11,248,507
Quebec City	3,847,824	14,231,210	14,886,189	98,988,167	131,953,390
Regina	1,520,816	6,389,996	7,221,202	4,688,700	19,820,714
Saint John	350,000	2,495,234	2,154,303	1,771,847	6,771,384
Saskatoon	865,244	4,112,553	8,765,267	16,201,000	29,944,064
St. John's	1,091,401	10,603,095	9,256,837	32,074,000	53,025,333
Thunder Bay	450,000	3,483,888	2,434,000	3,669,999	10,037,887
Toronto	36,344,000	175,706,000	297,437,000	279,356,000	788,843,000
Vancouver	31,650,000	56,495,000	123,180,000	167,941,000	379,266,000
Victoria	898,630	4,984,595	8,687,495	15,044,487	29,615,207
Winnipeg	6,578,000	24,408,000	28,514,000	24,323,000	83,823,000
Totals	**153,248,458**	**514,033,898**	**857,111,353**	**1,110,826,642**	**2,635,220,351**

Figure 10: Economic contribution of the AA's to their local communities in 2017.

Unless specifically attributed, the comments and observations herein are those of the author.

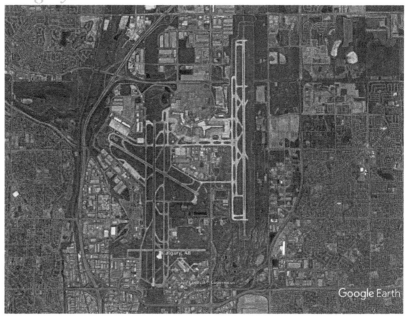

Figure 11: Image courtesy of Google Earth Pro, 10-18-2018. The pin marks the location of the original BCATP aerodrome.

The first airport to serve Calgary opened in 1914, in the neighbourhood of Bowness, 10 km to the west of the city. It occupied a square area 300 yards on a side and consisted of a hut and a grass runway. In 1928 operations shifted to a new airport (named Old Banff Coach Road Airport) southwest of the city and located on a bluff overlooking the Bow River. However, issues with turbulence in the area prompted

Figure 12: The curved-top building is an original hangar from 1928.

117

another airfield to be built the following year in Renfrew. This site was known as Calgary Municipal Airport and was operated by the City Electrical System. One of the airport's original hangars still stands at the corner of 12th Avenue and 6th Street NE.

As the city of Calgary grew in the area surrounding the Renfrew airport, the city government decided to relocate operations another time. It purchased 640 acres (1 section – 259 hectares) of land north of Calgary in 1938 for about $31,000. And, finally, here is where the airport stayed. Construction started in 1938 with a single paved runway (02-20) and a combined hangar and administration building. The airport opened on 25 September 1939, three weeks after Canada entered WW2. The BCATP assumed control of the site in 1940, using it as a wireless school, and an EFTS. When the United States entered the war in 1941 the airport became very busy as elements of the USAF became active along the northwest airway to Alaska, using Calgary as a fuel and maintenance stop for aircraft involved in the war effort. The USAF built hangars and other facilities to service their aircraft, and also the large concrete ramp that influenced the decision to place the new terminal there in 1948.

Regular passenger flights continued during this period.

At the end of the war, the airport had expanded to include four runways, five additional hangars, an ILS and much other infrastructure, all built by the BCATP, the RAF and the USAF. When the city resumed managing the airport in 1949 it got a whole lot of infrastructure for free.

The ILS and the extended runway 07-25 (now 6,200 feet – 1 800 m) allowed the airport to become part of the national transportation system when in 1948 TCA moved its operations from Lethbridge to Calgary because its acquisitions of Lodestar and North Star aircraft meant that it could now fly over the Rockies immediately to the west. The relocation of TCA coincided with severe flooding of the Fraser River in BC, and Calgary became the centre for Operation Sandbag. All military aircraft in the area were used to fly sandbags to Vancouver and as a result the main runway (16-34) took a terrible beating. After only a single landing by a TCA North Star TCA moved its operations back to Lethbridge.

While runway 16-34 was being rebuilt, and extended to 6,440 feet (1 963 m), the terminal facilities were moved out of the old hangar and moved to two existing buildings on the west side located beside the USAF ramp. These were renovated and adapted as a "new" terminal. In 1949 TCA again moved its main line services from Lethbridge to Calgary, giving direct service to Vancouver, Winnipeg and Toronto for the first time.

Canadian Pacific Airlines began flying from Calgary to Cranbrook, Castlegar and Penticton in 1950. This created more passenger traffic and the city agreed to build a new terminal on the west side. A bylaw provided the money and the new terminal opened in 1956. However, when jet aircraft landed at the airport for the first time in 1961 the new terminal, opened just five years earlier, became obsolete as it could not accommodate the increased passenger loads.

Flights from Europe commenced in 1962 and the city renamed the airport "Calgary International Airport – McCall Field".[183] Between 1962 and 1966 the terminal received five expansions, a new runway (10-28 at 8,000 feet (2 438 m)), and an extension of runway 16-34 to 12,675 feet (3 863 m). Pacific Western began its airbus service between Calgary and Edmonton. These additional services strained the terminal beyond its limits and a new terminal was needed if the needs of Calgary and its users were to be met.

Eventually the city government did not have the funds to cope with rising traffic. It sold the site to the DOT in April 1967 for $2 million in return for a promise of a new terminal. The first priority for the DOT was to meet the burgeoning passenger load and the existing terminal underwent major renovations which added 10 gates, holding rooms and additional facilities. This was completed in 1968.

The DOT began a refurbishment of the runways, renamed the aerodrome to "Calgary International Airport" and began construction of a new curved terminal at a cost of $130 million.

---

[183] The airfield had originally been named "McCall Field" in honour of Calgary flying ace Capt. Fred McCall, who had been instrumental in commencing flying operations in Calgary after WW1.

The new terminal opened in 1977. Attached to it was a Canadian Pacific hotel and a car parkade.

In 1982 the Executive Flight Centre completed its third-phase expansion to become the largest corporate and general aviation centre in Canada. Shell completed its Aero Centre hangar that same year. Air Canada built a new commissary building in 1984, Avis Rent-A-Car a new service centre in 1985, Tilden Rent-A-Car a new service centre in 1986, and, also in 1986, Purolator a new office/warehouse.

In 1987 DOT moved the concessions from the mezzanine to the departures level resulting in significant increases in revenue and a doubling of concession operators.

In February 1988, when Calgary hosted the XV Winter Olympic Games, the airport handled 85% of all Olympic-related travelers. A total of 156 Olympic-related charters passed through the terminal resulting in a total of 400,000 passengers in the month of February alone.

A new air traffic control tower was in operation by 1990 to coincide with the installation of new radar equipment.

The Authority

Prior to devolution, getting anything done, even moving a picture on a wall, required getting approval from Ottawa. Having the local authority meant that the decision could be made right then and there.[184]

From a TC perspective Edmonton was to be the centrepin for airports in Western Canada, and Calgary was to be the smaller airport. The folk in Calgary thought differently. Their strategy was how to get Calgary to be the leading airport in the West. TC had been instructed to get as much work as they possibly could into Edmonton, political hanky-panky all the time. So the Airport Committee of the Calgary Transportation Authority (ACCTA) came up with all sorts of ideas how to combat the work at

---

[184] Myrna Dubé, interviewed by Shirlee Matheson, 29 February 2016.

Edmonton. It was a big political battle and David Dover was the guy to do battle.[185]

The federal government would be saying this, and the provincial government would be saying that, the political regimes were doing this, and business was doing that – and all of sudden it would blow up. The federal government, the provincial government, the people of Edmonton, would suddenly be upset with the ACCTA. They would say: "You can't do that, you don't play ball like that, you're dirty!". The problem with Edmonton was that it thought it owned the right to fly airplanes and that Calgary was done, not in the game at all.[186]

The ACCTA did everything it could to keep the Edmonton municipal airport operating for as long as possible, because it realized that as long as the "muni" was in operation, the international airport at Edmonton, way out in the boonies, was going to be a millstone, and not a pretty thing to behold. The ACCTA played to the airlines to keep them going into the "muni", because every day they did that gave another day for the ACCTA to solidify business between Calgary and Europe and onward into the States.[187]

There was also at the same time as the ACCTA an Aviation Committee of the Calgary Chamber of Commerce (AC4) chaired by David Dover. He approached Mazankowski (former Minister of Transport) and asked him if he would work with the AC4. Maz said he would. So the AC4 organized a pro-forma Board comprised of Calgary businessmen and put together a proposal to TC to form the Airport Authority. The main issue was money. The Board insisted that it not use any federal money "because you don't borrow money from the landlord."[188] So the Board raised its own money and organized the line of credit well in advance. It knew that if this idea of an airport authority was going to succeed it would need some serious money. So the Board went to the

---

[185] Dr. Michael Mahar, interviewed by Shirlee Matheson, 2 November 2015.

[186] Ibid.

[187] Ibid.

[188] David Dover, interview with Shirlee Matheson, 8 June 2015.

Alberta Treasury Branch and got them to allow the Board to borrow money as if it were a municipality.

The Calgary Chamber of Commerce, the Calgary Transportation Committee, the city of Edmonton, and the City of Vancouver were all in the same boat: they were far away from Ottawa, and that eventually they would have to look after their own interests. At the time TC was glad to get rid of the responsibilities, but it still wanted the revenue.

Each Board member had a committee, with a specific job, with a mandate to do its work and report back to the Board as a whole. There were Board members with an interest in aviation, business, community affairs, transportation. Moreover, because the air routes were actually international trade agreements, and the cities were not involved in setting the routes, the Board decided it had to get into the game. How would a Calgary AA fit into the national and international scene?[189]

Mazankowski called one day and said "We're going to do this [give the Calgary airport to the nascent airport authority], and we're going to give you $3 million just to get you going". The Board had a lobbyist in Ottawa, named Jim MacEachern, the "go to" guy to get things done in Ottawa. He knew everybody. So Dover called Jim and said they had $3 million from Mazankowski. MacEachern said "Hang up the phone. Call Mazankowski back right now and tell him you cannot take the money." So Dover did that, and then called the Board to tell them that they couldn't accept the money. Mazankowski called back and said "you've been speaking to MacEachern. How are you going to finance this thing?"[190]

By this time Alistair Ross was in charge and he said "Well, if you want money, you go to where the money is: you go to the bank." Dover said "OK, Alistair, what are you doing tomorrow?" So off they went and pulled down $200 million from a line of credit with the Alberta Treasury Branch.[191]

---

[189] Ibid.

[190] Ibid.

[191] Ibid.

At the beginning the Board was quite small, made up of volunteers. And in order to keep its independence it accepted no gifts, no tickets, nothing, from the airlines. If a Board member had to go to Ottawa, or anywhere else to look at an airport, that person paid their own way. That kept the Board on an independent basis. And because the Board members were volunteers that allowed them to keep their links with the community of Calgary.[192]

The Board was sensitive to community issues, the environment, people affected by the airport. It had to be perceptive as to how the airport affected those who use it, and who live and work around it. Board members had to be sensitive to other Board members. They were not a bunch of guys trying to make a fast buck out of this. They had differences of opinion but they were sensitive to each other's understanding and perspective. They had differences of opinion and when that occurred they'd say "we have to resolve this." They tried not to leave a meeting with someone upset or mad at somebody else. They always left with a handshake. They knew they had a mission and they were going to do it.[193]

The Board had to get the people running the airport (the management staff) aligned with the Board, and to ensure that everybody the confidence that what they were doing was right, meaningful and worthwhile. They had to work in cooperation, for there was no room for celebrities and stars. They had to be innovative, but in a cooperative manner.[194]

The Board had no idea of how to work together at the beginning. Some board members had no idea of what a Board should look like, or what the Board's function was, or what it should be doing in any particular thing. Some of the Board members came riding in on a big white horse, or a black one, with no sense of relevance. The Board did not need, nor want, people on the board who told people how great they were. It wanted performance from the Board members. It needed results, not words.[195]

---

[192] Ibid.

[193] Mahar.

[194] Ibid.

[195] Ibid.

The Board had to be concerned with being competitive – with Edmonton, the trucking companies, the airlines. It had to understand the airlines and what is important to them, so as to allow them to be competitive. It had to organize the airport so that it served the airlines, but also at the same time the travelling public. That's not an easy task. Sometimes the demands the airlines made of the Authority made economic and business sense to them, but would have made life worse for the travelling public. It became a balancing act.[196]

Diversity was an issue on no one's radar at the beginning, but eventually the Board had to address it and develop appropriate policies.[197]

Negotiating with TC was difficult because they would not have their decision-makers at the table. They would always say they had to go back to the Treasury Board Secretariat in Ottawa. It would have been a better outcome for the Authority if the Board could have had tougher negotiations with the federal government. But the negotiations couldn't have had a win-lose result because the Canadian people win when the Authority pays a fairly good ground rent to the federal government, such as a portion of the rent for the airport land that the Authority leases to commercial operations. That is where the Authority has done a good job in generating revenue so the passenger doesn't have to pay high fees.[198]

The whole issue of ground rent was extremely contentious, and the federal government agreed to a revision of the rental formula in exchange for the right to nominate two persons to the Board.[199]

Working with a lot of people who were basically civil servants. It was difficult for them, especially for those who had been with TC a long time, because all of a sudden things started to change very fast. Everything with government takes such a long time – everything is so process-driven and there are rules and regulations – and it takes a long time to get information circulated, to get

---

[196] Ibid.

[197] Ibid.

[198] Bob Wellin, interview with Shirlee Matheson, 18 June 2015.

[199] Peter Wallis, interview with Shirlee Matheson, 30 Nov 2016.

approval from whoever, whereas the Board could now make a decision so much faster.[200]

When the Authority took over running the airport there were still a lot of staff who thought of themselves as civil servants, and who were still working in a public sector mindset. They would say "we're civil servants," and "you can't treat us that way," and "we're not here to do that." But in the opinion of some Board members they weren't very civil and they weren't servants. Some of the new guys who came in to run the airport must have taken a lot of aspirins because of the headaches the old staff gave them. Sometimes you just had to shake your head. The management staff had to put up with a lot of grief at the start. But things settled down after a few years, especially when the Authority started to push innovation "This is not a government job you've got here, guys. You're serving the community and you are building the town. This is what Calgary is all about."[201]

Ernie Caron set up a series of town hall meetings and discussions with the old Transport staff who had transferred to the new authority. Mostly he spoke about attitude, and transitioning to being entrepreneurs – a big jump for them. He was the right guy to do that because he had spent his life as an entrepreneur. Some of the people he had to deal with were a pretty hard sell, because they had been civil servants for so long. What was lacking in the civil servants, especially on the management side, was their inability to make a decision, because they had in the past never had to make big decisions. In the past everything had had to be referred to Ottawa, and they did not have to exercise those decision-making skills. But Ernie could strike like lightning. He would make a decision as you were standing there talking with him. Gradually, over time, he introduced that element of free enterprise into the staff, some of them kicking and screaming, that was so necessary if the airport was to succeed.[202]

The airport bought a piece of the Bilben ranch which was on the airport side of Airport Trail for $40 million. That purchase

---

[200] Dubé.

[201] Ernie Caron, interview with Shirlee Matheson, 4 August 2015.

[202] Caron.

allowed the airport to develop the YYC Logistics Park. Some of the Bilben land included the escarpment down to the Deerfoot Trail and some wetlands. The land will remain that way. "The big thing that still sticks in everybody's throat today – the airport bought a lot of extra land. The minute you buy land it goes into the lease and you pay ground rent on the land you just bought. It seems unfair but it is fair to the people of Canada, and that's what counts – isn't it?"[203]

The Authority has done a good job of developing the land for warehousing – 1,200 acres in the north east – for FedEx, Purolator, UPS and DHL. The future bodes well – the biggest problem will be the rent – heaven forbid if the people of Canada get a federal NDP government; they might re-negotiate the rents. The current rent structure is a good deal for the Canadian people. But to change to a system whereby the bigger airports pay for the smaller ones in unfair.[204]

In the concessions, the Authority insisted on street pricing for stores at the airport – no higher prices than in downtown Calgary. It built a Mac's milk so that people could buy groceries on their way home from arriving at the airport.[205]

At one point the Authority stole the cargo business from Edmonton. It dressed people up overalls and had them walk around the Edmonton hangar to see who were the customers. They came back and the Authority made good proposals to the shippers since it was cheaper for the shippers to deliver to Calgary and then ship back west, rather than direct to Vancouver. That made Calgary an air freight hub.[206]

Then the Authority built Springbank airport in order to get all the piston-engined aircraft out of Calgary and into Springbank. Having a big jet come onto final with a little Cessna 172 ahead of them was a mixture just didn't work. The Authority got the city to

---

[203] Wallis.

[204] Ibid.

[205] Roger Jarvis, interview with Shirlee Matheson, 31 August 2015.

[206] Tom Walsh, interview with Shirlee Matheson, 29 July 2015.

expropriate the land because the owner wouldn't negotiate.[207] After the land was purchased by the Authority, the land became part of the ground lease with TC (and subject to ground rent). Springbank had one runway east-west and another runway north-south. Eventually the runways at Springbank were lengthened which allows jets to operate there. There is also a large helicopter operation managed by Great Slave Helicopters.[208]

At the beginning the Chair felt there was too much emphasis put on developing the ATB, and not enough on the running the airport operations. More than once the Chair had to remind the Board that they were running the Calgary Airport Authority, not the Calgary Terminal Authority.

At the beginning the Board was very concerned about money, and were telling the staff "don't do this. Don't do that." That changed under Tom Walsh (the CEO) who encouraged the staff to "go visit! Go to these airport functions, go everywhere you can. See how the other guy operates, then you don't have to re-invent the wheel."[209]

One day the TC "language police" came out from Ottawa, six or eight guys, looked around, and said there wasn't enough French on the signage. So the Authority converted all the signs with French and English on them to symbols. A lot of people from many countries transit the Calgary airport; symbols are better than just a sign with English/French on it.[210]

A big change was when the Calgary city police took over from the RCMP. The Authority and the staff noticed that almost immediately communications between the security forces and themselves were greatly improved.[211]

Another excellent improvement was the Cell-Phone Parking Lot. Although almost as soon as it was completed people were saying

---

[207] Ibid.

[208] Jarvis.

[209] Walsh.

[210] Ibid.

[211] Jarvis.

"and what about putting in Wi-Fi so I can download stuff while I'm waiting?"[212]

From the perspective of an air carrier in 1992 the questions would have been "are these airport authorities going to be good for us or are they going to be bad for us? What is the biggest bang for the buck for us as an air carrier?" Originally the airports were run by Transport Canada and any major developments at an airport had to be approved by the Minister of Transport. The Minister determined what he or she thought was a good investment. An airline could not always be sure how successful it would be if there was indeed a political element to a decision to be made "here" versus a decision to be made "there". The airline could lobby the government through the Canadian Transport Commission (now the Canada Transport Agency), make a case for public convenience and necessity, and get a regulatory approval for a route which then the airports had to accept. However there was always the political aspect which could completely reverse a "sound" business decision at the local level.[213]

Consequently it made more sense to the airlines that the creation of an Authority would have more local focus, and less political interference from Ottawa, and therefore be more susceptible to the influence of the air carriers as to the activities the Authority would undertake. The thought process of the airline would have been to conclude that local authorities made sense, coupled with the sense that this creation was going to happen anyway, because once the machine got going it was simply a matter of who got there first: Vancouver, Edmonton, Calgary or Montréal.[214]

The more than two decades which have passed since the majority of the Airport Authorities were created show that although the airlines have a say in the operation of the airport, this influence has diminished over time as more and more of the Authority's revenues come from non-aeronautical sources (in 2017 at 17 of the

---

[212] Ibid.

[213] Wallis.

[214] Ibid.

21 Canadian Airport Authorities, non-aeronautical revenue was 60% or higher of total revenues).

It took a long time, but over the years the Board changed from being too involved with operations to become a policy board. "We're here to set policy, not to run the airport!" The first Board Chair was a frustrated former airport manager and it showed. We'd say "Let's get back to policy, please, and let Ernie (Caron) run the airport. That's what we hired him for."[215]

One of the mistakes the Board made was that it wanted to turn Calgary into the supersonic hub of North America by running the Concorde from London to Calgary to Houston twice a day. The Board worked with British Airways and Air France and got an agreement. But then some Board members went to the United States and told them what the Authority wanted to do, and the U.S. said "we will never allow a supersonic foreign flag carrier over the main part of the United States, but you can go around if you want." So Concorde service to Calgary didn't work out. Concorde of course didn't last. It was OK on the Europe to the Eastern seaboard run, but it was a small plane, only 120 people. The Board did get the Concorde to land at the airport once though.[216]

The airport is the economic driving force in southern Alberta, not just Calgary. Some of the Board members would get stuck on the terminal, but it is important to see that the airport as a whole is the economic driver.[217]

At the start the Authority took the airport as it was, in the condition as TC left it. And the Board said "now we can improve on this. So what do we need to do?" And the Board did that over the first eight years. It took its time and did things in a logical, orderly way "you don't just go and start pouring concrete. You have to have a plan and take each step slow and easy. You build up people, and you build up operations, and you make it so that the people working there want to make a career of it, and you're

---

[215] Ken Lett, interview with Shirlee Matheson, 9 August 1995. Supplemental interview 30 Nov 2015.

[216] Dover.

[217] Lett.

responsible to the people, the community, and the banks. And just because you have $200 million you don't spend it."[218]

The other thing was that if the Authority didn't provide good service people would not come, and that affects the economy of Calgary and the surrounding areas. The airport is a huge benefit to the city and the basic well-being of the people who live here.[219]

Some Board members thought the ground rent was too high. When all the airports are put together, this was the biggest land transfer in Canadian history, and the Canadian government is responsible to the people of Canada. The government had an asset, and there was a value to that asset, and the people of Canada deserve to get a reasonable return on that asset. The Board negotiated hard, but the TC folk negotiated harder because they were the representatives of the owners, the Canadian public. It was their job to get the best deal for Canadians. You never hear an airline say "I'm not paying enough for my landing fees."[220]

In 1992 there were no terms for Directors, but then the Public Accountability Principles came along in 1995 and the Board changed to term limits for Directors.[221]

There were some big egos involved in the transfer – it was not all a bed of roses, and when asked why they had become a Board member, almost all of them said "to be able to be in a position of change agent, have an impact, and drive something to conclusion."[222]

But in the end, a great many of them said that Jacques Pigeon (the TC lawyer in Ottawa) was critical to the success of what happened at Calgary.

Nominators for the Calgary Board are:

---

[218] Dover.

[219] Ibid.

[220] Ibid.

[221] Walsh.

[222] Ibid.

- The Long Range Planning Committee of the Calgary Chamber of Commerce, which has 10 members appointed to the Board;
- The Corporation of The City of Calgary, which has three members appointed to the Board;
- The Government of Canada, which has two members appointed to the Board; and,
- Rocky View County, which has one member appointed to the Board.

The Authority strives to achieve an optimal level of public and stakeholder accountability. The processes involved in achieving this level of accountability include:

- A public Annual General Meeting;
- A published Annual Report, including audited financial statements;
- An independent review of management operations and financial performance every five years, including a published report;
- Individual annual meetings with all Appointer organizations which are attended by the Board of Directors, senior management and external auditors;
- Compliance with the Canada Lease;
- Regulatory compliance;
- Meetings with key stakeholders;
- Public notice of fee changes;
- A community consultative committee;
- An accessibility advisory council;
- Meetings with airport operators and tenants; and,
- Meetings with civic officials and community organizations.

Figure 13: Calgary Airport

Since 1992 the Authority has invested more than $4 billion in infrastructure. In 2017 alone the Authority paid almost $41 million in ground rent to the federal government, had a construction program of $131 million (almost all of which was spent locally), and contributed more than $165 million to the local economy through wages, the purchase of goods and services, and property taxes.[223]

---

[223] Source: YYC 2017 Financial Report, http://www.yyc.com/Portals/0/CALGARY%20AIRPORT%20AUTJORITY/Publications/2017%20Financal%20Report.pdf?ver=2018-04-17-161254-537, accessed 26 January 2019.

Calgary, Alberta

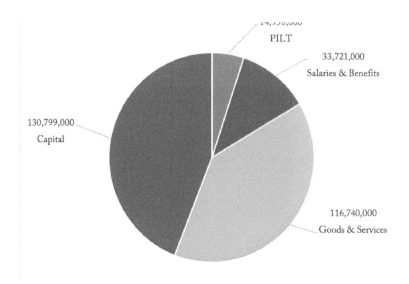

14,958,000
PILT

33,721,000
Salaries & Benefits

130,799,000
Capital

116,740,000
Goods & Services

Calgary, Alberta

Figure 15: Image courtesy of Google Earth Pro, 9-14-2017. The pin marks the location of the original BCATP aerodrome.

In 1931 a permanent airfield was built at Upton Field (later Upton Airport) and consisted of two turf runways 2,800 ft (850 m) and 1,600 ft (490 m) respectively, opening on January 16, 1932. Upton was a farming community located in the western part of Queens Royalty, northwest of Charlottetown. The airfield was leased to Canadian Airways Limited from 9 October 1932 to 9 October 1938, although the airfield was only licensed until 30 June 1938.

Throughout this time, Upton Airport received the first air mail service in Canada. Today the site is farmland and trees.

In June 1938 the city government asked the DOT to assist in the development of an expanded municipal airport. Upton Airport was considered a candidate, as was a 300-acre (1.2 km2) property east of Sherwood Station on the Brackley Point Road. Upton Airport was rejected due to lack of space and the Sherwood Station property in the central part of Charlottetown Royalty was purchased by the city government for $30,000. The provincial government contributed 50% to the development of the new airport in exchange for 50% of its profits while the city would operate it.

In December 1939 the city government offered the airport to the federal government for military use through the duration of WW2. The RCAF expanded the airport and enlarged the runways in preparation for using the airport to train pilots and aircrew. The runways were altered into a classic triangle configuration seen with most BCATP aerodromes across Canada[224]. The Royal Air Force used the airfield from 15 June 1941 until February 1944 during which time it was known as RAF Station Charlottetown. Following the departure of the RAF, the RCAF established training units at the airfield, which was renamed RCAF Station Charlottetown.

Figure 16: BCATP at Charlottetown - 1942

Following the end of WW2, the military presence at the airport diminished and by late 1945 the base was decommissioned and transferred from the RCAF to the federal Department of Transport on 1 February 1946, returning the airfield to civilian use.

Several expansions were subsequently undertaken, including an enlarged civilian air terminal off the Brackley Point Road on the

---

[224] The pin in the photo is in the middle of the old BCATP runway triangle.

west side of the airfield, as well as a lengthening and realigning of what would become runway 03/21 during the 1960s-1970s to accommodate jet aircraft. A major expansion during the 1980s saw the old terminal become a general aviation facility after a new terminal, control tower and emergency services building were constructed further to the north from a continuation of the Sherwood Road. This also saw runway 03/21 lengthened to its current configuration.

Charlottetown Airport saw extensive service during the 1960s-1990s from both Air Canada and Eastern Provincial Airways (EPA) to destinations in Atlantic and Central Canada. Following EPA's sale and merger with CP Air, Charlottetown Airport saw direct CP Air service from Central Canada for several years, continued by Canadian. The creation of Air Canada subsidiary Air Nova and Canadian subsidiary Air Atlantic saw the beginning of a downgrade in direct service by the major carriers from Central Canada and an increase in service from hub airports such as Halifax and Moncton.

The opening of the Confederation Bridge in 1997 coupled with capacity improvements at Moncton and Halifax airports saw many changes to air traffic through Charlottetown. Initially the bridge was seen by many as sounding the death knell of the airport. Moncton was only one hour away, and had more choices for a flying public than were available at Charlottetown. However, business and political leaders on the island recognized a viable airport in Charlottetown was an important economic development infrastructure and decided to work for that end.

The Authority

In 1995 TC called a meeting with the Greater Charlottetown Area Chamber of Commerce and the City of Charlottetown. The purpose was to discuss the transfer of management and operations of the Charlottetown airport from federal to local control.[225]

A Transition Committee was formed with Gerry Gallant as the Transition Coordinator. The group had representation from the Chamber of Commerce, the City, labour organizations, as well as

---

[225] Most of this section was created with the able help of Gerry Gallant, telephone interview with the author, 14 September 2018.

several local business leaders. The group met with TC many times over the next year to discuss how the divestiture was to proceed, and who was going to pay for what, and when. The government's policy was to commercialize the National Airports System through the transfer of responsibility for the operation, management and development to Canadian Airport Authorities (CAAs). Local management and operations was the primary objective since it was believed to be more cost-effective, more responsive to markets and better able to match levels of service to local demands.

It was not very long after the meetings began that it became clear to the Transition Group that Transport Canada was divesting itself of a liability, while retaining the assets. This issue of how to shift the airport from a losing proposition to a profitable one dominated the discussions.

One of the first orders-of-business for the Transition Group was the formation of a not-for-profit company which would assume the operational control of the airport. The Charlottetown Airport Authority Inc. was incorporated in 1996.

Meetings with the Transport Canada negotiators continued through 1995-6. The Transition Group had prepared financial projections, a capital plan and a business plan for the first five years of operations. These projections and plans were dissected and discussed at great length and in great detail, but it seemed that the issue always came back to what was the current condition and value of the assets, and what was Transport Canada going to put on the table in order to safely maintain those assets for the forseeable future. Deferred maintenance by Transport Canada was an issue, particularly after the airports' divestiture program was launched. From the Authority's point-of-view, it seemed to them that they were dealing with a parsimonious Scot, who had not opened his purse for so long that when he finally did, moths would fly out.

Discussions became heated on several occasions as the Transition Group believed the Transport Canada staff were not negotiating in good faith.

Eventually the Transition Group engaged Deloitte Touche to assist them in the negotiations.

A deal breaker for the Transition Group was the amount of money being offered by Transport Canada as funding for the first five years of operation. Transport had put $8 million on the table, based on a passenger volume of 160,000. Apart from the issue of whether or not this was enough money, the Transition Team was concerned about what would happen if passenger volume went down. In 1997 the Confederation Bridge opened and quite a few folk on PEI were saying that they would now go to Moncton where there were more airlines, and better connections and routes. If passenger volumes dropped, would there then be enough revenues to cover the operating costs?

During these negotiations, the Transition Group proposed that if passenger volumes dropped below 150,000 then the fledgling Airport Authority could come back to Transport Canada and reopen the transfer contract. Nobody was more surprised than the Transition Group when TC agreed. This condition was viewed at the time as an insurance policy to mitigate the risk of declining passengers. Notwithstanding the fact that the Authority was confident it could grow the passenger numbers, this strategy was more to do with establishing a comfort level within the community.

The Transition Group still had concerns. Was it even possible for the Airport Authority to succeed? Had the financial plan set aside enough money to fund the necessary upgrades and improvements that TC had for so long delayed in doing? Would passenger volumes remain at 160,000 annually? Would the Province, City of Charlottetown and islanders support the venture? Would local businesses get on-side?

The TG went on a communications and publicity campaign.

For the next year you could not pick up a paper, nor listen to the radio, nor watch TV without hearing at least one reference to something that was going on at the airport, or with the transfer, or with the new AA. Everything and anything that was to do with the AA somehow got mentioned in print or on the air.

Once the Authority felt it had the community on side, it began to address the issue of human resources. The existing airport staff were all unionized, and there was an unease amongst them as to what was going to happen when the airport went "private". The most vocal were the firemen, who were employed to respond to a plane crash or to be the first responders on airport property. The last airplane crash on PEI had occurred on 31 March 1977, and that had been an RCAF Argus at CFB Summerside. The TG was concerned that a dedicated staff of firemen waiting for a plane crash was a financial luxury the new AA would not be able to afford. However, the TC safety rules and regulations under which the AA would operate made it mandatory for the AA to maintain fire services in compliance with federal regulations that TC had always followed. The AA were committed to those policies and regulations. What to do?

A proposal was made to the fire hall that the firemen cross train as support workers for the airport. When trained as heavy equipment operators they would be an invaluable addition to the airport operations staff, and would be available to respond to an emergency when required. The firemen considered the proposal and, with the exception of three members, the rest accepted. The Charlottetown AA then became the first NAS airport to have firefighters who were cross-trained and had other responsibilities.

Since this "innovative approach" began not one emergency call has been missed due to a lack of trained personnel.

And the other AA's were quick to notice.

The transition from TC to AA was not without its minor hiccups. As with all the other AAs, the staff suddenly found themselves responsible for everything. Purchasing, paying the bills, marketing the airport, human resources, keeping track of the finances, even implementing a payroll system to pay themselves - everything was new.

What was not new was the commitment to safety. It all continued, as it had done for 50 years before.

Finally, on 28 February 1999 Transport Canada transferred operational and financial responsibility for the Charlottetown airport to the Charlottetown Airport Authority.

The decision to create the AA was a good one. Since the AA assumed control of the airport in 1999, it has invested more than $40 million in capital expenses, earns annual revenues over $6 million (six times more than its first year of operations), built new customs facilities and an international terminal, expanded the main terminal to accommodate additional airlines, expanded the terminal's apron to accommodate more scheduled flights on the ground at the same time, and made a major expansion to runway 10/28 in order to have two 7,000 ft (2 134 m) runways. Passenger traffic has grown from the 160,000 at transfer to 370,688 in 2017.

In 2017, the Airport Authority partnered with the Autism Society of Prince Edward Island to host the first ever Autism Aviators event at YYG. Developed by the Halifax International Airport Authority, Autism Aviators is a mock travel day for individuals on the autism spectrum and their families. The event saw 12 families gain the familiarity and confidence they need to take future trips. The morning was a major success and will become a signature event for the airport moving forward.

Another significant achievement was the 5th annual *flypei* Runway Run in support of Cystic Fibrosis Canada – PEI Chapter. Over 300 participants took part to help raise $5,000 for the local organization.

Each year, the AA supports numerous other special events and charities on Prince Edward Island. Other organizations that the Authority and its employees partnered with in 2017 include:

- Queen Elizabeth Hospital Foundation
- Prince County Hospital Foundation
- Holland College Tourism & Management Program
- Big Brothers, Big Sisters
- Rotary Clubs of Charlottetown
- Hope Air
- Mayor's Cup Golf Tournament in support of Stars for Life Foundation
- Easter Seals
- COPA for Kids
- Fusion Charlottetown
- CBC Feed A Family

Figure 17: Charlottetown Airport

As an economic engine to the local community, the AAs impact is felt far beyond the walls of its terminal. Direct employment at the airport rose to 685 jobs in 2016, bringing $36.5 million in wages and salaries each year. The economic impact of the airport is $115 million a year. In 2017 alone the airport contributed more than $10.8 million in direct spending (salaries & benefits, property taxes, goods & services, and capital investment) to the local community.[226]

---

[226] Source: Charlottetown Airport Authority Annual Report, http://www.flypei.com/admin/Editor/assets/pdf/CAA_AnnualReport2017.pdf, accessed 26 January 2019.

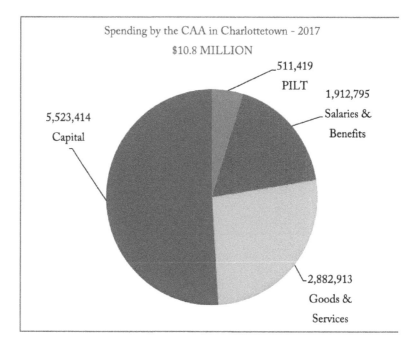

Spending by the CAA in Charlottetown - 2017

$10.8 MILLION

511,419
PILT

1,912,795
Salaries &
Benefits

5,523,414
Capital

2,882,913
Goods &
Services

Charlottetown, Prince Edward Island

Figure 19: Image courtesy of Google Earth Pro, 8-8-2018. This was a "green field" aerodrome built in 1960 and was not a BCATP aerodrome.

Originally opened in 1927 to house a flying school, the airfield just northwest of downtown Edmonton became the city's primary scheduled airport and an important military airfield during WW2. Number 16 EFTS opened on November 11, 1940 at the Edmonton Municipal Airport. It was operated by the Northern Alberta Flying Training School Ltd. under the supervision of the RCAF. The school closed on July 17, 1942.

Number 2 Air Observers School (#2 AOS) operated from August 5, 1940 until July 14, 1944. W.R. "Wop" May, a well-known Edmonton pilot, was appointed general manager of the school. Canadian Airways operated the school until 1942 when Canadian Pacific Airways took over.

It didn't take long for aviation and the city of Edmonton to outgrow the airport. With a city all around, there was no room to extend its less than 6,000-foot-long propeller-age runways.

By 1955, it was obvious that the downtown airport was inadequate for the coming jet airliners, which would need two-mile runways and spacious terminals to handle 100-plus passengers per flight.

145

That same year a site for Edmonton International Airport was selected near Leduc and the Department of Transport purchased 7,600 acres (30.76 sq km) of land for a total cost of $1,469,657. By an unwritten "gentleman's agreement," the original owners were allowed to lease back and continue to farm the land until it was needed for the airport. In terms of land area, Edmonton International Airport remains Canada's largest airport.

Turning farmland into runways had some interesting complications. Weeds overtook the construction area and polluted the surrounding farmland. A stubborn clan of beavers outwitted many human attempts to prevent them from flooding the site. Airport security in those days meant keeping livestock off the runways.

When the airport opened on November 15, 1960, its first terminal was an arch hangar. Today, that hangar is in use by Canadian North. In 1963, a passenger terminal, built in the international style, was opened. It remains in use as the North Terminal. Artwork, fired by Alberta Natural Gas, adorned the departures area exterior. A large mural, commissioned by the Canadian government in 1963 for $18,000 titled "Bush Pilot in Northern Sky" by Jack Shadbolt, remains to this day. An appraisal in 2005 indicated that the mural was worth $750,000, and a restoration of the mural was undertaken in 2007.

During the 1970s, the airport experienced a rapid growth in traffic as the city of Edmonton grew, and served approximately 2 million passengers annually by 1980. However, from the early 1980s until 1995, traffic declined. This decline was attributed to the continued usage of Edmonton City Centre Airport as well as to a slowing economy. Edmonton City Centre did not have the facilities to accept large wide-bodied long-haul aircraft, thus airlines used City Centre to fly short-haul flights to hubs in other cities where connections to many locations were available.

The Edmonton International airport had service to Europe soon after it opened.

In 1960, Canadian Pacific Airlines operated nonstop flights to Amsterdam with Bristol Britannia turboprop aircraft several times a week. By 1961, Canadian Pacific had introduced Douglas DC-8 jetliners on its nonstop service to Amsterdam. In 1962, Trans-Canada Airlines operated direct flights to London's Heathrow

Airport once a week via a stop in Winnipeg and also to Paris Orly Airport three times a week via stops in Toronto and Montréal with Douglas DC-8 jets.

During the late 1960s and early 1970s, Pacific Western Airlines operated Boeing 707 charter flights from the airport to the UK and other destinations in Europe.

In 1970, Air Canada operated nonstop Douglas DC-8 service to London-Heathrow twice a week while CP Air flew nonstop DC-8 service to Amsterdam three times a week. CP Air then introduced Boeing 747 jumbo jet service nonstop to Amsterdam with two flights a week being operated in 1976. By 1978, the airline was also flying nonstop Boeing 747 service to Honolulu. Air Canada had also begun daily nonstop Boeing 727-200 service to both Los Angeles and San Francisco by 1979.

In 1983, both airlines were operating wide body jetliners on their respective services to Europe with Air Canada flying Lockheed L-1011 TriStar long range series 500 model aircraft three days a week nonstop to London Heathrow while CP Air was flying Boeing 747 jumbo jets three days a week nonstop to Amsterdam. Wardair Canada also operated scheduled and charter flights to Europe as well as charter service to Hawaii from the airport and in 1979 was operating nonstop charter service to London Gatwick Airport and Prestwick in the UK as well as to Amsterdam and Frankfurt.

In 1989, Wardair Canada was operating scheduled nonstop service to London Gatwick and Manchester in the UK and was also operating nonstop charter service at this same time to Frankfurt and Honolulu. The Wardair nonstop service to London Gatwick was being operated with Airbus A310 jets with two flights a week in 1989.

Several US-based air carriers served the airport over the years as well. In 1975 Northwest Airlines operated nonstop Boeing 727-100 jet service to both Anchorage and Minneapolis/St. Paul while Western Airlines operated Boeing 727-200 and Boeing 737-200 jets direct to Denver, Salt Lake City and Great Falls (with all of these flights first stopping in Calgary). Hughes Airwest also served the airport with Douglas DC-9-10 and McDonnell Douglas DC-9-30 jets on nonstop flights to Spokane as well as direct flights to Las Vegas and Los Angeles.

By 1980, Hughes Airwest was operating five daily departures from Edmonton with Boeing 727-200 and McDonnell Douglas DC-9-30 jetliners with direct service via Calgary to Los Angeles, San Francisco, Las Vegas, San Diego, Phoenix, Tucson, Burbank, Reno, Boise, Spokane and Palm Springs. I

n 1981, Western Airlines was operating a daily nonstop Boeing 727-200 flight to Denver with continuing direct service to Phoenix and Los Angeles while Republic Airlines, which had acquired Hughes Airwest, flew daily nonstop Douglas DC-9-10 service to Las Vegas and Spokane.

By 1982, Republic Airlines was operating all of its flights to the U.S. from Edmonton via an intermediate stop in Calgary with direct service to Las Vegas, Los Angeles, Phoenix, Spokane and Palm Springs. United Airlines operated a daily Boeing 727-100 nonstop flight to San Francisco with direct one-stop service to Los Angeles in 1983.

Western Airlines operated a Boeing 727-200 nonstop to Salt Lake City in 1987 with this daily flight providing direct one stop service to Los Angeles. Delta Air Lines then acquired and merged with Western with Delta continuing to operate nonstop service to Salt Lake City from the late 1980s to the mid 1990s, first with a Boeing 727-200 and later with a Boeing 757-200 with these flights providing direct one stop service to Los Angeles as well.

In 1999, Canadian Airlines International flew daily nonstop Boeing 737-200 service to Chicago O'Hare Airport while Air BC flew nonstop British Aerospace BAe 146-200 jet service to Denver. In 1999, Horizon Air began nonstop Fokker F28 Fellowship jet service to Seattle.

The Authority

In 1979 the Haglund Report was released by Transport Canada. The report was the product of an internal task force headed up by Mel Haglund to explore options for the future management of airports in Canada. There was some support for the formation of independent airport authorities. Key task force members included Gordon Hamilton and Robin Monroe.[227]

---

[227] I am indebted to Ron Gilbertson for a great deal of the history of the Edmonton Regional Airports Authority, not only from his unpublished *"An*

In the early 1980's the Edmonton Air Services Authority (EASA), for a period chaired by Ross McBain and with Ron Gilbertson as Executive Director, reviewed the Haglund Report and was in general support of its findings. EASA made enquiries as to whether the report's recommendations would be supported by the current Government, but concluded that the Liberal Government was not interested in proceeding with the airport authority concept at that time.

In 1984 a Conservative Government of Brian Mulroney was elected. The new Government included as Minister of Transport the Honourable Don Mazankowski from Vegreville, Alberta.

Thinking that the new Conservative Government may support the concept of independent airport authorities, EASA formed a special task force to further explore the formation of an airport authority for Edmonton. The Task Force was co-chaired by Ev Bunnell and Bob Chapman, with the EASA Executive Director Ron Gilbertson providing support.

In January 1985 Ev Bunnell, Bob Chapman and Ron Gilbertson went to Ottawa to meet with Mazankowski to discuss the creation of the AA. Also present at the meeting was Janet Smith, the DM of TC and who had a reputation as being aggressive and difficult to deal with.[228] Chapman and Gilbertson outlined what they were planning to do and their timeframe, and, almost as an aside, said they needed some seed money to get things going. Mazankowski agreed with their request for funding and asked "How much?". Chapman and Gilbertson had not expected a positive response to this and had not thought through beforehand what amount they might ask for, so Gilbertson gave the first number that popped into his head: "$100,000 might do it" he said. And that is what happened. TC gave them the money. The other airport transition teams got wind of this and also wanted $100,000. TC said: Hang on, we need a policy here." So TC said to Vancouver, Calgary and Montréal: "you get $50,000 per airport. Edmonton gets $100,000 because it has two airports. So Vancouver, Calgary you get

_____

incomplete history of the airport authorities in Edmonton and Canada", but also the telephone interview he granted me on 19 September 2018.

[228] Several people I spoke with were a little less polite, calling her a "dragon".

$50,000 each and Montréal gets $100,000 because of Dorval and Mirabel."

Late in 1985 the EASA Task Force completed a preliminary study to determine the feasibility of the airport authority concept serving the Edmonton region and concluded that an airports authority would be financially viable.

On 18 February 1986 the Regional Airports Task Force Association (RAFTA) was formed as the successor to the EASA Task Force on airport authorities. The initial members were Ev Bunnell and Robert Chapman, who served as co-chairman. Ron Gilbertson was appointed Executive Director of RAFTA. The RAFTA team had gone to the 25 municipalities surrounding the new airport and asked for funding to the get the thing going. Five municipalities agreed to give $30,000 each, and the City of Edmonton gave $150,000, for a total of $300,000.[229] That was enough to get the Royal Bank of Canada to provide an operating line of credit for $500,000.[230] The other 19 municipalities refused.

So when the Board composition of the EAA was being determined it was decided that those municipalities who had supported the Transition Team in the creation of the EAA would each get at least one seat on the Board. Together with the federal government, the Board composition ended up as:

- City of Edmonton (6 Directors);
- City of Leduc (1 Director);
- Strathcona County (1 Director);
- Sturgeon County (1 Director);
- Leduc County (1 Director);
- Parkland County (1 Director);
- Government of Canada (2 Directors).

In May 1987 Mr. Bunnell and Mr. Chapman resigned from RATFA and were replaced as co-chairmen by Peter Watson and John McDougall.

---

[229] After transfer the AA paid all the monies back to the municipalities. Ron Gilbertson, email 11 January 2019.

[230] Before the transfer was completed, the line of credit with the Royal Bank eventually exceeded $4 million. Ron Gilbertson, email 11 January 2019.

In 1988 the federal government appointed Gerry St. Germain as Minister of State for Airports Authorities. St. Germain was assigned primary Cabinet responsibility for implementation of the airports authority concept across Canada. His first job was to form the Federal Airports Authority Task Force based on the results of the Edmonton feasibility study, and a growing interest from other communities in Canada (principally Calgary, Montréal and Vancouver). The task force further explored the concept of establishing independent airports authorities in Canada, and assists Transport Canada in the development of an airports authority policy. Ev Bunnell was appointed as the Edmonton region representative.

In April 1988 additional Directors were appointed to the Task Force. These were: John Askin; John Craig; Bill Grace; Jim Hansen; Jim Keefe; Leslie Mabbott; Ross McBain; John Prentice; Neil Reimer; Wayne Romank; Sydney Wood; and Don Dewar. In September, Hugh Robertson and Cort Smith were appointed to fill vacancies created by the resignations of Bill Grace and Sydney Wood. A permanent office for RATFA was established with two employees, Ron Gilbertson serving as Executive Director and Karen Croll as Executive Assistant. The offices were located in the Capital Square Building on Jasper Avenue.

Later that year, in consultation with the Edmonton and Calgary airports authorities advocates, the Province of Alberta decided to put in place special legislation that would govern the formation of airports authorities within the province. The province worked together with the Edmonton and Calgary representatives in preparing this legislation.

On 14 June 1990 the Alberta Airports Authority Act was proclaimed. The Act and its Regulations established legislation to govern airports authorities in Alberta.

In response to the Act, on July 26 1990 the Edmonton Regional Airports Authority (ERAA) was legally constituted as the first formal independent airports authority in Canada. An initial 11 member Board of Directors was appointed by the six municipal government appointers. The founding Directors included: Peter Watson; Jack Peat; Bill Stephenson; Lloyd Malin; Sid Hanson; Allen Williams; Jim Hansen; John Prentice; Gilbert Soetart; John Craig; and John Friesen. The Board later added two Directors as

Members at Large, with these being Pierre Jeanniot (former president of Air Canada) and Robert Joerger (a highly respected airports consultant from the U.S.). Peter Watson was elected by the Board as its first Chairman. After a national recruiting campaign, Ron Gilbertson was appointed as the President and CEO of ERAA.

In 1991 TC told the ERAA that when the Authority was formed it would be non-taxable. The federal Finance Department disagreed. ERAA argued that the tax laws for the AAs were punitive. Finance ignored them.

By that time Mazankowski was the Finance Minister. The ERAA wrote to Mazankowski explaining the situation. He replied that the ERAA should write what they wanted to see as an amendment to the Tax Act and send it off to the Finance department.[231] Tax policy is always secretive, so nothing was heard for several months, until amendments were published in the Canada Gazette, and there was the submission from the ERAA, word for word, amending the tax treatment of the AAs. Possibly the first time that an organization outside the federal government has written a change to the Tax Act. ERAA, and in particular Ron Odynski and Ron Gilbertson, played a pivotal role in drafting key provisions of the amendment which made the authorities federal corporate tax exempt and which applied to all airport authorities.

By 1991 the Transition Teams at Vancouver, Calgary and Montréal had hired one of the large accounting firms (Price Waterhouse or Deloitte Touche) to conduct the valuation studies of the assets to be transferred. The ERAA decided a different route, and hired the Royal Bank of Canada to do the valuation study. The thinking of the ERAA was: "any value you [the bank] arrive at, we will ask you to finance." The bank agreed and at the end of its valuation said the assets were worth $180 million. At the meeting with TC where the value of the assets was to be discussed, TC stated that in their opinion the assets were worth $300 million, and that was the federal government's asking price. The ERAA stated their position that the assets were worth $180 million. TC disagreed and tempers started rising. Finally the Western Region VP of the Royal Bank stood up and leaning over

---

[231] Ron Odynski, email to the author, 15 October 2018.

the table said: "I'm writing a cheque for $180 million. If you think it's worth $300 million, you come up with the difference." TC agreed to the $180 million.

On 21 December 1991 Gilbertson (CEO) and Odynski (Counsel) were on a conference call to Ottawa to work out the final details of the financial terms of the lease. There were several items on the agenda and as they went through each item the TC negotiating team would give a number that was the government's offer and ERAA team would answer with what they thought was a fair response. The first item was the value of the operating subsidy. TC offered $4.4 million a year. The ERAA proposed $8.6 million a year, a difference of $4.2 million a year (representing a total of $105 million loss to the EAA over the 25 years of the lease). The TC negotiators said that the government couldn't possibly agree to $8.6 million, but were willing to meet in the middle at $6.5 million. ERAA agreed. The next item was security. TC proposed a subsidy of $3.8 million. Prior to the meeting Gilbertson had prepared a spreadsheet with all the costs and his number for security was $3.9 million. To his surprise, and to the other members of his team, he blurted out: "we make it $6.7 million for security." The TC team had some discussion and agreed to saw off in the middle. This dealing continued for the entire meeting with TC proposing a number and the ERAA counter-proposing with their number and then both parties agreeing to meet in the middle. By the time the negotiations were completed Gilbertson calculated that the ERAA was going to be ahead by $250 million at the end of the 25 years. When the call concluded, Gilbertson was absolutely certain that his spreadsheet was wrong and that he had upset the negotiations (there was no way the AA could get the better of Transport Canada's high-powered team). He dreaded talking to Peter Watson the next day to inform him of what had been agreed to.[232]

A Memorandum of Understanding for the financial details was signed 24 December 1991.

In April 1992 the Finance Department called and said they were cancelling the deal – the TC negotiators had been taken advantage of by the ERAA team. Peter Watson (ERAA Board Chair) and

---

[232] Gilbertson, email 11 January 2019.

the Board (and especially Peter who is a very principled individual) were furious[233] and passed a motion to suspend negotiations with the federal government. As a consequence of that decision, the Edmonton AA essentially went from the front of the pack in negotiations to the back of the pack. Gilbertson had to inform the Royal Bank of the Board's decision. The bank was quite concerned because the AA owed the bank over $4 million but had no assets and at that time no reasonable means of repayment.

After some discussion the Finance Department agreed that the financial part of the lease would be modified so that the ERAA would end up with an operating "profit" of $85 million over 25 years. The other three leases signed that year had different financial outcomes: Calgary and Montréal were a "net" outcome to the AA (TC subsidies and AA revenues were equal), Vancouver was a net loss to the AA (TC subsidy did not equal the projected revenues over the 25 years).

In 1992 the Canadian Airports Council (CAC) was established to represent the interests of independent airports authorities in Canada. The four founding members of the CAC were the airports authorities in Calgary, Edmonton, Montréal and Vancouver.

In March 1992, as part of its strategic planning process and in response to a request from the City of Edmonton, the ERAA released a report entitled *An Airline Service Action Plan* for Edmonton's Future. The report, jointly prepared by the Board and management of ERAA, concludes that the Edmonton market can only justify one scheduled airline service airport, and that consolidation of all scheduled airline service is a precondition for improved airline service for the Edmonton region. Following the release of the report, ERAA held public meetings to gauge the community's reaction to the report and its conclusions. Utilizing the input received from its public meetings, the ERAA made recommendations to Edmonton City Council on the future role of the Edmonton Municipal Airport.

---

[233] Ibid.

On 2 August 1992 the long term lease of the Edmonton International airport took effect and the Edmonton Regional Airports Authority assumed control of the airport.

In October 1992 the City of Edmonton held a referendum on the future of airline service at the Edmonton Municipal Airport. The referendum was approved by 54% of the electorate and called for the continuation of scheduled airline service at Edmonton Municipal.

In 1993 Air BC announced that contrary to the City of Edmonton policy restricting scheduled airline service from the Edmonton Municipal Airport to points within Alberta, the airline would begin offering non-stop service from the Municipal Airport to Vancouver. Canadian Airlines announced that it would respond to the Air BC move, and that it would shift roughly half of its Edmonton-Vancouver scheduled services to the Municipal Airport. The ERAA stated publicly that the shifting of traffic from Edmonton International to Edmonton Municipal would dramatically impact passenger volumes at the International Airport and would seriously impair the financial viability of the airport. Support began to build for a second City of Edmonton referendum on the future of airline service at the Edmonton Municipal Airport.

In December 1994 Ron Gilbertson announced his resignation as President of ERAA and in January 1995 the ERAA Board of Directors appointed Geoff Hutchinson as Acting President and began the search for a new CEO. After a nation-wide search Scott Clements (retired LGen, Commander, Air Command and Chief of the Air Staff) was appointed as President and CEO of ERAA.

Just after Clements began his new job, a second referendum was held, asking if the 1992 Edmonton Municipal Airport bylaw should be repealed and that all scheduled traffic be consolidated at the Edmonton International Airport. The referendum called for the Edmonton Municipal Airport to remain open, but that its use be restricted to general aviation and corporate traffic. 77% of voters approved the referendum and the consolidation of all scheduled airline services at the Edmonton International Airport went into effect on June 1 1995.

In 1998, the airport underwent a $282 million "1998–2005 Redevelopment Project". The three-phase project included the construction of a south terminal and central hall concept, a commuter facility, doubling of the apron, and a multi-storey parkade. This redevelopment project expanded the passenger capacity to 5.5 million.

In 2002, as a result of 9/11, the insurance underwriters for the AAs hiked the liability insurance premiums to unheard of levels. Cort Smith, the Chief Financial Officer (CFO) for the EAA lead a team on behalf of all the AAs in Canada to find a way to reduce the premiums for liability insurance. This was a first in Canada. The team negotiated with Lloyd's of London and their agents in Canada and, in 2003, were successful in negotiating substantial reductions of the liability insurance premiums.

Figure 21: Control & Office Tower

By the time the ATB expansion project was completed in 2005, continued passenger growth triggered planning for another expansion. A new 107,000-square-foot control and office tower was added in 2009.

Further expansion was completed in 2013 including seven new passenger gates, 14 boarding bridges, moving walkways and advanced baggage handling and scanning systems. A new

Figure 22: International arrivals & departures wing added in 2013.

Renaissance Hotel was another major addition to the airport landscape.

The airport played a major role during the 2016 Fort McMurray Wildfire, operating as hubs for aerial firefighting and Medevac. The airport became a way-station and temporary shelter for thousands of Fort McMurray evacuees. The Emergency Operations Centre in the airport ran for 112 hours, organizing the arrival and departure of hundreds of aircraft. During the month of May 2016, the airport saw more than 300 additional daily flights on top of their regularly scheduled service.

In August 2016, the Government of Alberta announced $90 million in funding to begin twinning Highway 19 and that it had protected the area needed for a third runway. The airport also plans to extend Runway 12/30 by one-third its current length from 10,200 feet (2 100 m) to 13,220 feet (4,030 m) to increase accessibility and capacity tied to Port Alberta Developments Intercontinental routes.

Since the ERAA assumed control of the airport in 1992 passenger traffic has increased from 1.5 million annually to 7,807,384 annually in 2017, a 400% increase in 25 years.

Although the intent at the outset was that the ERAA operate an effective, efficient, safe and secure airport, over the intervening years the airport lands have come to be a major asset. At 10 square miles, Edmonton has by far the largest land area of any airport in Canada and the ERAA has actively promoted non-aeronautical businesses to locate there. As a result there is commercial, retail, office, logistics, entertainment and hotel operations, also Canada's largest cannabis grower.

Perhaps a final word on the economic asset the aerodrome has been to Edmonton and the surrounding area. The ERAA is an economic driver in the local communities and spends an average of $141.5 million annually in the Edmonton area on wages, taxes, operations and capital.

Since 1992 the ERAA has spent more than $1.2 billion on capital improvements to the aerodrome. Approximately $347.5 million of this expense was disbursed in the years 2012 to 2016. All of those monies were spent in the Edmonton area. These capital expenses were funded, in part, by the collection of an Airport Improvement Fee (AIF).

A 2014 economic impact study concluded that despite all the challenges that the aviation industry has faced since 2000, Edmonton has maintained its employment base, with 6,400 jobs in the Edmonton area directly related to the aerodrome operations. On-going operations at the ERAA make a considerable contribution to local employment and the provincial economy, representing an annual economic output in the Edmonton area of approximately $2.2 billion as a result of the direct, indirect, and induced jobs attributable to the ERAA.

The operating environment for the ERAA is both dynamic and complex. The ERAA maintains active relationships with stakeholders representing operational engagements, financial engagements and commercial engagements. While some of these are bilateral arrangements the majority of them are multilateral multiparty stakeholder activities.

As an economic engine to the local community, the ERAA's impact is felt far beyond the walls of its terminal. An economic impact study[234] conducted in 2010 showed that direct employment at the airport was 4,408 jobs, paying $169 million in salaries. Almost all of that was spent in the Edmonton area. The airport generates about $2 billion yearly in economic output. Since transfer the Authority has spent more than $1.2 billion on infrastructure development.[235] Almost all of that expense was spent locally.

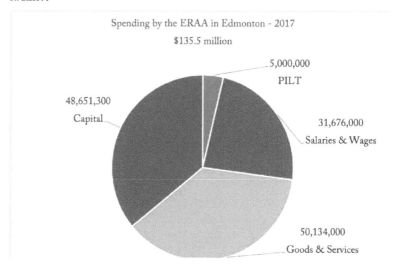

Figure 23: Spending by the Authority in Edmonton - 2017

---

[234] *The Economic Impact of the Edmonton Airports System*, InterVISTAS Consulting Inc, 7 October 2010.

[235] *Five-Year Performance Report*, Rideau Consultants Inc., 4 May 2017.

Edmonton, Alberta

Figure 24: Image courtesy of Google Earth Pro, 9-14-2017. This was a "green field" airfield and was not a BCATP aerodrome.

The Fredericton airport was built in 1949 by the DOT on land provided by the city, after much effort by the city to establish a municipal airport had met without success.

In 1920 the city of Fredericton asked Ottawa to build a municipal airport. The request was refused. In 1922 Fredericton appears as a public seaplane base in the List of Air Harbours Available for Use. In October 1929 the city made further enquiries of Ottawa for the creation of a municipal airport. Several sites were examined, including one at Embleton, northwest of the city and across the Saint John river, but nothing came of it. The city asked again in 1937, and more sites were examined. The one at Nashwacksis was recommended as a BCATP site, but it was felt that development there was too expensive.

In 1941 F. Hardwick obtained a license for day operations of light aircraft at Barker's Point. The following year he applied for a

161

license to operate a passenger and mail facility but it was declined as the field was felt to be "unsuitable".[236]

In 1943 the Mayor of Fredericton again asked the DOT for permission to use the Barker's Point Aerodrome for mail and passenger service. The request was denied but this time the District Inspector was instructed to find a site suitable for a main line airport to serve the capital of New Brunswick. A site was found at Rusagonis, which came to naught.

In May 1945 the city again asked for a site survey and this time a possible site was found at Lincoln. Comparative surveys were done on the Lincoln and Rusagonis sites. Costs and zoning restrictions favoured the Lincoln site and, on 25 April 1947 the Minister of Transport announced that the DOT would build an airport at the Lincoln site, provided that the city would provide the land. It had taken 27 years for Ottawa to act.

Work began in September 1948 and by March 1950 two runways had been constructed: 15-33 and 09-27. That same month the DOT announced that it would finish the airport if the city would build the terminal and ancilliary buildings and be responsible for operations and maintenance. The city agreed and an airport licence was issued to the city on 11 April 1950. The DOT paid an operating subsidy of five cents per square yard of paved surface (185,320 sq yds (154,927 sq m)). The subsidy was increased to six and a half cents in 1954.

In 1958 runway 15-33 was lengthened to 6000 feet (1829 m) and high-intensity approach and runway lights installed.

However the financial burden was too great for the city and after extended negotiations the DOT assumed control and responsibility for the airport on 7 November 1959. The city received payment of $118,000 for the land, buildings, installations and equipment.

An ILS was built in 1959 and a second taxiway in 1961.

An one million dollar expansion program in 1963 provided a new terminal building; maintenance garage and firehall; pump house;

---

[236] *History*, p. 101

water, sewage and fire hydrant system; extended ramp area; roads, and a car park.

A second expansion program in 1988-89 of $3.6 million remodelled and enlarged the ATB since the airport was now seeing 208,000 passengers per year.

The airport serves a larger land area than any other airport in New Brunswick: from Edmunston and Grand Falls in the north, to Houlton, Maine in the west, to St. Andrews and St. George in the south, and to Cole's Island, Minto and Chipman in the east.

The Authority

Unlike the other chapters on the airport authorities in this book, David Innes, first CEO of the Fredericton AA, offered to write a first-person account of the transition of the Fredericton Airport from being a facility operated by Transport Canada to one being operated by an airport authority. What follows below in italics was written by David himself.

I was the airport authority's first Chairman of the Board and its first President and CEO. It was a great privilege to be a part of the project of transferring and revitalizing the airport. The transition itself was a most exciting journey.

I became involved with the airport transition process in the early months of 1998. There had already been a first board which had been organized by Transport Canada mainly through the local MP, Andy Scott.

Andy had approached the City of Fredericton to nominate a first board but the city refused to be linked to the airport apparently fearing the implications of accepting any responsibility for it. Afterwards, Andy, working through the Fredericton Chamber of Commerce, found three directors willing to be responsible for developing the corporate structure and bylaws for an airport authority. It was a small committee of three people including Len Hoyt, who was a lawyer and Andy Scott's friend, as well as two local prominent businessmen Ken Bartlett and Gordon Simpson. None had any airport experience but all well-understood the importance of the airport to the future of the community.

At that time there was very little enthusiasm in the community to move towards airport privatization and much of the local narrative held that the Government of Canada was responsible for airports and that the

163

community should resist this "downloading of responsibility" by the federal government. Certainly that was the emphatic position of the City of Fredericton mayor and council. So while other airports were being "privatized" across Canada, little was happening in Fredericton in this direction.

An aspect of this lack of interest can be linked to the New Brunswick political scene at the time which was under the leadership of Premier Frank McKenna. Earlier in McKenna's tenure, Transport Canada shut down the Control Towers at Fredericton and Saint John and replaced them with Flight Service Stations. This move was generally interpreted within the provincial government as being an indicator that these two airports were in trouble and would eventually be shut down or at least lose commercial services.

As well, Premier McKenna had grown close to [the City of] Moncton as a political success. It was in terrible shape economically when he came to power he put a lot of money and political capital into [the City of] Moncton, and the city turned around. Its economy was really doing well. He had turned a mess into a real success. It was a great political narrative.

The Moncton Airport was part of that success and the province put a lot of energy into the Moncton Airport. In terms of privatization, the Moncton Airport had been quick out the starting block and transferred in 1997. With provincial support, it was doing very well. The province led the marketing effort for the Moncton Airport at that time which resulted in many important gains. This again led to a sense and a reality that the Fredericton Airport was lagging behind.

And of course, on December 17, 1997 an Air Canada CRJ crashed on the runway at Fredericton which really called into question the adequacy of the 6,000 foot runway for the "new" RJ.

After that incident, operationally Air Canada frequently imposed load restrictions on the RJ on the 6,000 foot runway. It was not uncommon to see a 50 passenger RJ headed to Toronto with as few as 12 passengers on it due to the load restrictions associated with the 6,000 foot runway. A wet runway, a warm day, any number of circumstances would result in serious load limits. The rest of the passengers who had purchased tickets would be told that the flight had been "oversold". Nobody was happy and the only solution was a longer runway.

It's fair to say that in the late 1990's, there wasn't a lot of enthusiasm for jumping into the operation of the Fredericton Airport.

In the early months of 1998, I was approached by Andy Scott, MP to be a member of the Airport Authority Board of Directors. At that time I was a professor of Civil Engineering at the University of New Brunswick where I was teaching aviation and airports planning and design. I had been at the university for over 20 years and I had at one time been a Civil Aviation Planner with Transport Canada so I had a good sense of the environment of aviation.

Andy also appointed Lyle Smith who was the retired Deputy Minister of the New Brunswick Department of Transportation and had a lot of credibility across Canada and inside Transport Canada. His third appointment was Norah Mallory, a communications consultant.

Appointments to the board were also made by the City of Fredericton, the Town of Oromocto, the Province of New Brunswick, the Fredericton Chamber of Commerce and the Greater Fredericton Economic Development Corporation. All of these had the power to nominate and we had a broad representation of the community probably more oriented toward business than government. There were some who left the board in the first few months but after that, the board was stable until the transfer occurred.

The board included Randall Hazlett (former military officer and investment broker) nominated by the Fredericton Chamber of Commerce, Andrew Steeves, (Consulting Engineer) nominated by the Greater Fredericton Economic Development Corporation; Jeff Toner, (School teacher) nominated by the Town of Oromocto, Michael Ircha, (Professor of Engineering at UNB) nominated by the City of Fredericton, Pat Bird (Businessman/Lumber Broker) also nominated by the City of Fredericton and Norman Ralston (retired Civil Servant) nominated by the province of New Brunswick.

To those board members, we added a local general aviation enthusiast as we considered that sector's representation on the board to be important. That person was Ernie McLean.

The board held its first meetings in the very early months of 1998 and I was elected as Chairman. We went through a few months of soul searching and trying to get a sense of the job in front of us. In our first quarter, some of the board members resigned because they were too busy with other commitments. The size of the task was becoming apparent.

Some adjustments occurred resulting in the above board composition which was in place for the whole of the negotiating period.

By the spring of 1998 we were ready to start the process in earnest. We began in early May, with a formal and public ceremony whereby we agreed to negotiate with Transport Canada for the transfer of the airport. Andy Scott was pleased to announce the start of the process.

One of the first things that we did was meet with New Brunswick Premier Camille Thériault to ask him directly if indeed there was a "one airport policy" for New Brunswick as was commonly believed. Frankly if there was, we had all agreed to stand down rather than start the process without the support of the province. That meeting happened in the early part of June of 1998. After being assured that "the Fredericton Airport is and will continue to be an important part of the NB transportation infrastructure" we moved forward. (Theriault was replaced by Bernard Lord as premier shortly after that and we repeated the meeting with Premier Lord with the same result) We considered this to be important to stem any assumptions that might be made within the NB bureaucracy.

We also began a conversation with our community to generate some enthusiasm for the airport. In fact, Fredericton was often thought of as a "government and university town" and it was often expressed that the airport maybe wasn't really vital to those functions.

However, a closer examination of the business community revealed a vibrant engineering consulting and IT sector as well as other sectors which were important to the future of the local economy. These businesses served a global marketplace and were highly dependent upon air service. There was also the Canadian Forces Base Gagetown next door which generated much air traffic.

So we started to communicate these ideas about "the new, connected, global economy" and how we could choose to be part of it or not and our key to participation in that economy was air service and the airport. There exist many communities in NB that had lost their train stations in the previous generations and had subsequently dried up economically. Those examples were repeated frequently and well understood by the audiences.

I became the public advocate for the airport and accepted speaking engagements far and wide to preach our message that the airport was vital to the survival of the community.

In November of 1998 we held the ultimate conversation with our community whereby we held a workshop entitled simply "It's Your Airport". We invited 175 community leaders to the local Sheraton hotel for a workshop and we asked our community for advice and pledged at the outset to take that advice.

Frankly if we were told to forget about it, we likely would have or at least we told the audience that we would. We also asked the participants to develop a vision for the airport and to help us define what we must do to be successful.

We had no idea at the time whether the workshop was a good idea but we needed to begin the conversation with our community. In the end, the day was a great success. There was a great conversation and all agreed that the airport should transfer and we should make a great success of it. The workshop also provided some definition of what success looked like.

The major issue that kept being raised that day was the length of the runways. Runway 15/33 was the longer runway and was only 6,000 feet long. It was not capable of handling the CRJ-100 and load restrictions were common especially after the crash of December 1997.

The Fredericton Airport had not been a high priority under Transport Canada ownership and the airport was not in a good state of repair. It had simply not been kept up over the years. The buildings and the runways would have to updated if we were to have any chance of future success.

We were given a community mandate on that day, a mandate to negotiate with Transport Canada. We, the board and the community, resolved not to accept any deal which did not provide enough money to solve the runway length issue.

Following the workshop, the negotiations began in earnest with Transport Canada. In order to accomplish the vision and specifically the runway extension, we wanted $20 million to fix the deficiencies. Transport was offering a package less than ten million. While we had an agreement with Transport Canada to have confidential negotiations and not to make public statements, then Minister of Transport David Collenette indeed made a public statement that Transport Canada would not be providing any money to Fredericton to extend any runway.

The negotiations with Transport Canada stalled in the early months of 1999. The airport authority had opened an office early in 1999 and had shut it down in the fall as no activity was taking place. No progress was made in 1999 and none through to the Fall months of 2000. It was a trying time for the board, for the community and a challenge for Andy Scott.

I have never really understood Transport Canada during these negotiations. They were emphatically not helpful. They came with a "take or leave it" proposition and after the Minister spoke, they said very little indeed. The minister's statement had made it difficult but there are always ways possible to work around statements like that. The additional money was not that significant and could be easily justified but there was just no effort on their part to recognize the issue and/or work with us.

It was our problem though and we eventually understood that we could count on Transport Canada for no financial support beyond their first position. They even did a study for us by one of their Ottawa-based consultants to show that a runway extension made no financial sense for us. We rejected the consultant outright and their conclusion would later be proven to be wrong.

One of my directors said at one point and probably spoke for us all when he said "I can't believe our own government is treating us this way".

With us, they were not helpful at all and their lack of sympathy for our predicament seemed to go all the way to the Minister's office. Interestingly I am aware that their behavior in the transfer of responsibility in other modes of transport, mainly marine ports, was not at all the same. I understand that Transport was quite generous with the maritime ports.

The Board evolved too during these negotiations. We had begun more or less feeling our way along though a strange process: unelected people negotiating with the federal government. As the process evolved however, the board became very unified, passionate and confident in their mission to revitalize the Fredericton Airport which we saw as the backbone of Fredericton's economic vitality. We had developed a very strong sense of mission and we had our community on our side.

But we had really made no progress in almost two years.

In November of 2000, with no real movement on the file, the Airport Authority board members were ready to offer our collective resignations

168

to our various nominators. We were tired of the lack of progress. At a rather dramatic meeting of all of our nominators in a single room, we challenged our nominators to resolve our financial conundrum. We saw little point in continuing to tread water.

Within 48 hours, a solution was found. We saw our political representatives from the federal, provincial and municipal governments come up with an assortment of funding mechanisms to provide the remainder of the money. The three levels of government put a patchwork of financial support together for the airport that got us to $16 million with which we were willing to move forward. All political stripes worked together to make this happen. It was a great and unifying moment for our community.

Transport Canada was completely unaware of these discussions as they had become irrelevant and simply held firm on their amounts. Everybody else worked around them. In November of 2000 then, we accepted the deal and began to prepare for the transfer which happened on May 1, 2001.

Fredericton was the second to last airport in the National Airport System to transfer. The Prince George Airport was the last.

As the months leading up to the transfer progressed, we turned our attention to the more operational issues. The runway extension design work started in the fall and winter of 2000/2001, that is before the transfer occurred. The transfer happened on May 1, 2001 and we filed the project with the Province of New Brunswick for environmental review on May 2. Work began on the extension of 09/27 to 8,000 feet in the fall of 2001. Runway 09/27 was ready for service when Queen Elizabeth arrived at the airport in October of 2002 as part of her Royal visit to Canada.

In the fall of 2000, the Greater Fredericton Airport Authority Board launched a search committee to find a new President and CEO. The committee approached me to take a leave of absence from the University of New Brunswick for the transitional first two years. I had become the public face of the airport and was quite impassioned with the project by then and agreed. In 2003, my two-year secondment was extended for a year and then finally I cut my ties with UNB to become the President and CEO until my retirement on April 15, 2015.

On the day of my retirement from the airport authority some seventeen and one half years after the "Its Your Airport" workshop, I reflected on our accomplishments. We had transferred the airport to an airport authority. We had the runway extended to 8,000 feet. The terminal was expanded to be capable of handling international traffic and had greatly expanded departure lounges. We had built a building to handle military operations. We had expanded the apron and the taxiway system. We had two domestic carriers and some international winter flights providing air service at the airport. We had significantly increased our annual passenger traffic. We had recovered all of our operating costs each year and had been able to invest more than one million dollars of our revenue per year into our capital projects. We were operationally self sufficient.

Remarkably, all of these accomplishments were elements of the vision that had been developed at the "Its Your Airport" workshop in November of 1998. The vision that had been developed that day had been largely accomplished.

Some Final Thoughts

The transition of the Fredericton Airport to an airport authority can be considered to be a qualified success.

At the time of transfer, Transport Canada had been exercising a policy of recovering their operating losses by increasing landing and terminal fees of airports that they still controlled by 25% per annum. It was clearly an initiative to have airports transfer or be made uneconomic. With the high fees and operational restrictions resulting from our short runway, the Fredericton Airport was well into "uneconomic" territory. One of the first things we did after transfer then was to reverse that trend and cut our fees by 25% to get them back into a normal range. This illustrates as well as anything the advantage of local control of a small organization to identify and resolve its own issues.

Small airports have done quite well within the airport authority model. Many would have predicted that airports like Fredericton would falter and fail. But the decades of experience have demonstrated that they are not only viable but they have grown and prospered and have demonstrated much creativity and initiative in conducting their business. Much has been accomplished and many successes evident.

And our communities are being better served by their airports. The local communities have stepped up and worked in partnership with the airport authorities in their mutual interest. The airports have provided a platform and have developed an expertise for enhancing air services for their communities.

While the above presents an overview of a largely successful story of a small airport under the Canadian National Airport System framework, some caution should be exercised in declaring success.

First of all, it must be understood that all of the major capital projects completed at the Fredericton Airport since transfer were completed with substantial capital assistance from the various levels of government. The funding agreement for each project was somewhat unique and usually required high levels of political involvement. Major capital projects at small airports can need community financial support. This puts smaller airports in a more tenuous position than their larger counterparts.

While the original National Airport Plan of 1994 recognized that "future capital requirements may result in some adjustments" in the self-sufficiency principle, development of programs by Transport Canada to recognize this principle has been slow to materialize. It has been almost 25 years since the National Airports Plan was developed and it is suggested that policies and programs should have been put in place long before now.

Keeping all the parts of the airport enterprise working together promises to be as challenging in the future as it has been in the past, but overall, the Fredericton Airport has greatly grown and prospered as an airport authority and the future of the airport now is most certainly significantly brighter than it was in 1998.

Some metrics

Since the AA assumed responsibility for the airport in 2001 it has invested more than $52 million in the airport infrastructure, and has seen passenger levels almost double from 200,000 per year to 400,000 per year.

The AA implemented a Safety Management System (SMS) and an Airport Security Program (ASP – previously known as a Security Management System (SeMS).

It is designated by Transport Canada as an International airport.

It undertook the development of the Community Air Access Strategy (CAAS) with the City of Fredericton and with the cooperation of stakeholders.

After a long and difficult 248 day strike in 2012, the AA came to an agreement with Local 60601 of the Union of Canadian Transportation Employees. Notwithstanding the impact of the strike on management staff, passenger traffic increased 3.5% in 2012;

Since 2001, it has increased air services to both domestic and international destinations, maintained military air traffic volumes, undertook a major rehabilitation of runway 15/33, upgraded Emergency Response Services to Category 6 as a result of increased traffic by larger aircraft, and hired new employees as a result of the Category 6 upgrading.

Figure 25: Fredericton Airport

As an economic engine to the local community, the AAs impact is felt far beyond the walls of its terminal. Direct employment at the airport rose to 279 jobs in 2016, throughout the region 513 FTE (full time equivalent) jobs are attributed to the Fredericton International Airport, bringing $13.2 million in consumer spending to New Brunswick each year –from employment alone. Taxes generated by the direct and indirect impact of the AA total $8.5-million yearly.

The impact of air access to residents' quality of life and the ability of the airport to attract and retain businesses cannot be overstated.

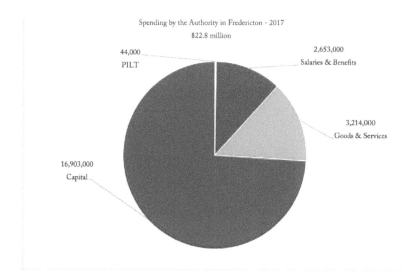

Spending by the Authority in Fredericton - 2017
$22.8 million

44,000
PILT

2,653,000
Salaries & Benefits

3,214,000
Goods & Services

16,903,000
Capital

Figure 27: Image courtesy of Google Earth Pro, 7-5-2012.

Gander's history as an airport begins with plans[237] drawn up on 23 February 1927 between J.A. Wilson, Secretary of the R.C.A.F. and Mr. Coolican, Deputy Postmaster General, for the establishment of the *Transatlantic Air Route* as part of the *Imperial Airship Scheme* to deliver air mail between England to Canada. The first step was to build a civil airharbour to accommodate an airship service. On 29 July, 1930 the inaugural flight of an airship was made between Cardington, England and St. Hubert, on the south shore of the St. Lawrence across from Montréal.[238] After one return trip of the R100, however, the service was cancelled.[239] And even though there was an undersea telegram cable, the demand for

---

[237] *History*, p. 283. In 1926 the Minister of National Defence and the Postmaster General had instructed staff to research the issues of air mail delivery, after it had been brought to their attention of the successful operation of air mail services in the United States, Europe and Australia.

[238] Public Archives Canada, MG 30 E243, Vol. 6, 866-8-1.

[239] The R100's sister ship, the R101, crashed on a trip from England to India on 5 October 1930. The British Air Ministry ordered the R100 grounded, eventually to be sold for scrap in 1931 for less than £600.

175

quicker delivery of letter mail was increasing. Ocean liners could cross the North Atlantic in less than five days, but an aeroplane could do the crossing in 24 hours.

In the Fall of 1930 representations were made by the United States government to Canada, on behalf of Pan American Airways, to allow a daily air mail service by Pan Am from Boston, Mass to Moncton, and then on to Sydney, NS and St. John's. This "intrusion" into Canadian air space caused great concern to the Post Office.[240]

Another issue was that Newfoundland at that time was not part of Canada, and was able to grant traffic and landing rights to foreign airlines. The British national airline, Imperial Airlines, had proposed to the United States national airline, Pan American Airways, to set up an experimental transatlantic air mail service using flying boats. Meetings were held in St. John's in July 1933 between Canada, England and the United States to discuss the proposed Atlantic service and the route to be followed. These meetings led to the governments of the United Kingdom, Canada, the Irish Free State and Newfoundland to sign an agreement which set out two stages of development. First, a survey of suitable sites for an experimental service, followed the creation of a regularly scheduled service.[241]

On 9 August 1935 the following was received by the Canadian Secretary of State for External Affairs:

> *His Majesty's Government in the United Kingdom has been giving prolonged consideration to the problem of establishing an air service for the carriage of mails and passengers by heavier than air aircraft across the North Atlantic between England and Canada and United States at the earliest possible date . . .*
>
> *......plans for Transatlantic flying must for the time being be based on the use of flying boats. It is however proposed ... that an experiment should also be made with landplanes.*

---

[240] From 1867 to 1981 the operating name of the Post Office Department was Royal Mail Canada.

[241] *History*, p. 38.

..... In order that the necessary ground organization be put into hand without delay, a preliminary survey is being immediately undertaken by Air Ministry experts to locate suitable bases in Newfoundland ....[242]

And that is why, soon after, a Mr. A. Vatcher arrived at Milepost 213 on the Newfoundland Railway, a stop called "Hattie's Camp", named after Mr. Hattie who cut wood in the vicinity, near Jonaton's Pond. It was a cabin in the woods, a "camp" to any Newfoundlander, and it was in the middle of nowhere, not a permanent town, village, or settlement within 50 miles. Mr. Vatcher asked the two men living there (Reuben Brown and Hebert Greening, both of Port Blandford, and who were there as fire rangers for the summer) if they knew of any flat land in the vicinity. Vatcher told the two men that all that day he and Lester Shea of Glenwood had surveyed the area of Whitman's Pond but to no avail. The area was too boggy and hilly. Brown and Greening said they knew of a spot not two miles down the railway line, and took him there the next day.[243]

They were right. It was flat land. A plateau some 500 feet above sea level. And in Newfoundland flat land is a rarity. Vatcher was thrilled and reported back to England that a suitable site had been found.

By June, 1936 work had begun in earnest, with a crew of 100 men clearing the forest and bush. By the end of 1937, a 900-person team had begun construction. Mr. T.A. Hall of the Newfoundland Department of Public Works was Chief Engineer, and Mr. Vatcher was Resident Engineer. They were assisted by F.C. Jewett[244] and R.A. Bradley[245] who had been instrumental in the building of the fourth Welland Canal, completed in 1935.

---

[242] Public Archives of Canada, MG 30 E243, Vol. 8.

[243] The Gander Area Historical Society website was invaluable in providing background for this chapter.
http://www.ganderairporthistoricalsociety.org/index.htm.

[244] Jewett later became the Chief Engineer for the BCATP, overseeing the construction of 190 airports during from 1940 to 1944.

[245] Bradley was airport engineer at Gander until the early 1950's when he became a regional construction engineer with the Ontario Department of Transportation.

On January 11, 1938, the first airplane landed at Gander. It was a Fox Moth VO-ADE, operated by Imperial Airways for the Newfoundland Government and flown by Captain Douglas Fraser. However, with the cancellation by Britain of the development of a trans-oceanic airplane (the Albatross) that same year, there appeared to be no immediate use for the airport. But contracts had been let, and monies committed, and construction continued to completion.

By 31 October 1939 the airfield had four paved runways, the largest paved area of any airport in the world at the time and the equivalent of 110 miles (177 km) of highway 20 feet (6 m) wide. The main runway was 4,800 long by 1,200 feet wide (1 463 m by 366 m), and the other three runways were each 4,500 feet long by 600 feet wide (1 372 m by 183cm).[246] The length and widths of the runways were determined by the fact that there was no alternate airport in Newfoundland, and an approaching aircraft had to be able to land no matter what the weather was doing. Unusual for the time, there were sodium vapour lamps as centre-line lighting and a Lorenz blind landing system from Germany. This was the forerunner of the post-war Instrument Landing System (ILS). It had a directional beam along the runway and an inner and outer marker beacon, but no glide path.[247]

The airport had one hangar, an administrative building providing office space and accommodation for single men, a diesel-electric plant (the sole source of electricity), twelve houses for married personnel, a general store, a central heating plant, an aviation fuel storage area, a fire station, and a railway station. There were no roads in the area, and the only link to the outside world was to fly, or the railway.[248]

By the outbreak of war in September 1939, Gander was ready for civil operations. Gander's location was on the Great Circle Route and almost equally half way between the airplane manufacturing plants in Canada and the United States. This gave it great strategic value since it was ideal refuelling and maintenance depot for

---

[246] *History*, p. 104.

[247] Ibid, p. 105.

[248] Ibid.

aircraft flying overseas. Consequently the airport became the main staging point for the movement of Canadian and American aircraft to Europe during the War.

In November 1940, Captain D.C.T. Bennett left Gander for Europe, leading the first fleet of seven Lockheed Hudson bombers across the Atlantic. The Battle of Britain had come and gone, but the need for fighters and bombers would only increase as the battle moved from Great Britain to Germany.

On 1 April 1941, the responsibility for operations at the Newfoundland Airport was transferred by the Dominion of Newfoundland to the Royal Canadian Air Force (RCAF) and on 5 May 1941 the airport was renamed RCAF Station Gander under the command of Group Captain Lewis.[249]

The U.S.A.A.F. arrived at Gander in May 1941 to conduct anti-submarine reconnaissance off the coast of Newfoundland. The Americans at Gander were tenants of Canada, which supplied the hangars and other administrative buildings on the "American" side of the airport.

Gander was originally planned as a transatlantic air terminal, and, in serving as a base for ferry operations during the war, it fulfilled that role. The airfield was heavily used by RAF Ferry Command and Air Transport Command for transporting newly built aircraft across the Atlantic Ocean to the European Theatre, as well as for staging operational anti-submarine patrols dedicated to hunting U-boats in the northwest Atlantic. Thousands of aircraft flown by the United States Army Air Corps through the changeover to the United States Army Air Forces, and the RCAF destined for the European Theatre, travelled through Gander.

The Royal Canadian Navy (RCN) also established Naval Radio Station Gander at the airfield, using the station as a listening post to detect the transmissions and location of enemy submarines and warships.

Following the war, the RCAF handed operation of the airfield back to the dominion government in March 1946, although the

---

[249] Ibid, p. 107.

RCN's radio station remained and the military role for the entire facility was upgraded through the Cold War.

In 1945, the Newfoundland government took over control of the airport again and on 16 September 1945 the first transatlantic proving flight, a Pan Am DC-4, departed Gander for Shannon in western Ireland. On 24 October 1945, the first scheduled commercial flight, an American Overseas Airlines DC-4, passed through Gander. By the end of the year, Pan-American World Airways, Trans-World Airline, Trans Canada Airlines (later Air Canada), and British Overseas Airway Corporation (later British Airways) begin regular Atlantic air service through Gander. The airlines occupied space on both the "American side" and the "RCAF" side. On both sides the civil airport administration converted some vacant military buildings into living quarters, offices and restaurants for passengers and other civilians.

On 14 September 1946 a new civil air terminal was opened in the former RAF hangar 22. Vacant living quarters nearby were converted to overnight passenger accommodation and named the "Skyways Hotel". Inside the hotel was the "Big Dipper Bar", open 24/7, which soon acquired a worldwide reputation as a meeting place.

During the war the population had grown to 15,000 (mostly military) people, but by 1947 the population had shrunk to about 2,000, about half of whom were employed by the Newfoundland government and the airlines. The airport administration was responsible for the entire community and supplied living quarters (mainly 544 apartments in converted military barracks), municipal services and utilities, a baker, a dry cleaning plant, stores, schools, churches and hotels.[250]

The Newfoundland and British governments had built Gander to serve the Trans-Atlantic Air Service and was to be financed by both countries. The two governments resumed their joint interest at war's end, but the intervening years had changed the concept somewhat and now Newfoundland played a more active role with the Civil Aviation Division of the Newfoundland Department of Public Works operating the airport. Newfoundland was administered by a Commission of Government, three of whom

---

[250] Ibid, p. 108.

were appointed by the U.K. and three by Newfoundland. Because finances were slim, the Commission decided that Gander would be operated on a cost-recovery basis. At one point landing fees were high, perhaps the highest in the world, were based on non-scheduled landing fees at La Guardia, New York, plus 50%, so as to recover the cost of snow clearing, etc. In 1946 the landing fee for a DC-4 was $80, and this increased by 50% on 1 October 1947.[251]

The financial position and management philosophy of the airport led to, for what was then, an unusual relationship between the airport and the airlines. When the airport could not meet all the demands of the airlines an agreement was reached whereby improvements to the airport required by the airlines would be funded jointly by the airlines. Rents and terminal use fees were paid by the airlines against their capital investment. The agreement worked well, although there were disagreements between the airlines and the airport management from time to time. The airport accounts for the year ending 31 March 1948 show revenues of $820,212 and expenses of $941,060 for an operating loss of $120,848.[252]

When Newfoundland joined Canada on 1 April 1949 the airport staff became civil servants of Canada, and the DOT assumed responsibility for what was then its largest airport, with a staff of 1,176. The operating and maintenance costs for 1948-49 were $2.9 million, and revenue was $3.2 million, an operating profit of $238,900. Putting those numbers into perspective, the total revenue from all airports operated by the DOT in 1947-48 had been $1.4 million.[253]

Airport management at Gander had a great deal of autonomy, far more than that usually allowed at a DOT airport. For one thing, it operated on the principle of cost recovery. And because of its isolation it was self-sufficient in many respects: it hired and fired its own staff and issued its own cheques. It took a while to integrate Gander into the DOT culture and for many years

---

[251] Ibid, p. 109.

[252] Ibid.

[253] Ibid.

Gander was "different" from the other DOT airports. By the same token, some procedures and practices at Gander became standard operating procedures at the other DOT airports; landing fees for one.[254]

Eventually Gander's cost recovery program was discontinued by the DOT, and the airport became one of many where the operating and maintenance costs came out of annual appropriations, and revenues were deposited into the federal government's Consolidated Revenue Fund. The Airlines' Agreement, whereby the airlines paid the full cost of the ATB operation, was also terminated.[255]

In 1950 the airport authorities decided to create a new town-site west of the airport and move off the airport lands all living quarters and other community necessities for the 4,000 people living there. There was a pressing need for housing, with many people wanting to own their own home. There was a demand for shopping facilities and private enterprise saw that Gander, by Newfoundland standards, was becoming a large population centre. New schools were required, and religious denominations wanted to replace the temporary facilities they had in surplus military buildings. In short, as Gander grew as a community, its people wanted a release from DOT control and dependency.[256]

For its part the DOT wanted to relinquish its responsibility for running a municipality, so it partnered with the Central Mortgage and Housing Corporation to build streets, housing, serviced lots, and rental accommodations. By the early 1950's all non-aviation housing and activity had been removed from airport lands. The town took the name of Gander and elected its own council in 1959.

Through the 1950's Gander was handling 13,000 aircraft and a quarter million passengers annually. Three runways were improved and extended: 13-31 to 8,900 feet (2 713 m), 09-27 to 6,180 feet (1 884 m), and 04-22 to 10,500 feet (3 200 m); one of the original runways was realigned, and the old no. 2 runway abandoned. A

---

[254] Ibid.

[255] Ibid, p. 110.

[256] Ibid.

new $3 million terminal was built and opened by Queen Elizabeth II in June 19, 1959. At that time Gander airport was one of the busiest international airports in the world, buoyed by trans-Atlantic traffic.

With the advent of jets with longer range in the 1960s, most flights no longer needed to refuel. Gander decreased in importance, but it remains the home of Gander Control, one of the two air traffic controls (the other being Shanwick Oceanic Control in western Ireland) which direct the high-level airways of the North Atlantic. Most aircraft travelling to and from Europe or North America must talk to at least one of these air traffic controls.

Some commercial transatlantic flights still use Gander as a refuelling stop; most notably, some American legacy carriers (United Airlines and Delta Air Lines in particular) who use the Boeing 757 to connect smaller European cities with their major US hubs. The 757 is particularly affected in this respect, as it was not an aircraft intended or designed for transatlantic flights. This practice has been controversial, since strong headwinds over the Atlantic Ocean during the winter months can result in the flights being declared "minimum fuel", forcing a refuelling stop at Gander in order to safely complete their journey.

In the early 1980's, IL-62s of Aeroflot (Russia), CSA (Czechoslovakia), Cubana (Cuba), Interflug (East Germany) and LOT (Poland) visited Gander daily on flights from Eastern Europe and the Americas. Interflug, Cubana, and Aeroflot also used Gander for the Moscow and Berlin to Havana route.

The fact that stop-overs were made at Gander soon became known to potential refugees, as it was one of the few refueling points where airplanes could stop en route from Eastern Europe or the Soviet Union to Cuba. It was not uncommon to have defectors declare political asylum at the airport. A number of persons from the former Warsaw Pact nations defected while their aircraft was stopped at Gander (including Soviet chess player and pianist Igor Vasilyevich Ivanov, Cuban Olympic swimmer Rafael Polinario, and the Vietnamese woman famously photographed as a naked girl fleeing a napalmed village (Phan Thi Kim Phuc).

The resulting tightening of customs and immigration policy served to effectively eliminate much of this traffic.

As time moved on, Gander International Airport adapted to changes in the industry. Today, technical stops remain a significant economic generator for the airport, especially with growth in the corporate/private jet market. In fact, twenty percent of business jets flying the North Atlantic stop at Gander.

The Authority

The creation of an Airport Authority at Gander[257] started when TC visited Gander in the mid-1990's and began discussions about the devolution of the airport. It soon became evident from the discussions that the TC folk had no interest in continuing to operate Gander as they felt it was too large, too costly, and in the wrong place. The local community had a different opinion and formed a Transition Team to see what could be done to save "their" airport with Terry Parsons as the President and Wilson Hoffe as the Vice President.

In 1997 TC commissioned PriceWaterhouse to look at the airport and make recommendations as to its disposition. Their 1998 report recommended that TC tear up most of the runways, demolish the ATB, and start all over again by making it a regional airport. Later that year John Cloutier and Daniel Paiement from TC came to Gander to meet with the Transition Team and discuss the findings of the PriceWaterhouse report.

It was an animated meeting.

The Transition Team felt that they had not been given enough opportunity to show what could be done. That TC had come to the meeting with its mind already made up that the airport was going to close. That, if given a fair shot at making it viable – between the "jigs and the reels" it was possible.

Cloutier didn't agree. He had a hard-nosed attitude to the AAs and was not well-liked by some in the Atlantic area airports. His bargaining technique was to take a very strong stand, argue vociferously for his position, and then, perhaps, accede to a minor adjustment. The folk in Atlantic Canada found that technique

---

[257] With many thanks to Wilson Hoffe, C.A. for a most informative chat on 18 September 2018. His recollections were a joy to hear.

offensive. Although they too could be hard bargainers, they thought his central Canada attitude a mite demeaning.

The Transition Team then prepared its own studies on the airport and its viability. The results were diametrically opposite to those from the PriceWaterhouse study and showed that there were several issues, mostly due to TC's lack of interest in operating the airport: first was the number of staff employed by TC and the concomitant costs associated with that; second was the airport lands and their total lack of development; finally the number of passengers was low since TC had done very little to attract carriers.

At the next meeting with Paiement and Cloutier the Transition Team asked: "How in the name of God has TC not done what was needed to be done?" Paiement replied: "No balls." No one in TC was going to stick his neck out and make Gander an issue, or to ensure that the necessary oversight and governance would happen. It was far away from Ottawa, in a place which had no strategic value, and was seen to be a mill-stone around the neck of TC, absorbing scarce resources.

The first issue to be resolved was the number of staff. TC employed more than 130 staff at the airport. The Transition Team thought it could operate with about 37 folk. Eventually the AA took on 42 staff. Twenty-five staff were taken on for a two-year period until they could find other work, and 69 staff were put on the shelf and given separation allowances.

The Transition Team had to find nominators for Board members. They solicited the municipalities nearby, and also the local Chambers of Commerce. The Public Accountability Principles required that three board members be from the federal and provincial governments. Eventually the Board comprised:

- Government of Canada (2 positions);
- Government of Newfoundland (1);
- Town of Gander (3);
- Town of New-Wes-Valley (1);
- Gander Chamber of Commerce (1);
- Lewisporte Chamber of Commerce (1);
- Exports Regional Chamber of Commerce (1);

- The Board in its own right (3).

On 1 April 2001 the AA took over the operations.

Gander has continued to remain as the refueling base for transatlantic flights operating between Europe and North America. Presently, there are two runways in operation at Gander. Runway 13-31 is 8,900 feet, and runway 03-21 measures 10,500 feet in length.

One of the most modern airports in the world, Gander International Airport has experienced many changes and has become renowned all over the aeronautical world. It is presently the North Atlantic Centre for communications and air traffic control.

Gander International Airport played an integral role in world aviation in the hours immediately following the September 11, 2001 attacks when all of North America's airspace was closed by North American Aerospace Defence Command (NORAD), and trans-Atlantic flights bound for the United States were ordered to land at the airport.

Figure 28: Gander after 9/11 - 38 airplanes grounded

By the end of the day, Gander International found itself playing host to 38 airliners, 6,122 passengers and 473 crew, as part of

Operation Yellow Ribbon. Gander International received more flights than any other Canadian airport involved in the operation apart from Halifax. The 6,595 passengers and crew accounted for the third highest total of passengers that landed at a Canadian airport involved in the operation, behind Vancouver and Halifax.

A major reason that Gander received so much traffic was its ability to handle large aircraft, and because Transport Canada and Nav Canada instructed pilots coming from Europe to avoid the airports in major urban centres of Central Canada, like Toronto Pearson International Airport and Montréal-Dorval. The reception these travellers received in the central Newfoundland communities near the airport has been one of the most widely reported happy stories surrounding that day, and was dramatized in the musical "Come from Away".

To honour the people of Gander and Halifax for their support during the operation, Lufthansa named a new Airbus A340-300 "Gander/Halifax" on May 16, 2002. That airplane is listed with the registration D-AIFC, and was the first aircraft of that fleet with a city name from outside of Germany.

The airport was the site for Canada's memorial service in 2002 to mark the first anniversary of the attack, over which Prime Minister Jean Chrétien, Transport Minister David Collenette, US Ambassador to Canada Paul Cellucci, and provincial and local officials presided. 2,500 of the 6,600 people that were diverted there the year before also attended the ceremony.

More than 700 military aircraft a year make technical stops at the GIAA, with military flight servicing accounting for more than $30 million annually in direct contribution to the local economy through the demand for fuel, accommodations, meals, and entertainment.

The domestic and military traffic (the aircraft movements which produce the most revenue) remained fairly constant over that same period.

Since it assumed management of the aerodrome in 2001, by 2017 the AA had spent approximately $36.1 million on capital improvements to the infrastructure. Almost all of that was spent in the Gander area and as such the AA is an economic engine to the whole region. Approximately one-half of the capital expense of

$36.1 million since 2001 has been funded by the AIF, with the other half funded by the federal and provincial governments.

Direct impacts of airport operations include 1,260 full-time jobs, $90 million in wages, $140 million in gross domestic product (GDP) and $240 million in economic impact.

Total economic impacts were 1,940 full time jobs, $210 million in GDP and $360 million in economic output.

Employment related to airport activity grew 10% over the period 2004-2012, with most gains in the airport support and airline services sectors. 95% of jobs directly related to airport activity are full-time positions and 20% of the total labour force in the Town of Gander can be attributed to direct airport activity.

The airport is also an important generator of taxation revenues to all levels of government. Total taxes paid on an annual basis, by passengers, employers, and employees are estimated at $46 million per year, including $27 million to the federal government and $19 million to the provincial government.

The airport authority is a regional employer with over 50% of the airport authority's staff residing in communities outside of Gander.

Over the period from 1996-2000, the airport under government management posted cumulative operating deficits of nearly $10 Million. Under GIAA management between 2012-2016, the airport posted profits of nearly $7 Million, a variance of $17 Million. The work once undertaken by Transport in 1995 required 97 full-time equivalents. While the airport has changed profoundly, that work is now done by a staff of 32.

Since assuming operating responsibility of the airport from Transport Canada, the airport authority has made it a priority to reduce its dependency on unpredictable aviation business cycles. The airport's investment in a 150-acre business park located on a prime tract of land for retail bears witness to this direction. Gander is the epicenter of a $2.5 billion retail market and the airport manages some of the highest visibility acreage in the community. In 2017, the airport confirmed new leases and Letters of Intent with developers and has every confidence going forward of securing greater occupancy. Commercial development provides a host of benefits, including generating employment and strengthening the community as a retail hub. Land leasing revenue the airport generates is invested back into the airport and provides a largely sheltered source of stable income in challenging times.

The airport and its partners continue to execute an international campaign to recruit and retain international technical stops traffic. Technical stops are a business segment that Gander has actively promoted since its inception. While the technical stop market for Gander remains well below historic performance, it remains a crucial business line. The competitive environment for a shrinking technical stop market has shifted importance to holding onto traditional customers in addition to prospecting for new ones.

The airport maintains a multi-media "Fly Gander" marketing campaign which includes promotions, print, radio, earned media/public relations, public space advertising and an ever-growing focus on social media.

Figure 29: Gander Airport

Since assuming responsibility for the airport, the Gander International Airport Authority has seen passenger traffic decrease from 465,252 in 2001 to 1.934 million a year in 2017. Revenues of $9.4 million and expenses of $8.1 million were seen that same year, for an operating profit of $1.3 million. Since 2001 the Authority has invested more than $36 million in infrastructure in the airport. In 2015 total taxes paid by passengers, employers, and employees at YQX, were estimated at $46 million per year, including $27 million to the federal government and $19 million to the provincial government.

Gander, Newfoundland & Labrador

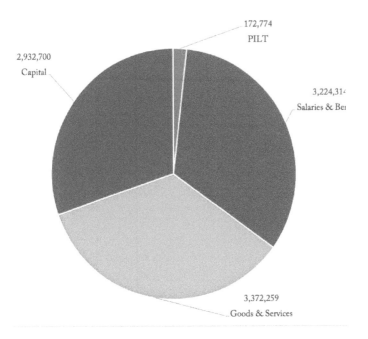

2,932,700
Capital

172,774
PILT

3,224,31⟨
Salaries & Bei

3,372,259
Goods & Services

Figure 31: Image courtesy of Google Earth Pro, 8-13-2017.

In 1955 Transport Canada began construction of the Halifax International Airport on land provided by the City of Halifax. It was not the first airport to service Halifax. That claim to fame belongs to a flying boat base set up at Baker's Point in 1918 to allow the Royal Canadian Naval Air Service (RCNAS) to operate Curtis HS-21 flying boats on anti-submarine patrol.

On 5 July 1919 the City asked the federal government to build a municipal airfield. The government's response was that it expected municipalities to build their own airfields.

Several years passed without any movement towards the construction of an airfield. On 19 January 1927 the Canadian Air Board (CAB) offered "technical assistance" if the City would provide the land. The City was indeed interested and offered several sites, all of which were rejected by the CAB due to technical reasons, cost or location. Finally, in September 1928 a site at Bluebell Farm[258] was deemed acceptable. The City held a

---

[258] "Bluebell Farm" between Chebucto and Bayers Road. Today the air field location is marked by Saunders Park.

191

Figure 32: Monument at Saunders Park denoting the first airfield in Halifax - "Bluebell Farm"

plebiscite and received approval to spend $190,000 for the land and construction of two landing strips: 1,800 by 600 feet (549 by 183 m) and 2,000 by 600 feet (610 by 183 m). An airport license was issued on 9 January 1931 to the City who then leased the airport to the Halifax Aero Club for operation and maintenance. Profits to be shared equally by the Club and the City.

In 1931 the Superintendent of Airways for the CAB wrote of Halifax: "the changes there in the last two years are miraculous; it is now a really good airport and has a good hangar and Club House. Pan American added a small passenger station last year and their daily service during August and September helped to establish confidence in the future of the airport on the part of Citizens."[259] Approximately $225,000 had been spent on the airport by then.

During 1938-39 studies undertaken to determine if the airport could be used for expanded airline use determined that it could not be adequately developed. It was decided to use the new airport at Dartmouth being developed for the RCAF. The new airport was

---

[259] Public Archives Canada, MG 30 E243, vol. 7.

ready in 1940 and the old airport closed in late 1941. The "new" airport allowed TCA to begin flying its trans-continental service to Halifax.

The city continued its interest in having its own municipal airport. Many sites were examined and, finally, in 1954 the Kelly Lake site (2,750 acres – 1 113 hectares) 37 km north of the City and recommended by TCA, was approved by the DOT, provided the City buy the land and transfer it to the DOT for one dollar. This was agreed. Construction began in November 1955 on two runways: 8,000 by 200 feet (2 438 by 61 m) and 6,200 by 200 feet (1 890 by 61 m); an air terminal building designed to handle 180,000 passengers annually; and administrative buildings and hangars. The Air Terminal Building (ATB) opened officially on 10 September 1960.

By the early 1970's the ATB was bursting at the seams and a new 54,000 sq ft (5,017 sq m) hold room was added in 1976. In 1988 two passenger walkways were added to improve customer service levels.[260]

Passenger loads continued to increase dramatically reaching 1.7 million a year in 1980 and, by 1990, over 2.5 million a year.

The Authority

In 1992 Don Mazankowski[261], father of the AAs, had come to Halifax to speak with the Chamber of Commerce about the AAs in Vancouver, Edmonton, Calgary and Montréal. A group of people then got together to form the Halifax Airport Study Group (HASG), which was incorporated under the provisions of the Societies Act of Nova Scotia on 28 October 1992.[262]

With the support of the City of Halifax, the City of Dartmouth, the Town of Bedford, the Municipality of the County of Halifax, the Halifax Board of Trade, the Dartmouth Chamber of

---

[260] *History of Halifax (Stanfield) International Airport,* https://halifaxstanfield.ca/wp-content/uploads/2015/12/History-in-English1.pdf, accessed 10 October 2018.

[261] Federal Minister of Transport, 1978-79, 1984-86.

[262] Jim Cowan, email, 31 January 2019.

Commerce and the Province of Nova Scotia, the Group began its work.

It was soon after that efforts stopped for a while as TC ceased most activity on devolution during the 1993 election campaign. After the change in federal government from Conservative to Liberal in 1993 the HASG got re-engaged, although there was a lull from 1993 to 1995 until the National Airports Policy and the Public Accountability Principles came into being. The issuance by TC of the Policy and the Principles caused an impetus to a number of Authorities across the country to get moving. Halifax was no different.

The HASG met from time-to-time to look at whether or not this might be something that would be good for Halifax. At one point it was agreed to engage the city in deliberations and the HASG received some seed money from them for due diligence. The Royal Bank stepped up and provided some funding, even though at that point there was no legal entity that could have ever paid back the bank if the thing had never panned out.

Jim McNiven was a member of the first group that attempted to negotiate the transfer. He had previously been Deputy Minister of Economic Development for the Province, and was Dean of the Faculty of Administration at Dalhousie when the first group was formed. He had an interest in economic development and thought the airport would be a major economic driver to the community if only given the opportunity. The group began negotiations with TC but were unable to reach a common view of the environmental liabilities[263] arising from the siting of the airport and negotiations ceased.

---

[263] The airport lands sit on a large deposit of pyritic slate. Pyritic slate is a sulphide-rich slate of the Halifax Formation of the Meguma Group of Nova Scotia. When exposed to water, oxidation of the sulphides occurs which generates acid drainage. Construction within the area of the Halifax International Airport since 1955 caused the most serious problems and expensive measures were required to avoid fish kills in rivers draining from airport lands. Previous studies assumed that the mineral responsible for the acid drainage was pyrite (FeS_2) but work at Dalhousie University showed that the most abundant sulphide is monoclinic pyrrhotite (Fe_7S_8).

On 30 March 1995 the name of the Group was changed to the Halifax International Airport Planning Group.[264]

The spark that got the second effort going was Mary Brooks. In the Fall of 1995 she was Chair of the Transportation Committee of the Metropolitan Halifax Board of Trade. There were several sub-committees of the Transportation Committee (Port and Rail, Air, etc.), and at one of the committee meetings she said, to the then airport manager, Janet Shrieves, "Janet, all these other airports across the country are being transferred, and nothing's happening in Halifax. Why is that? I know there was a previous effort that failed, but why is nobody talking to TC?"[265] and she said "why don't you call them?" and Mary thought, OK, there is a speaker phone here, so she put it in the middle of the table, and called the Airport Transfer Team at TC and said "why aren't you talking with us?" and TC said "well, no one's asked." So Mary asked what they could do for the next step, and took some notes. The next thing Mary knew, Jim Cowan was organizing a Board. The process had gone through some political channels in Nova Scotia since it seemed that the Provincial government had decided to get involved. Jim was well-known in the Provincial Liberal party and had good connections in the Province. In nominating the Board, the Chamber received a number of Board positions. The initial Board had 15 members, 12 by nomination and three members at large.

Three members of the Board (Jim Cowan, Bernie Miller, and Jim Radford) and the new Executive Director (Neil Raynor) went out to a conference in Edmonton organized by Western Economic Diversification. At that point Winnipeg had just transferred and the lawyer for Winnipeg spoke, saying that it took five years to negotiate the transfer, and he produced five or six volumes of transfer documents, including the "rent clause" of 174 pages. The group looked at each other and said "that's impossible. What could possibly take that long?"[266] Little did they know what they were about to undertake. The Halifax International Airport Authority was incorporated under the provisions of the Canada Corporations

---

[264] Cowan, 31 January 2019.

[265] Mary Brooks, interview with the author, 18 December 2018.

[266] Jim Cowan, interview with the author, 20 December 2018.

Act on 23 November 1995 and on 1 February 2000 it assumed responsibility for the airport – it too took five years!!![267]

From the beginning all legal service work was provided pro bono, until transfer. The Board had an accountant from KPMG who agreed to provide accountancy services, and it got some seed money from the city, which was used to pay for due diligence. Apart from Neil Raynor, there were no paid staff until 1999 when Dennis Rogers (employee number 001) was hired as CEO and then Joyce Carter (employee number 002) was hired as Vice President Finance.

The first full Board was formed in 1995. Prior to that time the members of the HASG were all male, and Jim Cowan called Mary Brooks and said to her "we looked around the table and realized we would need some alternate perspectives."[268] The Board had produced a skills matrix for the three members to be appointed by the Board: a union member; a transportation expert; and female. Two out of the three new members would be female, which made Halifax the only AA to have such a large percentage of females on its Board at formation.

There was a lot of volunteer work. Mary was putting in sometimes 20 hours a week, and she wasn't even chairing a committee. The preparations for negotiations ate up the time, at a significant burn rate, of 15 people, who all volunteered. Jim Radford (the Chair), Jim Cowan (Secretary and counsel), and Neil Raynor (the first Executive Director the Board hired), were the ones who actually conducted the negotiations.

Apart from environmental issues, the Board was involved in decisions about pensions, benefits, among other items, before and after the transfer. Bill Black and Dick Crawford, who both worked at Maritime Life, helped with the pension discussions. The Board had people in the community who volunteered their time and expertise, so it wasn't just paid consultants, but people who wanted this transfer to succeed who were involved.

---

[267] Negotiations with TC began 18 December 1995. Transfer took place on 1 February 2000.

[268] Brooks.

At transfer the ATB was in horrible shape and there was no doubt that an Airport Improvement Fee was needed immediately. Although it took quite a while, the Board made some good decisions on the structure of the airport and how it would work.

What to do with the staff was a difficult issue because TC would not let the Board see the personnel records prior to transfer. TC's position was "you have to take everybody on, and you have to offer them similar terms and conditions as they had under TC." And the Board said "OK, let us see the personnel records." TC refused. From the point-of-view of Board it was "OK, you're asking us to hire an office worker, and if they don't work out then we can deal with it, but we're taking on someone to operate heavy machinery around aircraft, people to work on the field, firefighters, etc. What training have they had? How do we know they are competent, and have received all of the training necessary to do what they do?" TC still refused as the records were "confidential".[269]

The Board found those kinds of things difficult, but it took everybody on and overall there were no real issues. Some of the TC employees embraced the challenge and became very good employees, and some never really adapted to the move from a public sector mentality and moved on. In hindsight getting the employees involved was the only way it could have been successful – the employees had to be behind it.

Negotiations with TC were a frustrating process for the Board. When the group had heard in Winnipeg that it took five years to transfer, they thought to themselves "we're smarter than that. We can do this more quickly."[270] Unfortunately, they found the negotiations to be a very, very difficult process. TC would say "now look, this is a 'take it or leave it' proposition. This is what we're offering and we're not going to change it in any way. This is what you have to take. And, by the way, you can't talk to any other Authorities who might be negotiating. This is all confidential."[271] That statement from TC was just an invitation to talk with the other groups negotiating at the same time. Which the Board did,

---

[269] Ibid.

[270] Ibid.

[271] Ibid.

197

and it found that although those groups were being told by TC the same thing, TC was conducting separate side deals with each of them. The side deals complicated matters.

The environmental issue with respect to pyritic slate had not gone away, and was particularly contentious when negotiating the second time around. TC had tolerated the acid run-off for many years, and during the negotiations TC said "you're taking this over, so now this is all your responsibility, and you have to indemnify us against any claims."[272]. The Board refused, for their position was that when a body of land is transferred from federal to provincial government, there is no environmental issue because the Crown can still not sue the Crown. But the minute a non-governmental organization assumes control of that land, then the Board of that organization can be sued for environmental damage. TC knew it had built on the pyritic slate, knew it had had an environmental issue for years, and had determined that the risk was not worth the avoidance cost. Eventually the Board negotiated the construction of a remediation plant to treat the runway runoff from a "one hundred year storm", for which the federal government paid a significant portion of the construction cost. The construction of that plant was considered to be adequate for the environmental signoff.

Another environmental issue arose when it was discovered that a rare orchid was growing on one of the airside lots: the "Southern Twayblade".[273] The Authority set aside the lot from any development plans but after many years discovered that the plant had disappeared.[274]

There was also the issue of a half-built, abandoned construction site that was to have been a 375 room hotel at the airport. Located immediately across from the airport terminal building the hotel was considered an eyesore, and a liability to anyone foolish enough to go near it. As part of the negotiations the Board demanded that

---

[272] Cowan.

[273] Of 11 species of orchid found in North America only four reach Nova Scotia, and the Southern Twayblade is one of the rarest.

[274] Joyce Carter, interview with the author, 28 January 2019.

TC take the structure down prior to transfer. This did not happen, but the issue became a useful bargaining item.[275]

The transfer terms offered by TC were generally the same terms as were being offered to other transfer groups across the country. The pace of negotiation was frustrating, and there was dissatisfaction and concern with TC's hard-nosed attitude. Moreover, from the Board's point-of-view, not only was it negotiating with TC, but it also had to bring the Halifax community along with it. At the beginning the community was not at all sure that transfer was the right thing to do, and so there was a lot of community education that had to be done and the Board made a point of doing a lot of consultation with the community during that period.

Part of that consultation process was to persuade community and business leaders that transfer was something they should back. Getting the community involved turned out to be a good move, because on a couple of occasions, it looked to the Board like the transfer was not going anywhere,[276] especially when the Minister of Transport said to Dennis Rogers "look, you have three months to make a deal, and if you don't make a deal in three months then I'll go and start dealing with another group of 20 people."[277] At that point the Board had a public awareness campaign to get a fair deal for Halifax. The support of the political and business leaders was important in getting some breakthroughs in the negotiations. The Board obtained some lapel buttons for people to wear; it said in ransom style cutout letters: "A fair deal for Halifax." The pièce de résistance was that the Board took out two billboard advertisements with the same message: one on the highway access road from the airport the week the Minister of Transport was visiting Halifax; and the other on the Airport Parkway in Ottawa. He could not miss either one.

---

[275] Cowan, 28 January 2019.

[276] At one point just before transfer Joyce was seriously wondering if she had made the right decision to leave her previous job and join the nascent Authority, as things were not going well in the negotiations with TC and there were doubts as to whether the transfer would actually occur. Interview with the author, 28 January 2019.

[277] Collenette.

The original date for transfer had been set for 1 January 2000. Throughout 1998 and 1999 there had been a lot of discussion as to what would happen to all the world's computers when the year changed from "99" to "00": "the Y2K issue". So the transfer team thought "we'll move the date to one month later, and that way TC will have all the headaches of dealing with Y2K." And they did. Transfer took place on 1 February 2000.[278]

Just over one year after transfer the bargaining unit went on strike. The AA was surprised by that. On 12 April 2001 support staff at the airport went on strike after their last contract had expired in February 2000. Job security, wages and the length of the contract were the main issues in the dispute.[279] Collective bargaining had begun in the fall of 2000, but by the spring of 2001, negotiations had come to naught and staff began a four-week strike. This was eventually was settled to the satisfaction of both parties.[280]

Negotiating the transfer with TC was a long, drawn-out, aggravating process, and there were some difficulties in getting the rent clause re-negotiated, but by-and-large the devolution of the airports been one of the more successful public policy initiatives that the federal government has undertaken. When one looks at the Port Authorities, and when one looks at how far the Airports Authorities have progressed compared to the Port Authorities, that progress has a lot to do with the governance structure. In Halifax, as it has evolved, the airport's nominators consult with the Authority before they make nominations, and over time the nominations just keep getting better and better, and the Board gets better over time. And over time the AA's Board has used its appointments to fill in the gaps so that the Board is as balanced as it could be. It has worked well.

The level of investment in the airport would never have happened if it had been left in the hands of government. Twenty years ago it would have been impossible to imagine that Halifax airport would be the airport it is today. That would not have happened had it not been privatized. That's not a criticism of the TC folks, it is a

---

[278] Carter.

[279] https://www.cbc.ca/news/canada/travellers-not-held-up-by-halifax-airport-strike-1.292861, accessed 12 February 2019.

[280] Halifax Airport Annual Report, 2001.

reality that there was just no way that TC could have advanced Halifax in the same way that they did Montréal, or Toronto or Ottawa. TC had to deal with the airports as they saw them and Halifax would never have progressed.

Halifax was a small airport in 2000, but it is no longer, for the Authority went out and got new airline routes and negotiated with the airlines. At transfer, there were three tails (logos of carriers served) seen at Halifax airport. Within five years, the airport marketing department under Jerry Staples was boasting of 21 tails to the local community. The Authority convinced companies to locate on airport lands. It re-built the airport terminal building and made it possible for concessionaires to be profitable. For example, the amount of capital investment since transfer at Halifax is approaching $635 million. That level of capital investment never would have happened under TC's management. There may have been some, but nowhere near that amount because any amount spent by TC would have come out of the federal budget, and there would have been a reluctance to spend in Halifax if the federal government could not also spend in St. Johns', or Québec City, or elsewhere in Canada. It would have been impossible for TC to have invested even $50 million, a tenth of what the Authority has invested. That $635 million investment is a remarkable economic driver to the city and the Province and has accomplished the following:

- State-of-the-art water treatment facility;
- Airside subdivision;
- Expansion of the international and domestic arrivals areas and public parking areas;
- Creation of the Flight Deck – a public observation area;
- Creation of the Airport Square – a major expansion of the retail and main lobby area;
- South end commuter aircraft facility;
- U.S. preclearance facility;
- Reconfiguration of the terminal front roadway to improve the flow of passengers and vehicles by creating separate roads for picking up and dropping off passengers and construction of a new one-way loop roadway system to improve traffic safety and wayfinding, reduce congestion and increase the road network capacity;
- Complete airfield restoration of airport runways and taxiways;

- Construction of a 2,300 space Parkade adjacent to the north end of the terminal building, including an over-road pedway, and Nova Scotia's first moving sidewalk;
- Construction of a Leadership in Energy and Environmental Design (LEED) certified, energy efficient combined services complex that houses the airport's emergency response services and airfield maintenance teams;
- Extension of Runway 05/23 to 10,500 feet; and,
- Renovations to the domestic/international check-in hall to accommodate a new baggage handling system and an industry-leading self-serve bag drop system.

When the Province goes on trade missions it always ensures that the airport is involved.

The AA was able to implement "pre-clearance", the ability for a passenger to clear U.S. Customs and Immigration while in Halifax, which now allows passengers to fly to any U.S. airport serviced by airlines from Halifax.

At the beginning it wasn't clear that it made economic sense to transfer responsibility for the airport to a local organization. TC had made it quite clear how much they spent in maintaining the airport, and how much they made in revenues from landing fees and terminal fees. The revenues just weren't there. But when one sees how closely the city is engaged, how closely the Province is engaged, how both the city and the Province look to the airport as a key economic driver, and how the Province supports the airport[281] through its International Air Service Investment,[282] that is something that TC could never do when it was the operator. It hasn't been entirely smooth sailing, but it has been a remarkable success story.

---

[281] Carter.

[282] An $11.1 million investment announced by the government of Nova Scotia on 15 March 2018 to improve air connections to key markets in Asia, Europe, and the northeastern and central United States and increase trade, tourism and immigration. https://novascotia.ca/finance/site-finance/media/finance/new%20investment%202017-18.pdf, accessed 29 January 2019.

Figure 33: Halifax Airport

As an economic engine to the local community, the AAs impact is felt far beyond the walls of its terminal. An economic impact analysis[283] conducted in August 2018 by estimated that in 2017 a $3 billion contribution to the Province of Nova Scotia could be attributed to the airport and its operations. Direct employment at the airport was 14,270 jobs in 2017. Throughout the region another 10,625 jobs are attributed to the airport. In 2017 alone, the Authority spent $79.5 million in the Halifax area for salaries, goods, supplies, services, property taxes and capital investment. Since transfer in 2000 the Authority has spent more than $635 million on infrastructure development. Almost all of that expense was spent locally.

---

[283] https://halifaxstanfield.ca/airport-authority/media-centre/airport-facts-and-stats/airport-statistics/, accessed 12 February 2019.

Halifax, Nova Scotia

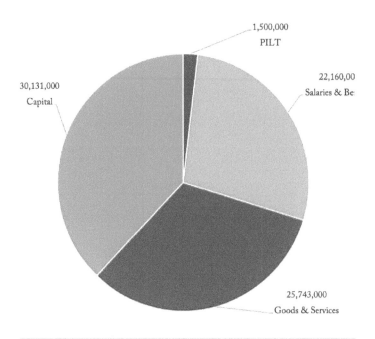

1,500,000
PILT

22,160,00
Salaries & Be

30,131,000
Capital

25,743,000
Goods & Services

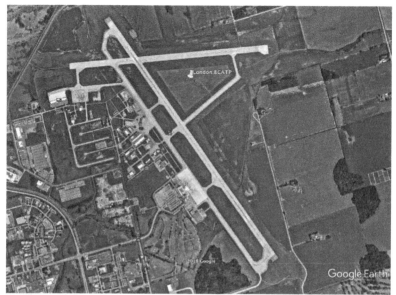

Figure 35: Image courtesy of Google Earth Pro, 7-2-2018. The pin marks the location of the original BCATP aerodrome.

In January 1927 the City of London selected a site for an airfield at Lambeth, Ontario and proposed a bylaw for $28,000 to purchase the land. The bylaw was defeated on 5 December 1927. A group of local businessmen acquired the site in 1928 and by 3 May 1929 an airport license was issued to London Airport Ltd. The London Flying Club was formed in 1928 and became a tenant of the new airport. The airfield was used for flying instruction, private aviation, and for air mail. By 1933 it had become too small for the three-engined aircraft used by Trans-American Air Lines on that route (the original grass landing strip may still be seen from the air).

The London Flying Club continued to use the Lambeth airfield until 7 August 1942.

In 1935 the city asked the Civil Aviation Branch to conduct a survey of the airport to determine if it could be expanded or if a new airport needed to be developed at a more suitable location. Site surveys and consultations took place over the next four years and in May 1939 the DOT recommended three possible sites: one near St. Thomas (south of the city); one near Rebecca (6½ km northeast); and one near Crumlin (3 km east). The DOT proposal was that if the city purchased the land, the DOT would develop the airport, exclusive of buildings. The city purchased the Rebecca site and on 9 September 1939, at the start of WW2, work began on a new airport. The city leased the new airport to the Government of Canada on 24 January 1940 for the duration of the war. Runways 14-32 and 05-23 (each 3,100 feet, 945 m) were paved and ready for use by 27 July 1940. The Royal Canadian Air Force built three hangars, barrack blocks and administrative offices for RCAF Station Crumlin on west of the airport. RCAF Station Crumlin was host to No. 3 Elementary Flying School and No. 4 Air Observer School, both part of the British Commonwealth Air Training Plan.

In 1941 an aircraft overhaul plant was built by Central Aircraft Ltd. to service Lysanders, Ansons, Fleet trainers, Fairey Battles, and Mosquitos. This plant is still in use by Diamond Aircraft.

In 1942 the Honourable C.D. Howe, Minister of Transport, opened a civilian terminal which also housed the civil radio and Trans-Canada Air Lines.

In 1943 runways 05-23 and 14-32 were extended to 4,145 and 4,000 feet respectively (1 263 and 1 219 me) and runway 08-26 (3,800 feet – 1 158 m) was added to create the classic BCATP "triangle" (see the triangle in the top of the photograph). DND also added two hangars.

Commonwealth Air Training Plan operations ended on 31 December 1944 with the closure of No. 4 Air Observer School.

After the war the city refused to accept responsibility for the airport so it remained under the control of the Department of Transport.

In 1947 TCA began flying DC-3s and the terminal was enlarged to accommodate the increased passenger loads.

RCAF Station London opened in 1950 to support a NATO Induction and Training Centre, later moved to Centralia. The station closed on 30 September 1958.

In 1955 TCA began using Viscounts and runway 14-32 was reinforced and lengthened to 6,000 feet (1 829 m). Runway 08-26 was reinforced and lengthened to 5,200 feet (1 585 m) in 1957.

As passenger loads increased steadily the DOT has been planning a new terminal as early as October 1953 but the city was not interested. Eventually, in December 1960 DOT asked the city for title to land on the south side of the airport for a new terminal. The city sold the land to DOT and a new terminal opened on 10 April 1965. The old terminal was demolished in 1969.

In 1973 runway 08-26 was extended to 6,300 feet (1 920 m), runway 14-32 to 8,800 feet (2 682 m) and runway 05-23 shortened to 3,174 feet (967 m). Runway 14-32 could now accommodate DC-8, Boeing 707 and 747, and L1011 aircraft. The long runway allowed for the first non-stop London, ON to London, England flight to be made on 11 September 1975 by a Boeing 707 of Laker Airways.

Economic regulatory reform in the 1980's allowed for more airlines, more destinations, and greater choices at the airport, which in turn created more demand and increased aviation activity. The need for something to be done about the passenger processing areas of the terminal became more and more pressing and from 1983 to 1985 a number of refurbishing and expansion projects were undertaken to meet the increased demand.

In April 1988 runway 05-23 was decommissioned and converted to a taxiway, a change which permitted the construction of new facilities and the development of new commercial lots.

On 1 August 1998 control of the airport was transferred from Transport Canada to the Greater London International Airport Authority

The Authority

The years prior to the transfer had been "interesting".[284]

The City of London had been involved in airport operation from 1927 to 1945, however after the war the City declined to accept responsibility for the airport and TC operated the airport until 1998.

The City of London was very supportive of regaining local control via an Airport Authority. This occurred in February 1995 when

---

[284] With thanks to Steve Baker for his email on the creation of the London AA.

Geno Francolini, Bill Loyens, Tom Gosnell, and David Atkinson met to form the London Airport Planning Group (LAPG). Their task was to develop a structure for a Board of Directors that was representative of the Community, and to draft corporate bylaws for an Airport Authority that were acceptable to the Federal Government.

The LAPG was comprised of dedicated community leaders who volunteered for a task that had no job description, They believed in the concept of local people making local decisions on the future of their airport. This was in stark contrast to the sixty years of centralized Government operations.

The LAPG operated from Feb 1995 to December 1995, by which time it had enough information to incorporate the Greater London International Airport Authority (GLIAA) as a private corporation with no equity shareholders. Once the GLIAA incorporated the LAPG dissolved itself.

The LAPG had excellent support from the local municipalities and the region. Board members represented the region and ensured broad community and regional support. The City of London embraced the ambitious plans and worked closely to align economic development initiatives.

Negotiations were demanding as TC wanted a detailed business plan describing how the National Airport Policy would be supported and how the Government would end all investment. The Board was required to accept a detailed lease of over 400 pages that covered far more than a property lease or normal commercial transaction, with much of the language dealing with the policies and roles of the federal government.

TC had developed a lease plan and corresponding terms. Except for some negotiated capital funding the terms were fixed and meant to apply to all airports. There was little room for negotiation.

The Authority had to determine its ability to pay since operations started on day one with a cash register and a dream. A few basic operational assets and chattels were conveyed at market value. The Board spent much time preparing detailed cash flow projections based on several scenarios to determine the actual revenue requirements. Consequently the airport was operated in a lean and proactive approach to cover all operational costs. This was a first in the recent history of the London airport as it went from an annual deficit to break even status. The Board realized that an AIF was required to fund capital improvements, and that a diversified revenue base was required to ensure overall success.

In accordance with the Public Accountability Principles promulgated by the federal government in 1995 the initial directors asked the nominators to propose the required additional directors. These Principles, applicable to all Airport Authorities formed after 1995, required the Board to consist of a broad range of skills and experiences. Board members were nominated by designated nominators: the federal and provincial governments, the City of London, the Chamber of Commerce, a representative of Labour, a Consumer group, and a member at large.

Initially the Board was both a management board and a governance board, as during the start-up phase the Chair of the Board was appointed as the first CEO. However, a year later the Board developed into a governance board, as it had intended, and the President and CEO positions were combined to a single position on the management team.

Negotiations between the GLIAA and TC were very slow. Three years elapsed from initial overtures to a final signing of documents, primarily because the Federal Government was negotiating several airports at the same time as a group. The London airport was significantly undercapitalized and had had no infrastructure investment for several years. It was also losing money through operations. During negotiations the Board requested infrastructure improvement funds based on TC's planned capital improvements. Some regard was placed on the condition of facilities and an attempt was made to level the field amongst transferred airports.

For almost 60 years the union had had experience of a single operator at the airport. It now had a very different private sector operator with which it had to negotiate. The bargaining unit staff wanted local changes in agreements to make them more local based than national. Through some open and fair negotiations the first agreement was concluded in the first year. Since then there has never been a labour disruption.

At the beginning the staff was apprehensive about changing employers and pension plans, notwithstanding the pleasantries and words from TC. However, almost all the staff remained with the Authority and later remarked how wonderful was the experience of local people making local decisions. For the first time the bargaining unit was involved in decisions on developing local services rather than meeting the national policy needs of TC.

The biggest difference was that the new Authority had a vision of strategic planning, customer service, creating area economic growth, integrating planning of airport lands and adjacent city lands, aggressive pursuit of air services and becoming the hub of aviation for south western Ontario. This contrasted greatly with the TC's mandate of "similar essential services" at airports across Canada.

Recently, the Province of Ontario divested itself of all airport support and operations primarily in the north and smaller communities. Although for many years it had no evolving policy on airports, the Province worked closely with the Authority to establish a fair and predictable property tax system. Previously the federal government had provided an annual Grant in Lieu of Taxes to the City of London.

Since 1997 the Authority has been a substantial contributor to the economy of South West Ontario in general, and the economy of the London area in particular.

Figure 36: London Airport

On an annual basis the GLIAA operations contribute immensely to the local economy of the City of London and its surrounding communities:

- More than 1,000 direct full-time equivalent (FTE) jobs annually;
- More than 50 businesses are located at the aerodrome; and,
- Approximately $357 million created in the area economy.

210

In 2017, the Authority alone spent \$8.6 million in the London area.[285]

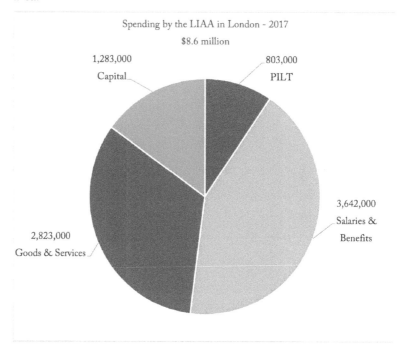

Figure 37: Spending by the Authority in London in 2017.

---

[285] Source: London International Airport Authority, 2018.

Figure 38: Image courtesy of Google Earth Pro, 9-21-2017. The pin marks the location of the original BCATP aerodrome.

As with almost every other airport in Canada, the raison d'être for the creation of an airport at Moncton was to deliver the mail faster. And so, on January 11, 1928, the first scheduled air flight out of the Greater Moncton area took place. This flight was carrying mail and passengers to the Magdalen Islands. It is interesting to note that at the start of air travel the mail was important, passengers were extra revenue, and there was very little, if any, cargo. Today, cargo is important, and both passengers and mail are extra revenue.

After much discussion as to the need for a permanent airport facility, Leger's Corner was chosen because of more favourable landing conditions.

In 1929, a local private company[286] bought the land at Léger's Corner airstrip and built two grass runways (1,500 feet and 900 feet) as well as structures for aircraft maintenance. It was also in 1929 that the Moncton Aero Club was founded, as was the

---

[286] Moncton Airport Ltd., owned by Dick McCully, Charles Baxter, John Humphrey, William Creaghan, Timothy O'Brien, and Dave Houston.

International Airways Flying School. These later became the Moncton Flight College, one of the pre-eminent flight schools in Canada. Also in the same year, the airport expanded its air mail service to include Prince Edward Island and Montréal.

The first Maritime Provinces Air Pageant was held on 1-2 July 1929 and attracted 45,000 spectators. Profits from the air show allowed the company to pay for the land and improvements.

On 29 October 1929 the company transferred ownership of the airport to the city, and Moncton became a municipal airport. The city graveled the runways in 1930.

In 1936, the Department of Transport and the Provincial and Municipal governments discussed the possibility of the construction of an airport suitable for trans-Canadian routes. The Léger's Corner site was unsuitable for expansion and instead a site in nearby Lakeburn, 6 ½ km east, was selected in May 1936 as the new site for the airport.

In 1937 the city entered into discussions with the DOT as to the development of the Lakeburn site. A plan was agreed upon with the city contributing $192,000 and the DOT $162,000. A paved runway 3,200 by 150 feet (975 by 46 m) and two additional dirt landing strips were to be constructed. On 26 March 1938 the city agreed to buy the site. DOT would undertake to pay all construction costs and operate the airport. The city would share any operating profit until it had been reimbursed for the cost of the land.

In March 1940, the Department of National Defence opened a flight training school under the auspices of the BCATP. A new hangar was also constructed at the airport during the war to serve as a repair and maintenance facility. The BCATP triangle is located in the lower left of the aerial photograph of the airport.

During the 1940s, civilian air services expanded and became available serving Montréal, Halifax, Charlottetown, Sydney, Saint John, Fredericton and Newfoundland. The hangar of Trans-Canada Airlines became the location for the first air terminal. In 1952, the larger Clark Ruse hangar was being converted into a modern air terminal when it was destroyed by fire. In 1953, a replacement air terminal was constructed.

In 1958 runway 07-25 was lengthened to 6,150 feet (1 874 m).

Further expansion in 1964 brought an air traffic control tower and a new operations building.

In 1968 runway 11-29 was lengthened to 8,000 feet (2 438 m).

In 1976, the air terminal was again expanded.

In 1980 runway 07-25 was renamed to 06-24 due to magnetic variation.

The Authority

Moncton had been a railway town for well over a century until the closure of the Canadian National Railway (CNR) locomotive shops in 1986.[287] Even before that time, Len Lockhardt, Chair of the Economic Development Corp (later Enterprise Moncton), had organized people from the universities, business and the local communities and had got them to agree that the airport was necessary to Moncton.[288]

The Greater Moncton Chamber of Commerce was also at the forefront of promoting the airport through its work with the Air Transport Committee. In 1988 Bill Whalen became the Executive Vice President and continued that focus on the airport.[289] Led by a gentleman named David Smith, the Chamber formed an exploratory committee to follow on with the National Transportation Act of 1987 since a major principle of the new Act was the devolution of the airports to the private sector. Not very long after the exploratory committee was formed David Smith was appointed to the bench, and Doug Windsor took over the task of continuing to look at the idea of the Moncton airport transferring.

In 1990 Robert Basque and several others from the exploratory committee went to a airport conference at Harrison Hot Springs, British Columbia. The Minister of Transport was a speaker and he mentioned that the next transfer was going to be Dorval and Mirabel, and then the Government was going to look at the Tier 2

---

[287] In 1986 CN Rail closed its repair shops, later demolished in 1988. When the shops closed, CN relocated 5,000 jobs from Moncton to other parts of Canada. Source *Historical Footprints,* http://www.tracestudio.ca/historical-footprints/, accessed 25 January 2019.

[288] Robert Basque, interview with the author, 23 January 2019.

[289] Bill Whalen, interview with the author, 8 January 2019.

airports, which included Moncton. At that conference the group met with YVRAS and Michael Tretheway, who became an instrumental part of the Moncton transfer. Because Moncton was not a very big airport the group felt that YVRAS could assist the transition team throughout the whole process.

But in 1990 the federal government made the decision that it was only going to deal with the big four and the committee folded until 1994, when Doug Young (the MP from Bathurst and Transport Minister in the Chretien Cabinet) introduced the National Airports Policy.

In 1994 George Rideout approached Bill and said "I'd like Moncton to get on this bandwagon. Would you be prepared to sit on a committee?"[290] So Rideout and Whalen put together an exploratory committee and Whalen was elected to be the Chair. It was at that point that they started down the process to look at what was involved. Was TC actually going to deal with the so-called "midsize" airports? By 1995, when it became apparent that it was more than a notion that TC was going to deal with the mid-sized airports, the committee legalized the entity as the Greater Moncton Airport Authority.

The committee then met with the three municipal councils of the day, Moncton, Riverview and Dieppe, told them what it was looking at doing, told them why it was looking at doing it, and asked them for some level of interim funding so that the committee could properly study the issue. The committee also met with the Province. Frank McKenna was the Premier in those days and Frank was a big supporter of airports in general, but certainly the Moncton airport.

The three municipalities gave the committee enough preliminary funding to start the process. The committee knew it would have to go to the banks at some point, but had no idea at the time just how long and involved the process would be, how difficult the TC folk would be. Their argument was "if we don't do this, it won't get done".[291] TC made it very clear that the Moncton airport was running at an operating loss of about $2 million a year and they

---

[290] Ibid.

[291] Ibid.

were not going to put even $20,000 into the airport, for if they did then all the other airports would also want $20,000, and TC could not give preferential treatment.[292]

The airport at Moncton had two runways at the time, one of the runways needed to be re-surfaced and the terminal building was badly in need of renovation. TC made it very clear that they had no plans to do that, that their vision was a 'hub and spoke' system based on Halifax, with regional airports, including Moncton, feeding the hub using Dash 8s or smaller. So TC was just going to do away with the second runway because it wasn't needed for propeller-driven aircraft.

One of the people hired by the committee to help investigate the transfer process at the local level was John Strugnell, who had been the Moncton airport manager and had retired a short time before. John coined the term "airports in the 21st century are going to be like railway stations of the 19th century. Towns that don't have one are going to have a difficult time economically, and to grow and develop."[293] The committee firmly believed that, being a fairly small community. Moncton had been a railway town, and the committee knew the benefits that came from that.

Soon after, in 1995 or 1996, TC said to the committee "look, here's the situation. Moncton's losing $2 million a year. And we're committed to continue to fund that airport until the year 2000. In the year 2000 it has to be break-even, that's the directive we've gotten from the Government. If, at that point nothing has happened, it's going to become a 9 to 5 airport. Now, we are prepared to give you the $2 million a year from now until 2000 if you take over the airport right now." So if the airport had gone to a 9 to 5 operation, it would then effectively be a hub-and-spoke because the airport wouldn't be able to service flights late at night.

So the committee decided that it was to their advantage to get that airport transferred to the Airport Authority as soon as possible so that the committee could get the airport out of TC's hands and then run it as a business, as it should.

---

[292] Basque

[293] Whalen.

At an early committee meeting they got the CEO of the Edmonton airport to meet with them and describe some of his experiences of transfer. He gave some examples of the efficiencies that the Edmonton AA had been able to implement. For example, the Edmonton AA was one of the first airports to put in a playground. He said "under TC, I needed 52 different authorizations to get that done. After the transfer, I needed two, my safety officer, and me."[294]

The committee was quite confident that it could take the $2 million a year for the four years from 1997 to 2000 and do more with it than if the airport had been left with the civil servants of TC. The committee believed absolutely that it could put in operational efficiencies and turn the airport around so that it made an operating profit. This decision ensured that Moncton was one of the first Tier 2 airports to transfer. YVRAS agreed with the committee's decision and helped it to get going.

The committee had no idea that the process would be as long and as costly as it turned out to be, and that the negotiations would be as difficult and frustrating as they were. The majority of expenses were for legal and consulting fees. The committee hired a couple of people from Price Waterhouse Coopers to help them understand the deal, the offering, the concept behind TC's thinking. There was nobody in the region at that time that the committee found who really understood what TC was trying to do with this whole deal. So legal and consulting fees were the most of it. The Board was not compensated. It had some travel expenses, to go to the national conferences, and one or two short ventures into some of the northern U.S. towns to look at similar sized airports to see how their operations went so that it could get an understanding of what opportunities there might be for us.

Negotiations with TC were "frustrating".[295] The committee thought that because TC did not wish to invest any money into Moncton, it then also did not wish to invest in the negotiations. There wasn't a great deal of focus on "Isn't this great that

---

[294] Basque.

[295] Basque.

Moncton is stepping up to the plate."[296] The negotiations were frustrating. The TC negotiating team would arrive in Moncton, negotiate terms of the contract, get everyone's agreement, go back to Ottawa, and then come back to Moncton and say "no, we can't do that. Our bosses won't agree." And the Moncton team would say "look, you come down here, you say you have authority to negotiate, we agree on something, and then you come back and say no." TC's response was "well, take it or leave it". So even though the committee didn't like all the terms of the lease, they thought they would have to take it as it was in order to take advantage of the $2 million a year.[297]

At the time Moncton was the first of the medium-to small-sized airports that were going down the transfer road. Others were not far behind, but Moncton was one of the first.[298] There were others that were certainly larger than Moncton, both as a community and as an airport, but being the first Airport Authority in Atlantic Canada was difficult, frustrating, and unfair, both in terms of negotiations and in the deal that Moncton ended up with.

The TC staff were nice enough. Sometimes a few of the participants could go afterwards for a beverage at the end of the day and have a pleasant conversation. But TC had a direction that they had been given, and everybody was frustrated. The committee would go to a national meeting and everyone expressed frustration. There was certainly a sense that Moncton was getting the back of the hand.

From a labour negotiations point-of-view it was very different. One of the things that was required was that one of the Board members had to be a labour representative. The Board took that seriously and engaged Greg Murphy as its labour rep. Greg was a long-time CN worker, retired, and had been a long-time labour rep during his working career. He was active in labour issues even in retirement. And he was, the Board felt, the person who, while carrying an interest in the labour issues because of the transfer from government to private, would help the Board understand the

---

[296] Whalen.

[297] Basque.

[298] Victoria, Thunder Bay and Ottawa would also sign Agreements to Transfer that same year (1997).

challenges and work with the Board in its fiduciary responsibilities, to help move and accept and satisfy the needs on both sides. Labour negotiations, for the most part, went fairly smoothly, to a great extent because of Greg's explanations to the Board, but partially because a lot of the airport employees, knowing John Strugnell, and having worked with him, and having him deliver some of the messages, of what happens to the Moncton airport if transfer doesn't happen, were fairly amiable to the transfer, as long as they were going to be treated fairly. The labour issues at transfer were not as contentious as they were at other airports.[299]

One of the issues was the defined benefit pension plan. Employees at time of transfer were guaranteed continuation of their benefits as they were before transfer. But the Authority could not afford to put in a defined benefits pension plan going forward so it put in a defined contribution pension plan for any employee hired after transfer

Initially the transfer went quite smooth because the Authority had to guarantee everyone employment for two years. When the two years were up and it came to negotiating a new collective agreement a couple of Board members with labour experience took on the challenge and got to the 11th hour on the eve of a strike. Basque was called in to negotiate. One of the big issues was the guarantee of employment. The Authority said "look, we're a small airport. We can't continue the employment guarantee. We just want to get this thing going." So a clause was negotiated into the collective agreement that said the Authority would guarantee the jobs of all the employees who were employed at time of transfer unless one of either Air Canada or Canadian Airlines ceased operations. The union said "ah, that'll never happen" and signed the agreement.

Just a short while later, after the collective agreement was signed, Canadian Airlines went under. The Authority had the opportunity to get WestJet into Moncton and went to the union and said "look, even though the collective agreement says that job guarantees are off the table once one of either Air Canada or Canadian Airlines goes under, we are not going to use that clause, because we have WestJet here." The Authority is still reaping the

---

[299] Basque.

benefit of that to this day. And Moncton has had no strike since transfer. The only one in Canada.

Initially the union's position was to protect the jobs of the people who transferred. The Authority respected that position. It told the union that it was not trying to lay people off, it was trying to grow the airport in a responsible way. A mutual respect developed and since then there has been a very positive relationship between the union and the Authority, no question.[300]

Moncton had a very strong Board, made up of nominees from the three municipalities, the province, the federal government, the Chamber of Commerce, and the labour representative. From Day One the Board did a fair amount of work in engaging the skill sets that it felt that it needed during the investigation, during the negotiations, and during the aftermath of actually running the airport. It was a governance Board once transfer occurred. The Board had made the decision, fairly early in the negotiations, that when transfer occurred, it was not going to run the day-to-day operations of the airport. After transfer YVRAS was hired to be the managing directors of the airport. YVRAS in turn hired four individuals who were the senior management team. The Board's governance aimed at the milestones it created with the YVRAS.

Rob Robichaud was the first CEO, and made an excellent job of making the airport part of the community. Prior to his arriving as CEO the airport was something way out there in Lakeburn, where you went every now and then to take a plane. There was no connection of the airport with the community, and the Board said, very clearly, in its mind that the airport was now the number one asset that the community has. The airport has to feel, for the citizens, that it's part of the community and that the community understands where the Board was trying to go with the airport. Rob did a first class job of that, among many things.

The Board had always said that TC had no vision for the Moncton airport. That irked the Board, and it tried to make sure that its message to anyone who would listen was "this is the number one economic tool this region has, and if we let it go, or if

---

[300] Basque.

we don't help it realize its full potential, we will be the poorer for it."[301]

The Board also had the Premier of New Brunswick, Frank McKenna, on its side. He understood the vital role that the Moncton airport played in the economic development of New Brunswick, On more than one occasion, when it was suggested to him to designate the Moncton airport as **the** airport in New Brunswick, because Saint John had the port, and Fredericton, with the seat of government, with two universities and the civil service, had a built-in economic development engine, his response would be "that's never going to happen."[302] McKenna understood the importance of the airport, but did not show demonstrative favoritism of a substantial nature to Moncton. He knew the significant role that the airport played in the economy of Moncton.

Soon after the Authority took over the airport the City of Dieppe's expressed interest in developing an industrial park on the northeast side of the airport. To develop the area would require an access road along the northern border of the airport lands. When the city discussed their thoughts with the Authority the Board decided that it would be an ideal opportunity to build a new ATB.

When the Authority took over the airport the ATB was a disaster. The Chamber had complained to TC about the condition of the ATB many times, and TC's response would always be "no,no, we're not spending any money.".[303] However, within a month of the Authority taking over operations, the TC inspectors arrived at the airport and cited over 20 code violations on the ATB. It was yet another example of the Crown not able to sue itself and that TC was not subject to the same rules as the Airport Authorities. The Authority was left with little choice but to work towards a new building for it made no sense to spend millions of dollars fixing up a pig from a different generation. The decision to build anew was easy. It was also a pretty easy decision for the Province, for the tax revenue generated by the industry that has been built on

---

[301] Whalen.

[302] Ibid.

[303] Ibid.

the airport land has more than offset the cost of the road. From an economic development perspective it was a no-brainer.

Throughout the years, many renovations were made to the air terminal building. A large landing apron was constructed on the opposite side of the airport in a location which would later become the site of the new international airport terminal. This landing apron would be pressed into service in a dramatic manner on 11 September 2001 when airspace over North America was shut down following the World Trade Center attacks. A dozen flights with over 2,000 passengers were diverted to the Greater Moncton Airport.

In May 2001, the new, state-of-the-art international air terminal was completed and officially opened in 2002 by Queen Elizabeth II.

Figure 39: Moncton Airport

Since transfer the AA has spent $108 million on capital for infrastructure. It employs 142 full-time and part-time seasonal employees, and more than 390 people work at enterprises located on airport land. The AA contributes more than $430 million to the local economy every year through salaries, taxes, utilities, and other payments. It has paid more than $1.3 million in rent to the federal government since transfer and contributes more than $11 million annually to the local economy of the Greater Moncton Area.

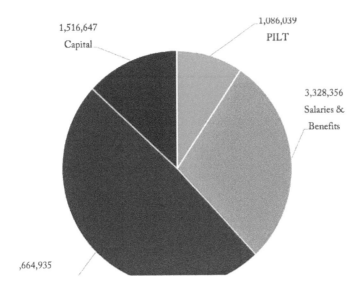

Figure 40: Spending in Moncton by the Authority - 2017

Figure 41: Image courtesy of Google Earth Pro, 6-2-2018. The pin marks the location of the original BCATP aerodrome.

Montréal has had a long association with things aeronautical, from 31 July 1879 when Charles Paige, Richard Cowan and Charles Grimley made one of the first balloon ascents in Canada, to the Aviation Meet at Lakeside[304] in 1910. The first official air mail flight was from the Bois Franc Polo Grounds[305] on 24 June 1919.

Although there was an airport at St. Hubert from 1927, by 1939 the Department of Transport (DOT) had begun to look for a better site since it was felt that the St. Hubert location was "too far from the city to make it attractive for short haul, as passengers have to spend too much time getting to and from the airport."[306]

The aerodrome at Cartierville was discounted from the outset because it was too small and hemmed in by obstructions, even

---

[304] The meet was held in Pointe Claire, QC. A memorial commemorates the site, located immediately behind the City Hall on Blvd. St. Jean.

[305] The Polo Fields were located in the area where Blvd. St. Laurent and Chemin Bois Franc merge.

[306] Canada, Department of Transport, file 5168-817, vol. 1, memo, 6 July 1939.

though the Canadian National Railway line ran right beside it giving good access to downtown.

Eventually the area where the Dorval race track was located was thought suitable. The land was flat, the site was large, and there was little habitation and no obstructions nearby. But the war intervened and although the DOT shelved any ideas of building a new airport at Dorval the Department of National Defence (DND) had need for many new airport sites through its involvement with the British Commonwealth Air Training Plan (BCATP). The site at Dorval met those needs admirably. On 20 May 1940 the BCATP asked the DND for a site near St. Hubert for a wireless training school. The DOT suggested to the DND "a site under consideration as a civil airport to serve Montréal, with a view to possible development to make the aerodrome suitable for Wireless School Aircraft and an Elementary Flying Training School, the balance of development necessary to meet Transport requirements to be carried out after the war."[307]

An Order-in-Council of 24 December 1940 said:

"to develop an airport at Dorval for an Air Observer School and Wireless School under the British Commonwealth Air Training Plan, the said airport to be developed also as a Civil Air Terminal for the metropolitan area of Montréal in place of St. Hubert airport which is now used for that purpose and which would then be placed at the disposal of the Department of National Defence for use as an aerodrome for a Service Training School under the Commonwealth Air Training Plan, the cost of the work at Dorval to be borne jointly by the Department of Transport and the Department of National Defence in accordance with the interest of each Department, taking into consideration the transfer of the St. Hubert Airport to the Department of National Defence".[308]

Fifteen hundred acres of land were purchased. The first contract to build infrastructure was awarded to Dibblee Construction Company on 10 October 1940 with completion by August 1941. The contractor was to build a classic BCATP triangular runway

---

[307] Canada, Department of Transport, file 5168-817, vol. 2, memo, 20 May 1940.

[308] Canada, Department of Transport, file 5168-817, vol. 4.

configuration of three paved runways, each 4,000 by 200 feet (1 219 m by 61 m), capable of being extended to 5,000 (1 524 m).[309]

In a statement to *The Montréal Star* on 25 October 1940, the controller of Civil Aviation said that it was necessary to acquire such a large piece of land since "the Dorval site is so near the city that it is essential to secure enough property to provide for future developments and prevent the building of homes, facilities and other obstructions in the immediate neighbourhood of the flightways."[310]

The airport opened on 1 September 1941, 10½ months from contract signing to end of construction! During construction the BCATP had requested changes to the runway lengths, with the final configuration as:

- One N-S runway   5,270 x 200 feet (1 606 x 61 m)
- One E-W runway   5,000 x 200 feet (1 524 x 61 m)
- One NE-SW runway   5,000 x 200 feet (1 524 x 61 m)

However, Dorval was not to be used by the BCATP as their plans had changed in the interim and instead the facilities meant for them were handed over to the Royal Air Force Ferry Command. At the same time all civilian operations at St. Hubert were transferred to Dorval, with St. Hubert becoming a strictly military airport for DND.

The conditions under which Ferry Command occupied Dorval were set out in a letter dated 26 May 1941:

"H. M. Long, Esq.
Ministry of Aircraft Production, United Kingdom
Royal Bank Building
Montréal, Québec

Dear Mr. Long:

Thank you for your letter of My 23ʳᵈ, accepting responsibility on behalf of the Ministry of Aircraft Production for an estimated sum of $1,385,640, covering the original commitment of the BCATP,

---

[309] *History*, p. 147.

[310] Canada, Department of Transport, file 5151-817, vol. 1, 25 October 1940.

now transferred to the Ministry, and compensation for extensions to runways, etc., detailed estimates, which are to be submitted by this Department to your office in due course.

I confirm that the above figure is an estimate and that, when the actual cost of construction is known, financial adjustment will be made in accordance with this. Action has been taken to authorize Dibblee Construction Company to proceed immediately with the extensions and revisions in the specifications in regard to strengthening the pavements, etc., and work will proceed with the utmost vigor to completion.

It is also agreed that the use of the airport will be limited to civil air transport operations and trans-Atlantic flying and will not be used for other purposes without the joint consent of this Department and your Ministry; further, that your Ministry shall have the right to erect, at its own expense under conditions acceptable to this Department, any buildings, hangars, etc., necessary for the conduct of your operations, and that any structures erected for this purpose will be part of your Majesty's equity in this airport, such equity to be the subject of negotiation between the Canadian and British governments at the close of hostilities, when a general adjustment of accounts between the two governments is effected.

Yours faithfully,

C. P. Edwards,
Deputy Minister"[311]

This understanding was later formalized by agreements between the Canadian and United Kingdom governments in Agreement No. 32705 July 30, 1941, and Amendments No. 31149 January 26, 1943, and No. 35939 June 5, 1944.[312]

Ferry Command became the largest operation by far at the Dorval airport. They built three large hangars (the last of which was demolished in 2012), a headquarters administration building, numerous small operations buildings, and were responsible for the

---

[311] Pubic Archives Canada, J. A. Wilson Papers, MG30 E243, vol. 9.

[312] Pubic Archives Canada, RG 24 5240, file 19-55-1, vol 2.

fire crash and ambulance services and airport security. DOT maintained and managed the airport, including the control tower. Trans-Canada Air Lines (TCA) built its own hangar.

The civilian Air Terminal Building (ATB) opened in December 1941 with a curved front that resembled the ATB at Washington National Airport.[313]

Originally there were six hangars on the airport: no. 1 was built by the DOT and leased to TCA; no. 2 was built by TCA and later sold to Québecair; nos. 3, 4 and 5 were built by Ferry Command and had a total of 12 bays; no. 6 was built by the RCAF and was destroyed by fire in 1956.[314]

In June 1944 Ferry Command handed over all its infrastructure to TC "without compensation" on the understanding that it would enjoy use of the facilities until six months after the end of the war and that TC would maintain the airport at the appropriate standard.[315]

As an indication of the level of activities at the time, *The Montréal Star* reported on 8 September 1945 that four airlines operating 22 schedules and handling 500 passengers a day were using Dorval. More than 10,000 aircraft had been delivered from Montréal during the war, and there had been more than 20,000 trans-Atlantic communications flights.

When the war ended in August 1945 the transition to full civilian service began. Since 1941 TCA, Canadian Colonial Airlines, Northeast Airlines and Québec Airways had been operating at Dorval. Canadian Pacific Airlines began operations from Dorval in 1942. BOAC had operated the Return Ferry Service to England for the RAF Ferry Command since May 1941, and TCA had operated the Canadian Government Trans-Atlantic Air Service (CGTAS) since July 1943. BOAC's service was demilitarized in September 1946, and CGTAS demilitarized in May 1947. Both companies began to offer commercial transatlantic scheduled services from the former RAF Transport Command

---

[313] John Stroud, *Airports of the World*, Putnam, 1980, p. 57.

[314] *History*, p. 149.

[315] Pubic Archives Canada, RG 24 5240, file 19-55-1, vol 2, 5 June 1944.

administration building; the main terminal was used for domestic traffic.

On 16 February 1946 the DOT took over the buildings, hangars and facilities, valued about $4.5 million, in a transfer made by Air Vice Marshal G.R. Beamish (Air Officer Commanding, Transport Command No. 45, Group RAF) to C.P. Edwards, Deputy Minister, DOT. The RAF Group disbanded at midnight that same day. During the hand-over Beamish presented a bronze plaque to the deputy minister to commemorate the work of both the civil organizations and the RAF Transport Command formations that had been based there.[316]

The permanent airport licence for Dorval, no. 231, was issued 11 December 1946.

Air traffic began to increase dramatically following WW2. In 1946 a total of 246,359 passengers passed through Dorval. Bilateral agreements with other countries saw more and more airlines landing at Dorval: BOAC (1946); KLM (1949); Air France (1950); Lufthansa (1956); SAS (1957); Sabena (1957); and Alitalia (1960). By 1952 passenger loading was 589,216 annually.

A new terminal opened in December 1960 which eased congestion greatly.[317]

Dorval airport is associated with several "firsts" in airport operations:

- Ground transportation: on 1 September 1941 the Murray Hill Limousine Service was granted the first ground transportation concession at any Canadian airport. It provided ground transportation between Dorval and downtown Montréal.
- Restaurant: the Canada Railway News Co. operated the Tea Wing Restaurant in the original terminal – the first airport restaurant in Canada.
- Airport hotel: the Canada Railway News Co. also operated the nearby Dorval Inn, used by crews from Ferry Command. The

---

[316] *History*, p.149.

[317] Transport Canada built five identical terminals across Canada: Gander, Montréal, Toronto, Edmonton and Vancouver. The only one left standing is at Gander which, complete with 1950's chrome furniture and equipment, is now used for period movies.

company paid TC 5% of gross revenues for the use of the concession.

- Liquor License: the first liquor license to an establishment in a Canadian airport was to the Montréal Airport Restaurant and Bar, in 1956.
- Flight kitchen: the Canada Railway News Co. operated the first flight kitchen at any Canadian airport. Opened in 1941, adjacent to the RAF Ferry Command mess. Prior to that meals had been prepared at the Bonaventure Railway Station in downtown Montréal. Ferry crews were pleased with the change.

Although not a "first" in Canada, the Tilden Drive Yourself company received the first car rental concession at Dorval in 1952. It was an exclusive concession and, at the time, Tilden was a Hertz licensee. In 1953 Tilden left the Hertz organization but because the concession was in Tilden's name it continued as Tilden-Rent-A-Car. Hertz received a concession in 1957 and Avis in 1959.

The first car parking concession at Dorval was granted to Stanley Realty Co. (a subsidiary of Tilden) in 1952.

In March 1948 TCA announced it would soon introduce its DC-4M North Star aircraft on the North Atlantic route and expressed concern about passenger congestion at the existing terminal. BOAC was soon to introduce Constellations. Already two aircraft would arrive simultaneously and caused overcrowding at the Inspection Service. "Peaking" was a problem and the airlines were asked to revise their schedules.[318]

On 27 January 1950 the District Inspector for Eastern Airways (that was a staff position in the DOT – not the American airline) recommended to headquarters in Ottawa that consideration be given to the problem of jet aircraft noise that could be anticipated at the Dorval airport. His concern was prophetic, for the first noise complaint was received from Pointe Claire on 18 May 1951, but it was not for a jet aircraft.[319] The problem worsened and on 9 September 1959 the City of Dorval asked the DOT to prohibit jet

---

[318] Peaking is a problem that has not gone away.

[319] *History*, p. 150.

aircraft from operations during "normal sleeping hours". The DOT then did some studies at Dorval, Toronto and Winnipeg and, as a result of those studies, in 1960 implemented noise abatement procedures between the hours of midnight to 0700. The noise problem was one factor which led to the decision to build a new airport at Mirabel rather than expand Dorval.

By 22 January 1952 the two main runways had been lengthened to 7,000 feet (2 059 m).

In May 1952 Colonial Airlines and Northeast Airlines expressed an interest in having pre-clearance inspections (provided by the U.S. Inspection Services) established at Montréal. Such pre-clearance was working well in Toronto (for American Airlines) and Colonial and Northeast saw the facility in Toronto as a competitive threat. The DOT said "no" since the ATB was overcrowded. Colonial and Northeast ignored the DOT and on 23 November 1953 U.S. Immigration staff arrived and began working at the airline counters. One year later, on 22 December 1954, the Deputy Minister of the DOT ordered the pre-clearance to stop until new facilities could be provided and in February 1955 the airlines were told to discontinue pre-clearance. The travelling public had a different idea. They liked the possibility of clearing U.S. customs and immigration in Montréal and then going to any airport in the U.S. served by the airline. Consequently, the airlines ignored the order and in April 1955 the Department agreed to let pre-clearance continue on an "interim" basis.[320]

A new terminal building was begun in 1956. It was badly needed, for in that year Dorval was the busiest airport in Canada with 1,092,000 passengers. Unfortunately, the decision to build a new ATB was a bit of a knee-jerk reaction to the airlines and the new aircraft coming into use and construction began before all of the users and all of their needs were considered. Consequently the construction costs rose dramatically through the many major design changes imposed by the airlines, DOT and the concessionaires as construction progressed. As one design engineering company owner said "Those change orders made me a rich man."

---

[320] Ibid. p. 151.

The completed terminal finally opened in December 1960 as the newly renamed Montréal International Airport. It had cost more than $30 million and at that time "was one of the largest and finest air terminals in the world."[321] It had been planned to accommodate growth in airlines and passengers well into the future. It had several restaurants and bars, and many shops, in accordance with DOT's new airports concessions policy aimed at increasing non-aeronautical revenue.

By 1968 passenger loads were at 4.5 million per year and the airport was suffering. A long-term planning study[322] found that over the next 20 years:

- airline passenger traffic would double every eight years;
- air cargo volumes would double every three to four years;
- general aviation traffic would double every ten years;
- 10,000 people were employed in the aviation industry in metropolitan Montréal in 1968. That number was expected to grow to 40,000 by 1985;
- By 1985 the airport would need 7,500 acres (3 037 hectares) for aviation activities, plus a reserve of 2,500 acres (1 012 hectares) for future use. It currently occupied 3,900 acres (1 325 hectares);
- Air activities would have to occur 24 hours per day to accommodate the growth in air traffic;
- Noise disturbance to neighbouring towns would only grow. A night curfew was already in effect and would be difficult to remove.

The study had two solutions: move the people away from the airport, or move the airport away from the people. Moving the people was considered a political disaster right from the outset as it would mean expropriating more than 6,000 acres (2 470 hectares) of land from the adjacent cities of Dorval, Pointe Claire and St. Laurent. The only other choice was to build a new airport far enough away from current population centres and where there was

---

[321] Ibid.

[322] Madeleine Lasnier, *Aeroport International de Montréal / Montréal International Airport (Dorval)*, Department of Transport (Québec Region), September 1968, pp. 10, 12, 22, 26, 28.

land to accommodate the foreseen growth. Also, going far out into the country meant there would be relatively few people who might be bothered by the noise, and even if they were they would not have a large enough political voice to do anything about it.

Building a new airport meant that Dorval could continue for use by short-haul inter-city aircraft, by business and general aviation aircraft, and for aircraft maintenance and servicing (in 1958 Air Canada had built a large maintenance base in the northeast part of the airport). Air traffic would be more evenly spaced out during the day and the night curfew could be maintained. After much discussion, a new Montréal International Airport was built at Mirabel. It opened in 1975.

Although in 1960 the new terminal building was thought to be sufficient for demand well into the future, by 1975 Dorval was failing in many ways. The 800,000 sq ft (74 320 sq m) air terminal building had to accommodate domestic, trans-border and international air traffic, airline operations and administration, airport management, U.S. and Canadian customs and immigration, weather, air traffic control, restaurants and shops. It had 38 aircraft gates, and parking for 2,400 cars. By 1989 there were 44 aircraft gates and parking for 5,700 cars.

Air Canada installed its first passenger loading bridge in December 1966.

In May 1970 Air France landed its first Boeing 747 at Dorval. The sudden influx of so many passengers at once overwhelmed the facilities and demonstrated the need for expansion to accommodate such large single aircraft loads.

By 1975 more than 8 million passengers used the Dorval airport and there were more than 10 million visitors. 14,000 employees worked at the airport, either for the DOT or for the many businesses occupying airport land.

When Mirabel began operations in October 1975 all international air traffic for passengers and air cargo destined to Montréal was moved there, leaving domestic and transborder air traffic at Dorval. The intent was that Mirabel would grow substantially and by 1995 be operating a near full capacity for the runways and terminal already built. However, the amount of land available was enormous[323] and expansion for five additional terminals and four more runways was not an issue.

As with the best-laid plans of mice and men, that did not occur.

In hindsight there were several reasons why Mirabel never achieved its potential, even though many pilots thought it "the best airport to land at and take off from".[324] The energy crisis of the 1970's affected airline operations dramatically. The political issues of the Parti Québecois and the passage of Bill 101 in 1975 greatly affected the English-speaking community and many businesses moved down Highway 401 to Toronto. The provincial government failed to build a promised rail link.

But perhaps the most important issue was Mirabel's loss of status as the sole eastern gateway to Europe as other bi-lateral agreements were established at other Canadian airports. In return for Canadian air carriers to land at European gateways, Canada had to allow the European air carriers landing rights at airports other than Mirabel. Almost immediately passenger traffic patterns changed dramatically, as passengers previously landing at Mirabel and then transferring to a domestic carrier to fly to Toronto, now could fly directly to Toronto. Also, the longer range of newer aircraft now allowed direct flights from Europe to the western cities of Winnipeg, Edmonton, Calgary and Vancouver.

In 1980 Canadair (now Bombardier) built an aircraft assembly plant in centre field, near the Air Canada maintenance hangar.

In 1985 the Québec Regional office of TC moved from the old RAF Transport Command hangar it had occupied since the end of WW2 into new offices located west of the ATB parking lot. The old RAF hangar was demolished immediately and the space freed up used for aircraft parking.

The Authority

Montréal was always different[325], especially when the federal government decided in 1966 that there would be two airports

---

[323] 97,000 acres (39 250 hectares).

[324] Clint Ward, Air Canada Captain, interview with the author, 15 November 2018.

[325] Jean-Jacques Bourgault, interview, 2 October 2018.

serving the Montréal area: Dorval and Mirabel. Unfortunately the provincial government never did build the high-speed rail link to connect the two airports. Federal government policy was that Mirabel would handle the International traffic and Dorval the domestic and trans-border traffic.

The Québec government was never interested nor involved in the airport at Dorval, only in the airport at Québec City. Not like in Ontario where the Provincial government had an active involvement and interest in Pearson. Under the Québec Liberal government of Daniel Johnson and also the Québec PQ government of Jacques Parizeau there was never any interest shown in the formation of the AA. But the local municipal politics showed some interest – Dorval, Montréal, Laval, Mirabel. Also the Board of Trade.

In 1986, convinced as they were by the importance of the Dorval and Mirabel airports, a small group of politicians from the greater Montréal area and representatives of the business community, led by the mayor of Montréal, Jean Doré, went to Ottawa to urge the Minister of Transport to allow the transfer of the Dorval and Mirabel airports to an LAA. They were not alone as organizing groups from Vancouver, Edmonton and Calgary were also urging the federal government to allow LAAs. The work of these four groups of concerned citizens caused the federal Minister of Transport to announce the policy of airport devolution on 9 April 1987.

The political and economic fortunes of the Montréal region were quick to react to the opening created by the federal government and, on December 4, 1987, a group of concerned citizens formed what would become the Société de promotion des aéroports de Montréal (SOPRAM), a regional consultative body involved in the care and development of both airports. SOPRAM was made up of members appointed by the following organizations:

- the city of Montréal - Marcel Lesieur and John Gardiner;
- the city of Laval – Gilles Vaillancourt and Lucien Desrochers;
- the Conference of Suburban Mayors – Peter Yeomans and André Gamache;
- the Montréal Metropolitan Chamber of Commerce – Jacques Ménard and Luc Lacharité;
- the Montréal Board of Trade – John Pepper and Alex Harper;

-   the Corporation for the Promotion of Mirabel (COPAM) –
    Hubert Meilleur and André Gamache; and,
-   the Mirabel and Montérégie Development Corporation jointly
    with the City of Longueuil – Pierre D. Girard and Claude
    Bachand.

As it had done with the organizing committees of the Edmonton,
Calgary and Vancouver LAAs, TC lent SOPRAM $100,000 to
form the LAA.

SOPRAM worked hard through the next two years and, in 1989,
incorporated a not-for-profit company, the Aéroports de Montréal
(ADM), as a local airport authority mandated to negotiate with
the federal government for the assumption of responsibility for the
Dorval and Mirabel airports and, subsequently, for their
management and development. It also had to involve the mayors
of Mirabel, St-Laurent, Pointe-Claire and Dorval and keep them
apprised of the negotiations.

On 31 July 1989 ADM signed a letter of intent with Benoit
Bouchard, Minister of Transport to transfer the operations and
management of the Dorval and Mirabel airports from TC to the
ADM.

The Air Transport Association of Canada (ATAC) was very
concerned with the ability of SOPRAM to finance the transfer.
However SOPRAM kept its cards close to its vest and eventually
ATAC realized that the airport was a monopoly and would have
no trouble raising money.

One major issue to resolve was that of provincial and municipal
taxation. Under TC's management the federal government would
make Payments in Lieu of Taxes (PILT) to the local municipality.
In the case of Dorval airport this was about $7.7 million in 1990.
However, the provincial government had informed the ADM that
the new amount to be paid to the province, the municipalities and
the school board would be in the region of $20.7 million a year.[326]

---

[326] As it turned out, the provincial and municipal governments gave the ADM no
relief from PILT. Consequently, today the ADM pays the highest PILT of any
AA in the country: $40.2 million in 2017.

Not very many people involved at the beginning understood the economic benefits the airport brings to the local communities.

Eventually the LAA had to merge the management of the two airports. The intent was to use Mirabel to create the biggest economic centre in the region but that didn't work out.

The creation of ADM was the result of a long-standing regional dialogue that was part of a broader societal project aimed at bringing regional business management closer to local decision-makers. The transfer of the airport to ADM was an extraordinary opportunity for the greater Montréal region to take over strategic assets essential to its economic development.

The ADM had to undertake an enormous amount of work as due diligence prior to takeover. Over a period of three years it conducted the following:

- offers of employment and conditions of employment to 550 public servants (250 at Dorval, 250 at Mirabel, and 50 office staff);
- traffic forecast and study by Peat Marwick;
- airport capacity study by Sypher Mueller;
- infrastructure repairs and improvements study by Bouthillette, Parizeau and Assoc (mechanical, electrical); Dessau Inc, (civil) and Lemay and Assoc (architecture);
- rapid transit study – Dorval Mirabel, by Samson, Belair, Deloitte, Touche;
- insurance and risk analysis by Wyatt;
- municipal taxation study by Martineau Walker, Samson, Belair, Deloitte, Touche
- research study on airport financing by Richardson Greenshields;
- tax statutes study by Martineau Walker
- management information systems study by Samson, Belair, Deloitte Touche; and
- study of the future organization and evaluation of senior management positions.

The ADM assumed responsibility for the Dorval and Mirabel airports on 1 August 1992. It was not lost on the ADM that the situation with respect to passengers arriving and departing from the Dorval and Mirabel airports was a situation requiring the utmost effort and expediency to resolve.

There was a 17-year history to unravel.

When Mirabel was built and international passengers began arriving in 1975, it was not long before passengers realized that they had a long and tedious transfer to Dorval for any continuing domestic flight. And domestic passengers arriving at Dorval had a longer and more tedious transfer to Mirabel for their international flight since those flights almost always left at the evening rush hour time and the road route to Mirabel was usually jammed with highway traffic. This fact took a long time for management in the TC Québec Regional Office to appreciate through the late 1970's and all through the 1980's. They could not believe that their building Mirabel had been a mistake.

Eventually the management at ADM successfully overcame the errors and mistakes it inherited in 1992 and was able to put in place a management regime to develop and enhance services at Dorval far in excess of what TC had thought possible in the 1980's.

The first CEO, and the first permanent employee of the ADM, was Jacques G. Auger. He was supported by a Board consisting of:

-   Arthur P. Earle, Chair
-   Claude Lefebvre, Vice-Chair
-   Paul-Yvon Lesage, Treasurer
-   Nycol Pageau, Member
-   Gordon Fehr, Member
-   Normand Guérette, Member

Jacques Auger also performed the duties of Secretary to the Board.

The $716 million expansion of Dorval from 2000 to 2005 gave it the ability to serve 20 million passengers a year, accomplishing one of the goals that was to be met with the construction of Mirabel. (In the 1970s, the federal government projected that 20 million passengers would be passing through Montréal's airports annually by 1985, with 17 million through Mirabel). Aéroports de Montréal financed all of these improvements itself, with no government grants.

As an economic engine to the local community, the AAs impact is felt far beyond the walls of its terminal. Direct employment at the airport was 26,800 full-time jobs in 2015 and throughout the region another 27,900 full-time jobs are attributed to the airport. This number of jobs brings $5.4 billion in consumer spending to Montréal each year from employment alone. In 2017 the ADM paid $40.2 million in property taxes to the City of Montréal and $61.4 million in rent to the federal government. Total spending in 2017 by the ADM in the greater Montréal was in excess of $448 million.

Over the 2018-2022 period, ADM expects to invest close to $2.5 billion to increase capacity to respond to growth in volume and to renovate or rebuild end-of-life infrastructure. This investment will greatly increase the value of the infrastructure assets (and also its tax base).

Figure 42: Montreal Trudeau Airport (Dorval)

The Montréal-Trudeau airport will soon reach a volume of 20 million passengers. Even though the ADM recently inaugurated a new international jetty this passenger volume will most likely mean the AA will have to construct a new ATB.

ADM will begin work in 2019 to connect the terminal building to the Réseau express métropolitain (REM). This mass transit rail

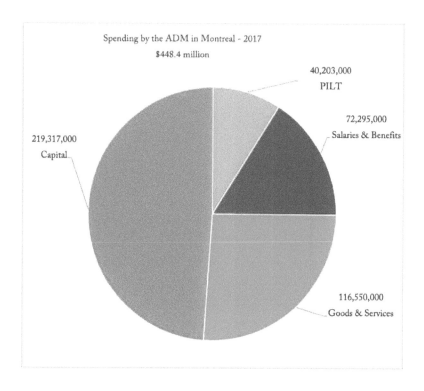

Spending by the ADM in Montreal - 2017
$448.4 million

40,203,000
PILT

72,295,000
Salaries & Benefits

219,317,000
Capital

116,550,000
Goods & Services

Figure 44: Image courtesy of Google Earth Pro, 9-21-2017.

In 1966 TC began a study[327] on the aviation needs of the Montréal area over the next 25 to 35 years. The study established that the existing airport at Dorval would be at capacity by 1975 and, even if expanded, would meet that expanded capacity by 1985. If greater expansion than was possible was needed there was no more land, and the acquisition of land to meet any greater need would be very expensive indeed.

Consequently the federal government entered into a series of negotiations with the Provincial government as to the location of a new airport to serve Montréal. Several options were considered and presented: Saint-Jean-sur-Richelieu 31 miles (50 km) to the southeast), Vaudreuil-Dorion 25 miles (40 km) to the west), Joliette 43 miles (70 km) to the north), St-Amable 19 miles (30 km) to the southeast), and Ste-Scholastique 37 miles (60 km) to the northwest).

---

[327] Lasnier.

The federal government proposed that the airport should be located at Vaudreuil-Dorion. Not only was it well served by existing road and rail routes, but it was close enough to both Ottawa and Montréal to serve as the gateway for both cities[328]. However, Québec provincial Premier Robert Bourassa, who had a frosty relationship with the federal Prime Minister Pierre Trudeau, reportedly did not want such an important project to be placed so

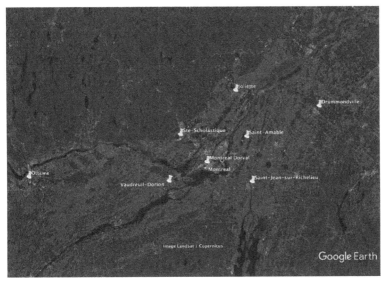

Figure 46: Locations of a new airport for Montreal as proposed in 1966. The location at Ste-Scholastique was eventually chosen for Mirabel.

close to the Ontario border. The Bourassa government preferred that the new airport be situated in Drummondville (100 km (62 mi) to the east).

In March 1969 the federal and provincial governments reached a compromise to locate at the Ste-Scholastique site, and proposals were drawn up to expropriate 97,000 acres (39,250 hectares), an area larger than the entire city of Montréal. This area is served only by a long road link via Autoroute 15 and Autoroute 50. An additional link via Autoroute 13 was planned but never completed. Also planned was the connection of Autoroute 50 to the

---

[328] However some pilots thought that the best location would have been somewhere in eastern Ontario, near the Ontario-Québec border and about halfway between Montréal and Ottawa.

Ottawa/Gatineau area, a goal which would not be achieved until decades later, in 2012.

The federal government expropriation resulted in making Mirabel the world's largest airport by property area. (King Fahd International Airport near Dammam in Saudi Arabia later surpassed Mirabel as the world's largest airport by property area, a record it still retains). The airport's operations zone, which encompassed what was eventually built plus expansion room, amounted to only 6,880 hectares (17,000 acres), about 19% of the total area of the airport. The federal government planned to use the excess land as a noise buffer and as an industrial development zone. This attracted the ire of the people of Ste-Scholastique who protested vehemently against the expropriation of their land. Nevertheless, construction started in June 1970 under the auspices of BANAIM, a government organization formed to build the airport.

High-speed rail transit (the system was to be capable of speeds from 100 to 120 kilometres per hour (62 to 75 mph) for the Montréal–Mirabel run), initially to be called TRRAMM (Transport Rapide Régional Aéroportuaire Montréal–Mirabel), was intended to be completed at a later date. However, it never got beyond the drawing board. The TRRAMM system was also intended to eventually be expanded to other parts of the Montréal region. The major stumbling block for the TRRAMM project was funding. The federal, provincial, and municipal governments never managed to find enough cash to fund the highly ambitious and expensive rapid transit project. Thus, Mirabel was forced to cope with an inadequate road system and non-existent rail transit, supplemented only by express buses.

Montréal–Mirabel International Airport opened for business on October 4, 1975, in time for the 1976 Summer Olympics. In the rush to get the airport open in time for the Olympics, it was decided to transfer flights to Mirabel in two stages. International flights were transferred immediately, while domestic and US flights would continue to be served by Dorval airport until 1982.

Transport Canada had predicted that Dorval would be completely saturated by 1985 as part of its justification for building Mirabel. It also projected that 20 million passengers would be passing through Montréal's airports annually, with 17 million of those through

Mirabel. However, three factors dramatically reduced the amount of projected air traffic into Dorval: long-range jets; cheaper jet fuel; and poor policy.

After 1976, Mirabel and Dorval began to decline in importance because of the increasing use in the 1980s of longer-range jets that did not need to refuel in Montréal before crossing the Atlantic; the use of longer-range aircraft was made more attractive by national energy policies that provided Montréal refineries with feedstock at prices substantially below world prices, starting in 1975 and ending in the 1980s with the drop in world oil prices.

In addition, the simultaneous operation of Mirabel for international flights and Dorval for continental flights made Montréal less attractive to international airlines. A European passenger who wanted to travel to another destination in Canada or fly to the United States had to take an hour-long bus ride from Mirabel to Dorval. The complicated transfer process put Montréal at a significant disadvantage. The planned but unbuilt highways and incomplete train routes compounded the problem. The international airlines responded by shifting their routes to Toronto. There was also the issue of Air Canada's desire to keep flights in Dorval so as to be close to their workshops and connections to Pearson Airport.

By 1991, Mirabel and Dorval were handling only a total of 8 million passengers and 112,000 tons of cargo annually, while Toronto was handling 18.5 million passengers and 312,000 tons of cargo. Mirabel alone never managed to exceed 3 million passengers per year in its existence as a passenger airport. It soon became apparent that Montréal did not need a second airport.

To ensure Mirabel's survival, all international flights for Montréal were banned from Dorval from 1975 to 1997. However, public pressure in support of Dorval prevented its planned closure. As a result, Dorval's continued existence made Mirabel comparatively expensive and unattractive to airlines and travellers alike. While Dorval was only 20 minutes away from the city core, it took 50 minutes to get to Mirabel even in ideal traffic conditions. Passengers who used Montréal in transit had to take long bus rides for connections from domestic to international flights, and Montréalers grew to resent Mirabel as they were forced to travel far out of town for international flights.

Many international airlines, faced with the stark economic reality of operating two Canadian points of entry, opted to bypass Montréal altogether by landing instead in Toronto with its better domestic and American connections. The simultaneous operating of both Montréal airports resulted in Dorval being overtaken in traffic first by Toronto, then Vancouver and finally relegated to fourth by Calgary, as international airlines were slow to return to Dorval after it resumed handling international flights in 1997. Only Air Transat held out at Mirabel until the very end, operating the last commercial flight which departed to Paris on October 31, 2004.

Over time, the decreasing passenger flights began to take a toll on businesses within Mirabel.

Various incentives were tried to get Mirabel going[329], including minimal fees to get cargo planes to land there, and no fees for technical flights, but, at the end of the day, Mirabel was just not meant to be. ADM did a study at Mirabel, with Doug Wilson of Sypher Mueller from Ottawa, because all of a sudden Mirabel was losing all its carriers, such as KLM, who were going to pull out of Montréal. Their load factors were high, but they were getting no yield.

At about that time Robert Milton, Air Canada VP Marketing under Hollis Harris, was walking with Benoit through the Dorval terminal discussing various ideas about Dorval and Mirabel, and Milton suggested turning Mirabel into a super-hub, of bringing aircraft in from airports all over North America and Europe.[330] That didn't happen.

So ADM thought "what are we going to do with this place?" The study brought forth some interesting facts:

- Montréal had far more service than it deserved, in terms of the market size for Montréal and its surrounding area. The former bi-laterals had caused a great deal of traffic into Dorval. If you were going to fly into Canada you had to stop at Dorval.

[329] Paul Benoit, interview with the author, 30 November 2018.

[330] Ibid.

- The DC-8's in use at that time could not make it all the way to the west coast and so they had to stop to re-fuel. KLM had a flight: Amsterdam, Montréal, Houston, Mexico. Essentially Dorval was a combination destination/fuel stop.

- The economic decline of Québec and Montréal due to the political situation, the rise of the nationalist Parti Québecois, and Bill 101 (the Act which made French the official language of the Province). Maybe there was going to even be a border crossing at the Ontario-Québec border? Who knew? When Canadian Pacific Railways, the Royal Bank of Canada, the pharmaceutical companies, and several hundred other companies left, they took thousands of jobs and people with them.

So at the end of the study it came down to "we've got two plants here, both running at less than 50%. What do we do?" Benoit recommended that all airport operations be moved to Mirabel and the land at Dorval sold for housing. That was not the final decision, influenced in great part by Air Canada and the 4,000 folk they had working at their maintenance base in Dorval. For Air Canada, making domestic passengers take ground transport of over an hour to Mirabel was uncompetitive. And having to ferry planes to and from Mirabel to Dorval for maintenance was insane. The cost as well to split manpower both on the ground and in the air was killing the profitability of Air Canada of operating in Mirabel.[331]

ADM said "OK, we're going to allow carriers their own choice as to which airport they will service".[332] That decision essentially bid one airport goodbye. Which is what happened and all passenger traffic had ceased at Mirabel by 2004. As it turned out, there is now more employment at Mirabel, due to the aerospace industries there, than there was when it was a passenger terminal. But at the time it was hard.

A major issue was that if a passenger was trying to make connections from Winnipeg to Heathrow, through Dorval and Mirabel, they had to pick up their bag in Dorval, get it to a bus,

---

[331] Bill Bredt, email, 15 January 2019.

[332] Benoit.

battle the rush-hour traffic on Hwy 13 or Hwy 15 to Mirabel, because most of the planes left Mirabel at 7 or 8 in the evening, and then have to re-check their bag in Mirabel. It just wasn't viable. The whole story of Mirabel was that the plan was never followed. The original plan was to move the international carriers from Dorval to Mirabel, then the U.S. carriers, then finally the longer-haul, domestic carriers. The will wasn't there to go to Step 2 and then Step 3 so Mirabel got stranded out in the middle of nowhere. Because if the federal and provincial governments had actually followed through with the plan for Mirabel, Ottawa was going to become a feeder for Mirabel by means of a high-speed trains from Ottawa to Mirabel, and from Montréal to Mirabel, then Mirabel would have had a chance. As it turned out, Mirabel had no chance whatsoever as soon as it became a political issue.[333]

At the beginning the Authority was running buses from Mirabel to Ottawa. It started with British Airways and their Canadian Director, Tony Searsley, as he wanted to attack the Ottawa market. Tony said "what if we put a bus in there?"[334] At this time the BA flight used to go London, Montréal, Detroit. And the beauty was that the plane would land in Mirabel at 1400 hrs and by 1500 hrs you had the passengers for Ottawa on the bus on their way. Now the plane would go on to Detroit, spend a couple of hours there, and come back to Mirabel. By that time the bus had dropped all the passengers in Ottawa, loaded passengers for London, driven back to Mirabel, and they would be in the ATB ready to board the plane which departed early evening for the overnight flight back to London, and arrive there early the next morning. The brilliance of this was that the bus cost $475, and Mirabel got a bus load of passengers who normally would have flown out of Ottawa. The Authority got an award from TC, called Top Hat, under Dave McQuarrie, for the idea. When Benoit went to Ottawa in 1996, that was one of the first questions the Board asked him "who the hell came up with the idea of stealing passengers from Ottawa?"

The Authority also looked at the possibility of a train from Ottawa to Mirabel. The problem was that the tracks were on the wrong

---

[333] Ibid.

[334] Ibid.

side of the Ottawa river. The Authority wanted a system such as exists in Switzerland, where you can bring your bags to any station and they are checked through to your destination. The idea was that a passenger would arrive at the Ottawa train station, check their bags, take a train to Mirabel, board their plane, and pick up their bags at their final destination.

By 2005 passengers no longer used the Mirabel airport.

In 2014 the terminal building and its parking structures were demolished.

Today, Montréal–Mirabel International Airport is used almost exclusively for cargo flights, with passenger operations having ceased on October 31, 2004, 29 years after the airport's opening and many years of limited, primarily charter service.

The Authority

Mirabel is operated by the airport authority: Aéroports de Montréal (ADM).

Figure 47: Image courtesy of Google Earth Pro, 6-1-2018. The pin marks the location of the original BCATP aerodrome.

While the first powered flight over Ottawa occurred in 1911, it would be nearly the 1920's before the landing field at Bowesville Road would become known as the Hunt Club Field.

Early in its history, the Hunt Club Field made its mark in aviation when, on July 2, 1927, twelve P-1 airplanes under command of Major Thomas G. Lanphier, United States Air Corps, proceeded from Selfridge Field (Harrison Township, Michigan) to Ottawa, acting as Special Escort for Colonel Charles Lindbergh, who was to attend the opening of the Dominion Jubilee (the 50th Anniversary of Confederation). Col Lindbergh arrived in his "Spirit of St. Louis" Ryan N-X-211, landing on the small field, welcomed by some 60,000 spectators. Tragedy occurred when First Lieutenant J. Thad Johnson, Air Corps, commanding 27th Pursuit Squadron, was killed in an unsuccessful parachute jump after a collision with another plane of the formation on arrival over Ottawa.

With the incorporation of the Ottawa Flying Club on January 14th, 1928, the industry gained momentum; the first airport licence was granted to the Club on July 26th of the same year, and

251

the airfield's name was once again changed – this time to the Uplands Aerodrome.

In November 1936, the first Ministry of Transport was formed by the federal government, with C.D. Howe at the helm. Minister Howe was tasked with developing connections to the rest of the country and with the British Commonwealth. To accomplish this daunting task, he established Trans-Canada Airlines in April 1937. The success of Trans-Canada was contingent on establishing a cross-country service, which would require suitable landing fields along the way. The Ottawa Flying Club, not financially able to make the necessary improvements to the landing strip, eventually abandoned the site. Fortunately, Laurentian Air Services, one of the oldest bush flying services in Canada, saved the day when they leased the airfield site in 1937.

Over the next few years, enhancements were made to the site by Laurentian Air, including a hangar and other facilities, and the Ottawa Flying Club returned to the site under an extended lease. Ultimately, the work required to serve Trans-Canada Airlines proved too much and the Department of Transport purchased the 300-acre aerodrome from Laurentian Air. DOT set about, almost immediately, to construct new facilities and two hard-surfaced runways. On August 20th, 1938, Transport Minister Howe cut the ribbon inaugurating the Uplands Airport.

With the outbreak of WW2, the Department of National Defence acquired the airport land and established its own facilities. Uplands became a Service Flying Training School for the Royal Canadian Air Force (RCAF), and additional lands to the east of the airport were acquired for the eventual construction of five hangars and a military camp.

On 1 August 1940, the BCATP school opened at Uplands. The sky was filled with RCAF Harvards and various other training aircraft during the war, and many pilots earned their wings and took their newfound talent to the skies over Europe.

At the end of the war, the military activity at Uplands did not diminish. In fact, with Canada's commitment to the North Atlantic Treaty Organization (NATO), Ottawa was set to become an important base for international flights. Runways 14/32 and 07/25 at 8,800 and 6,200 feet respectively, became operational at the end of 1951. One of the more enduring military roles that played out at Uplands was the 412 Squadron of the RCAF, which continues to provide transport for many important visitors to the nation's capital.

During the 1950s, while the airport was still named Uplands and was still a joint-use civilian/military field, it was the busiest airport in Canada by takeoffs and landings, reaching a peak of 307,079 aircraft movements in 1959, nearly double its current traffic. At the time, the airport had scheduled airline flights by Trans-Canada Air Lines (Toronto, Montréal, and Val-d'Or), Trans Air (Churchill), and Eastern Air Lines (New York via Syracuse, and Washington via Montréal). With the arrival of civilian jet travel, the Department of Transport built a new field south of the original one, with two much longer runways and a new terminal building designed to handle up to 900,000 passengers per year. The terminal building had been scheduled to open in 1959, but during the opening ceremonies, a United States Air Force F-104 Starfighter went supersonic during a low pass over the airport, and the resultant sonic boom shattered most of the glass in the airport (including the entire north wall) and damaged ceiling tiles, door and window frames, and even structural beams. This mishap added approximately one year to the construction schedule, and $300,000 to the budget of $5 million. As a result, the opening was delayed until April 1960. The original terminal building and Trans-Canada Airways hangar continued in private use on the airport's north field until the Fall 2011 when it was demolished.

The terminal was finally opened by Prime Minister John Diefenbaker on June 30th, 1960.

The terminal, which was designed by local architects Gilleland and Strutt, was built to accommodate up to 900,000 passengers per year. To better accommodate larger aircraft, the two main runways were extended in 1961; 14/32 to 10,000 feet and 07/25 to 8,000 feet.

The airport's official designation was changed to Ottawa International Airport on 24 August 1964.

1975 was an important year for the region and the airport; the National Capital Commission opened the Airport Parkway, as an extension of Bronson Avenue, thereby providing a vital link between the community and the airport.

By 1980, approximately 2 million passengers per year were travelling through the airport – more than double its design capacity. A renovation plan was announced in 1982 and ultimately unveiled in 1986. The renovated space included extensive use of skylights, glass and steel. According to architect Patrick Murray, "we wanted to bring back the excitement of coming to the airport".

Further evolution included the airport's control tower and radar service moving to the Combined Air Navigation Facility and Regional Training Centre, located off Limebank Road, in 1991.

In June 1993, the federal government officially renamed the airport Ottawa Macdonald-Cartier International in honour of two of Canada's Fathers of Confederation.

The Authority

In 1992, when TC transferred the first four airport authorities,[335] the federal debt was massive. Huge amounts of infrastructure money were needed and the government didn't have it. Included in that federal infrastructure were the airports, and they were in pitiful condition. So what better way to lower expenses and the debt but to drop these airports off the federal books, let go a few thousand employees, and then charge the new AAs rent. It was a "no brainer".

Ottawa had tried to form an Authority along with the first four but the election of 1993 and the subsequent political issues with the Toronto Pearson airport caused TC to cease all negotiations. But by 1995 the political air had cleared, the National Airports Policy had been formulated, and the Public Accountability Principles for Canadian Airports had been published. TC put out feelers to the remaining airports saying "we're open for business, if you're interested."

Ottawa was interested and the Ottawa MacDonald-Cartier International Airport Authority (OMCIAA) had formed a Board with David Gavsie as the Chair. A lot of the credit to form an Authority in Ottawa must go to David. He was a very good lawyer, who singlehandedly put together a very good volunteer Board. David and the other members of the Board saw the

---

[335] Vancouver, Edmonton, Calgary and Montréal.

condition of the airport and told themselves they had to do something about it. That is when it got to the point of, "well, now things are getting serious, let's bring in some people who know the business".

Which is why, in October 1996, Paul Benoit came to Ottawa to take over as CEO.[336] His job at the start was to get the financing lined up, get the employee transfer agreements done, and get the senior management team working as a team, with a target of transferring on 1 February 1997. That was only four months after he started!!

When Benoit began it was just him and a part-time receptionist. So the first thing he did, with a lot of help from Gavsie, was to hire an attorney from Ogilvy Renault to handle all legal affairs. The second person Benoit hired was an HR guy to handle the employees, and AON for the financial studies.

At the same time as Benoit was getting the administration team organized, Gavsie was getting pre-clearance to the U.S. The Ottawa airport did not have pre-clearance to the U.S. in 1996, but it did have the ability to organize it within the bi-laterals established between Ottawa and the U.S. So, at the same time as negotiations were happening with TC for the airport transfer, the Board was saying "let's design for pre-clearance and get the U.S. Embassy on board".[337] Five months after transfer on 1 February 1997 the pre-clearance opened for business, built, staffed and operating, with a duty-free store.

The board at the beginning was a volunteer board, and they were very much community activists. They had a marketing committee, an operations committee, and several other committees. Benoit and his team said, "now look, you brought us in to run the place, and those committees are essentially operations, either you're a managing board, or you're a governing board. Let's make up our mind right now." The Board said "well obviously we want to be a governing board." Benoit was fortunate to have a few really good Chairmen running the Board. There was David Gavsie, when the

---

[336] Paul Benoit, interview with the author, 30 November 2018 and 10 December 2018.

[337] Ibid.

Board really needed his legal expertise at the beginning when doing the transfer. Then when it came to do the construction the Chair was Regis Trudel, a VP at Minto Construction, and because of his construction background he was immensely useful when the Board got into the nitty gritty. Regis came up with suggestions that Paul never would have thought of. For example, make sure that you hire someone from the outside as the owner's representative to keep an eye on your contractors. Because you have your general contractor, and your managing contractors, but you need somebody who is "your man", someone who has your best interests in mind and who looks at it just from your perspective. The Board very quickly accepted its role as a governing board.

The "negotiations" with TC for the Ottawa airport were hard. TC's position was "this is what is on offer. There is nothing else." This was understandable, to a point, because the federal public servants had their instructions and the negotiating team realized that any proposal had to be discussed in great detail. But TC had set a very high value on the chattels, and TC's position was that it was mandatory that the new Authority accept all the chattels. For example, there was a snowblower from the 1950's, and TC put a high, non-negotiable value on it. A final offer. The snowblower was old, and in dire need of maintenance, and was worth practically nothing. But TC was adamant "that's the price of the snowblower. Take it, or leave it." The negotiating team did the best it could with, basically, someone it was negotiating with who wanted to make sure that the government was no worse off at the end of the day.

Sometimes the negotiating team found TC's attitude difficult to understand, especially when it seemed that an idea would come at the team from out of the blue and they would find themselves saying "now what on earth is TC getting at?".

For example, there was a clause in the ground lease that said that TC would not permit a competing airport within 75 km of the existing airport. The negotiating team felt that this was fair as it would preclude any competition within a reasonable radius of Ottawa.

However, on 31 January 1997, a Thursday, the day before transfer was to occur, TC was prepared to totally ignore that clause. That day, on the day prior to transfer, everyone was in the Boardroom with dozens and dozens of binders, everyone was ready, the employees were all in "go" mode, and just before all the signatures were to happen, TC was on a conference call and said "we want to run TC's own fleet of aircraft as a shuttle service back and forth from Toronto as a service for our employees, and run it out of the TC hangar at YOW."

The room went silent. Finally someone said "whoa, whoa, whoa. You want to set up your own passenger terminal here? In your hangar?" And TC said "yeah, we'd like to do that." And the negotiating team said "Well, you can't do that. Remember, the lease has this rule – no competition within 75 km." And TC replied "the rule applies from the fence. What happens within the fence is excluded."

Well, the negotiating team all had a bit of moment over that one. A recess was called and the negotiating team left to discuss the issue. After some animated back and forth TC finally realized that them having their own terminal wasn't such a good idea and they dropped the request. But it was tense for a while because if TC had not dropped the request the transfer would not have happened the next day.[338]

One of the interesting things about the transfer was the attitude of the airport employees: they had security; they had benefits; they were set. And then suddenly this group calling themselves an Airport Authority, that they didn't know, came along and promised them a good, or even better deal. The employees did not have to transfer. If they wanted to stay with the government, they would be offered a job. But any employee that did transfer would have the same benefits package as was offered to them by the federal government: a defined-benefits pension, for example. This was really hard on some of the smaller airports. But the employees took a gamble. They gave the Authority their pension funds. Benoit was floored that they had that confidence. They were good employees who were working in a system which at that time was choking them off, and they believed in the new Authority.

One of the things that has happened with the coming into being of the AAs is the effect on airport staff training and experience.

---

[338] Benoit, email 13 January 2019.

Prior to 1992 a TC employee might begin their career in a small airport, may have progressed to a larger airport, may have ended up at Pearson, depending on the job they had, and then they would go to HQ. By that time they had an extensive aviation background. But one of the downsides of devolution is that there are now very few folk at TC who have actually worked in an airport.

Consequently YOW, together with a TC employee, Ian Henderson, began to run courses on how an airport is managed and operates. The Authority and Ian got together and said "this is ridiculous. Here we have Lease monitors who never set foot in an airport until they arrive to conduct a lease review. We have got to do something."[339] So the Authority set up a series of courses, which ran yearly. The course consisted of five Tuesdays, in the Fall, and people would arrive from TC, from Privy Council, from Finance, from across all government departments and agencies, and the instructor would say "look, we're going to give you Airports 101. It may be biased, because it's from our perspective, so you take it the way you want, but here's what it is." So the first Tuesday might offer them a day on Lease Management, on the second Tuesday they might spend a day with a Duty Manager and learn about Airport Operations, on the third Tuesday it was a day with the Marketing Group, all to try and give the federal employees a bit of a basis from which to build their knowledge of an airport, and also, equally important, to give the airport staff an exposure to government employees and how they work and see things. Today that is the biggest problem that TC has. They have people in their early 20's coming out of Carleton,[340] who come to people at the airport who have been working in the business for 40 years, and saying "well, now this is how you're going to do it." And there is a disconnect, an unsafe disconnect. When Ian retired there was no one to take over and the program died.

When the airport transferred TC had put a net book value of $67 million on it. Today the Authority has paid that amount at least

---

[339] Ibid.

[340] Carleton University, located on the Airport Parkway, immediately to the north of the airport.

four times over, plus, invested more than $600 million since transfer. The government got a pretty darned good deal.

From the start the Authority decided that it was going to build a new ATB. It invited the banks into its discussions and asked them who wanted to be the lead financing agent in the Authority's plans? Effectively the Authority had beauty contests with them all. The Royal Bank arrived with quite a show, and they had brought a cheque with them for millions of dollars, which they threw on the table saying "we believe in this organization, and we believe in you, and we're prepared to put money on the table right now."[341] And then when the Authority did its first bond issue, it went out in a couple of hours, and was over-subscribed almost immediately, way over-subscribed, to the point where the bank came to us and said "do you want another $100 million?", and the Authority said "no, we want to cut it off at $300 million."

And then the Authority did something very different when it came to building the ATB. Some of the AAs have been accused of over-building, with some of the smaller ones spending all that money and then they can't put a RESA[342] at the end of the runway, or they can't groove the runway, because that's too expensive.

In Canada the regulations call for a 60 m RESA. When the ICAO standard is 150 m, and the ICAO recommendation is 300 m, why in Canada are we doing that? Why? Because we just built a $400 million ATB and now we have no money. This is not a good use of money. The responsibility of the AA is to provide a safe and secure facility to the travelling public, not a palace. The glitz has a community impact, but so does the absence of RESA or grooving when a plane skids off the runway. The problem with RESA and grooving is that it's not sexy – who's going to see it? But until then, just look at this amazing, beautiful building we've got.

---

[341] Benoit.

[342] Runway End Safety Area – "the surface surrounding the runway prepared or suitable for reducing the risk of damage to airplanes in the event of an undershoot, overshoot, or excursion from the runway." Fourteenth Meeting of the CAR/SAM Regional Planning and Implementation Group (GREPECAS/14). International Civil Aviation Organization. April 2007.

The Authority decided to run the ATB as a business. There were four building options. After much discussion one option was finally decided on. When the CFO revealed the construction costs for that chosen option the senior management team said, "can't do that, it's too much." So senior management decided on a less expensive option, but, to finance that option the Authority would run two revenue streams: one for operations, and the other for construction. 100% of the construction project had to be financed by the AIF, and 100% of operations had to be financed by landing fees, terminal fees, and concessions and rental revenues. That imposed a financial discipline on the Authority. Other airports would use both operations money and AIF money to build, and that brings forth risk, especially when the economy goes south. Because the Authority was able to manage its funds, it went from having the highest landing fees of the largest eight airports, to having the lowest of the eight, because things were run separately. Benoit could not overstress that the solution to those who accuse airports of over-building, and that's more than half of the AAs in Canada, is to tie construction finances to the AIF, not to other revenue. There were times when building the ATB when the Authority said, "you know those nice skylights, well we can't afford them right now, so maybe we pull them out."[343] And then perhaps the steel came in cheaper, so now the skylights could be put in. Essentially the new ATB was under budget, and came in early. Benoit attributes that "to a hell of a team."

Benoit found it difficult when the architects came in and said "traditionally you've got your baggage claim area, your departure area, and you've got your offices over and above. We want to put your offices in the middle." His first reaction was "you're crazy, you can't do that." But he was wrong, and they were right, because as it turned out that was a brilliant solution as it put the management staff close to everything.

Once an airport in Canada reaches a certain size[344] it must have an on-site police force, paid for by the Authority. The police are very expensive, and the costs of security for Canadians, foreigners and

---

[343] Ibid.

[344] Two million passengers a year.

diplomats are borne exclusively by the AA. ICAO Annex 17[345] says that security against terrorism is the responsibility of the state, and the state has a responsibility to protect, not to pass the responsibility and the bill on to a private organization such as an AA.

After the devolution the AA's relationship with the staff at TC was strained. There were a lot of people at TC who would look at the Ottawa staff, and look at the salaries the Authority was paying. There was some resentment on the part of TC. There was a lot of "well, we could have done the same thing, if only we had had 'x'." At the most senior level the relationship with TC was good. At the Deputy Minister level the Ottawa airport was not a priority anymore. The airport was no longer a TC responsibility and the DM was on to other things. At the Director General level things were good, but at the TC staff level there was resentment, and a lot of "these are the rules, and by God I'm going to make sure you follow them." One of the clauses was the Crown may not be any worse off than it was before, and that all facilities provided to the Crown by the AA must be rent-free. Suddenly, the Ottawa airport, and several other airports, got notice from TC that they were going to transfer their Regional people into the ATB and that the AA's would have to provide office space to these folk. TC's thought was "It's free. We're moving in." There was a big fight over that - and TC lost.

For the construction the Authority used a formula that really helped. In Canada railways do not pay municipal taxes for the real estate occupied by their track. At transfer the Ottawa airport was paying Grants In Lieu of Taxes (GILT) to the city of Ottawa and the Authority approached the Ontario government saying "we need to build a new ATB, but we can't afford to pay the municipal taxes that would be levied on it at the current rate. We're building something for 20 years down the road, we're not going to use its

---

[345] Standards and Recommended Practices (SARPs) for international civil aviation are incorporated into the 19 technical annexes to the Convention on International Civil Aviation, also known as the Chicago Convention. Of critical importance to the future of civil aviation and to the international community at large are the measures taken by ICAO to prevent and suppress all acts of unlawful interference against civil aviation throughout the world. SARPs for international aviation security were first adopted by the ICAO Council in March 1974, and designated as Annex 17 to the Chicago Convention.

capacity for a very long time, so why should we pay for it today?"[346]
So the Ottawa AA said "last year we paid you 'x' in GILT. Here's
how we would like to go forward. We would like to take that
number 'x', divide it by the number of passengers, and pay
something near that number based on the number of passengers
that go enplane through the ATB." At that time the number was
about $1.18 per passenger. "We will pay you that amount every
year going forward, that is the base amount, based on the number
of enplaned passengers. If our passenger volumes increase, the
taxes paid will increase. If our passenger volumes decrease, an
economic downturn, the taxes paid will decrease. We will pay what
we can afford to pay. What's in it for the city? In return, we are
going to carve out of the airport certain non-aviation facilities,
such as a hotel. Under the old formula, the hotel was included in
the airport's taxes. Under the new formula the hotel was carved out
of the land value, and the hotel, taxed at the city's standard rate,
will pay taxes to the city directly. So the more the airport develops,
the more tax revenue the city will receive." The Authority had to
convince the City of Ottawa, then to convince the Regional
Government for Ottawa, then the Province. The proposal was
approved.

There was also the Airport Operating Influence Zone – the
AOIZ. The Authority was tired of having studies come forward
that said "well, you know, if the wind is blowing in a certain
direction, and you put a double-paned window in your house, the
aircraft noise isn't going to be that bad." And then immediately
having people moaning and groaning about the noise. So they
took the Noise Exposure Forecast and a map, and drew hard lines
on roads, and said "you're not going to build residential housing
within that area." The first group to bring on board were the
builders. The Authority explained to them, "look, this doesn't'
work. You're coming to us with all kinds of excuses, 'if the wind
isn't blowing', 'if we build this way', then it's all OK." The builders
eventually came on-board. The Authority then went to the city
and said "the builders want this, the airport wants this, what's your
problem?" and the city said "well, if everybody wants it, how can
we object?" There's been a couple of infills since then, and a couple

---

[346] Benoit.

of sites that the AA lost, but there's been a lot of pro-active things that the team at the AA put in place in Ottawa.

One issue that has arisen since transfer is a train to the airport. The question is: how many passengers per hour is the LRT going to carry to the airport? The Authority had been accused of not wanting the LRT because it was going to hurt parking revenue, but that's wrong. It had done a study very early on, and updated that study later. The results did not change. Both the early study, and its later update, said the LRT will have very little, if any, impact on the airport.

For example: the LRT runs every 20 minutes, and the train has just left the airport. You're a businessman, you've just flown in from Toronto, you're on an expense account. You're going to have to wait 20 minutes for the train to take you to Tunney's where you have to take another train, and then that train is probably not going to stop where you want to go anyway, so you will have to take a taxi. Will you wait the 20 minutes? Probably not. And this example is for only one certain client. The example does not consider anyone going south, nor south-east, nor west, nor Kanata, nor over the river to Gatineau. The Authority said "build it. We'll reserve the land. We'll even build the terminal." Now there's nothing wrong with a train. It works at Vancouver, it's getting better at Pearson-Union, and Montréal desperately needs one to reduce the congestion. But in Ottawa?

At the end it's great employees, great Board members, and a great team. That's what makes it work.

Figure 48: Ottawa Airport

In 2011 direct employment at the airport 4,964 jobs, with a labour income of $271 million, almost all of which was spent in the National Capital Region (NCR). The direct gross output of the airport is $1.1 billion annually. Economic contribution of YOW to the NCR was $461 million over the period 2013-2017.

30   31.2   35

Figure 49: Economic contribution of YOW to the NCR - source OIAA

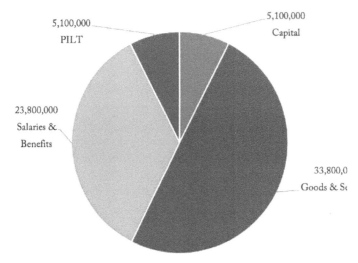

Spending by the OIAA in the NCR - 2017
$97.7 million

5,100,000
PILT

5,100,000
Capital

23,800,000
Salaries &
Benefits

33,800,0
Goods & S

Figure 51: Image courtesy of Google Earth Pro, 7-29-2018. The pin marks the location of the original BCATP aerodrome.

An airport at Prince George opened in 1920, and until 1932 the airport's site was the bypass highway that ran from Tenth Avenue to Eighteenth Avenue. The airport served as a stopover for aircraft including US Army Junkers JL-4's and de Havilland Fours going to Alaska. In 1932, the airport was moved to the intersections of Highway 97 and Highway 16, near Carney Hill (the same site is now the Prince George Golf and Curling Club). At this second, newer airport, US planes also flew in large numbers to Alaska prior to the United States declaring war on Japan. Planes seen included Douglas B-18's and Martin B-10's. This airport was used until about 1942 and was closed for good on March 31, 1944. During the 1930s and early 1940s, it contained Pineview Elementary School, which was renamed the Airport School.

On November 14, 1940, the Canadian-American Permanent Joint Board of Defence set out a need for a number of new Northwest airports, including Prince George, for the support of a new Northwest Staging Route. This new staging route would provide protection, permit aircraft to be deployed rapidly to northwestern Canada and Alaska in time of emergency and allow men and

265

supplies to be moved into the region by air. In late 1940, Canada's Department of National Defence contracted to build a new (third) Prince George airport on a bench at the top of the hill about three miles south-east of the city on the old Cariboo Highway, across from the Federal Government's Experimental Farm. This location is now the site of today's airport, YXS.

The Department of Transport built single family homes, an unmarried staff residence, a diesel electric power plant and vehicle maintenance garage. A small administration building and radio range station was built by Pan American World Airways (Pan Am) and a few years later (1944) this was replaced by a new, larger DOT administration/radio range terminal and a large hangar was built (burned down in 2009) about the same time. The resident DOT staff were housed on the airport and the Pan Am staff were accommodated in houses built on the East side of the old Cariboo highway, across from the airport.

In 1942, the United States Army Air Force (USAAF) started construction of a number of buildings for their people and for RCAF staff. The buildings included troop dormitories, a medical clinic, a gymnasium and a cafeteria. The latter was also used for USO shows and movies for airport staff. The US staff component included an Army Airways Communication Station, an 11th Air force detachment (1452nd AAF Base Unit - detached from Edmonton Municipal) and a small detachment of US Navy staff. The US Navy had a contract with Pan Am to fly men, equipment and everything else from Seattle to Juneau and Fairbanks via Prince George and on to Kodiak, Dutch Harbour, Adak and back in periods when coastal weather conditions were poor. The 11th Air force 1452nd Base Unit at Prince George airport were Air Transport Command, charged with facilitating aircraft and supply shipments from mainland US to Alaska on the Northwest Staging route.

The new airport comprised 2034 acres, was completed on August 9, 1945 and had three runways arranged in a triangle. In 1941, after the completion of runway 14/32 (now 15/33), U.S.-based Pan Am operated from the Prince George Airport as a stopover location on its Seattle to Fairbanks route ferrying men and equipment for the U.S. Navy. In 1942, Canadian Pacific Air Lines began offering scheduled flights six times a week into Prince George. Canadian Pacific and its successors CP Air and Canadian

Airlines International served the airport for many years. During 1942, 1943, and 1944, the airport was used as an alternate airport (to Edmonton municipal) by the USAAF for United States to Russia Lend-Lease aircraft flown primarily from Great Falls, Montana to Alaska and on to Russia. Planes seen in the new Prince George airport were mostly P-39 Airacobras, P-63 Kingcobras, B-25 Mitchell bombers, and C-47 Skytrain transports. Also seen were RCAF Hawker Hurricanes and Bristol Fairchild Bolingbroke bombers.

During the war years, the RCAF ran the airport with close assistance from the Department of Transport and the USAAF. In 1946, with the war over, the airport was turned over to the Department of Transport by the RCAF and the USAAF and RCAF buildings were torn down, leaving the DOT buildings and homes as well as the Pan Am housing. These lasted until the early 1950s when they were either moved or torn down. The hangar was used until 2009 and the DOT Admin building - terminal was replaced with a new, modern terminal in 1973. In the mid-forties, the Airport School was re-established at YXR and served resident Department of Transportation children and children from neighboring farms until the early 1950s. The school had up to three teachers and up to 25 students in grades one to six, at various times.

Over the years, Canadian Pacific operated such twin engine prop aircraft as the Lockheed Lodestar, the Douglas DC-3, the Convair 240, and the larger, four engine Douglas DC-6B propliner and Bristol Britannia turboprop. In 1953, the first lights were installed along runway 14/32 (now 15/33). Later that same year, a United States Air Force B-29 Superfortress was forced to make an emergency landing along the same runway. It landed 18 in (46 cm) deep inside the tarmac.

Prince George Airport was commercialized in 1963 when Mrs. P. Richardson opened the first coffee shop in the terminal. Wildlife such as moose or deer can be seen occasionally from the runway. During the WW2 years, wildlife near the airport was largely wiped out due to airport soldiers hunting in their free time.

CP Air operated jet service into the airport during the 1970s primarily with the Boeing 737-200 jetliner with nonstop flights to Vancouver, Fort St. John and Whitehorse as well as direct, no change of plane service to Edmonton, Grande Prairie, Fort Nelson and Watson Lake. CP Air also operated nonstop Boeing 727-100 jet service to Vancouver as well as direct to Edmonton via a stop in Grand Prairie during the mid 1970s. Pacific Western Airlines also served Prince George at this same time with Boeing 737-200 jet service to Vancouver, Edmonton, Kamloops and Dawson Creek, and de Havilland Canada DHC-6 Twin Otter turboprop and Douglas DC-3 propliner flights to Kelowna, Penticton, Prince Rupert, Smithers, Terrace, Quesnel and Williams Lake. CP Air and Pacific Western would continue to compete with nonstop service to Vancouver into the 1980s with both airlines flying Boeing 737-200 jetliners on the route. Pacific Western acquired CP Air and the combined airlines then operated as Canadian Airlines International.

The Authority

My thanks to John Backhouse (who was Mayor of the City of Prince George at that time) for these notes on the airport transfer on the part of Prince George City Council and the Regional District of Fraser Fort George. This dialogue with Transport Canada took place sometime between 1994 to 1996 as the National Airports Policy came into being in 1994.

Prior to transfer some Transport Canada NAS airports had a Community Advisory Committee and Mayor Backhouse Chaired that Committee from 1990 to early 1996. Messrs. Blake, Paul, Wilson and Backhouse had met frequently from 1995 to 1997 and noted the success that other small Airport Authorities had achieved since they transferred.

In 1997 Mayor Backhouse became the Chair of The Prince George Region Development Corporation and remained in that capacity until 2000. At the request of the Regional District of Fraser Fort George Board of Directors the Prince George Regional Development Corporation established an Airport Transfer Planning Committee in 1997. The Committee was composed of Dale McMann (CEO of the Development Corporation), Jerry Deere (formerly a member of the TC Advisory Committee and local business person), Robert Leverman (lawyer), Lynne Fehr (Commercial Manager Scotiabank), George Paul (City Manager) and Dave Wilson (Chief Administrative Officer for the Regional District of Fraser Fort George.

The Planning Committee hired Intervistas Consulting to assist them in the process. After two years studying the question the conclusion of the committee and the consultants was that the airport, if transferred, might be marginally viable. Passenger levels at the time were in the 300,000 to 400,000 range.

The Planning Committee represented by Messrs. McMann, Leverman and Deere made application, on July 26,2000, to incorporate the Prince George Airport Authority. Shortly after incorporation Mayor Backhouse was elected Chairman of the Airport Authority Board of Directors and negotiations commenced with Transport Canada.

The Board negotiated as a full Board. Members were Valerie Giles (Secretary) and Scott Pollard, both Federal Government appointees; Bob Leverman and David Wilson (Vice Chair), both Regional District of Fraser Fort George appointees; Prince George Development Corporation appointees Jerry Deere and Neil King; Jim Blake (Chair), Ron Epp (Treasurer), and Valerie Kordyban; these three were the City of Prince George appointees. The PGAA Board itself appointed Lynne Fehr and Neil Meagher as Board members.

The PGAA Board then enlisted the services of PriceWaterhouseCoopers and Pryde Schroppe and McComb to assist them with the negotiations. The major sticking points were the operational viability of the airport and the amount of badly needed future capital expenditures as Transport Canada had incurred minimal capital expenditures over the previous five years. Negotiations failed and Transport Canada then hired Peter Strum as a consultant to advise them on the contentious issues. Strum to some extent concurred with the PGAA concerns. Agreement on an acceptable offer from TC was finally achieved in late 2002 and the Prince George airport (the last NAS airport in Canada to transfer) was transferred on March 31st 2003, one day before the expiration of the National Airports Policy.

The Board composition changed on the day after transfer as Valerie Kordyban and Bob Leverman had both recently moved to other communities. They were replaced on April 1st, 2003 by Dave Wilbur and Michael Tkachuk.

It is to be noted that major improvements to buildings and infrastructure have happened since transfer and the airport has moved from an annual operating deficit under TC of approximately $1 million per year to recurring operating surpluses since 2009. Since 2014 operating surpluses have exceeded $1 million each year.

It is important to note that all NAS airports under 500,000 passengers have struggled with ongoing capital improvements costs as these airports do not qualify for ACAP funding[347]. Within the past few months (mid-2018) there has finally been some recognition of this struggle by the Federal Government with one-shot capital infusions to the six airports (Prince George, Charlottetown, Saint John, Fredericton, Gander and Moncton) however there is still no ongoing federal program to meet this need.

Figure 52: Prince George Airport

An economic impact study[348] conducted in 2011 found that the direct impacts of YXS were 430 direct person years of

---

[347] ACAP (the Airports Capital Assistance Program) is a policy of TC whereby regional airports may petition for capital to help them in a major project such as a runway renewal, or a new ATB. Although regional airports play an essential role in Canada's air transportation sector, they can struggle to raise enough revenue for operations. The program addresses this issue by funding projects that: improve regional airport safety; protect airport assets (such as equipment and runways); and, reduce operating costs.

[348] InterVISTAS Consulting Inc., 23 November 2011.

employment, $32 million in gross domestic product (GDP), $57 million in economic output; and $17 million in wages.

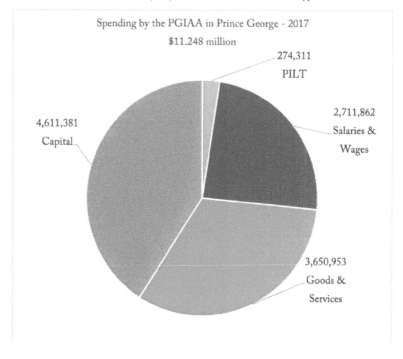

Spending by the PGIAA in Prince George - 2017
$11.248 million

Figure 54: Image courtesy of Google Earth Pro, 8-16-2017. The pin marks the location of the original BCATP aerodrome.

In early May 1928, the controller of Civil Aviation visited Québec City to meet with the Mayor, at his request, to discuss the establishment of an aerodrome to serve the city. The Mayor hoped that the federal government would provide the facility. The controller wrote a long letter[349] back on 15 May 1928 to the Mayor saying:

- the provision of air facilities was the responsibility of local authorities;
- if the Department paid for an aerodrome at Québec it would be called on to pay for an aerodrome at any town or city that wanted one;
- that the purpose of an aerodrome was to facilitate air mail, and if Québec wanted to do this it must build the airport on its own;
- the question posed by His Worship as to why Montréal and Rimouski had aerodromes that were built by the federal

---

[349] Public Archives Canada, MG 30 E243, vol. 9, memorandum, 15 May 1928.

government was irrelevant as the purpose for which they had been built did not apply to Québec; and

- if Québec wanted an airport it should ally itself with a commercial organization wishing to build such an aerodrome.

In 1928, without the assistance of the Mayor, Canadian Transcontinental Airways built an airport near chemin St. Louis in the municipality of Ste. Foy, west of Québec City, with two strips 3,000 feet (914 m) long. This was in response to a contract the company had received to operate an air mail service from Montréal to Rimouski, along the north shore of the St. Lawrence. The company constructed three hangars and other facilities on the site. In 1930 the company was acquired by Canadian Airways who almost immediately ceased operations from the airport at Ste. Foy because it no longer delivered air mail to Rimouski.

Things remained dormant until 1936 when the city Clerk of Québec sent a telegram to the Minister of National Defence strongly endorsing the view of the Québec Chamber of Commerce that the Québec airport be made part of the National System, and that the "Dominion government operate and maintain it."[350] The minister replied that the RCAF had no plans which would involve the establishment of an airport at Québec.

On 7 March 1938 Romeo Vachon, the District Superintendent, Canadian Airways, advised the DOT that his company would close the airport on 1 May 1938. On 6 May 1938 Mr. Vachon indicated that he had had further discussions with Mayor Borne about the continued operation of the airport and that the Mayor had indicated that the city would not intervene in its closure. Mr. Vachon also reported that the boundary markers had been removed and the land was ready to be ploughed up. He reported also that "the present site provides fair facilities in an east-west direction, but, owing to the slope of the land, the north-south aspect is not good, and it is doubtful if a field for first-class air line operations could be built on the site."[351] He continued in his report to say that surveys of nearby sites had not found anything better, and that to "attain a really good site it may be necessary to move

---

[350] *History*, p. 179.

[351] Public Archives Canada, MG 30 E243, vol. 9.

further out from the city, probably a distance of 10 or 12 miles out."[352]

Late that month, May 1938, surveys confirmed that a site at L'Ancienne Lorette would be suitable. Located 10 miles to the northeast, it had easy access to the city. But the surveys were to no avail, nothing went forward.

And then the outbreak of war finally gave the city authorities what they had been asking for in vain for years.

In October 1939 the DOT, on behalf of the DND, asked for options on the land identified at L'Ancienne Lorette. However, the price asked was too high and the DOT let the matter die. However by the middle of 1940 the exigencies of war intervened and the DND had begun to construct an airfield for the BCATP. It had three paved runways: 12-30 at 3,000 feet (914 m); 06-24 at 3,300 feet (1,006 m); and 02-20 at 2,800 feet (853 m). All three runways were 150 feet (46 m) wide. The airport had no lighting and operated only during daylight hours.[353]

Figure 55: The BCATP aerodrome at Quebec City in 1948. Photo tirée des collections de la Bibliothèque de l'Université Laval, Québec. Used with permission.

---

[352] Ibid.

[353] *Aerodrome*, p. 56.

In early 1941 an AOS and an EFTS were in operation at the field. The flying school was operated by the City of Québec Elementary Flying Training School Ltd and had Ansons and Fleet Finches as training aircraft. The AOS was operated by Québec Airways. By 1942 the airport had become the largest training school in eastern Canada.[354]

In 1943 operating facilities were greatly improved with the installation of approach lighting, runway and taxiway lights, and a radio beacon. In September Canadian Pacific Airlines began regular service between Montréal, Québec City, Mon Joli and Sept-Iles.

On 31 March 1945 the BCATP ceased operations and the airport's sole customer remained Canadian Pacific Airlines for several years. The DOT took over operations at the airport while the land remained under the ownership of the DND. Because the city of Québec had no interest in assuming responsibility for the airport, on 11 December 1946 the airport was formally transferred from the DND to the DOT.[355]

A gradual growth in passenger traffic caused runway 12-30 to be extended at both ends to a length of 5,700 feet (1,737 m). In 1954 runway 06-24 was lengthened to 6,000 feet (1,829 m). In 1974 it was lengthened to 7,500 feet (2,286 m) and in 1979 it was added to again to achieve a length of 9,000 feet (2,743 m).[356]

In 1955 construction began on the first ATB, ramps and loading areas as a result of TCA and Québecair operating three flights a day using DC-3 and Lockheed aircraft. The ATB was officially opened on 17 December 1957. The airport was designated as an alternate for the North Atlantic air route.

In 1959 an ILS was installed along with high-intensity approach lights, and an Airport and Airways Surveillance Radar for air traffic control.

In 1964 a weather radar system was installed and, in 1965, a VHF Omnidirectional Range (VOR) navigation system came into

---

[354] Ibid.

[355] *History*, p. 179.

[356] Ibid, p. 180.

operation, followed by a Tactical Air Navigation (TACAN) system.

Jet aircraft arrived in 1964 and in 1965 runway 02-20 was closed, thus bringing to an end the triangular set of runways which were the classic configuration for a BCATP airfield.

The volume of air traffic continued to increase and a new ATB opened in 1973, with the old ATB transformed into an administration building.

In 1981 a new access road was built and aprons were upgraded, followed by, from 1982 to 1984, more expansion of the ATB, car parking areas and aprons and ramps for aircraft.

The Québec City airport was renamed to Jean Lesage International Airport in 1993, and, with the inauguration of a new international zone at the airport in 1996, the airport's international character was confirmed once again. The following year, a new control tower and the NAV Canada Aviation Complex were unveiled.

The Authority

In 1992 the Québec City Chamber of Commerce became interested in the idea of privatizing the management of the airport. Some members of the Chamber thought this would be a good idea so they created a company, the Société aéroportuaire de Québec, which later became Aéroport de Québec Inc.[357]

For the next eight years the Société worked with TC to analyze the situation: how could they do this? or what to do about that? It took some time for the members of the Société to fully understand and be confident in several issues: What amount of money would be needed in order to successfully take over the airport? What kind of contract would the Société have to sign with TC? What would the Société do with the TC employees? The Société was also aware that many staff who worked for the airport were not located at the airport, they were in Montreal or Ottawa. The only staff located at the airport were operating staff. There was no marketing

---

[357] I am indebted to Gaëtan Gagné, President and CEO of the Aéroport de Québec Inc. (Quebec City Airport Authority), for his time in allowing me to interview him on 11 December 2018 and again on 7 February 2019. This chapter could not have been possible without his input.

department, no finance department, nothing, except the operational side, and the Société would have to build that side of the airport's management and operations from scratch.

Once the Société and TC had agreed on the conditions of transfer, the Société announced on 1 November 2000 that the airport was privatized. The Board of Directors appointed a management committee, together with a general manager, and assumed control of and responsibility for the management and operations of the Quebec City airport. At that time, the budget was around $4 million a year and profitability was near zero.

The people who lived in Quebec City knew, and had known for many years, that what was good for air transportation was also good for them. For many years Quebec City had had a minimum of air service. By the time the Société assumed responsibility for the airport it was overdue for repair and maintenance, by many years.

There was also the issue that since the service from the Quebec City airport was minimal many people living in Quebec City chose to travel by road to Montreal in order to fly somewhere. This lack of service caused the Chamber of Commerce to get involved because business people needed an airport to develop their business and to travel the world.

Throughout the transition period the Province and the city governments wanted nothing to do with the Société and its negotiations with TC. They were supportive, but the Province, and especially City of Quebec, declined to help the Société in any way because there was no particular political will to get involved, because both the city and the province believed that TC was just dumping their problem onto another jurisdiction.

At the time of transfer in 2000 there were 672,800 passengers travelling in and out of the Quebec City airport.[358] In fact, more than $500 million dollars was required to renew the ATB, the equipment, the runways, the taxiways, the fire station, and the parking lot. Almost all of the infrastructure had not been maintained very well since 1984 and was in drastic need of renovation or re-building.

---

[358] Today there are close to 1.8 million passengers annually.

The Société had an executive committee which did the actual negotiations with TC. The Société found that TC was collaborative in its negotiations, and generally things were fine during the whole of the transition process. At the end it became apparent that TC was in a hurry to transfer the airport, but since the Société didn't know the details of how things were going it was difficult to analyze the risk until TC gave the Société more information. Although prior to transfer the provincial and municipal governments were not very helpful, after transfer the federal and provincial governments were very collaborative.

The TC employees at the airport were apprehensive at the beginning, and as an employer the AA did very badly in those first few years. Only four years after transfer, in 2004, it had a 110-day strike. During the strike, some employees occupied the offices of a few Board members, and the situation was not good. This has since changed, and today the working climate has dramatically turned around as demonstrated by the current five and six-year contract agreements with the unions.

At transfer the employees were worried and concerned. What is going to happen? They were no longer protected by the federal government, and even though they still had their union, they were still concerned that the AA would cut jobs. Would the new AA look for profit, and consider only the bottom line? To counter this the Société created a committee and learned about the staff, and in turn the staff learned about the Société. This took some time but today the relationship is good.

After transfer the reaction of the airlines was rather negative. They did not agree with the AA. They argued that the AA fees were too expensive. They said the AA should not build, that there was no reason to undertake such a large and expensive construction program. The airport was adequate as it was.

However, in the opinion of the Airport Authority the airlines were forgetting one thing. The airport is the same as a highway. It is no different. If we go back to the beginning of the 20th century, to 1908, when Ford was just beginning to build his Model T and 1911, when the first highway was built in the United States, and then in 1915 when the first highway was built in Canada, those who were lucky enough to be on or near those highways benefitted economically from the business which passed by their door. Those with no highways did not benefit. As the highways were extended around the country the more people created an economy. It is the same thing with airports. If air traffic is centralized into one place, as say in a major hub, and other airports are not built, the local towns will not benefit from that economy. However, the airlines will benefit because with a single central airport they now can concentrate their traffic and reduce their costs, particularly because there is no competition.

When the Quebec Airport Authority built its airport it had only one major carrier who was renting all the counters, there was no competition. So the AA said, "in the future we will have 'common use' counters", which means that the carriers uses the counter for the time they need it, and then it will be available to another airline for the time that they need it. The AA created competition, prices went down, traffic went up, and the passengers in Quebec City were happy.

In 2008 the AA constructed a new domestic terminal and the AA received subsidies from the provincial and federal governments of $15 million each, for a total of $30 million for its first project costing $68 million.

In 2010 Gaëtan Gagné proposed to the Board that a building program costing $50 million a year for the next 10 years should be undertaken. It was an aggressive program. The AA wanted $100 million from both the federal and provincial governments to help finance the project, and it would borrow money from the market for the remaining $315 million. The Board agreed with the proposal. So Gagné asked the Premier of the provincial government, Mr. Charest at that time, "Would you put $50 million into our project, with the condition that the federal government matches your money?"[359] And he said "Yes". Gagné then went to the federal government and, thanks to then federal Minister Josée Verner[360], it came in with $50 million. Gagné then

---

[359] Gagné, interview with the author, 7 February 2019.

[360] At that time Mme Verner was Minister of Intergovernmental Affairs, President of the Privy Council for the Queen of Canada, Minister for La Francophonie as well as Minister responsible for the region of Quebec

went to Yonge street and asked the financial institutions for $315 million, and got it.

In 2018 the AA added a new international terminal. It has also received authorization from the Canadian federal and US governments to add a pre-clearance facility to allow direct flights to all US airports. The Quebec City airport will then be quite competitive and able to develop its community. Business people will be able to cultivate their businesses from Quebec City because they will then have connections to the United States and Europe, and most other destinations.

Labor relations are an important part of the AA's management philosophy. In order to monitor employer/employee relationships the AA uses a system called *Officevibe* [https://www.officevibe.com]. Every employee provides feedback and, on a weekly basis, the AA analyzes the results. The results show an engagement rate of 78% (According to some studies, the typical average engagement rate of Canadian workers is 33%). The engagement of the employees is a large part of the AA's success. There is also the fact that from the get-go Gagné posed the critical question: "Who are our primary customers?" In 2000 it was not unusual, in Canada, for the primary customer of an airport to be the airline. But, in 2006, Gagné said "No. The primary customer for the Quebec City airport is the passenger. Because the passenger has the most value-added of all kinds of customers that we have." From that point on every decision the AA made was for the benefit of the passenger. If an undertaking could not be supported for the benefit of the passenger, that undertaking did not happen. It took time to implement that philosophy, but today "Passenger first®" is a valued part of the AA's philosophy.

As an example of "Passenger first", consider this episode which took place early one morning when a man and his wife arrived at the terminal. They had driven about a 200 km and had arrived at about 3 in the morning for a flight at 6 am. One of the staff found him sitting in the terminal, very upset, and said to him "Can we help you?" He said he could not fly with his wife because he had forgotten his prescription medicines. The staff member called a pharmacy in Quebec City and got them to open up and fill his prescription so that he could go on his trip. This commitment to service is "passenger first" at its best.

The expectation of the AA is that people do not travel every week. More than half of the AA's passengers are tourists who perhaps fly once a year. They are not business people, who might fly once a month, or even more. And for the business people the AA operates its own VIP room. The AA refused to let an airline operate the VIP room so the AA can have in its VIP room whomever it wants. The AA has received several prizes for its construction program: the best VIP room in North America; and green energy.

According to TC, no entity other than the Authority should control an airport. Because at the end the airport belongs to no one. TC created the Authorities to benefit the local communities. Board members are not there to represent their communities, they are there to offer advice to the Authority, and to do fiduciary duty to the airport. Their duty of care is to the airport and its passengers, not to the City, not to the Chamber of Commerce, nor to nobody else.

At the end of the lease the AA has to hand back the airport in first-class operating condition, and with no debt. The AA has a 60 year lease, and has not exercised the 20 year option. In 2019 there are 41 years left on the lease. This time factor was one of the reasons why the AA had to push hard to build at the beginning of the lease, because it needed time in order to amortize the investments necessary to bring the airport to a first-class condition. If the AA had waited till the last 20 years it would not have had time to repay the whole debt. And even though the AA must maintain the building in first-class condition, it may be with the building it now has, with no expansion.

However, over the long run the requirement that the building be handed back in first class condition and with no debt is not sustainable, according to the AA. The large airports, such as Pearson, Montreal, Calgary or Vancouver will still have investment in infrastructure that they must do, and how will they repay that cost before the end of the lease? If the condition remains mandatory that the buildings be handed back with no debt and in first class condition, the only solution may be that they are allowed to privatize. For example, the Quebec City AA borrowed money from pension funds and the banks, and those financial institutions lent the AA money at 4.25%, but they do not participate in the profits of the airport. It is highly probable that a pension fund will be very interested in investing $100 million to get a $5 million benefit every year. It is better to have a large institutional investor put in 25% to help an AA increase traffic. In Toulouse, for example, the Chinese have purchased 49% of the airport. And an airport with investment creates the potential of more traffic, creates the potential of increased economy in an industrial park, a commercial park, building skills. The local economy then becomes connected to the world.

In the next 10-12 years the world's traffic is expected to double. Since the AA now has basic facilities it will be very easy to amend those facilities to meet the increased demand. The last phase of construction allowed the AA to meet a capacity of 3 million passengers a year. Any passenger loading more than that will depend on the airline's scheduling because the AA has two peak markets, one in the morning and one in the evening. If the AA could spread flights over 24 hour then the passenger loading would be more evenly distributed and the AA could increase capacity to 4 million passengers annually. In that case more gates would be needed. But because of the ATB and its design, adding additional gates would be very easy.

Since transfer the AA has done exceedingly well, both in operations and in finances. It now has assets exceeding $600 million, a cumulated surplus of $135 million, and ended 2018 with an $11 million surplus. According to a Conference Board study, the airport contributes more than $ 600 million to the Canadian economy. Over the last 15 years, it has had a compound annual growth in passenger traffic of 7.2%. This result proves that the Quebec City airport was quite behind the market and that there was a substantial demand that was not being met. The Chamber of Commerce was right, as business people, to form a Société and take charge of that airport.

The airport supports 1,863 direct jobs and a total of 5 675 jobs in Canada.[361] In 2017 alone, the Authority paid some $33 million for salaries, goods and services, and grants in lieu of taxes. Moreover, as an illustration, since 2011 alone, the Authority has paid more than $24 million in rent to the federal government.

---

[361] Conference Board of Canada, June 2017.

Figure 56: Quebec City Airport

What is of interest in proving the thesis of this book is the graph on the next page. It demonstrates, dramatically, the change in passenger growth after the airport was taken over by the Airport Authority – after the Authority began its program of reconstruction and development centred on the passenger - "Le passager avant tout®" (Passenger First®). As may be seen, for the 13 years prior to takeover by the Airport Authority passenger volumes hovered around the 670,000 per year mark. Since takeover passenger volumes have soared to close to 1.8 million per year, more than doubling the number of passengers annually.

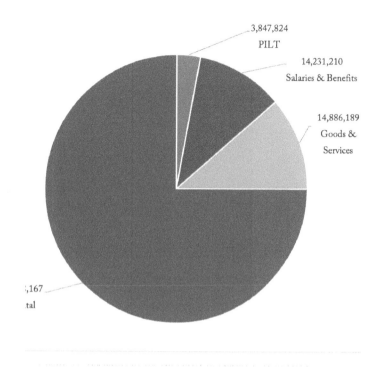

3,847,824
PILT

14,231,210
Salaries & Benefits

14,886,189
Goods &
Services

,167
tal

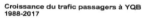

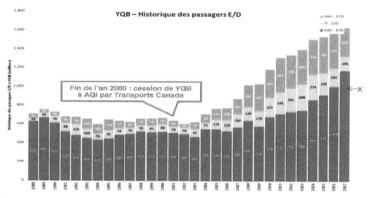

Figure 58: Graph courtesy of l'Aeroport de Québec Inc.

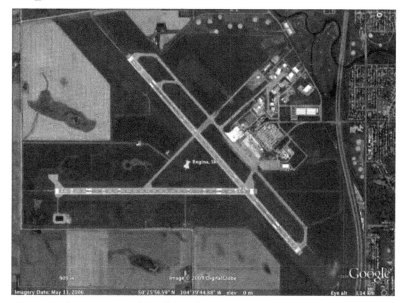

Figure 59: Image courtesy of Google Earth Pro, 7-2-2018. The pin marks the location of the original BCATP aerodrome.

Regina had an airport as early as 1919, located at the corner of Mill Avenue and Cameron Street on an 800 square yard field (669 sq. m). A second airfield, Lakeview Aerodrome, was opened by Jack Wright and R. J. Groome in 1927. The City also got in the act and set aside 40 acres (16 hectares) for a future airport. Almost immediately this purchased was overtaken by events as the Regina Flying Club, in order to qualify for benefits under the government's plan to assist light aeroplane clubs and associations, bought a quarter section (65 hectares) of land two miles (three kilometres) to the west of the city. The city now had three airports. The city bought the land from the club in 1928 and the Regina City Airport was opened officially on 15 September 1930.

The Prairie section of the Trans-Canada Airway was the first to be built, due to the relatively flat and easy terrain, and a radio beacon was built at the airport as part of the navigation chain. Over the next few years a hangar was built, the two runways were paved (in 1932, the only paved runways between Montréal and Vancouver), and airport lighting was installed. In 1938 a radio range was built,

Figure 60: The ATB and Control Tower, 1938

runway 07-25 (3,740 feet – 1 140 m) was constructed and runway 12-30 (3,725 feet – 1 135 m) rebuilt. An administration building with control tower was needed, but since the city was unable to finance it, the DOT paid the cost.

In 1940 the DOT took over operation on behalf of the DND so that the airfield could be used by the BCATP. The DND then built a new runway (03-21 at 3,300 feet (1 006 m)) to create the standard triangular system of runways, three hangars and other maintenance and administrative buildings for the use of No. 15 Elementary Flying Training School. At the end of the war the airfield was given back to the DOT, which continued to operate it until 1955.

In November 1952 runway 07-25 was re-built and re-aligned to 08-26. An Instrument Landing System was installed in 1955 and a new ATB opened on 12 October 1960.

In 1967 runway 12-30 was extended to 7,900 feet (2 408 m) and runway 08-26 extended to 6,200 feet (1 890 m).

In 1955 the City of Regina resumed operation of the airport, with an operating subsidy from DOT. Even with the subsidy, the city had financial difficulties in operating the airport and in 1972 the DOT bought the property from the city for $2.3 million. In 1986 a renovated and enlarged ATB opened.

Figure 61: ATB and Control Tower, 1955

In 1988 the airport served 601,700 passengers and had 50 employees. The day before transfer, on 30 April 1999, the airport had 55 employees and had seen 749,000 passengers the year before.

The Authority

Prior to TC operating the airport, the City of Regina had operated it. So when TC wanted to transfer the airport it was sort of "déjà vu" for some of the folk.

In 1996 Muir Barber was the Chair of the Regina Economic Development Authority[362] when the City of Regina was contacted by TC to say that TC was interested in transferring the airport. The Mayor called Muir and asked him if he'd be interested in looking into it, and he said "sure". He contacted TC and they gave him a few fuzzy details. He said "Well, send us some numbers and we'll look into it." TC said "no, you'll have to form an AA in order to be given the numbers." Muir said "well, that's not how this is going to work. We talked with Winnipeg and they told us their costs for transfer had been in the order of $600,000. So, no, until we see the numbers we have no interest whatsoever." And TC said

---

[362] Muir Barber, interview with the Author, 9 January 2019.

"well, we can't give you the numbers." And Muir said "well, fine." And things just went dark.

Close on to a year elapsed before Muir heard from them again. TC called and said "we're getting down to the short strokes[363] and you are one of the last airports remaining. We'd very much like for you guys to partake. In fact we're talking with Saskatoon as well." Muir said "well, send us the numbers." And TC said "we can't. Not until you form an AA." Muir said "we are not going to spend that kind of money until we know there's an inkling of a reason why we would get involved." And TC said "well, we may have no choice but to close the airport." And Muir said "really? Go ahead."

A little bit later TC called and said "well, we're prepared to give you some of the numbers on the understanding that you form an authority if it's warranted." And Muir said "sure". So Muir, Paul Hill and Dick Rendek formed a committee. Muir was the Chair (by then he had left REDA and had some time on his calendar, or at least he thought he did!!). Dick Rendek was there because they thought they might need some legal help. Dick was a great guy and legal mind. Paul had the political connections. It was just the three of them at that point. Dick was in the twilight of his career, had been a great community guy, and fit the bill for the team.

Eventually TC sent the numbers. The committee then heard the spiel from TC about what a great deal it would be for Regina. TC also said how much money it wanted from the nascent authority in order to transfer the airport.

The committee got into the numbers and started meeting with the airport manager, Steve Burchi, and his staff. The committee talked to the Winnipeg Board, who were a great resource. They also talked to Vancouver Airport Services (VAS), who did some consulting to help figure out pros and cons, and to educate the committee a little bit. The options before the Authority took over were to hire VAS and have them run the airport as 3rd party managers, or for the Authority to run it themselves. Steve asked that he and his management team be hired and allowed to continue the running of the airport. The committee threw those ideas around and eventually decided to do it on their own and hire

---

[363] 14 out of 22 airports had been transferred to Airport Authorities by this time.

Steve and his crew. The Board continued to use VAS for statistics and as 3rd party consultants, and found them very helpful.

The transfer team got some money from the City of Regina, and some from TC. Most of the money went on the formation of the AA, all the legal requirements. It didn't cost $600,000 like it did Winnipeg, but certainly the transition team didn't get paid. For secretarial help the team stole from each other. Muir couldn't remember if he got reimbursed for his expenses.

Negotiating with TC was frustrating at times. Paul and Muir were in the business of negotiating with real estate, and at some point they realized that while airports are a complicated business, at another level it just a whole bunch of real estate that people have activities on. They were able to figure out the real estate piece pretty fast. But they discovered that TC was not results driven as much as they were process driven. If the process was proceeding, the committee's impression was that TC was happy. Paul and Muir, however, were in the results business. For them, if there was no end in sight then they walked away. That difference of understanding made it frustrating for both sides. Muir just wanted TC to tell him the numbers, he'd figure it out and get back to TC. But TC's response was "well you should do this, and you should get that study, and that study." Muir's response was "we don't need all that stuff. If I want to know what our equipment is like I'll go talk to the guys in the garage and ask them." It was frustrating on that level, but Muir knew that ultimately there was no question that TC had to transfer. TC could bluster and storm as much as they wanted but in the end Muir didn't care. Regina had a Cabinet Minister in the city at that time [Ralph Goodale] and the transition team was able to talk to him on a personal level and say "tell these guys to smarten up" and Goodale would phone somebody and there would be a change.

One day the transition team was at a meeting with all the other AAs. The meeting's purpose was to explain the birth of CATSA and how that was going to help the AAs. As the "suits" explained how they were going to roll out CATSA, the AAs became increasingly appalled at the costs and the way CATSA was going to be run: the pre-board screening function was now to be operated by a Crown Agency with triple the number of employees and double the average wage. CATSA had a huge impact on the Authority's finances as the space requirements for pre-board screening became known and better understood. Every time a budget item related to a CATSA requirement arose, the Board's reaction was "how are we going to pay for this?" because under the lease any government department or agency was to be provided with the necessary space in the airport terminal at no cost. The Regina Authority was not alone, for the rest of the Canadian Airport Authorities were in the same boat. When they complained to CATSA about the costs, the reply was "well, it's not your money. Just put in on the departure fee". The Authority felt there was little responsibility, and no accountability nor answerability, on the part of CATSA in terms of the regulations they were imposing on the airport authorities and the impact those regulations had on costs to the Canadian travelling public.

The committee had to negotiate with the union prior to transfer. Dick had a lot of experience and expertise in the labour relations area, and that was primarily why the Board elected him as the first President of the airport. He had become the de facto CEO throughout the formation period, so he was the one that got tasked with negotiating with the union. Muir knew a number of the employees, the fire chief, the maintenance shop supervisor, and had a pretty good idea of what the pulse was. The employees were good guys and liked working at the airport. Negotiations went well for a year or so but then the union in Ottawa sent out a few "heavies" who tried intimidation and the negotiations got ugly pretty fast. Dick was authorized to make a very good offer, but the union guys from Ottawa refused it and starting negotiating through the press. Dick knew exactly the ground that he had to stand on, and the negotiating team also published its offer to the union in the newspaper. That action really upset the Ottawa heavies. The local employees had had no idea how good the offer was, for the Ottawa heavies had kept them in the dark, and eventually the local employees voted to settle for the original offer. Before that, however, the negotiating team was in the room and the union heavy from Ottawa, a big blustery guy, was pounding his fist and swearing that "this was gonna happen, and that was gonna happen" if the offer wasn't made better. The lead negotiator for Regina sat there, calmly, then suddenly got up, leant over the table, and in a very quiet and controlled voice said "do not, ever, raise your voice to me again." And the union guy sat down, leaned back in his chair, and went white.

After the date of transfer the TC inspectors started getting very picky about the Civil Airport Regulations – the CARs. The Authority's response was always "fine, take it back. We don't need it." And the inspectors would equivocate and back off. It was good that the Authority has hired its own management team, rather than use VAS to manage the airport for them, because the staff gave the management team, and the Board, a heads-up of what was likely on the horizon with regards to TC and the Regulations. The staff also provided an extensive list of what was deficient prior to transfer so that the negotiating team was able to get enough money from TC to fix the deficiencies. With no financial surprises the Authority was able to construct an apron replacement and renew some equipment. That was all figured out in advance.

After transfer the largest complaint was with Air Canada. The airport terminal building had five bridges. Air Canada owned one or two, and the airport owned the rest. After transfer Air Canada had to give the bridges to the Authority, take them away, or pay rent. In the event, Air Canada was totally unprepared and did not see why this was their problem. About a half dozen people came out from Air Canada headquarters in Montréal and after some discussion the Authority gave Air Canada a one-year extension saying "you've got to get this thing out of here or pay us to have it hooked onto our building." Air Canada's response was "well, you can't make us do that." The Authority said "yes, we can. We will just tear it down. You do not have standing here anymore." There was a flurry of letters back and forth and when the one year was up Air Canada asked for another one-year extension. Muir said "get a quote from a demolition company and send it to them". And then everything started going smoothly.

At transfer TC ended up giving the Authority about $3 million to cover the cost of some old equipment, deferred maintenance, and a few things that needed updating. On the last day that TC operated the airport they had 50 or 55 employees and the next day, when the Authority took it over, there were 30, and Muir thought that number fat.

When the deal was finally completed and the dust had settled Muir was at a meeting of all the AAs. John Cloutier was there also and he said "you know, if we had had some time we could have turned this around." Muir said "John, you guys screwed it up. The only way to fix it was to start over."

Before transfer there was little sense in the community of the airport's importance. Most Regina residents just thought of it as a utility they were entitled to. The transition team too underestimated its importance until they started talking to their constituency. For example, IPSCO, one of Regina's biggest employers, needed service to Chicago, because that's where their headquarters were. It was at that point that the new Board found out how hard it was to get airlines to land. It was an important lesson and the Board quickly became cognizant of the economic importance of the airport. The municipal politicians had only looked at the airport as a revenue source. They got Grants in Lieu of Taxes and totally underestimated its economic importance. There was an education needed and it took some time, but the efforts of the Board in communicating its message of the economic importance of the airport to Regina and the surrounding area eventually paid off.

By 2004 Muir and Dick had left the Board and it now had the following members:

Name	Title	Nominator
Murray Westerlund	Chair	Government of Canada
Larry Schneider	Vice Chair	City of Regina
Patricia Warsaba	Member	Government of Canada
Duane Beaudry	Member	City of Regina
Campbell Brass	Member	City of Regina
Vacant	Member	City of Regina
Frank Flegel	Member	City of Regina
David MacLeod	Member	City of Regina
Steve McLellan	Member	City of Regina
Ann Phillips	Member	City of Regina
David Rooke	Member	City of Regina (Moose Jaw)
Myron Popp	Member	RM of Sherwood
Al McDonald	Member	Province of Saskatchewan
Kelly Hague	Member	Regina Airport Authority
Jack Ritenburg	Member	Regina Airport Authority

Figure 62: Regina Airport

As an economic engine to the local community, the AAs impact is felt far beyond the walls of its terminal. Direct employment at the airport rose to 1,078 jobs in 2015, throughout the region 3,497 FTE (full time equivalent) jobs are attributed to the airport, bringing $354 million in consumer spending to Regina each year – from employment alone.[364] Property taxes in 2017 were more than $1.5 million. Rent payments for the Ground Lease have totalled more than $8.5 million since they began in 2006. Since transfer in 1991 the Authority has spent more than $185 million on infrastructure development. Almost all of that expense was spent locally.

---

[364] *THE ECONOMIC IMPACT OF THE REGINA INTERNATIONAL AIRPORT: 2015*. RP Erickson & Associates Aviation Consultants Calgary, June 2016.

Regina, Saskatchewan

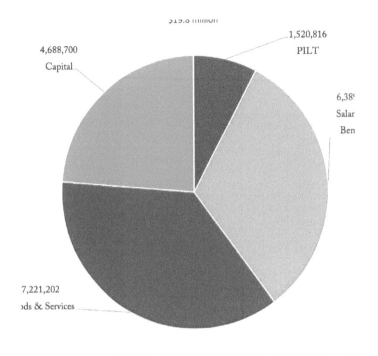

$19.8 million

1,520,816
PILT

4,688,700
Capital

6,38
Salar
Ben

7,221,202
ods & Services

Figure 64: Image courtesy of Google Earth Pro, 12 May 2017.

The first airport at Saint John was built at Millidgeville. The Air Board chose this 102 acre (41 hectares) site following an exhaustive survey of the district, made at the request of the city. Atlantic Airways Ltd. operated the airport and its two runways: 1,800 feet (549 m) and 2,200 feet (610 m). [365]

In 1931 Pan American Airways began to operate a daily air mail service from Portland, ME to Saint John, Halifax, Sydney and St. John's. Their permit to operate in Canada did not allow them to carry passengers or mail between points in Canada, a regulation that did not please the local residents.

In November 1931 the Superintendent of Airways reported that he found the Saint John airport much improved. He also reported that it was very much underused as Pan American had discontinued it service.

In the early 1930's the Millidgeville airport acquired a reputation as an international airport since it was used by aviators attempting

---

[365] Helmer Bierman, *Millidgeville – The Dream of a Great Airport*, The Atlantic Advocate (September 1980), pp. 18-23.

to fly across the Atlantic. Several flights landed there enroute from New York to Harbour Grace, Newfoundland, which was their departure point for Europe.

In June 1931, the American Ruth Nichols hoped to be the first woman to fly the Atlantic solo. As she arrived at Millidgeville in her gold and white Lockheed Vega she crashed on landing. She was injured and flown back to New York.

On the same day two other Americans, Hoiriis and Hillig, left the Millidgeville airport for Harbour Grance in their Billanca Liberty. They crossed successfully and landed in Germany on 25 June 1931.

Figure 65: The airport at Millidgeville in 1930, showing the runway locations. Image courtesy of Google Earth Pro, 12 May 2017.

On 19 May 1932 Amelia Earhart, with Bernt Balchen, arrived at Millidgeville in her crimson Lockheed Vega, *Friendship*. She had been the first woman to fly, as navigator, across the Atlantic with pilots Wilmer Stultz and Louis Gordon in a tri-motor Fokker seaplane in June 1928, and now she wanted to be the first woman to fly the Atlantic solo. She succeeded when she flew from Harbour Grace to Londonderry, Ireland on 21 May 1932.

On 23 August 1932 George Hutchinson landed his Sikorsky Amphibian, *City of Richmond*, at Millidgeville. He, his wife and two children, were on their way to Scotland by way of Labrador,

Greenland and Iceland. The plane was wrecked upon landing in Greenland but no one was injured.

The Controller of Civil Aviation. DOT, in a report of 28 March 1938 wrote:

Millidgeville was chosen as the best site available within a reasonable distance of the City. Development has, therefore, been somewhat costly and the airport limited in size. Up to 1932 the City spent a total of $183,175 on the site and adjacent seaplane base at Millidgeville. Recognizing that the City had backed the project wholeheartedly when times were good and that certain improvements were required to make the site safe, and in view of the acute unemployment situation in the City, the Department of National Defence established a project on the airport for the relief of single, homeless men and further expenditures were made. The project was closed in the fall of 1935... the City would be entitled, on the basis of their original expenditure, to a grant of approximately $61,000. If they decide to proceed with further improvements, it is recommended that these involve the removal of certain outcrop of rock, the diversion of Milledge Avenue, and the extension of the east-west runway across the existing road into clear country beyond. Though the site will never be one which will permit of its use by very large aircraft in all conditions of visibility, the airport has already proved itself a safe airport for smaller types of aircraft and with the work recommended can be greatly improved to permit safe use by medium class aircraft under fair conditions of visibility.[366]

During WW2 an RCAF airport was constructed at Pennfield Ridge, 50 miles (80 km) southwest of Saint John and operated under the BCATP as No.2 Air Navigation School and N0. 34 Operational Training Unit. At the end of the war the DOT assumed responsibility for the airport and for a time Saint John was served from both sites: with Maritime Air operating from Millidgeville and TCA from Pennfield.

During the war there was a dramatic increase in the size and number of aircraft and an ever increasing volume of air traffic and cargo. By early 1943 the City realized that the airport at Millidgeville was inadequate and asked the DOT to build a larger

---

[366] Public Archives Canada, MG 50 E243, vol. 9.

airport. A search was commissioned and by December 1943 an engineering survey selected the site of the current airport, 10 miles (16 km) east of Saint John. The site consisted of 1,776 acres (719 hectares) and on 26 February 1946 the City paid $200,000 for the title. The DOT agreed to construct the airport, but maintenance and operation were to be the responsibility of the City.

By the end of 1950 runway 05-23 at 5,500 feet (1 676 m) and runway 14-32 at 5,100 feet (1 554 m) had been built. The terminal building was completed and opened on 8 January 1952. The aerodrome was named Turnbull Airport, after W.R. Turnbull of Rothsay, a pioneer aeronautical researcher and inventor.[367]

The Millidgeville airport license was cancelled in 1951 and the site later became a housing estate (as may be seen in the photograph above).

By 1951 the City was finding it problematic to fund the operations and maintenance of the airport, so beginning on 1 January 1952 the DOT paid the City an operating subsidy.

Turnbull airfield hosted its first air show on Dominion Day, 1 July 1953. More than 40,000 people came to the airfield to see participants from across Canada and from many foreign countries. It was an outstanding success.

Air travel through Saint John grew at a rapid pace and by 1954 an extension to the air terminal was proposed to accommodate the increased passenger loads and an international Customs service. A new control tower was also proposed. Construction was completed by July 1956.

The City's Airport Commission notified DOT that, commencing January 1956, the DOT would be charged $9 square foot for space that it occupied in the control tower. This caused quite a stir in

---

[367] Turnbull built a wind tunnel in 1902 to test wings and wind flow over them. It was the first of its kind in North America. He was the first Canadian to tackle the theoretical aspects of aeronautics. He later took an interest in the design and construction of air propellers and in 1918 began experiments with variable pitch propellers. He was the first person in the world to successfully build a variable-pitch propeller and demonstrated it to the DND at Camp Borden, Ontario, in 1927 (see F.H. Ellis, *Canada's Flying Heritage*, University of Toronto Press, 1961, pp. 3, 13-15).

Ottawa and, after considerable negotiation, the DOT bought the control tower, and the land it sat on, from the City for $102,000.

In 1958 an Instrument Landing System (ILS) was commissioned.

At the same time as the public side of the airport was being developed, the private sector was also becoming interested in the site. In 1953 the Irving Organization built a square hangar 120 feet (30 m) on a side, 30 feet (9 m) high. Sliding doors took up 70% of the east wall.

On 14 May 1957 the Airport Commission proposed that $432,000 be spent on an extension to the air terminal. Discussions between the Commission and the DOT as to who was going to pay for what and when took some time but eventually, in the spring of 1960, a contract was awarded for the demolition of approximately 40% of the existing terminal, to be replaced by new construction that effectively doubled the size of the terminal. The work was completed in June 1961.

With the arrival of jet passenger service runway 05-23 was lengthened by 2,000 feet (609 m) at the 05 end of the runway. This was completed in September 1964.

In 1967 Carrigan Insurance Company built a combined hangar and club rook from which they operated a scheduled air service throughout New Brunswick under the name of Air Brunswick. This operation was later bought out by Air Canada.

After nearly ten years of intermittent, on and off again, negotiations, on 1 April 1968 the City and County of Saint John agreed to sell the airport lands, premises, and equipment to the DOT for $835,000.

In June 1973 the air terminal was enlarged, this time by 3,400 sq ft (316 sq m) and again in 1977, this time to accommodate baggage pick-up and a passenger exit.

In the Fall of 1975 Fundy Aviation built a metal hangar on a concrete slab. The door had not yet arrived when a hurricane lifted the hangar off the slab and blew it 150 feet (46 m) over a hydro line and into a nearby field. The hangar was reduced to rubble. The five aircraft housed inside the hangar were miraculously unharmed.

In 1980 a combined services building was constructed at a cost of $1,560,500 to house the vehicle maintenance garage, general trade shops, and fire hall.

Passenger volumes continued to increase and a $1.2 million refurbishment was done to the air terminal in time for the Canada Summer Games, hosted by Saint John in 1985.

In 1988 DOT employed 28 full and part-time employees at the airport.[368]

The Authority

Around 1995 there was a risk that the Saint John airport might not be part of the National Airports System (NAS). The Mayor of the City of Saint John, Elsie Wayne, supported by the Saint John Board of Trade, fought hard to ensure that the airport retained its status and remained part of the NAS. Through her political connections she persuaded Doug Young, the Minister of Transport, to keep the airport open.[369] The business community also exerted pressure on the provincial and federal politicians.

Soon after that political work TC notified the city of Saint John that it wanted to begin negotiations about transferring the Saint John airport to the control of a local airport authority. The Mayor telephoned Lino Celeste and asked if he would head up a committee to negotiate the transfer. He had no experience in airports, but he had previously been asked a number of times to do something similar for the City, when they wanted to build a new aquatic centre, and similar things. So he put a transition team together to negotiate the terms of the agreement.[370]

The transition team comprised:

- Lino Celeste, Chair

- Bill Fitzpatrick, CA

- Pat Riley, President of Saint John Longshoreman's Association

---

[368] *History*, p. 201.

[369] Bob Creamer, interview with the Author, 2 January 2019.

[370] Lino Celeste, interview with the Author, 4 January 2019.

- Sylvie McVey, CEO from Sussex

- Jim Russell, Comptroller

- Larry McGillivray

- Christianne Vaillancourt, CBC producer

- Graham McDougal, financial investor

- Darrell Guoyasch, Director, Saint John Board of Trade

- David Ames, lawyer

Supporting the transition team and providing legal advice was Bob Creamer.

The first task for the transition team was to assess the viability of the airport as an independent business. Could it survive, even though it would be a not-for-profit? And to ensure that it would be "profitable" in the sense that it could pay its bills and not run in the red. The transition team did not, at the beginning, see the airport as a monopoly. The passenger numbers were not there. The main question was: is this viable? They were not sitting there thinking that it was going to be a cash cow, their primary concern was "could we run it, break even, and pay the bills?"[371] Although the traffic was in the order of 250,000 passengers a year, they had to make sure that they were not going to take on a problem. They ended up doing our own forensic examination of the books, and then hired PWC to do a financial analysis and a forensic accounting to see if it was viable. They concluded that the airport would be OK on the operating side, but that the capital investment needed would be in the order of $7.5 million because the runways were in bad shape.

Whether or not there would be a PFC caused a great deal of discussion and when it was implemented would the PFC be a "stand alone" charge or be on the airline ticket.[372] Initially the PFC was collected by the AA, but eventually it became a fee collected by the airline and remitted to the AA.

---

[371] Creamer.

[372] Ibid.

One of the major issues was when the new Authority was going to have to start paying rent to TC, because that depended on calculations of passenger loads. Lino had in mind that once the passenger volume got to 200,000 passengers a year the Authority would have to start paying rent.

Over the next year or so negotiations continued. TC gave the Authority some money for capital improvements, and the two parties came to an agreement as to when the rent would start. The next thing was to transfer the airport so now there had to be a Board of Directors to run it. Lino was the first Chairman of that Board. The members couldn't come just from Saint John, they had to come from the area the airport was serving. So the Board had members from Sussex and from the southwest.

One of the hot issues was that an airport at Saint John. Moncton and Fredericton didn't make sense and there should be a single airport in Sussex serving all three cities. Lino was never in favour of that and didn't give it much consideration. Moreover there wasn't any pressure from the negotiating committee to do that. In his opinion it was a pretty short drive to the airport from just about anywhere in the Saint John region −15 or 20 minutes at the most. So building an airport at Sussex had no appeal. Why would anyone want to travel further when the Saint John airport was pretty handy for all of the Sussex region and most of southern New Brunswick. The one factor he didn't consider was that he never thought Moncton would amount to a substantial competitor because it was too close to Halifax. And Halifax had the planes, flights and connections that appealed to people. If you were in Moncton and you wanted to choose more frequent service you weren't that far from Halifax. But as it turned out Moncton wound up with a big freight business and that pushed that airport to a point where it had a lot of everything it needed to attract a lot of the carriers, and Moncton became a pretty good hub for passenger traffic.

The Board was concerned over money. It spent a lot of time saying "how are we going to be able to afford this airport? What are we going to be able to do to attract flights?"[373] Because back then all the airport had was Air Canada and if they didn't put in four

---

[373] Ibid.

flights a day you were in trouble. So the Board thought "why don't we make Saint John a centre for travel?" because we have the port here and we have passenger ships arriving, and we have the airport. So at one time the Board was in discussions with a travel firm from Germany and tried to get them to establish an office in Saint John to conduct a tour operation. It never happened.

The Board had a pretty good idea that initially it was going to spend money on needed maintenance to the runways. It had no plans to do much with the ATB because other AAs, when they had taken over the airport, the first thing they did was to build a new, modern ATB, just like Moncton did, but the Board never felt that was what it needed to attract flights into the airport.

Creamer received all the documents a few months before the takeover, including the ground lease, the rent clause, agreement to transfer, and all the schedules. His job was to review all the paperwork before the final negotiations with TC. So he locked himself into his home office for a full week to review the 30 or documents (about 1,000 pages) so that he could give a "high-level" explanation of what they meant to the transition team. He developed a system whereby he could give an overview of each document which explained its purpose and its important parts. There were four categories for each item in each document: critically important, important, not so important, not important. Once he had organized everything, he then addressed each provision of each document with the transition team.

Unique to the Province of New Brunswick is that the Saint John Airport Inc. was incorporated under the New Brunswick *Companies Act*, which is legislation different from the *New Brunswick Business Corporations Act* which most companies incorporate under. This was to ensure that the AA was truly a New Brunswick incorporated company, and also to ensure it was a company with its own Letters Patent (which also incorporated the federal Public Accountability Principles). The *Companies Act* is provincial legislation meant for charitable organizations and not-for-profit companies.

After Creamer had analyzed the documents, and had then reviewed them with the transition team, they quickly realized that there was not much left to negotiate, Cramer met for a day with Senzilet at the Halifax airport to go over the documents.

Creamer found John Cloutier to be a tough negotiator, and Michael Senzilet a consummate lawyer – "he knew the ground lease inside out."[374]

There was no doubt in the minds of the Board members that the Premier of New Brunswick (Frank McKenna) supported Moncton. Lino had told McKenna that the three airports in New Brunswick were all well under way with their negotiations with TC, and that he hoped McKenna was not going to start interfering with the process. McKenna swore up and down that he wasn't, but Lino believes Moncton couldn't have built a new ATB without the new road that the Province built to access it. That's where the politics came in.

A single airport for New Brunswick was an idea that had been around for a long time, but by this time Moncton was well established, Saint John was on its way, and Fredericton was doing well also. None of the three airports were pushing for a single airport to service all of New Brunswick, nor were many people, except for a lobby group that had something in mind for the Sussex area, rather than being concerned for the passengers who wanted service from the existing airports. There was never anything serious about a central airport, because the minute a proposal was made, and talk started about shutting down the local airports, the political side just squashed it flat. People would come up to Lino and ask why he hadn't supported a central airport, because it would have given them access to many more flights and destinations. He would tell them that if they took the 6:00 am flight from Saint John to Toronto, they then had access to flights to anywhere in the world, and they didn't have to arrive at the airport two or three hours ahead of their flight time in order to check their bags and then go through security.

Skip Cormier was the first CEO of the Authority and he had a different idea.[375] He tried to get the three airports together, Moncton, Fredericton and Saint John, and to build a new airport in the middle of all three. All three airport had cash at the time. Saint John had $7 million, Fredericton had $17 million, and Moncton had $30 million. That would have been a good down

---

[374] Ibid.

[375] Skip Cormier, interview with the Author, 3 Jan 2019

payment on a new airport. and Skip thought to himself "if we all got together and built a new airport in the middle, we'd all be 45 minutes from an airport. It would have one firehall, one set of runways to sweep, one set of equipment, and one ATB to maintain. It would have about 800.000 passengers a year, and with that passenger load we could get more airlines and more destinations. Individually we just didn't have enough volume to get these flights and destinations out of these small airports."[376] So he met with the three airport managers and Moncton expressed no interest whatsoever because they had InterVistas managing them. Moncton also had McKenna's ear and he was subsidizing low-cost carriers to them. But Fredericton was still interested so some members from the two Boards had several meetings to discuss using an airport in back of Petersville Hill, at the entrance to Gagetown, about halfway between Saint John and Fredericton. About 6 miles to the west of the highway is an airport, with a 4,000 foot runway, which had been used for spraying and forest fire fighting. When they were spraying there were some barracks for the workers to sleep in. Skip thought that would be the perfect spot if you were going to put an airport half-way between Fredericton and Saint John. And it probably would have led to more four lane highway along the route. All that was needed was a 6 mile access road from the highway. The two Boards had a few meetings, and it seemed as if it would be a go, but then Fredericton got their transfer done and they decided not to pursue it. A shared airport for Saint John and Fredericton was estimated at the time to have had a volume of 550,000 to 600,000 passengers.

To close the three airports now would require a great political will, or a very persuasive outside influence. The time to have done it was when the three airports transferred, but there has been too much investment since then.

TC had a set of conditions and documents they were working from and then it was left with the negotiating committee to go over the documents. The committee would say "well let's try for this." Lino thought that the Authority did extremely well on the contribution it got for capital. TC were fair negotiators. He

---

[376] Ibid.

doesn't remember himself or the committee being upset with what TC proposed.

"I was just there to do the negotiations. I didn't want to be the Chair of an airport authority."[377]

Money was needed for studies, and consultants, but the banks would not finance them. So some resources agreed to delay their billing until the transfer has occurred and the AA could pay the bill.

When Skip Cormier was asked what it was like to be the first CEO he replied "it was like starting a business from scratch. The feds had their own accounting systems, their own telephone systems, etc., so we had to set up new telephone lines, we had to set up an accounting system, general ledger coding, all the stuff you would need to run a business. So primarily the first order of business was to get all those pieces in place."[378]

He didn't find it difficult to do that, but it did take time. And TC didn't offer any help at all. What telephone system to use? What accounting system use? There was no help from TC at all. The Authority just went and did its own thing.

For the employees the transition from the public to the private sector went well at the beginning. They went in search of a Local for the union to be a part of, and until the time they signed on with PSAC and began negotiations the Authority had a reasonable time with them. People got along, and helped each other. Everyone had everybody's back. But once the negotiators from Ottawa arrived the situation changed totally. In Skip's opinion "it became ridiculous."[379] The whole union experience really poisoned the well. Before transfer it had been a great place to work, small, 24 employees, people got along, and they had each other's backs. But once the guys from Ottawa came in it suddenly became management against the world. Negotiations went on for almost two years, with the union making demands that the Authority

---

[377] Celeste.

[378] Cormier.

[379] Ibid.

could not meet. Eventually the union went on strike for 5 months, but finally settled for what they had been originally offered.

Before the strike, however, the Authority had resurfaced the runways, and had 90% of the terminal re-built. It was an old ATB, made up of a couple of buildings melded together. The Board decided a complete renovation was required. An old staircase was removed (it went to the roof for the days when you could go outside and watch the airplane come in) which greatly improved traffic flow. The existing floor plan was expanded to allow for a bigger baggage hold room, a new departure lounge, and a new customs facility that could handle larger planes. There was no business for that customs room at the time, but Skip knew that if they didn't build it they'd never get the business. There had been a small customs area before, but it would only handle the passenger load of a small plane, and the Authority couldn't attract any larger airlines or larger planes on the routes to the U.S. It took a few years for passenger loads to increase, but that expansion has proven to have been a wise decision.

Cormier had done ticket lift studies for direct flights to Boston because there was a lot of noise from the business community in Saint John, but there were only about 5,000 passengers a year and the airline wanted 30-35,000 passengers a year before they would consider a route, even for a Dash 8. The bleed to Bangor was about 25-30,000 passengers a year, and there was bleed to Fredericton too. For people who lived on the west side of Saint John, up around Grand Bay or Westfield, they are as close to the Fredericton airport as they are to the Saint John airport. So the Authority had to be very keen as to what it was going to do.

Cormier was insistent that was no debt. By the time it became necessary to do the runways enough money had been saved from the AIF to pay the $6 or 7 million to do the two runways. The Authority then started saving for the next round, to do the expansion and renovation of the ATB. It was all done without any debt.

At transfer nothing was in good shape. TC had done no maintenance in years, the runways needed rehabilitation, the equipment was in poor shape, the ATB was showing its age, and there were leaks everywhere.

In 2004, five years after transfer, the Board had the following members:

Name	Title	Nominator
David Barry	Chairman	Enterprise Saint John
Pat Riley	Director	Saint John Airport Inc.
Rod Cox	Director	Provincial Government
David Ames	Director	Saint John Airport Inc.
Harold Tennant	Director	Enterprise Fundy
D. Noel Wittrien	Director	City of Saint John
Charles Nelson	Director	City of Saint John
James Russell	Director	Fundy Region Mayors
Paul Doiron	Director	Saint John Board of Trade
Paul Harquail	Director	Federal Government
Christianne Vaillancourt	Director	Federal Government
John Buchanan	Director	Saint John Airport Inc.

Several of these people had been part of the transition team and had been there from the beginning. When I spoke with Lino a few days after New Year's 2019 to hear his recollections of the creation of the Saint John Airport Authority he said "we had no idea at the time, really, of what we were getting ourselves into. We all just thought it would be a good idea. Good social responsibility, I

Figure 66: Saint John Airport

guess."[380] There's that "they did the very thing that no one could imagine", again.

Since transfer the AA has spent $16 million on capital for infrastructure, and forecasts spending a further $30 million over the next 10 years. It employs 81 full-time and part-time seasonal employees, and more than 190 people work at enterprises located on airport land. The AA contributes more than $63 million to the local economy every year through salaries, taxes, utilities, and other payments.

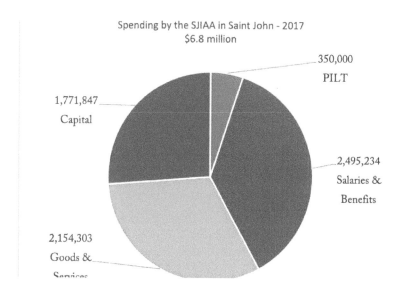

Figure 67: Spending by the Authority in Saint John in 2017.

Figure 68: Image courtesy of Google Earth Pro, 12 May 2017. The pin marks the location of the original BCATP aerodrome.

In 1911 a Curtiss airplane owned by Bob St. Henry arrived by train and made its flight at Saskatoon on 17 May 1911, from a prairie grass strip west of the city limits. Glenn Martin, later known as a designer and builder of bomber aircraft, came to Saskatoon in 1912 and flew a Pusher biplane, which he had designed and built, at the annual Exhibition. In 1913, when the city set aside a quarter section of land west of the exhibition grounds at the southwest edge of the city as an aerodrome, W. Featherstone set up an aviation school there with a Farman biplane. Then came World War I and all aviation at Saskatoon ceased.

In April 1919 Lt. Stan McClelland, ex RAF, established a commercial flying operation at a field on 22nd Street West and Dundonald Avenue, one mile (1 ½ km) north of the St. Paul's Hospital, and built a hangar for his Curtiss JN-4 biplane. Four DH-4B airplanes of the US Army Air Service used the airfield on 25 July 1920, on their way from New York to Nome, Alaska.

Three of the aircraft landed at McLelland Field on their return journey on 10 October 1920.[381]

At the same time as McLelland was setting up his airfield, another was established three miles (4 ½ km) north, near Hudson Bay Slough. Operated by Keng Wah Aviation, it was used to train pilots from China, the United States and Canada for Dr. Sun Yat Sen's Revolutionary Army.[382]

Saskatoon is shown in the 1922 List of Airharbours as having two public-commercial airharbours: one 400 by 600 yards (366 by 549 m) with Airharbour License No.49 in the name of R.J. Groome of Regina; and the other 300 by 400 yards (274 by 366 m) with Airharbour License No. 2 to McLelland Aircraft Ltd.[383]

In February 1920 the city asked the Air Board to establish an aerodrome in Saskatoon. The Air Board declined because government policy required that any aerodrome be the responsibility of the local municipality. The city took no further action.

Seven years later, in 1927, the situation had changed. The Department of National Defence, Civil Aviation Branch, asked Saskatoon to establish an airport since DND was considering air mail services and was launching its scheme to establish light aeroplane clubs across Canada. The city was interested and DND sent someone to help find a suitable site. In May 1928 a site was chosen and the city acquired a quarter section (65 hectares) of land in the rural municipality of Cory[384] in July. The site was licensed for day use on 1 June 1929. It had two runways: north-south, 1,760 feet (537 m); and east-west, 2,640 feet (805 m). DND installed lighting in June 1930. This airport now forms a small part of the existing airport.

---

[381] I was unable to find any record of the fate of the fourth aircraft.

[382] *Airports '79 – 50 Years in Flight*, Saskatoon Star Phoenix, 31 May 1979, supplement.

[383] *Canadian Airharbours, Aviation and Aircraft Journal*, 21 October 1921, pp 482 and 531.

[384] The Rural Municipality of Cory became part of the City of Saskatoon on 1 January 1971.

By 1938 Western Canada Airways was carrying air mail to and from Saskatoon, and Prairie Airways Ltd was providing daily passenger service to Regina, Moose Jaw, Prince Albert and North Battleford. About the same time the Saskatoon Flying Club agreed to provide primary flying training to provisional flying officers of the RCAF. In 1940 the club became part of the BCATP as No. 6 Elementary Flying Training School and the city agreed to lease the airport to the federal government for "the duration" of the war. By the end of 1940 the RCAF had established No. 4 Service Flying Training School, which continued operations until November 1945.

Work started immediately on building five large hangars, barracks, mess halls, classrooms, workshops, a hospital, and a control tower. By early 1941 most of the construction was complete. The economic lift to the community was immense.

Figure 69: WW2 hangar built by the BCATP. Photo by the author, 19 March 2019.

apparent that relief stations would be necessary and two auxiliary airfields were set up: No. 1 at Vanscoy and No. 2 at Osler.

BCATP operations ceased on 31 March 1945. Notwithstanding its agreement with the federal government of 1940, the city refused to accept responsibility for the airport so the DOT assumed maintenance of the airport in November that year. By 1948 instrument landing systems were installed on runways 08 and 32.

315

In 1950 the RCAF returned and established No. 1 Advanced Flying Training School (AFTS) to train RCAF, RAF and NATO air crews. By the end of 1952 Permanent Married Quarters (the, sometimes, infamous PMQs) and personnel and their families began to arrive. In addition to No. 1 AFTS there were No. 23 Wing HQ, No. 406 Auxiliary Squadron, No. 3043 Technical Training Unit and No. 4002 Medical Unit. These remained until 1964 when the RCAF closed the station and handed over its four hangars to the DOT.

TCA began scheduled passenger and cargo services in July 1947 using DC-3s. It changed to North Stars in 1950, Viscounts in 1955 and DC-9s in 1967.

The airport became a Customs Port of Entry in 1954.

Runway 08-24 was lengthened in 1954 and again in 1960 to 8,300 feet (2 530 m). Runway 14-32 was lengthened to 6,200 feet (1 890 m) in 1963.

A new air terminal was built by the DOT in 1955 (using the same plans as for the terminals in Windsor and Québec City). The city again refused to take over the new airport.

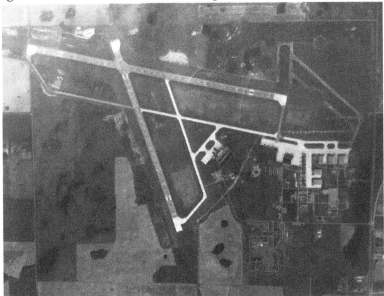

Figure 70: Saskatoon airport circa 1965. The original BCATP triangle is still there.

Twenty years later, in 1975, DOT built a new terminal and turned the old terminal into an operations building.

In 1989, on the seventieth anniversary of the airport, the Minister of Transport dedicated the Wall of Fame, celebrating the airport and its aviation pioneers.

Figure 71: Saskatoon Airport 2018, courtesy of the SIAA.

The Authority

In 1995 or 1996 Wayne Brownlee, David Ekmeyer, Peter McKinnon, Bob Stromberg, and Fraser Sutherland formed the transition team to look at what would be entailed in the transfer of the Saskatoon airport to an AA.

The group had heard rumours that transfer was going to happen so Bob Stromberg talked with a law firm in Alberta who had been involved in the privatization and development of their airport authority. Bob's interest was in supplying the group in Saskatoon with legal work. But, as he said, "I could have saved myself a whole bunch of time and done a whole bunch of other things that would have been really profitable if I had not gotten involved with the airport authority. But it worked out not too badly."[385]

Wayne Brownlee was in the business development side of the Potash Corp and Bob Stromberg was on the Board of Directors of Potash. So they knew each other. Brownlee had also been involved

---

[385] Robert Stromberg, interview with the author, 3 January 2019.

in a lot of business negotiations, mostly in the business development side of things with companies from other nations. Stromberg asked Brownlee to join the team to help with the negotiations with TC.

On the team were a lot of people who loved airplanes but not Brownlee. He liked negotiating. Planes were not a passion of his, unlike some other members of the Board. He was interested in ensuring that the airport represented the local community and he wanted to make sure the airport got a fair deal.[386]

The group was initially just interested in talking with TC to see what could happen, and how the situation would unfold. They also decided that it might be advantageous to speak with other AAs at that stage. Michael Senzilet of TC was quite helpful. A bright and smart lawyer, he'd been through all the transfers up to that point and he knew exactly where this was going to go.

Saskatoon was a small airport with a passenger count of about 800,000 a year. The transfer group had received word from TC that they were going to give the AA a whole bunch of money, but in the end the amount offered by TC really didn't amount to much.

Eventually, in 1998, the group applied for Letters Patent for the AA, and it was then necessary to form a Board. The group chose people who they thought would bring something to the table. Stromberg had this comment about his own experience and expertise as a Board member "I was a pilot, although I soon found out that that didn't give me the qualifications to sit on the committee for I didn't know a whole lot about TC and how it works."[387] He was not alone. Other members of the Board were Fraser Sutherland, who was involved in construction; Wayne Brownlee, who had a lot of financial experience from his work as CFO of Potash Corp.; the Dean of the Law School came aboard; Peter McKinnon, who was a partner in Peat Marwick Mitchell; and a labour union representative: Greg Trew. None of them really knew how TC worked, and how the transfer negotiations might proceed. Their initial task was to figure out what they had to do,

---

[386] Wayne Brownlee, interview with the author, 4 January 2019.

[387] Stromberg.

and how they were going to do it. They also needed to establish how to approach TC when TC finally decided they wanted to talk to the nascent AA.

Wayne Brownlee and Bob Stromberg got the mandate from the Board to do the negotiations. Their *modus operandi* was that once they came to what they thought was a fair agreement they would call a Board meeting and get the Board's approval.

Negotiations worked out really well, at the end. At the beginning negotiations were tense. Stromberg had spoken with someone from Victoria who had been the lawyer for the first AA to accept the TC proposal. That chap's attitude had been "we [Victoria] don't need a whole bunch [of money] so we'll just take what they offer us."[388]

At that time [1999] the Saskatoon airport had seen some growth in traffic and the numbers were going up, but the real issue was that the airport was by that time 24 years old and at the end of its life-cycle. For the previous 20 years there had been fundamentally no investment by TC in infrastructure, and the issue for the transition team was to get a capital contribution from TC. TC's starting position was "you take it over as is." And the transition team's starting position was "sorry, no, not without a substantial capital investment."[389] London and St. John's had transferred the year before, and Regina, Charlottetown and Saint John were well on their way in their negotiations. All had obtained an allowance for capital investment, and the Saskatoon team said "there has to be a level playing ground. It is not fair to put us under the gun to get money and retrofit the airport to a standard for Saskatchewan and its passengers. It would not be fair to expect us to find the money on our own"[390], not when, in the rest of Canada, the airports authorities had received capital monies for infrastructure renewal and development.

Brownlee's experience in negotiations told him there are a buyer and a seller. And the trick in finding a deal is to establish who has the greater incentive or motivation to conduct the transaction. His

---

[388] Ibid.

[389] Brownlee.

[390] Ibid.

job during the negotiations was to leave the federal government with the impressions that the transition team didn't really care if the airport transferred or not, even though he knew he had a Board that really wanted it.[391] TC was moving well along the road [to transfer] with other airports and by then they were a really motivated seller. So the transition team went through a period of time where they simply had to convince TC that the transition team was indifferent to transfer unless it got the right deal.

At the first meeting with TC, Michael Senzilet and his team came out to Saskatoon to make a proposal that the government give an amount of about $5 million as a capital contribution to the needed renovations. They met at the airport's conference room. On one side of the table were Senzilet and his crew, and on the other side were Brownlee, Stromberg and a few Board members. Between them was a very large pile of documents, from which Senzilet started reading. After about 20 minutes Stromberg called a halt saying "we [Stromberg and Brownlee] need to talk before this goes any further. Would you mind giving us some space?".[392] So the TC team left the conference room. There was some animated discussion amongst the Saskatoon team with a consensus that "hey, we're not going to sit here for six hours or more listening to these guys read to us from these 200 page documents."[393] So Stromberg called Senzilet and the other TC guys back inside the Board room to tell them to go away. They could leave the documents and the Board would read them and then after that everyone could have a discussion. Stromberg told them "now look guys, we can't go any further with this meeting. My Board isn't interested in having you read these documents to them."[394] Michael Senzilet just sat there listening to Stromberg, and after a short period of reflection he said "yeah. Now which part of 'fuck off' don't you understand." And Stromberg said "well, if you want to take it that way then I guess that's it."[395] And Stromberg,

---

[391] Ibid.

[392] Stromberg.

[393] Ibid.

[394] Ibid.

[395] Ibid.

Brownlee and the other Board members left the room. It was the only time during negotiations that the team walked out on TC.[396]

The Saskatoon airport was in really rough shape at the time and the negotiating team felt it just had to say "no" to the first offer. So TC went away and came back a second time with a larger amount. The negotiating team again said "no, we can't do it for that." And TC went away again empty handed.

Eventually TC got to the point where they wanted to close the deal, and offered about $11 million. The negotiating team had been ready to settle for $9 million, but when TC arrived the first thing they said was "now, stop this horsing around and let's get this deal done. Here's $11 million. Now sign." Stromberg thought that if they had tried they could have got a couple more million out of TC, but the Board was satisfied, and he was satisfied.[397] The Board knew what capital projects it was going to do when it first took the airport over because of the work Fraser Sutherland had done. He had a lot of construction experience. He had found a local architect, who was very capable, and with Fraser's help and explanations, over the period of a few months the Board knew what it wanted to do in order to renovate the ATB. After putting out a tender the Board was able to negotiate a contract with PCL. Sutherland was the right resource at the right time as he knew the construction business and the types of contracts that were needed to sign.

The Board knew that it was assuming control of a monopoly. As a result of that knowledge it knew it had a major obligation to the passengers, because it knew it could set the fees at a level to cover expenses. Brownlee saw the issue of a monopoly as an interesting question for it was on his mind throughout the discussions.[398] In his mind the airport is a utility, a monopoly, and there was no overriding governance requirement for people who manage that utility. In the first few years of the AA's administration of the airport, he was strongly of the view that landing fees and boarding fees be kept to a minimum, and that it would not be detrimental to

---

[396] Farquhar and Cloutier, 23 October 2018.

[397] Ibid.

[398] Brownlee.

the airport to carry a debt load. But there were many on the Board who wanted to increase the AIF and save the revenue from it until the AA could carry out a capital spend without creating debt. In Brownlee's opinion the way the federal government set the AAs up allows for almost a usurious relationship with the travelling public from the point-of-view of the AIF.[399]

The Board were fiscal conservatives and did not want debt, notwithstanding that the AA could raise debt at a very cheap rate [since effectively the airport, from a risk point-of-view, is the same as a municipality]. And Brownlee thought that debt would keep the cost of travel down since the AIF would be minimal, or even zero.[400] But debt as a financing vehicle was never used.

The AA had no debt because it had enough money to basically do everything. It had an AIF of $5, but only because the AA was told by TC that it had to have an AIF. TC suggested the AA start with a $10 AIF, but from the work of Sutherland the AA knew it didn't need that much money so the AIF started at $5.

A major problem at takeover was that the AA had only 19 employees, almost all of whom were conducting maintenance and operations. All the HR was done out of Winnipeg, and finance out of Ottawa so some extra staff were hired to do that work. The biggest concern of the Board was the attitude of the employees. They had always worked for the government and they basically had a public sector mindset. The Board spoke with the airport manager, Bill Restall to get an idea of the union and the employees. Bill wasn't the most popular fellow with the aviation community, but after talking and spending a bit of time with him the Board decided to keep him on as the manager, eventually CEO. But there were times Stromberg would have to call him in and say "Bill, you're starting to act like a godamned government agent again. Grow up! Otherwise you're not going to be here."[401] Bill was very capable, but every now and gain he would go back to his old ways, and he'd have to be talked to.

---

[399] Ibid.

[400] Ibid.

[401] Stromberg.

To fund the transition team Stromberg's law firm put up the money. There were no monies available to the transition team as no bank or financial institution would lend it money without any surety. Moreover the transition team couldn't open a bank account in the name of the AA because it didn't have an agreement with TC. So the members all paid their own little expenses but when it came to other expenses, studies or trips to Ottawa, Stromberg would use his expense account for that sort of thing. He kept track of it and when the AA took over it paid his firm back. It wasn't that much, only about $10,000 or so. It could have been a hell of lot more but it wasn't, because they were all careful about how much they spent on things.[402]

The transition team understood financial analysis with the help of Pat Pitka, who was a CA and a Managing Partner of Peat Marwick. It also had Wayne Brownlee, who was the CFO of the Potash Corp, and both of them used some of their people to help work through the numbers. There was also some business people, one of whom was Betty Anne Latrace-Henderson, who played a major role. Karim Nasser, professor of engineering at University of Saskatchewan, was very helpful.

Originally the Board was comprised of 15 people, but it was soon found out that that number was unwieldy and the number was reduced to 12.

This was the Board in Dec 2003.

Name	Title	Nominator
Mr. E. Robert Stromberg, Q.C.	Chairman	City of Saskatoon
Pat Pitka	Vice-Chair	Board
Fraser Sutherland	Secretary-Treasurer	City of Saskatoon
Betty Anne Latrace-Henderson	Director	Federal Government
Henry Dayday	Director	Federal Government
Gary Mearsty	Director	Provincial Government
Wayne Brownlee	Director	City of Saskatoon
Dr. Karim Nasser	Director	City of Saskatoon

---

[402] Ibid.

Saskatoon, Saskatchewan

Peter MacKinnon	Director	City of Saskatoon
Nancy Hopkins, Q.C.	Director	City of Saskatoon
Greg Trew	Director	Board

One of the AA staff members looked after human resources, including the contracts with the union. Within three months of transfer the union went on strike at the urging and instigation of the union leaders from Ottawa. Williams was the union guy from Ottawa and he was pleased with the strike, because the Ottawa union heads wanted to make an example of Saskatoon to the rest of the airports in the country. But it was poor timing for a strike. It was springtime, with no snow to be moved, no major work to be done. The airport was in OK shape, not good shape, but OK. So the AA just said "no" to the strikers' demands. The strikers picketed Stromberg's house, and did all kinds of annoying things. Stromberg would go to the airport and the picketers would be walking back and forth with their signs saying "Stromberg is a puppet master" or "Management is rotten". And Stromberg would stop and chat with them. They were a small group and he got to be quite friendly with them. The union guy from Ottawa got wind that Stromberg was talking to the strikers and he came out and said to the strikers "You may not really want to strike. But since you are on strike you have to be out here. And don't talk to management."[403] But, after almost 85 days of walking the picket line, the union finally agreed to settle for what the AA had offered them the first time around. Since then the AA has never had a problem with the union. As Stromberg said "We tried to look after them well. They were just a small group of 19. Now it's close to 40 people. It's a bigger building. More things to be done, I suppose."[404]

For most of the staff the experience of going from public sector to private sector employees was a tough time.[405] They were used to a

---

[403] Ibid.

[404] Ibid.

[405] Although some of the staff welcomed the change. They found the TC mindset "stifling". When it came to getting something approved the smallest change required reams of paperwork and signatures. After the AA took over the management of the airport, decisions could be made almost on the spot.

routine, used to the government way, used to not being required to think for themselves because they had a set of rules and they followed those rules. However the AA Board came from a very different mindset. They were experienced business people, all from the private sector and they expected people to use their initiative. The airport staff were in the service of the public so they had to have good public relations with everybody that walked in the door. Stromberg thought that they caught on to that real quick and they did a good job.

There was one time when the relations between the Board and management almost all fell apart. It was a hot summer's day and the entire senior management team was off playing golf. An employee phoned Stromberg saying "we have a hell of a problem out here." The covered walkways that go to the planes (the loading bridges) were 108 degrees F (42 degrees C) and someone had passed out while getting to a plane. Stromberg said "can't you open the doors?" and he said "Nope. It's against the rules. You can't leave the doors open." Stromberg said "Open the goddamned doors, get some air going through." He then went to the airport and asked "where is everybody?" "well they're out playing golf." And he said "how come there's no air conditioning on this thing?" "well, it's going to cost $6,000." "well, where's Restall?"[406] "he's on the golf course." On Monday morning they had the air conditioning contractor in there cutting holes in the loading bridges and installing air conditioning units. Stromberg said "you know, Bill, it's just a problem with you guys. You're going back to the old days. That's not how you operate an airport." Overall they worked well, but about every two years Stromberg would have to have a "come to church" meeting with him.[407]

The AA tried to have a governance Board but that only worked so far. Originally there were too many Board members – 15 people – as the transition team had been told the Board had to representatives from different groups. But the group was too large, so it was cut it down to twelve. That made for a more effective and efficient Board – a better Board. The first time the members were nominated to create a diverse Board, there were only two ladies on

---

[406] The CEO at the time.

[407] Stromberg.

it, but a better representation from the rural communities, not just the city. Even though governance was an issue, the Board wasn't really a management Board either. First of all it had "a whole bunch of people who didn't know a damn thing about airports"[408]. They knew that planes landed there, and they knew where the bathrooms were, but that was it. However some of them came in thinking they were going to change everything with the attitude of "I'm going to fire you." or "I'm going to change this, or that" because of run-ins with airport staff they had had in a past life. Stromberg found he had to rule the Board with an iron fist so that he could keep people away from the staff.

He made sure that if the Board wanted to do something it would make a decision in the Board room and then pass that message on to management and that would be it. There was the odd exception, but not very often.

Figure 72: Saskatoon ATB, 2018. Photo courtesy of the SIAA.

The major developments implemented since 1999 include the following:

- 1999 – The airport completed an Apron 1 restoration by replacing approximately 1/3 of the concrete pads on the apron.

---

[408] Ibid.

- 2000 - Nav Canada opened a new state of the art Air Traffic Control Tower.
- 2002 - The airport completed renovation and expansion of the Air Terminal Building including the addition of a fourth Aircraft Loading Bridge.
- 2005 - The airport relocated and expanded the Airline Ticket Counters and baggage make up system in the main terminal concourse. A fifth Aircraft Loading Bridge was added to the Air Terminal Building.
- 2006 - The airport completed an expansion of the Public Parking Lot and realigned Airport Drive and the entrance to the parking lot.
- 2008 – Restoration of Runway 09 / 27 was completed.
- 2009 - Apron 1 expansion completed to prepare for terminal expansion.
- 2010 – De-ice Pad developed on Apron 1.
- 2013 - Construction of Apron VI for GA aircraft.
- 2015 – $53 Million terminal renovation and expansion completed, providing 9 gates. Remote parking facility opened.
- 2016 - Construction of remote shuttle parking facility began.

Since transfer on 1 January 1999 the AA has spent more than $205 million on capital investment in the airport, almost all of which has been spent in the Saskatoon area. It employs 40 people to run the airport, and another 1,420 people work at businesses located on airport land. The AA contributes more than $346.5 million annually to the local economy of the City of Saskatoon through salaries, taxes and local purchases. Its economic impact is more than $1.0 billion annually. The airport began paying rent in 2006 and since then has contributed $10,259,734 million to the federal treasury. Since 1999 it has paid more than $13,247,979 million in taxes to the federal, provincial, and municipal governments.[409]

Figure 73: Spending by the Authority in Saskatoon in 2018.

---

[409] Source: Saskatoon Airport Authority, 10 January 2019.

Saskatoon, Saskatchewan

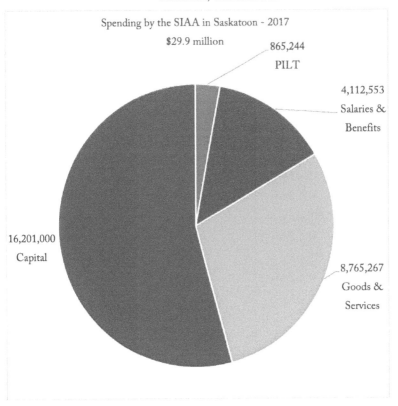

Spending by the SIAA in Saskatoon - 2017

$29.9 million

865,244
PILT

4,112,553
Salaries &
Benefits

8,765,267
Goods &
Services

16,201,000
Capital

Figure 74: Image courtesy of Google Earth Pro, 14 August 2017. The pin marks the location of the original BCATP aerodrome.

In 1939, at the outbreak of WW2, concern was expressed in the Canadian Parliament for the security of Newfoundland in the event of a German raid or attack. Prime Minister King, speaking in Parliament, stated: "the integrity of Newfoundland and Labrador is essential to the security of Canada"[410] and that, in contributing to the defence of Newfoundland, Canada would not only be defending Canada, but also assisting Britain.

Discussions on 29 February 1940 between Sir Edward Emerson, commissioner for Justice and Defence for Newfoundland and officials from the Department of External Affairs were concerned with the defence of Bell Island against German submarines. At that time 30% of the iron produced in Canada was smelted at Sydney, Nova Scotia from ore produced by Wabana Mines, Bell Island, Conception Bay, near St. John's. The defence of Bell Island was important to both parties. Canada because of the ore; Newfoundland because the mine provided employment for Newfoundlanders and revenue to the government. In his

---

[410] *Hansard*, 8 September 1939.

329

discussions Sir Edward raised the possibility of establishing an RCAF station for reconnaissance and anti-submarine aircraft.

Simultaneously the Joint Board of Defence (comprising Canada and the United States) was considering the responsibilities of the two countries for the defence of North America. Their report on 4 October 1940 recommended the establishment of a fighter base near St. John's.

Moreover, convoys to England from Canada and the United States were coming under increasingly severe attack from German U-boats. In 1940 shipping losses were averaging 150,000 tons per month and the lifeline to England was in danger of being cut if something was not done immediately to counter the U-boat threat. Air protection was imperative and it was essential to have an air base near St. John's.

Given the pressing nature of these three issues it was felt that a permanent airfield defense facility was needed to defend this outpost of the British Empire. Although there was an existing air base at Gander, the Canadian Government agreed to construct a second air base near St. John's. By 17 April 1941 a site was chosen near the community of Torbay, against the advice of local experts who preferred Cochrane Pond, to accommodate Royal Canadian Air Force (RCAF) operations.

The question of title to land at Torbay was the subject of much correspondence. The government of Canada wanted to acquire property title to airport lands it was to use, but the government of Newfoundland was only offering a lease. Canada thought this would lead to an unsatisfactory position, whereby property bought from private owners would be owned by Canada outright, while other parts would be under lease. A conference at St. John's on 27 October 1941 resolved the issue: Canada was to receive a grant in fee simple from the Newfoundland government to Crown lands needed for the airport. This arrangement was later re-affirmed by Article 4 of the Agreement between Canada, Newfoundland and the United Kingdom regarding defence installations, signed at St. John's on 8 April 1946.[411]

---

[411] *History*, p. 205.

On 28 April 1941 McNamara Construction Company began construction on the airport at a cost of $1,436,000. By the end of 1941 two 4,000 by 150 foot (1 219 by 46 m) runways (08-26 and 17-35), taxiways, aprons, hangars and other facilities had been built and were in operation. On October 18th, 1941, three American B-17 Flying Fortresses and one RCAF Digby made the first unofficial landing on the only serviceable runway available. The runways were still under construction and concern was expressed about the possible hazards to both civilian and military personnel from such unauthorized landings. Later that month a British Overseas Airways Corporation B-24 Liberator flying from Prestwick, Scotland, to Gander, made the first officially sanctioned landing during a weather emergency. A snowstorm, which prevented the landing at Gander, also closed down airports from New York to Montréal. As fuel was running low it was decided that one of the runways at Torbay could be used even though work on it was not completed. Due to the fact that the airport lacked instrument landing aids at the time, the pilot, Captain S.T.B. Cripps, used local radio station VONF as a homing beacon. The aircraft suffered minor nose wheel damage on landing but no injuries to its five crew and fifteen passengers were reported.[412]

The RCAF officially opened Torbay Airport on December 15th, 1941. It was jointly used by the RCAF, Royal Air Force (RAF), and the United States Army Air Corps until December 1946.

With the construction of the airport the government of Newfoundland was anxious to see commercial air services established between Newfoundland and Canada. When first approached TCA was not interested as they thought the route commercially unviable. With the consent of the Dominion office in London, the Newfoundland government began negotiations with Northeast Airlines to fly from St. John's to Boston and New York. That got TCA's attention. H.J. Symington, TCA's president, wrote to the Secretary of State for External Affairs saying that TCA was interested in providing service to Newfoundland, but wondered how he would provide service without any aircraft, since no more civilian aircraft could be acquired during the war. A subsequent meeting between TCA, the

---

[412] Ibid, p. 204.

DOT, Secretary of State and the RCAF resolved the issue. The RCAF had planes, but no pilots. TCA had pilots, but no planes. So TCA would fly RCAF aircraft to Newfoundland and provide the necessary air mail, passenger and cargo services from Moncton to Gander and then on to Torbay.

The first aircraft flown by TCA into Torbay, a Lockheed Lodestar, arrived at 1615 hours local time on 1 May 1942. It carried Canadian Army Nurse Baker, Nurse E.E. Buffet, Sergeant F.B. Cahill, RCAF, J.L. Courtney and J.P. Courtney. The crew consisted of Captains Trerice and Fowler and the stewardess, Dorothy Reid. It departed one hour later with passengers Mrs. F.J. Quinn, M.T. Rogers, W.M. Knapp, Tas Whipper, A.L. Malloy and L.K. Chaplin.[413]

Torbay Aerodrome – 1943
Runway Layout

November 1941 saw the arrival of No. 11 Bomber Reconnaissance (BR) Squadron, the first RCAF Squadron to take up duties at the Torbay Air Base. In April 1942 Lysander aircraft of No. 5 Coastal Artillery Co-operation Flight, which was later renamed No. 1 Composite Detachment in July 1943, took up duties at Torbay. Until its disbandment in June 1945, the Flight busied itself with search and rescue, target towing, photo reconnaissance, blackout observation, dive bomb and machine gun practice, mail drops, and

---

[413] Ibid, p. 205.

once late in December 1944, a turkey drop over an RCAF radar site on Allan's Island on Newfoundland's south coast.

In May 1942, No. 11 (BR) Squadron ceased anti-submarine operations at Torbay and was replaced by No. 145 (BR) Squadron, RCAF. In June 1942, Hurricane fighters and Harvard trainers of No. 125 Fighter Squadron, RCAF, arrived at Torbay.

In 1943 runway 08-26 was lengthened to 5,000 feet (1 524 m), and runways 02-20 (4,000 feet – 1 219 m) and 11-29 (4,900 feet – 1 493 m) were added to the two existing runways.

One event of note that occurred during 125 Squadron's tenure at RCAF Torbay involved some British made Spitfire aircraft. Late in December 1942, the S.S. Empire Kingsley, en route from England to Africa with a deck load of aircraft, diverted to St. John's due to inclement weather. The winter weather had severely damaged three Spitfires on the ship's deck. The three aircraft were brought to Torbay where the Station Maintenance Wing salvaged enough parts to build one aircraft. Spitfire ER824 was test flown in March 1943 by 125 Squadron's Commanding Officer, Squadron Leader R.W. Norris. Once word got out that there was a serviceable Spitfire at Torbay, Air Force officials ordered it shipped overseas. Before ER824 left, however, the mechanics who rebuilt her stenciled the name "Miss Torbay" on the engine cowling. "Miss Torbay" survived the war, ending its days with 17 Group Communications Squadron, RAF.

On 3 June 1945, for the last time, St. John's residents saw the familiar parade of air force blue uniforms as the RCAF held its final formal march. Following services at the Church of England Cathedral and St. Bonaventure's College, the parade moved to the War Memorial where the RCAF's Air Officer Commanding in Newfoundland, Air Commodore F.G. Wait, took the salute at the march past.

The United States Air Force also had personnel at Torbay, mainly in the fields of communication and transportation, in addition to, and in support of, their base at Fort Pepperell.

On 1 April 1946, the airport became a civilian operation under the jurisdiction of the Canadian Department of Transport[414]. Confusion was caused by the presence of American military personnel at a civilian airport and consequently on 1 April 1953, control was turned back to the Department of National Defence.

On 15 April 1953, the RCAF Station at Torbay was reactivated and RCAF personnel started to move in and began providing the necessary administration and operation of the facility to support the mission of its co-tenant, the USAF. Early in 1954 a rental agreement was signed between the USAF and the RCAF and the USAF acquired use of additional buildings. The 6600th Operations Squadron of the USAF was activated in July 1953 and moved into existing Torbay Airport facilities. The USAF rented over thirty buildings at a cost of over $210,000 per year. The USAF operations at Torbay Airport, from 1953 to 1958 - when

---

[414] From 1949 to 1951 the Airport Manager was Tom McGrath, whose history of Canadian airports written in 1984 was invaluable to this book. Born in St. John's, Newfoundland in 1913 he was educated at St. Bonaventure's College in that city. As a small boy in 1919, he was taken to see the aircraft then assembled at St. John's for the first attempts to fly across the Atlantic, stimulating what would become a lifelong interest in aviation. He obtained a pilot's licence at Air Services Training school in England in 1934. Returning to Newfoundland, he went to work as a clerk-secretary to the Chief Engineer of Marconi's Wireless Telegraph Company at Gander in 1937. In 1938, he was appointed operations officer with the Civil Aviation Division of the Newfoundland Government and served at Botwood and Gander during the operation of the experimental commercial trans-Atlantic flying boat service. During WW2, Tom McGrath served with the Royal Air Force Ferry Command at Goose Bay, Bermuda and Gander and held the post of Senior Flying Control Officer. Following the war, he returned to service with the Newfoundland Government as Operations Manager at Gander International Airport. When Newfoundland joined Canada in 1949, Tom McGrath transferred to Civil Aviation Branch of the Canadian Department of Transport and served as Airport Manager at St. John's Airport. He later became an Airways Inspector with Transport in Moncton, New Brunswick, and was moved to Ottawa in 1951. In Ottawa, he became responsible for the development of airport revenue and was the first Superintendent of Property Management for Transport's airports across Canada. He later served as Director of Airport Services and Security, Director of Operations Review (Air), Special Advisor to the Director General of Airports and Construction, and finally Deputy Director General, from which position he retired in 1978. Tom McGrath had a lifelong interest in the history of Newfoundland and trans-Atlantic aviation; collecting, researching and writing on the subject. He was the author of *History of Canadian Airports* an internal publication for Transport Canada printed in 1984. He died in Ottawa in 1994.

the Northeast Air Command was deactivated, were notable achievements. Thousands of tons of cargo were handled by Torbay in support of the many bases and satellite stations throughout the Command.

The DOT maintained control over the terminal building in the southwest corner of the airport. The facility remained RCAF Station Torbay until 1 April 1964, when it was returned to the jurisdiction of the DOT under the name St. John's Airport.

The first terminal building at the site was constructed in 1943. A small wooden structure, it was replaced by a larger brick building in 1958.

In 1954 runway 11-29 was lengthened by 2,100 feet (638 m). It was lengthened again n 1968 by another 1,500 feet (457 m). It was now 8,500 feet long (2 588 m).

Construction of runway 11-29 began before formal permission had been obtained from the Newfoundland government. Part of the runway was on land the government of Newfoundland had granted to the United States to meet its requirements. This was a concern for the Canadian government as it felt that facilities constructed by or for the United States government should be on land owned by Canada. Discussions between Canada and the Newfoundland government resolved the issue and on 18 June 1943 Newfoundland granted the land to Canada.

In 1958 runway 17-35 was lengthened to 7,000 feet (2 134 m).

In 1981, the terminal building housed the offices of the airport manager and staff. There were ticket offices for Eastern Provincial Airways (EPA), Air Canada, Gander Aviation and Labrador Airways, a waiting area, a departure lounge, a self-serve restaurant, a licensed lounge, a number of food concessions and rent-a-car facilities. In 1981 a small museum was being prepared to house the story of aviation in Newfoundland and related memorabilia.

The control tower originally constructed during the war burned down in an extensive fire at the airport on 17 March 1946, which caused one and a half million dollars worth of damage. Construction did not begin on a new tower until 1951; it was then opened in June 1952. A new Tower/Communications Building replaced that structure in March 1976. The tower was equipped with radio navigation and landing aids including precision approach radar, non-directional beacon and VHF omni-directional range.

Although the airfield was not used as much as Argentia, Gander, Stephenville, and Goose Bay Airports in the movement of large numbers of aircraft to England, it was still busy. The RAF had its own squadron of fighters, surveillance and weather aircraft stationed there. The RCAF personnel strength on the station during the peak war years was well over 2,000. Through an agreement between the US and Canadian governments early in 1947, the United States Air Force took over the use of the airport facilities and utilized about ten of the buildings located there. The US Military Air Transport Service (MATS) needed Torbay Airport in order to complete its assigned mission at that time. Maintenance of the airport and facilities was done by the DOT.

One item of note is that, from the point of view of the weather, the airport is undoubtedly located in a less than ideal place. The small point of land on which the airport is located is surrounded by water on three sides: the Atlantic on the east and north, and Conception Bay on the west. Because of the hilly terrain, and the nearness of open water, weather conditions vary greatly and are affected by small changes in wind direction and speed. The cold Labrador Current flows south along the east coast of Newfoundland, curves westward south of the Avalon Peninsula, and meets the warm Gulf Stream southeast of the airport. This can cause extensive fog, even when windy. To counter the weather the airport is only one of four in Canada equipped with a Category III instrument landing system. This allows an aircraft equipped with an automatic landing system to land safely in zero visibility; the pilot in command being effectively blind.

The Authority

In 1992 TC came to the City of St. John's with a proposal to turn the airport over to the private sector[415]. The city was at a loss as to what to do with the proposal so it handed the job over to the Board of Trade, which had a Transportation Committee chaired by Rex LeDrew. The Transportation Committee's principal role

---

[415] Most of this section is based on a telephone interview with Rex LeDrew, the first Chair of the St. John's International Airport Authority, and also its first CEO.

was to oversee bus routes and other city-related transportation issues, and it had no idea as to what to do with the airport. So the Transportation Committee formed a Board of Trade Airport Planning Committee (BTAPC) with Rex as the Chair and with members from the City of St. John's; the St. John's Board of Trade; the Town of Conception Bay South; the Provincial government; the City of Mount Pearl; and the Mount Pearl Chamber of Commerce.

The BTAPC was in place by 1994 and began discussions with TC about the transfer. It soon became clear to some members of the BTAPC that the fundamental issue was the money, not the running of the airport – that was a technical issue that could be handled by those with experience in such things. The issue faced by the BTAPC was how much would it cost to run the airport, and how much would it cost to take the existing St. John's airport and bring it to an acceptable standard.

For many years both the local population and the Provincial government had been complaining to TC about the sorry state of the St. John's ATB - described by some as "3rd class rough". Many folk in St. John's and the surrounding towns and villages felt that TC rarely thought of the airports in Newfoundland and Labrador, "those places out on the Rock", and as a result had let the airports fall into "rack and ruin". With the exception of Gander ("which had a gorgeous building and no passengers"), the other airports in Newfoundland (Deer Lake, Stephenville, St. Anthony - "just a barn"; and St. John's) were the poor cousins of the rest of Canada.

The BTAPC got to work, but, as is usual for most committees, only a few members of the BTAPC actually did anything. Most of the members had been nominated by their organization due to their political connections, not because of their ability to understand the issues surrounding the transfer of the airport to a local AA, and Rex found himself and two or three other members up most nights and weekends working on the project.

It was an exhausting task. And they had no guidelines.

The BTAPC was faced with trying to estimate what it would cost to run the airport on a daily basis, and to renovate the airport to the standard required of an "international" airport. When they questioned TC about the costs of running the airport, TC would not give them a straight answer – "it might cost this" or "it might cost that" or "this is a good estimate for that cost", but never a firm response. When they asked what studies TC had done on the necessary repairs and maintenance, the answer was "none".

The BTAPC decided it needed some financial, legal, and engineering advice and determined that a budget of $5 million might suffice to buy the necessary expertise to do the due diligence required. But where to get $5 million? By this time it was 1995, and only three years had elapsed since the federal government had closed the cod fishery. Newfoundland was reeling from the failure of the cod fishery and the downstream effects. And the last thing people were interested in was giving money for a project which a lot of folk had no interest in, or thought would never work.

So the BTAPC went to the banks. Several asked many questions about cash flow, and credit and financial planning, and where the guarantees were if the bank lent the five million dollars. The BTAPC had to reply: "There is no guarantee. There is no surety for the loan. But if you lend us the money, then once the AA gets going, you will be the AA's bank." And the only bank that came forward with the money was the Canadian Imperial Bank of Commerce.

As the BTAPC went forward it became apparent that the environmental assessment required to establish a baseline was going to cost an awful lot more than anyone had imagined. There were so many questions: "Where are the spills and contaminated areas?"; "Are there underground fuel storage tanks?"; "Where did the fire training take place?", and on, and on, and on. No one had any answers and at times it seemed to Rex that it was a situation of "you don't know what you don't know, so hope for the best." So the BTAPC went back to the bank and got more money.

Meanwhile the negotiations with TC were becoming a "long, drawn-out and painful process" as some of the negotiators on the TC team were determined that every single line was to be examined in the minutest of detail. For the BTAPC this was a "nightmare" as the legal fees increased almost exponentially. But some of the TC folk were there to help. Michael Senzilet got kudos from Rex LeDrew over Michael's knowledge of the process. As Rex said: "Michael would pick you to death on the details, but he was like a really good preacher. He could quote you chapter and verse on where you could find the answer to your question."

Rex thought that success came when "both sides finally developed a common lexicon" for it was only at that time that the two sides began to understand each other.

Finally the day came when the lease was to be signed (apart from the lease, there was a 2 cubic foot box containing all the documents relating to the discussions over the past five years). As the folk from the BTAPC and TC were signing the lease Nancy Healey noted to all assembled that immediately TC signed the lease it no longer had management responsibility for the airport and the new St. John's International Airport Authority would be constituted as managers on 1 December 1998. However she pointed out that it was 29 November 1998 – so what was to be done for the one day in between? There was a bit of a huddle off to one side and it was decided that since Nancy was the only permanent employee of the BTAPC that had formed the SJIAA, she would be the CEO of the airport for the one day. As she said: "Thankfully nothing happened."[416]

Rex summed up the situation: "The traveler was never really concerned about the cost of walking through the ATB. And with the AIF, the cash flow is truly mind-boggling. With the creation of the AAs TC never lost its income stream, and Canada got some amazing infrastructure."[417]

St. John's International Airport 's strong military ties continue to the present day with approximately 1,300 military aircraft stopping at the airport each year to refuel or for crew rests.

The Airport Authority and 150 RCAF (North Atlantic) Wing of the Air Force Association of Canada have preserved the military history of the airport in a display located on the main level of the Airport Terminal Building. The display features photos and models of the aircraft associated with the military operation at what was formerly called RCAF Torbay. It also holds a memorial to the Newfoundlanders who died during WWII in the service of the Allied Air Forces and a memorial to those Canadian and American airmen and women who lost their lives while either

---

[416] Nancy Healy, interview, 7 November, 2018.

[417] Rex LeDrew, interview, 1 October 2018.

stationed at or travelling through RCAF Torbay (St. John's International Airport), then considered an overseas post.

Figure 76: The St. John's terminal building in 2005.

Since transfer on 1 December1998 the AA has spent more than $328.6 million on capital investment in the airport, almost all of which has been spent in the St. John's area. It employs 85 people to run the airport, and another 1,900 people work at businesses located on airport land. The AA contributes more than $20.95 million annually to the local economy of the City of St. John's through salaries, taxes and local purchases. Its economic impact is more than $608 million annually. The airport began paying rent in 2008 and since then has contributed $16.5 million to the federal treasury.[418]

Figure 77: Spending by the Authority in St. John's in 2017.

---

[418] Source: Five Year Performance Review, Rideau Consultants Inc, December 2018.

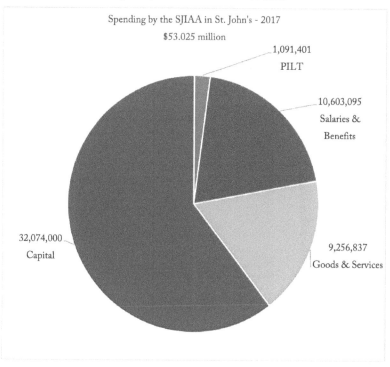

Spending by the SJIAA in St. John's - 2017
$53.025 million

1,091,401
PILT

10,603,095
Salaries &
Benefits

32,074,000
Capital

9,256,837
Goods & Services

Figure 78: Image courtesy of Google Earth Pro, 22 July 2017. The pin marks the location of the original BCATP aerodrome.

In January 1927 the Air Board in the Department of National Defence wrote to many towns and cities across Canada, including Fort William, suggesting that they provide aerodromes to serve their communities. Fort William showed interest and, with the neighbouring city of Port Arthur, [419] asked the Air Board to find a suitable site for the aerodrome.

A suitable location was found seven miles (13 km) west of Fort William, near the municipal golf course, and on 19 March 1929 an airport license was issued to the Fort William Aero Club to operate an aerodrome with a 2,000 foot (609 m) runway. By 1931 the condition of the airport had deteriorated so much that the Air Board requested the city repair it at a cost of $1,200. The club let the lease lapse in 1935.

In October 1937 the city asked the DOT for help in building a new airport. A site was selected 3/8 mile (0.5 km) south of Arthur

---

[419] Fort William, Port Arthur and the townships of Neebing and McIntyre joined to become the city of Thunder Bay in January 1970.

Street in the nearby township of Neebing and in May 1938 the department agreed to assist in building a new airport. The impetus for all this was because the Canadian Car and Foundry Co. (CC&FC), a division of the British airplane manufacturer Hawker Siddley, had been awarded a large contract to build two-seater aircraft for Turkey. The new airport was very close to the CC&FC plant. The city bought 240 acres (97 hectares) and by March 1939 one runway was in operation.

In 1940 the city asked the federal government if it wanted to use the airport as a training field for the duration of the war. The BCATP thought this was a good idea so on 2 July 1940 DND leased the field from the city and the RCAF established No. 2 Elementary Flying Training School. By this time the airport had three grass strips in operation.

Additional land was acquired allowing two of the existing runways to be lengthened: runway 12-20 to 4,120 feet (1 256 m) and runway 07-25 to 4,700 feet (1 433 m). All three runways were re-built in concrete.

The EFTS closed in June 1944 and the RCAF turned over the buildings to the CC&FC. The DOT took over from the CC&FC in February 1945.

In March 1946 the DOT offered to return the airport to the city, who politely declined the offer. Since the airport license was in the city's name this license was cancelled on 18 October 1946 and a new one issued to DOT that same day.

On 28 May 1947 the airport name was changed from Fort William Municipal to Lakehead Airport. The name changed again in 1970 to Thunder Bay Airport. TCA began service to Lakehead Airport on 1 July 1947. A new terminal building was opened in March 1953.

In 1952 DOT bought the land from the city of Fort William. At the same time DOT bought additional land to extend runway 12-30 to 5,300 feet (1 615 m) and runway 07-25 to 6,200 feet (1 890 m). In 1968 another 98 acres (40 hectares) of land was purchased bringing the overall area of the airport to approximately 790 acres (320 hectares).

Improvements to the landing systems continued throughout. In 1948 a low-intensity approach lighting system was installed on all runways. In 1950 an ILS was commissioned. In 1956 high-intensity lighting was installed on runway 07-25 and high-intensity approach lighting installed on runway 07.

The terminal building was extended in 1964, and again in 1978.

By 1980 the airport has scheduled services offered from Air Canada, Nordair, Norontair, Bearksin Lake Airways and Austin Airways. Charter services were offered by the Thunder Bay Flying Club, Lakehead Flying School and Austin Airways. The deregulation of airlines in 1987 caused Thunder Bay to become a "hub and spoke" airport, linking northwest Ontario to Winnipeg in the west and Toronto in the east.

Figure 79: Thunder Bay Airport

The Authority

In 1992 some folk in town[420] heard of the four Local Airport Authorities in Vancouver, Edmonton, Calgary and Montréal, and thought it would be a good idea if Thunder Bay looked into the possibility of an AA taking over control of "their" airport. The Nordic Winter Games were to be held in Thunder Bay in 1995

---

[420] With many thanks to Jack Jamieson and Scott McFadden for allowing me to interview them. This chapter owes a lot to them for its facts. Any incorrect interpretation of what they had to say is my error.

and TC had announced in 1991 that it would renovate and essentially re-build the existing ATB in time for the games.

The leader of the Thunder Bay group was Gerry Cook, a professional engineer and local building contractor. He got Robert Patterson and Bill Smeljanick involved, together with Jack Jamieson as counsel, and the four of them proceeded to negotiate with TC.[421] The negotiations continued over the next year, but in 1993 a federal election was held and the Conservative Government was replaced by a Liberal one.

A lot of news during the election campaign had centered around the awarding of a contract by the Conservatives for the building of a new terminal at Toronto Pearson. The Liberal leader, Jean Chretien, made the contract award an election issue and promised that if the Liberals formed the new Government it would immediately cancel the contract award and impose a review of not only the Pearson airport, but of the previous airport devolutions to the four LAAs.

The Liberals won the election, and the net result to the Thunder Bay group was that negotiations with TC came to a screaming halt.

The Liberal Government then tasked TC to review the existing AAs and how they were governed. The result was the Public Accountability Principles for Canadian Airport Authorities, issued in 1995, and a re-start of negotiations between the Thunder Bay group and TC.

By this time the negotiation group had crystalized into a more formal organization and was fundamentally the group that eventually became the Board, with John Walker as Chair, and Gerry Cook, Bert Baumann, Ian Angus, Charlie Grant, Don Hutsal, Karen Pappin, and Tom Walsh as members. Jack Jamieson remained as the Board's counsel.[422]

The Board was very "hands-on" and struck committees to attack the issue and do the work, rather than hire consultants. For example there were committees to address the environmental and

---

[421] Jack Jamieson, interview with the author, 8 December 2018.

[422] Ibid.

human resource issues, as well as a committee which conducted the negotiations with TC.

There was also the small matter of money. How was all the preliminary work required going to be paid for? The Board went to the various financial institutions in Thunder Bay and made their proposal. They would explain that they were trying to form an Airport Authority which would take over the operations of the Thunder Bay airport, but that they had no money, no assets, no security, and no personal guarantees. All the banks and financial institutions told them to take a hike, with one exception, the TD Bank, who said "OK, how much do you want?" That bank eventually became the AA's banker.[423]

Negotiations with TC continued through 1996 and most of 1997. They were hard times.

The Bylaws were the first sticking point. Jack Jamieson recounted that many times he would draft changes to the Bylaws and send them off to Michael Senzilet, who would send them back to Jack with many changes.[424] One major point was that TC would not proceed until it had a letter from the City of Thunder Bay saying that the city was satisfied with the Board's appointment process. This letter was a long time coming, but it eventually appeared at TC, the Bylaws were approved, and the Board received agreement from TC that negotiations could proceed.[425]

The Board found that TC was essentially a fair and transparent negotiator, and provided the Board with much needed direction and advice. As one the of the TC staff put it "If you guys are crazy enough to take this on, then this is what you need to do."[426] The Board discovered that you could haggle with the TC team, but they were fair and forthright. TC had by this time gained much experience in conducting negotiations with many airport transfer groups across the country. The negotiations in the late 1980's and early 1990's with the first four airports were quite different and unique to each airport, but by this time TC had the Public

---

[423] Ibid.

[424] Ibid.

[425] Ibid.

[426] Ibid.

Accountability Principles, and was ensuring that all the airports were treated in the same manner.

Although TC had basically built a new ATB at Thunder Bay in the early 1990's, by 1996 the runways were in bad shape and needed a substantial capital infusion. Who was to pay for that was a major point of contention between the Board and the TC negotiating team (John Cloutier, Michael Senzilet and Sandy London). Eventually the negotiations settled on a $1 million one-time payment for capital expenses, a limited term for subsidies to be paid, and the transfer of TC employees to the new Authority with no loss of salary or benefits.

Jack Jamieson recounted that at one negotiating session he pointed out that the lease document was unclear, and that Michael Senzilet immediately corrected that loophole. Jack eventually learned not to say anything about unclear issues in the lease.[427]

At one point the Board spoke with a board member from the Victoria airport about the difficulties they were having with TC over the lease negotiations. His comment was "TC is not about to change anything. The document is fixed. That's the way it is. So why not just sign it?"[428]

Which is what the Thunder Bay Airport Authority (TBAA) did on 1 September 1997 with Scott McFadden as its first CEO.

TBAA was the first small airport to transfer as all transfers up to that date had been large airports with 2 million or more passengers annually. TBAA saw approximately 500,000 passengers in 1997. It was a far different business from the large airports and although TC by then had had five years of experience with devolution, that prior experience had nothing to do with the economics of a small airport. TC did not understand the practicalities of operating a small airport outside the government remit.[429]

The TBAA was suddenly faced with the practical issues of running a business, not just the operation of the airport, and with limited fiscal and human resources to do that. There was a small

---

[427] Ibid.

[428] Ibid.

[429] Scott McFadden, interview with the author, 5 December 2018.

and capable team at TBAA (mostly formerly TC staff) but the more private sector "business" aspects of running an airport were new to all. How to bill the airlines for landing and terminal fees? How to produce a payroll, or to produce financial statements, or provide pension and benefit administration? These aspects of Airport operations had been managed centrally from Ottawa prior to transfer. Notably, there did exist a culture of cost saving, within the limitations of a centrally managed government operation. The cost of developing and implementing all this was the responsibility of the TBAA, and there was no support from TC. And no recognition nor awareness from TC of the need to do all this. So the TBAA went and developed the systems it needed to operate as a business, and then commercialized that expertise to sell to other airports.

To fund the expected capital expense the TBAA implemented an AIF. McFadden was against the concept of AIFs as it was seen as having many flaws. It is expensive to implement, and expensive to collect. And in an economically depressed area, such as Thunder Bay, it does not make sense to add unnecessary costs to the travelling public.[430] After only two and a half years, in September 2001, the TBAA removed the AIF. This was not a popular move amongst the rest of the AA community in Canada, nor with the airlines or the government. The other AAs had begun to rely on the AIF to a great extent to fund capital expansion. The government saw this as a reduction in revenue to the Consolidated Revenue Fund since the AIF was taxed. The airlines initially saw the AIF as de-stimulator but it gradually evolved to be seen as a "no cost" revenue, not only for the 7.5% they retained as a charge to the AA for collecting the AIF, but also because the airline only remitted to the AAs an AIF for 95% of the passengers from which it collected such a fee.[431]

---

[430] Ibid.

[431] I found this to be an interesting comment as I was aware of the fact that the airlines retained a percentage (varying from 6% at a large airport – Pearson - to 7.5% at a small airport – Thunder Bay) of what they collected as an administration fee, but I was not aware that they only remitted AIF fees on 95% of passengers who travelled on their planes. Whenever I had spoken with the airlines about their fee for collecting the AIF they were quite strong in their defence of the costs they incurred in collecting the AIF fee. When now I see that they collect an extra 5%, their total charge is 11% to 12.5% of the AIF fees as an

It should be noted that the Government of Canada's original stated policy objective was "the Government should be **no worse off.**" With the passing of time (around 2005) this changed to "there should be an adequate return for Canadians" or similar. There appears to be no supporting policy statement from Parliament.[432] The evolution appeared to just happen within the bureaucracy. Needless to say Canadians have never seen any of the "returns;" in fact they've just had to pay more tax under the guise of user fees, Airport Rent, HST etc.

McFadden believes that many Canadian airports are overbuilt and are monuments to the egos which built them. "Jade canoes and gold-plated waterfalls"[433] do not make an airport more efficient. In the absence of a "tax & spend" AIF mentality, the best approach is the McDonald's model: clean, efficient and always in excellent repair. A Community's airport is often the first and last impression for visitors, business and leisure so it should be welcoming, comfortable, clean and efficient and provide some "flavour" of the local and regional culture and flare, but this doesn't necessarily mean spending millions on grandiose structures, custom fixtures and fittings, subjective artwork and costly high-maintenance furnishings.

Thunder Bay was perhaps fortunate in that the original Board was more concerned about efficiency, innovation and growth than politics and personal image building.[434] AA board members are typically patronage-type appointments / nominations, and of course there are no shareholders, so no "skin in the game." There are some inevitable conflicting objectives!

"administration fee". This is, in my opinion, unconscionable. It costs an airline nothing, nada, zero, rien, to collect the fee. It is all bits and bytes, done by a computer. Admittedly there was a one-time cost to program the computer system to recognize the fee and make some sort of allowance to send this to the airport concerned, but surely these one-time costs have been recouped since 1997. As an on-going "cost" the airline is engaging in opportunistic gouging of the passengers and the AAs.

[432] McFadden.

[433] Ibid.

[434] Ibid.

The Thunder bay airport was the only "new" ATB in the system at time of devolution. The rest of the AAs in Canada believed this was the only reason Thunder Bay could eliminate the AIF. That was 20 years ago and the Airport still has no AIF and the lowest all-in fee structure in the country.

There is nothing particularly complicated about an airport and its infrastructure. You have runways, taxiways, aprons, an ATB, a parking lot, and access roads. Roads and buildings all exist in the world. But the "roads" in an airport are specific to purpose: i.e. a runway must be built to handle a 750,000 lb (340 000 kg) airplane landing on it at a descent rate of 25-30 feet per second (8-10 m/sec). A four-lane highway does not have this restriction. Aggregate must be a specific size and asphalt mixed to tight specifications, and there's a lot of it! So some of the costs for infrastructure are high when compared to a municipality, or a provincial or federal government, but can be planned for with a reasonable degree of confidence, even in a region like Northwestern Ontario with its economic uncertainties.

A normal business establishes and maintains forecasts for operations and capital, income, expenses, cash flow. Cashflow forecasts enable prudent debt management and timing of more discretionary capital spending. Nothing unusual here that should compel an AA to implement a non-traditional methodology like a permanent AIF-type fee. It is obviously easier (for a monopoly) to implement a big fee, but easy seldom means best.

Airports also have excellent access to capital. TBAA used debt to finance its capital program including runway rehabilitations, extensions, replacement/expansion of subsurface infrastructure, parking expansions, terminal building expansions, fleet renewals, etc. TBAA's cost of capital was always far less than its return on invested reserves (another efficient revenue source that few other airports took advantage of).[435]

Beyond the financial management side of the business there is far more complexity. Airports in Canada come under federal jurisdiction, for reasons that may not be well understood by some Canadians. At the time of transfer TC encouraged AA's to negotiate agreements with their respective municipalities.

---

[435] Ibid.

Fortunately (for Canada) such an agreement was not mandatory. However many AA's, including TBAA, voluntarily complied with municipal and provincial requirements and regulations under a *good neighbour* philosophy. This was the less contentious approach and suited an evolution of decision-making more rooted in politics than good practice.

When TC stopped owning the infrastructure, and became solely a regulator, it also stopped being concerned about the costs of the things it was regulating. Airport Emergency Response Services, for example, was a major cost to TC and at the time of devolution TC was about to totally change the way in which firefighters were costed and paid for. But devolution happened before the fire fighter regime changed, and the AAs inherited an expensive situation. Since devolution, Transport Canada has not been shy about implementing costly regulations to the airports and industry. There remains an obligation to perform a cost benefit analysis but the *costs* that TC does analysis on are limited to those potentially incurred by itself, not those incurred by the AA. Stuck with burdensome regulation TBAA developed an "Airport Operations Specialist" methodology wherein the regulatory requirements are met by Airport Operations Specialists (AOS) in place of firefighters. AOS's are effectively the frontline airport operators executing everything from the Airport's Snow Plan to Wildlife Management Program, pavement management, etc., and of course the Emergency Response Plan (ERS). It is a proactive methodology as opposed to the reactive traditional ERS model. The TC regulations remain restrictive and generally impede efficiency and proactive safety activities.[436]

Fortunately for the TBAA, TC had excellent records of what it had spent to build, maintain, operate the airport. These records were useful to the TBAA when it came to assume control of the airport. For example the TBAA knew what the new ATB had cost to build. There were records of what it cost to maintain the runways, taxiways, and aprons. Records existed for equipment acquisition and maintenance, and also life-cycle costs and life expectancy. These data formed a reasonable basis for business and capital planning into the future.

---

[436] Ibid.

There were unknowns at time of transfer. What future regulations were to be imposed on the TBAA? When the federal government removed itself from the equation, other levels of government stepped in and said "where is our piece of the pie?" e.g. the city of Thunder Bay wanted to tax the 880 acres of airport land as if it were a corporation. The Federal Government paid Grants in Lieu of Taxes to municipalities for services provided, which was typically a fraction of what a municipal tax levy would be, but it failed to clearly pass on this jurisdictional clarity to AAs. The proposed cost increase to TBAA would have been in the region of $800,000 per year (TBAA had gross revenues of < $4million at the time), other AAs paid much more. Fortunately the Thunder Bay, Toronto, and Ottawa airport authorities were able to secure a more reasonable formula with the Province of Ontario.[437]

The Aeronautics act gives the Minister of Transport the Authority to, for example, protect the airspace in the vicinity of airports. Since Devolution ministers have been reluctant to exercise this authority leaving Airport Authorities with long and costly battles through the courts. The Federal Government has these authorities/jurisdictions for a reason i.e. to develop and protect the critical infrastructure necessary to build and sustain the Canadian economy.

The TBAA was one of two small airports who were the first to transfer[438] and it was unable to look elsewhere when faced with a

---

[437] McFadden, email 18 March 2019. "Municipal taxation was one of those "surprise!" loose ends that the federal government could have relatively easily resolved but choose not to. Another example of the federal government failing to assert its jurisdictional authority.

Most AAs faced big tax bills as municipalities attempted to apply shopping mall rates to terminal and support buildings and hard surfaces including runways. TBIAA received a bill for $883,000 (compared to the approximately $175,000 TC had been paying in PILT). Other airports had it much worse.

I got together with the Ottawa Airport Authority and the GTAA and worked on both the federal and provincial governments. In the end it was Ernie Eves (as provincial minister of finance) that agreed to a formula based on passenger throughput and capped the annual increases to 5%. This formula applied to London, Ottawa, Toronto and Thunder Bay. 5% per annum increases compounded is still a big number considering AA's build their own infrastructure and provide most of their own services."

[438] The other was Moncton. Both transferred the same day – 1 September 1997.

problem, because there was no one else who had seen this problem. This caused it to become innovative and responsive, all in a very short time frame.

The price sensitivity of demand for air travel is well understood and documented. When the original WestJet arrived on the scene Canada saw the pent up demand for air travel balloon passenger volumes at every airport WestJet served. An unintended consequence perhaps was that the dramatic drop in air fares created an opportunity for others to take advantage of the perceived *headroom*. For example, as hidden costs and fees were implemented by airport authorities, Nav Canada, governments and ultimately the airlines themselves, all-in airfares returned to higher levels, the reasons for which were unclear to the travelling public. Largely due to that inflexible cost structure, many smaller communities that had scheduled air service no longer do (a severe impediment to the economic wellbeing of Canada's relatively remote small communities). Even communities the size of Thunder Bay now have no jet service, a significant step backward in safety and comfort.

In 2017 passenger volumes exceeded 800,000 per year and the airport contributed $0.2 million to the local economy.

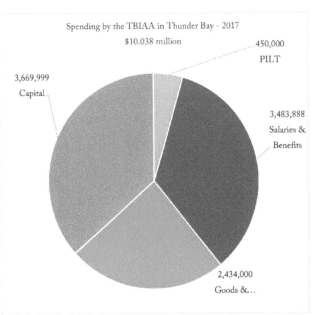

Spending by the TBIAA in Thunder Bay - 2017
$10.038 million

450,000 PILT

3,669,999 Capital

3,483,888 Salaries & Benefits

2,434,000 Goods &...

Figure 81: Image courtesy of Google Earth Pro, 7 May 2018. The pin marks the location of the original BCATP aerodrome.

By 1937 Toronto had already had 27 years of experience with airports (De Lesseps Field[439] in 1910; Leaside in 1917; Downsview in 1929; and the Toronto Harbour Seaplane Base in 1932) and more than two intense years of discussion as to where a new airport was to be located.

Two years previously, on 1 February 1935, the federal government had announced that it would build the finest airport in all of Canada and that it would cost a million dollars. This caused some upset amongst the city councillors who thought they had much better uses for a million dollars, especially in the midst of the Depression. The city needed housing, roads, and a new courthouse, not a fifth airport!! Eventually the new DOT and the city agreed on a way forward, and on 14 December 1936 Ottawa committed to spend $150,000 towards construction.

---

[439] The site of the first air meet in Toronto in 1910, hosted by William Trethewey, engineer.

By August 1937 the city had decided on a site to the northwest and 13 farms totaling 1,411 acres (571 hectares) were purchased for a new airport at Malton. The farmers from whom the land was bought owned Lots 6-10 on Concessions 5E, 5W and 6. They were:

- Horace C. Death - 99 acres (Conc. 5E, Lot 6)
- John Dempster - 100 acres (Conc. 5E, Lot 7)
- John H. Perry - 100 acres (Conc. 5E, Lot 8)
- Wilbur Martin - 100 acres (Conc. 5E, Lot 9)
- A. Schrieber - 100 acres (Conc. 5E, Lot 10)
- Lydia Garbutt - 100 acres (Conc. 5W, Lot 8)
- Mack Brett - 150 acres (Conc.5W, Lot 8,9)
- David J. Lammy - 150 acres (Conc. 5W, Lot 9)
- W.A. Cripps - 200 acres (Conc. 5W, Lot 10)
- Frank Chapman - 50 acres (Conc. 6, Lot 6)
- Rowland Estate - 100 acres (Conc. 6, Lot 7)
- Frank Chapman - 100 acres (Conc. 6, Lot 8)
- Robert H. Peacock - 100 acres (Conc. 6, Lot 9),
- Thomas Osborne - 100 acres (Conc. 6, Lot 10)

Figure 82: 1880 map showing approximate location of current runways. Runway location drawings by the author.

Work began immediately and by September 1938 Malton Airport had two paved runways, each 3,000 feet (914 m), a grass landing strip, lighting, weather reporting, and a radio range.[440]

In 1939 TCA built a hangar near the old Chapman farm house (the building on the right, near the road) as Malton had become the main operating base for TCA's transcontinental service.

Figure 83: Malton Airport, 23 April 1939

The northern part of the airport property quickly became a site for aircraft manufacturing. The National Steel Car Company built a plant in 1938. In 1939 Canadian Associated Aircraft Ltd. built a plant in the north-east, but very quickly leased it to near to National Steel Car who then went on to build Lysanders, and Hampden, Anson, Lancaster and Lincoln bombers. In 1945 A.V. Roe took over the greatly enlarged plant and began designing and building the Avro Jetliner, the CF-100, and eventually the Avro Arrow.

The war had a large effect on the Malton airport. First came the establishment of aircraft manufacturing on a very large scale. Then the BCATP chose the site for the No. 1 Elementary Flying Training School and then, soon after, chose it as the location for

---

[440] *History,* p. 229.

the No. 1 Air Observers School. And through all of this Malton continued to operate as a civilian airport.

A new brick terminal was built in 1949, with a design capacity of 400,000 passengers per year. Enlarged in 1954, and again in 1959, it served until the aeroquay opened in 1964.

The Canada Railway News Company[441] opened the first food and beverage concession at Malton in 1941.

The first car rental concession opened in 1950 with Hertz Rent-a-Car. Tilden opened a second car rental operation in 1954.

Paid car parking began in 1951, the first such operation in any of the DOT airports. By 1957 parking space had grown to 1,050 spaces.

Passenger traffic grew steadily[442]:

- 1946   180,307
- 1952   558,820
- 1962   1,480,00
- 1968   5,091,700
- 1971   6,423,500
- 1975   9,076,000

In 1958 TC began a program to modernize and update the major airports in Canada: Gander, Montréal, Toronto and Vancouver all received "modern" air terminal buildings designed to last for the foreseeable future[443]. The airport at Toronto was the first in Canada to receive an ATB which took into consideration a very long-term plan for development. Designed by John C. Parkin, the plan was to build four "aeroquays" joined together by a central hub, a separate administration building, a cargo-handling facility, and a road network tied to the Provincial road system. It was a radical design – circular in concept, no more than two minutes was required to go from any gate to any other.

---

[441] The 2nd such operation in Canada. The first was at Montréal Dorval. Founded in 1883, this eventually became Cara Operations Ltd.

[442] *History*, p. 231.

[443] Of which only Gander has an ATB from this period.

"Aeroquay One" began construction in 1958. It took six years to complete with its official opening on 28 February 1964. By this time it had become known as "Terminal 1" and was already nearing capacity. Designed for 3.5 million passengers per year, it saw 3.7 million in 1966 and 4.6 million in 1967: Canada's Centennial Year. In 1968 TC announced plans for a second airport for Toronto at Pickering, and a second terminal at the existing airport. Building for Terminal 2 commenced in 1969 and was completed in 1972. By that time 6.7 million passengers arrived at or departed from Toronto International.

Three years later, in 1975 after much discussion and a Royal Commission, plans for a second airport at Pickering were shelved and over 11 million passengers arrived at or departed from Toronto International. Although expansions to both Terminal 1 and Terminal 2 had increased passenger capacity to more than 15.5 million passengers per year, maximum passenger handling capacity was again raising its constraints.

By 1986 the Toronto airport had two large terminals in operation: Terminal 1 and Terminal 2, both of which were at, or very nearly at, capacity. To meet this demand the federal government issued an Expression of Interest to design, build, finance, and operate Terminal 3. Four consortia responded and prepared proposals. The Airport Development Corporation was selected and an agreement was signed in 1987 to construct and operate a world-class passenger terminal serving domestic, transborder and international airlines. In addition to the ATB, a 3,000 car parking garage, a first-class hotel, offices, trade and convention facilities, and office development along Airport Road. A 40-year ground lease for the terminal property was signed in 1988, and construction began on May 2 of that year.[444]

In July 1989, the federal government released a strategy report on aviation in southern Ontario. The report recommended that Toronto Pearson be developed to its optimum capacity so that it could continue to serve as the major airport. The federal

---

[444] *History.* p. 233.

government began the environmental assessment of the Toronto Pearson site, appointing a review panel.[445]

In 1990, a $40-million expansion enlarged the international section of Terminal 2, increasing capacity to 1,800 passengers per hour.

When the large, horseshoe-shaped, state-of-the-art Terminal 3 opened in 1991, it garnered international attention, not for its modern design, but for its operator: PaxPort had built Terminal 3. It was the world's first airport terminal designed, built, financed, and operated by a private sector corporation on land which it did not own. The transaction was so successful that TC wanted to get a second consortium to build and operate T1, and a third to operate the runways. The impression of those who wanted to form an AA would be that if all these consortia existed the only job left for the AA would be to cut the grass.[446]

In 1991 two reports had been written for the Toronto City Council highlighting the economic benefits that accrued to a municipality because of its airport. The reports came to the attention of the Chairman of Metro Toronto who then tasked the Toronto Economic Development Commission to see what could be done to assist in the creation of an AA. At that time TC was taking about $50 million a year out of Pearson airport and using it to maintain other airports in the NAS and the local impression was that that cash flow could be put to much better use if it stayed in the GTA and was used to maintain Pearson.

In 1991, the federal government held public hearings regarding the findings of the Environmental Impact Study conducted in relation to the expansion of Toronto Pearson. The appointed Environmental Assessment Review Panel deliberated on the findings throughout 1992 and in November of that year recommended against airport expansion.

Notwithstanding that recommendation, in February 1993 the Minister of Transport announced that the federal government would move ahead with the Toronto Pearson expansion, including

---

[445] Ibid. p. 243.

[446] Steve Shaw, interview with the author, 25 September 2018.

a new fourth runway. Preparatory construction began that summer.

In 1993 the local politics were very strong. Mayor McCallion was adamant that the Pearson airport was not going to be transferred to an AA until the issue of the Toronto Island (Billy Bishop) airport had been resolved.[447]

The Toronto folk had seen the creation of the four LAAs and how they had been successful. But apart from the local politics, Montréal also wanted to get the jump on Toronto and began bilateral discussions with TC about having all International traffic from Europe land at Mirabel.

The Regional Chairs said "Pearson is a regional airport. It serves not just Toronto but the entire area including Hamilton and Pickering."

By 1994, Toronto Pearson International Airport had three terminals, three runways, and was seeing 20.9 million passengers a year. The existing facilities were forecast to reach capacity by the year 2000, with passenger demand continuing to increase. The federal government looked once again to the potential of the Pickering lands[448], and began deliberations over new ways to sustain Toronto's aviation demands.

In 1994 the newly-elected Liberal government cancelled the contract for the new T1 and instructed TC to ask the former members of the AA organizing committee to assemble a proposal for creating an AA to take over Pearson airport. Finding members to form a Board for an AA was an exciting time as not just a few wondered what they would be getting themselves into, given the political interference in the past. Potential Board members were told that:

- An AA would be good for the GTA.
- There was a certain 'glamour" to being associated with such a high-profile organization.

---

[447] Ibid.

[448] *REPORT OF THE AIRPORT INQUIRY COMMISSION*, Information Canada, Ottawa, K1A OS9, 1974.

- They had achieved a lot in the professional/business lives, and it was time to give back to the community.

The present Greater Toronto Airports Authority (GTAA) was subsequently created under Bill C-28, the Pearson International Airport Agreements Act, in 1996.

Figure 84: Toronto Pearson Airport

The Authority

However, the birth of the GTAA did not occur without some extensive intervention of a helping midwife.[449]

The folk in Toronto had not been sleeping while the airports at Vancouver, Edmonton, Calgary and Montréal had been given over to Local Airport Authorities. Metro Toronto Chairman Alan Tonks[450] along with his regional chair colleagues began the process

---

[449] I thank Steve Shaw for his candid comments during our interview. I have used a 2006 publication of the GTAA: *Celebrating Success: 1996-2006* to flesh out his comments.

[450] The last Metro Chairman before the municipalities amalgamated in 1998 under the Mayor of the City of Toronto, Tonks was Mayor of York from 1982 to 1988, before becoming Metro Chairman from 1988 to 1997.

of establishing a Local Airport Authority. The process was fraught with political difficulty.

In the decades since the first landing at Toronto Municipal Airport at Malton, the surrounding farmland had become home to more than 650,000 Mississauga residents (Canada's sixth largest city) and more than 424,000 Brampton residents (Canada's 14th largest city) and their wealth of industries. The input and support of these municipalities would be necessary if anything was to be done.

Tonks and Peel Regional Chairman Frank Bean agreed to return to their councils to seek approval for the creation of a bi-regional task force that would attempt to form an airport authority. However, Peel Regional Council recanted at the last minute because of unresolved concerns over who would have more representation: Toronto or Mississauga. The matter of the Toronto City Centre Airport also remained outstanding.

Metro Toronto, keen to begin the process, went ahead and created its own community task force. Their two goals were to assess the federal government's airport transfer policy and to place this issue on the regional agenda.

The five members of the Metro task force were:

- Art Eggleton, Mayor of Toronto

- Bruce Sinclair, Mayor of Etobicoke

- Alan Tonks, Metro Chairman

- John Shepherd, member of Metro Toronto Economic Development advisory committee

- Gordon Riehl, President of the Metro Toronto Board of Trade

During the next seven months, the task force gained the support of the Metro Toronto Board of Trade for the airport authority concept and determined that they needed to gain broad community support before proceeding with a transfer proposal.

In 1988 the new Transport Minister, Benoit Bouchard, announced additional airport transfer guiding principles to supplement those originally announced in 1986. Minister Bouchard's main amendment was that a Local Airport Authority must have local and provincial support.

In August 1989, Minister Bouchard announced short-, medium-, and long-term measures to address a variety of southern Ontario air system problems. The proposal declared that Toronto Pearson had grown to "Canada's busiest airport, and one of the 20 busiest airports in the world." Renovations to Terminals 1 and 2 at Toronto Pearson were declared "top priority," Terminal 3 was "to be completed by mid-1990," and plans were announced to conduct technical studies and a public environmental assessment review regarding a proposal for two new runways.

Under the proposal, Transport Canada would retain responsibility for air safety, navigation, air traffic control, and security, but all other operations would be managed by a municipally-approved corporation with a mandate to use any and all revenue from operations for airport systems. The transition from Transport Canada to local control would be an enormous undertaking with a steep learning curve, but it would be the most exciting thing to happen at Canadian airports since first landings. And at Toronto Pearson International Airport it would spark a long battle for control of Canada's busiest and most lucrative airport.

"[Toronto] Pearson will continue as the major airport for Southern Ontario and be developed to its optimum capacity in terms of social, economic, environmental, and transportation considerations," the Transport Minister announced in August 1989. "The other airports in Southern Ontario should be developed to respond to the immediate demands for aviation infrastructure and ultimately be developed to fulfill their roles within the area airports system and eventually supplement the role of [Toronto] Pearson."

The announcement spurred a private consortium called PaxPort Inc. to present a well-publicized proposal to the federal government calling for the privatization of Terminals 1 and 2. This proposal distressed the government, who had not asked for a proposal and recognized that the proposal would compromise the plan to establish a Local Airport Authority.

PaxPort, formed from Matthews Group, CIBC Wood Gundy Capital, Allders International, and Ellis Don, were organized, publicity-conscious, and backed by Terminal 2's main tenant Air

Canada, which was itself becoming deregulated. At that time, 45 per cent of Air Canada stock was sold by the federal government and a second offering was proposed for the next year.

The PaxPort proposal impelled the Metro task force to accelerate their efforts to gather community support. They approached Gardner Church, Deputy Minister for the Office of the Greater Toronto Area (OGTA), who had realized that his office had overlooked airport infrastructure in its 1989 evaluation of Greater Toronto Area needs. Church agreed that OGTA needed to remedy this oversight, and he called together the heads of regional councils that surrounded the airport.

The OGTA task force convened to hear the results of the Greater Toronto Coordinating Committee's (GTCC) report on airport capacity and Greater Toronto Area (GTA) needs. The report recommended that GTA airports should be operated as a system and that a Local Airport Authority was the preferred method of operation.

Then another private consortium submitted an unsolicited proposal for terminal development, making it clear that the private sector believed Toronto Pearson worthy of interest. All told, the federal government received subsequent unsolicited proposals from Air Canada; the Airport Development Corporation, who operated Terminal 3; and Canadian Airports Limited, who were associated with the British Airports Authority.

This second proposal galvanized a regional committee called the Group of Seven. Its members were heads of regional councils in the area around the airport:

- Art Eggleton, Mayor of Toronto
- Bruce Sinclair, Mayor of Etobicoke
- Hazel McCallion, Mayor of Mississauga
- Reg Whynott, Chairman of Hamilton-Wentworth
- Howie Herrema, Chairman of Durham Region
- Peter Pomeroy, Chairman of Halton Region
- Ken Seiling, Chairman of Waterloo Region

At the same time, an Airport Technical Committee was formed by Toronto Pearson operations and management staff to provide input on the practical necessities of forming a Local Airport Authority.

In December 1990, the Group of Seven met with Doug Lewis, the latest Transport Minister, as well as the recently appointed Ontario Transportation Minister Ed Philip and the GTA transportation head Ruth Grier. At this meeting, Lewis indicated support for an airport authority as well as his support for terminal privatization.

Minister Lewis asked for input from the Group of Seven for the federal government's privatization terms of reference, scheduled for release in early 1991. The key point offered was that no terminal privatization should occur before an airport authority was formed.

Thereafter, the Airport Technical Committee made presentations to the Group to ensure they thoroughly understood airport issues, specifically those related to privatization and the formation of a Local Airport Authority.

As a result of their discussions, the issue of accountability was identified as a major barrier. The federal government's airport transfer guidelines were clear: a Local Airport Authority board could not contain politicians, nor public servants. But without political representation, the Group argued, how could an airport authority be accountable to the communities it served?

Unable to resolve this issue, OGTA informally approached Transport Canada staff to ask if the federal government would relax this edict in order to meet the special needs of a Local Airport Authority in the Greater Toronto Area.

But the government insisted that political involvement in an airport authority would not be allowed. For the latter half of 1991, its proponents discouraged and the OGTA now occupied with issues related to the new provincial government, the formation of an airport authority was put aside.

But not for long. In early 1992, there were whispers that the latest Transport Minister Jean Corbeil was preparing to announce a Request for Proposals (RFP) for the privatization of Terminals 1 and 2. The rumours roused OGTA, which began to solicit members for an airport authority that could draft a proposal.

On March 16, 1992, the RFP was released by ministers Corbeil, Wilson, and Martin, inviting the private sector to "finance the upgrading of Terminals 1 and 2 and to manage them under a lease agreement." The RFP was intended to "encourage private-sector initiative and innovation while ensuring safety, security, and fairness to users."

Minister Corbeil said: "The federal government is committed to expanding Pearson Airport's terminal capacity to adequately serve the growing number of users forecast over the next decade, while restricting the cost burden on the taxpayers."

The Request for Proposals gave interested parties 93 days to respond. Proposals were to be evaluated on the basis of the "airport's long-term development needs, operational advantages, and economic objectives for southern Ontario, as well as their overall financial value for Canadians," said Shirley Martin, then Minister of State for Transport.

The OGTA regional chairs had to move quickly if they were to submit a proposal by the deadline. They asked the Deputy Minister to facilitate the creation of a Local Airport Authority, called the South Central Ontario Airport Authority (SCOAA), that would serve as a bidder for the terminals redevelopment project. The regional chairs would provide names of prospective members, and the provincial government would provide a loan guarantee to cover start-up and bid-preparation costs. Alan Marchment, the Chief Executive Officer of Central Guaranty Trust, was selected as the SCOAA interim Chair.

But OGTA had moved too quickly for the liking of the Peel Regional Chair and Mayor McCallion, who were perturbed at being left out of the process, however unintentionally. So, led by Sidney Valo, President of the Mississauga Board of Trade, the Pearson Regional Airport Corporation was formed as a second proposed airport authority. Valo began to lobby for support from the regional boards of trade and chambers of commerce in the Greater Toronto Area, as well as with regional councils.

But having two rival airport authorities undermined either's chance to bid. Transport Canada made it clear that they would negotiate with only one duly constituted and politically sanctioned Local Airport Authority. Once again, something had to be done to create a united, viable airport authority, acceptable to everyone involved.

Prompted by the Metro Toronto Board of Trade, the regional chairs formed a private-sector task force to recommend next steps, to create an airport authority, and to assemble a proposal for the terminals redevelopment project. At this time, Hamilton withdrew from discussions and no longer participated.

The members of the task force were:

- Gerry Meinzer, Chairman, representing Metropolitan Toronto
- Sidney Valo, representing Peel Region
- James Bullock, representing Halton Region
- Robert Attersley, representing Durham Region
- Michael Butt, representing York Region

Steve Shaw, who worked for the Metro Chairman's office, became the task force's secretary, dedicated exclusively to the airport authority issue. He organized meetings of the task force, coordinated staff support, and pursued the Metro Board of Trade and Transport Canada for input.

The task force proposed that the regions and municipalities of the Greater Toronto Area approve the Local Airport Authority's draft nomination and board structure by February 1993. The board was to consist of 10 members, two representatives from each area. In addition, five members were to be appointed by the board.

"[The task force] went to each municipality and explained what an airport authority was, how we proposed to create it, and what we were proposing to do," Valo said. "We educated them about how the airport was a significant economic engine: the second largest employer in Ontario after the auto industry.

"We took the proposal to the regional chairs and they accepted it."

Finally, four years after Chairman Tonks's meeting with Peel Regional Chair Frank Bean, a working group was established capable of providing an alternative to a for-profit consortium: an airport authority that could manage the airport efficiently, enhance regional economic growth, and confer regularly with the surrounding communities; in short, an authority that combined sound business practices with a strong sense of public accountability.

But thanks in part to the outgoing federal government's rush to have the future of the airport sealed, another struggle was taking shape—this time under the watchful eyes of the media and public.

The task force had no time to rest. The regional chairmen and their private-sector working group had to make a case for the development of a Local Airport Authority and draft a proposal for the terminals' redevelopment, while consulting with the surrounding regions' political, business, and community representatives. There were four main issues that needed quick assessment:

- How could an airport authority be formed to ensure the interests of the regions were addressed?

- What area and number of airports could the authority be expected to oversee in the initial stages?

- What legislation, funding, and staff support were required to make the authority fully operational?

- What process should be instituted to unify the authority and raise the endorsement of municipalities, boards of trade, and chambers of commerce?

The private consortia bidding on the terminals redevelopment project, by contrast, were long established, accountable to none of the regional business or community groups, and had a significant head start in developing their proposals.

The Director of the Southern Ontario Area Airports Study (SOAAS) reported to the task force in September 1992. John Kaldeway, later appointed President and Chief Executive Officer of the GTAA in 2004, served as project director of the study, which was conducted by the Transport Canada Ontario Regional Directorate. The study considered the roles of 19 southern-Ontario airports around Toronto Pearson throughout a 20-year horizon. The study was eventually published in March 1995.

Central to the SOAAS was the confirmation of the regional, national, and international importance of Toronto Pearson as a gateway to North America and as a centre of world trade, and the recommendation that Toronto Pearson should continue to be Canada's central hub airport.

Also key to its recommendations was that the Pickering lands be developed into a reliever airport by 2012 to take over traffic from Toronto Pearson, which was forecast to reach capacity at that time. Pickering was chosen over Hamilton because of its proximity to Toronto population and markets, and its limited site constraints compared to Hamilton.

By October 1992, the task force of the regional chairs had produced a report describing the best way forward, and they circulated it to the municipalities for support. After an intensive effort, resolutions of support were received and on that basis the private-sector task force was incorporated as the Greater Toronto Regional Airports Authority (GTRAA) on March 3, 1993.

The inaugural board members were:

- Robert Bandeen, Chairman, nominated by Metropolitan Toronto
- Robert Attersley, nominated by Durham Region
- James Bullock, nominated by Halton Region
- Michael Butt, nominated by York Region
- Anne Edgar, nominated by Peel Region
- Peter Gilchrist, nominated by York Region
- Maureen Kempston-Darkes, nominated by Durham Region
- Gerry Meinzer, nominated by Metropolitan Toronto
- Sidney Valo, nominated by Peel Region
- John Walker, nominated by Halton Region

A non-profit corporation run according to business principles was a new concept for Toronto Pearson, but not for Transport Canada. Transport had already transferred some operations to Local Airport Authorities at the other four major Canadian airports: Vancouver, Montréal, Calgary, and Edmonton.

Nor was the concept new internationally. Britain had put three London airports under the aegis of the British Airports Authority in 1965 with great success. In addition, the Port Authority of New York was operating three airports to national and international kudos.

However, the initial plan for Toronto Pearson involved leasing Terminals 1 and 2 to one private interest, the airfield to another, while a third leased Terminal 3. In addition, the federal government wanted a Local Airport Authority to oversee these operators. Toronto Pearson was the biggest, busiest, and most contentious airport in Canada. And times were heady:

- The federal government was impatient for divestment.

- There was nervous expectation about a huge increase in travellers and cargo at the airport.

- A federal election loomed.

- Media and the public were becoming increasingly interested in the airport issue.

Before Christmas 1992, Minister Corbeil announced that PaxPort had delivered the "best overall acceptable proposal received for the redevelopment and operation of Terminals 1 and 2."

In negotiations, PaxPort developed a joint venture with its competitor, Claridge (a partner in the Airport Development Corporation that ran Terminal 3), to complete the deal. The partnership became known as T1/T2 Limited, then Mergco, and finally the Pearson Development Corporation.

With Claridge involved, the deal would result in a private-sector monopoly at Toronto Pearson, a situation PaxPort had warned the federal government against during the competition.

On August 30, 1993, eight months after PaxPort was announced as frontrunner, Minister Corbeil and Public Security Minister David Lewis announced that the PaxPort-led consortium, called Pearson Development Corporation (PDC), had won the opportunity to redevelop and run Terminals 1 and 2.

Under the $700 million agreement, PDC was to sign a 57 year lease (37 years with an optional renewal period of 20 years) with the federal government, and would take over the federal agencies' existing leases with airlines and concession operators. The closing date for agreements was set for October 17, 1993.

The needed improvements to the terminal buildings would not happen under government ownership though, because the government had made a commitment not to increase the deficit.

Minister Lewis, himself a former Transport Minister and a privatization pioneer, said the deal with PDC underscored his government's commitment "to let the private sector do what the private sector does best, which is operate ventures of this kind."

But not everyone was convinced. Federal Liberal leader Jean Chretien and New Democratic Party leader Audrey McLaughlin called on Prime Minister Kim Campbell to halt the deal, but she refused. A federal election was called on September 9, 1993.

During the election campaign, the privatization deal at Toronto Pearson became an issue.

"I'm warning everyone involved: if we become the government, [the deal] will be reviewed; and if legislation is needed [to overturn the deal], we will pass legislation," Chretien said.

On October 25, 1993, the Liberals won a landslide victory, and the GTRAA, so close to being edged out by private interests, had a new opportunity to make a difference in the future of Toronto Pearson.

Less than 48 hours after being elected, Prime Minister Chretien commissioned Robert Nixon, a former Liberal treasurer for Ontario, to review the agreement between the former federal government and PDC. All progress related to the deal would be halted until Nixon completed his report. The review also halted the move to privatize the airfield.

On December 3, 1993, Nixon's report was released. The findings were scathing. Among them:

-   The single-stage Request for Proposals and 93-day deadline created an "enormous advantage" for the firms that had previously submitted proposals.

-   Lobbying "exceeded permissible norms" creating heavy pressure on the bureaucracy, such that many civil servants requested transfer from the project.

-   No financial pre-qualification was required, a highly unusual freedom in a project of such magnitude.

-   There was an unacceptable constraint on alternative airport development within a 75 km radius of Toronto Pearson, which included Hamilton International Airport, until Toronto Pearson was processing 33 million passengers per year.

- Patronage "may have had a role in the selection."

Nixon concluded that "to leave in place an inadequate contract, arrived at with such a flawed process, and under the shadow of possible political manipulation is unacceptable." The PDC deal was suspended.

The suspension gave new hope to the GTRAA, which renewed its efforts to be recognized by Transport Canada.

On December 10, 1993, three GTRAA members, Peter Gilchrist, Sidney Valo, and Anne Edgar, along with Steve Shaw, met with Toronto Mayor Eggleton and the Minister responsible for the Treasury Board to discuss the urgency of the situation at Toronto Pearson. At this meeting, Eggleton asked three questions:

- Where did the GTRAA stand on the issue of terminal redevelopment?

- What was the GTRAA's position on funding?

- What was the GTRAA's view on the proposed new runways?

But the GTRAA had spent much of its time working on recognition, rather than developing airport plans. The group couldn't answer Eggleton's questions at that time. Eggleton suggested that the GTRAA meet with the Transport Minister and members of the Metro Liberal caucus to enlist their help in getting recognition and becoming a viable option for Toronto Pearson management.

A week later, the GTRAA received a letter from the assistant Deputy Minister of Transportation for Ontario, David Guscott, suggesting the GTRAA could take the initiative by influencing Metro and GTA caucuses; by displaying professional expertise, financial confidence, and political preparedness; and by examining the airport's market position and preparing a complete business strategy.

The GTRAA set to work. It sent a letter to the Minister of Transport embracing the recommendations relating to an airport authority in Nixon's report, especially those concerning the GTRAA board structure, that its five vacancies should be filled by two members appointed by the Ontario Minister of Transportation and three members, including the chair, appointed by the Minister of Transport. These members would not be elected officials nor government employees, and would be required to perform their duties in the best interests of the authority.

The GTRAA urged the new Transport Minister Doug Young not to let business at Toronto Pearson "continue as usual" as that would create a significant disadvantage to airport development, strategic marketing, and airline- and airport- related promotions. The GTRAA also pledged to accept some modifications to its policies in order to achieve rapid resolution.

The GTRAA, mindful that it lacked a clear position on terminal and runway development, decided it was impossible to take a position as it had not been part of the original discussions and processes. The authority would continue to work toward recognition with the Minister of Transport and then work as quickly as possible to develop positions on development and operational issues.

On April 13, 1994, the government introduced Bill C-22 to the House, the bill that cancelled the Pearson Development Corporation (PDC) deal officially and limited compensation to the companies involved to out-of-pocket expenses, preventing them from claiming lost opportunity or profits foregone.

Bill C-22 was passed in the House, but not passed by the largely Progressive Conservative Senate, which sent the bill back to the House for amendments. The PDC consortium, according to the Senate, deserved the opportunity to seek redress for compensation in the courts. The battle over compensation would continue for two years.

On July 13, 1994, days after the Senate's refusal to pass Bill C-22, the Minister of Transport announced the new National Airports Policy that, for the first time in Canadian aviation history, clearly defined the federal government's role in airports. Toronto Pearson was defined as one of Canada's 26 core airports that made up the National Airports System and would be managed by an authority in accordance with Canadian Airport Authority principles.

Essentially, the National Airports Policy changed the federal government's role from airport owner and operator to that of owner and landlord. Air traffic control and some airport security would continue to be provided by the federal government, but everything else from setting fees for parking, to the management of ground terminal services and concession operations would be managed by the authority. As a financially self-sufficient corporation, the GTRAA would receive absolutely no taxpayer money, and would be responsible for generating the funds required to develop and operate the airport, maintain the facilities, and improve the region's air transportation system.

To become Toronto Pearson's authority, the GTRAA had to comply with Canadian Airport Authority requirements:

- It had to be a not-for-profit corporation.

- Its board of directors had to consist of 15 members nominated by various community interests.

- Its senior managers had to hold regular meetings with a community consultative committee.

In November 1994, after making all the necessary bylaw changes and gaining resolutions of endorsement from all major municipalities, the GTRAA was reconstituted with a new name: the Greater Toronto Airports Authority (GTAA). It was officially recognized by Transport Canada as the operating authority for Toronto Pearson International Airport.

Steve Shaw, who had acted as secretary of the authority working from the Metro Chairman's office, became the first GTAA employee with the designation of Director of Strategic Planning.

At that time, the GTAA board of directors included:

- Robert Bandeen, Chairman, nominated by Metropolitan Toronto
- Robert Attersley, nominated by Durham Region
- Donald Blight, nominated by Durham Region
- James Bullock, nominated by Halton Region
- Michael Butt, nominated by York Region
- Ronald Dennis, nominated by Peel Region
- William Dimma, appointed by the federal government
- Anne Edgar, nominated by Peel Region
- Peter Gilchrist, nominated by York Region
- Gerry Meinzer, nominated by Metropolitan Toronto

- Joanne Thomas Yaccato, appointed by the federal government
- Sidney Valo, nominated by Peel Region
- John Walker, nominated by Halton Region

Shortly thereafter, the board was completed by Bonnie Patterson, appointed by the Province of Ontario, and Sharon Moss, nominated by Metropolitan Toronto.

Eight years after Minister Crosbie's deregulation announcement in 1986, Canada's largest airport had a professional authority financed without taxpayer money, operated according to the best business practices, and founded on the principles of public accountability. In December 1994, the GTAA signed a Letter of Intent to initiate formal negotiations with Transport Canada for the transfer of Toronto Pearson International Airport.

By January 1995, there were already differences of opinion on how to proceed. Transport Canada insisted that there be no substantive changes to the generic legal transfer document, but the GTAA argued that the nature and character of Toronto Pearson was unique and required a management structure not constrained by not-for-profit business conventions.

That month, after two years of service on the GTAA board, Sidney Valo was elected as chairman for a three-year term. His tasks were immense: to oversee the transfer of Toronto Pearson from Transport Canada, to build the GTAA into a viable administrator, and to find a Chief Executive Officer to lead the GTAA into its first term as manager of Toronto Pearson.

The board organized itself into three working groups: Operations, Business Planning and Transfer Process, and Organizational Development.

Operations studied current construction projects and began research on further airfield development, preparing for renewed public and media interest in airport policy. It established contact with every stakeholder group from limousine operators to residential neighbours.

Business Planning and Transfer Process developed a budget and established an office in the government Administration Building between Terminals 1 and 2. It negotiated the lease of airport lands with the federal government.

Organizational Development was talking with airport executives, looking for a Chief Executive Officer.

It was a steep learning curve. The federal government had slated approximately $250 million for redevelopment of the airport prior to signing the Letter of Intent. Many projects were already underway and several more contracts needed immediate attention:

- a new runway and associated taxiways

- existing runway restoration

- a central aircraft de-icing system

- parking lot reconditioning

- construction of a storm water quality control facility

The board developed a long-term strategic plan that would accommodate the expected number of passengers comfortably and safely. Though 1994 saw Toronto Pearson process 20.9 million passengers, demand was expected to increase to 40 million passengers by 2010 (and did reach 47.1 million by 2017).

In December 1995, the GTAA and Transport Canada signed a Memorandum of Understanding agreeing on the financial terms for the transfer of Toronto Pearson. The GTAA was the first Canadian Airport Authority to reach this stage of negotiations with the federal government after the 1994 National Airports Policy was established.

Meanwhile the Pearson Development Corporation (PDC) issue resurfaced in the form of a senate committee hearing. Bill C-22 had never passed, due to the objections of the largely Progressive Conservative senate. Formally nullifying the PDC deal required passing Bill C-22, and the GTAA could not assume operational control of Toronto Pearson until the bill had passed.

By April 1996 with a Liberal majority senate, Bill C-22 was passed. The PDC later sued the federal government for $662 million in damages related to lost profits, consulting, and lobby fees. The parties settled out of court a year later for $60 million, including $45 million in PDC out-of-pocket expenses and $15 million in legal costs and interest. When it was over, the last barrier to the ascension of the GTAA was finally removed.

In May 1996, Transport Canada signed the Agreement to Transfer. Four months later, the board of directors approved a financial plan that would act as a foundation for the GTAA's entry into the bond market, and satisfy the GTAA's obligation to Transport Canada. The revenue bond issue, one year later, would turn out to be the largest of its type in Canadian corporate history.

On 2 December 1996, the GTAA signed a Ground Lease with the federal government and assumed the operation, management, and control of Toronto Pearson for a term of 60 years, together with one renewal period of 20 years. Under the lease agreement, the GTAA is authorized to operate the airport on a commercial basis and set fees, rates, and charges for the use of Toronto Pearson.

The Ground Lease included all airport lands, buildings, and structures, as well as certain roads and bridges providing access to the airport, but excluded assets leased to others, such as Terminal 3 under a 40-year lease to the Airport Development Group, and assets owned by Nav Canada—the operator of Canada's civil air navigation system.

With the last pieces falling into place, the GTAA joined Calgary, Edmonton, Montréal, and Vancouver in the group of major Canadian airports under local control.

Within a decade of the first task force meeting, Canada's flagship airport was now governed by nominees representing all levels of government and reflecting the various interested parties: community, organized labour, and the business community.

The airport saw 49.5 million passengers in 2018, an increase of 5% over 2017, [451] and only ½ million passengers from Toronto becoming a "mega hub" airport.

---

[451] Source: GTAA.

Toronto, Ontario

As an economic engine the airport contributed more than $788 million to the greater Toronto economy in 2017 through its purchase of goods and services, property taxes, salaries and benefits paid to airport employees, and capital investments in infrastructure.

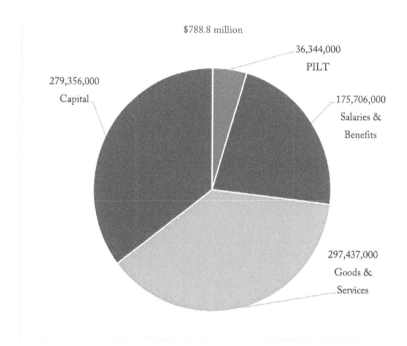

$788.8 million

36,344,000
PILT

279,356,000
Capital

175,706,000
Salaries &
Benefits

297,437,000
Goods &
Services

Toronto, Ontario

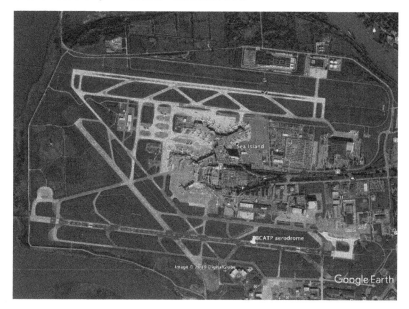

Figure 86: Image courtesy of Google Earth Pro, 27 October 2017. The pin marks the location of the original BCATP aerodrome.

On 25 March 1910 Charles Hamilton, an American, landed at the Minoru Park Race Track on Lulu Island, flying a Curtis pusher biplane. This was the first airplane flight in western Canada. In April 1911, also at Minoru Park Race Track, William Templeton and cousin, William McMullen, test-hopped their home-built plane. Templeton later became the first manager of the Vancouver Municipal Airport

In 1920 the Air Board established a seaplane base at Jericho Beach for the use of the Civil Air Operations Branch. The Branch flew HS-21 and F-3 flying boats on government patrols, forest protection, customs, aerial surveys, photography and transportation.

On 17 October 1920 a DH-9 aeroplane of the newly formed Canadian Air Force landed at the Brighthouse Park race track, near Richmond, at the end of the first cross-Canada flight. The trip had begun on the 7 October and the final leg was piloted by Capt. G. A. Thompson, who later became the district controller of Air Services for the DOT in Vancouver.

381

In 1928 Charles Lindbergh refused to visit Vancouver because "there is no fit field to land on"[452] That same year the city of Vancouver leased a field near Landsdowne Park on Lulu Island to create the city's first airfield, with two grassed runways: east-west 2,691 feet (820 m) and north-south 1,260 feet (384 m); and a waiting room. It was used by B.C. Airways for its service from Vancouver to Victoria.

Meanwhile the city was pushing ahead with a more permanent and satisfactory airport. A site on nearby Sea Island was recommended. The city of Vancouver approved the site and purchased 475 acres (192 hectares) for $300,000. The new airport was also to have facilities for seaplanes.

At the laying of the foundation stone for the new ATB on 13 September 1930, William Templeton, the first airport manager, said: "We had an airport, but no night lighting, no weather bureau, no radio aids, and no business."[453] The "no business" part did not last for very long.

The 1930's were the era of the barnstormers, the thrill ride, the aerial shows and air races and more than 2,500 people took sightseeing flights from the airport in 1931, while only 536 passengers arrived at the airport on 309 flights from other places.[454]

The new airport had a single east-west grass runway of 2,400 feet by 100 feet (732 by 31 m), an administration building and two hangars. A seaplane harbour was built on the south side of the aerodrome (which is still in operation as of 2018). An interesting comment on the operation of the airport was made by J.A. Wilson, controller of Civil Aviation in Vancouver "The municipal authorities do not realize the importance of making charges for the use of their airport as reasonable as possible so that the aircraft

---

[452] *Vancouver International Airport: Historical Information and Chronological Listing,* John Scott Mitchell, Vancouver Airport Planning Project, c. 1975

[453] *Flying High: The 50th Anniversary of the Vancouver International Airport 1951–1981.* Transport Canada, TP3118E, unnumbered page.

[454] Ibid.

operators will use the municipal airport rather than establish facilities of their own."[455]

Throughout the 1930's money was always an issue, even though new airlines began using the airport. Alaska Washington Airways, Canadian Airways and United Airlines were all flying scheduled routes but the revenues were not adequate to cover the operating costs and by 1935 the city of Vancouver passed a resolution recommending the Department of National Defence assume control of the municipal airport and use it as a national airport as part of the Canadian Airway System. The Controller of Civil Aviation was not in favour and wrote: "The policy of this Department from the beginning has been that each locality must provide and maintain its own airport. ... If the Department should now take over the Vancouver airport, similar demands would be made by many other cities. ... During the past few years, at least two and a half million dollars[456] have been spent by the cities of Canada on airport development. ... The maintenance of all these city airports would throw an intolerable burden on the Department and, as civil aviation develops, there would be continual pressure for the expenditure of more money to keep pace with the growing requirements of the airways."[457]

By 1938 the airfield had two hard-surfaced runways of 3,000 feet (914 m), a grass runway, taxiways, field lighting, and a low frequency, low course radio range.

In August 1940 the Department of National Defence took over the airport for the duration of the war and six months thereafter. That same year saw the establishment of No. 8 Elementary Flying Training School (EFTS) under the BCATP and thousands of pilots were trained there. Notwithstanding the large number of military aircraft on-site, the airport continued to function as a civil airport under the management of the DOT, using the pre-war city staff. During the war DND lengthened and strengthened the runways and constructed hangars and support buildings.

---

[455] Letter to Squadron Leader A.T. Crowley, 8 July 1931, Public Archives Canada, MG 30 E243, vol. 1.

[456] $46.6 million in 2018 dollars.

[457] Public Archives Canada, MG 30 E243, vol. 8.

The airport was returned to the city on 31 October 1947 and at that time the DOT began to pay an operating subsidy.

In 1948 the airport, at times called the Vancouver Municipal Airport or Sea Island Airport, was renamed as Vancouver International Airport. By this time Trans Canada Airlines, Canadian Pacific Airlines, Queen Charlotte Airlines, B.C. Airlines, Vancouver "UFly", Okanagan Air Service, United Airlines, British Commonwealth Pacific Airways (later to become Qantas) were providing scheduled services to Canada, the United States, Hawaii, Fiji, Japan, China, and Australia.

The original ATB was destroyed by fire in 1949. A temporary structure, the north terminal, was built by March 1950.

An Instrument Landing System (ILS) and high intensity approach lighting was installed in 1948. A new runway, 08-26, 8,600 feet (2 621 m) was built in 1953 to replace the old main runway, 07-25, and was later extended to 11,000 feet (2 353 m). In 1961 a cross-wind runway, 12-30, of 7,300 feet (2 225 m) was completed.

One source of income, unique in Canada to the Vancouver International Airport, was a tax of 25 cents per passenger inbound through Customs. This amount was added to the revenue of the airport. In 1953 the operating profit, after depreciation, was $55,979, an amount duly deposited in the city coffers.

By 1956 passenger traffic was 654,000 annually and the terminal facilities were expanded again. On 1 July 1957 the west terminal was opened. The north terminal was extended again in 1963, but it was very clear that a major terminal would be required to accommodate projected growth.

The city began its planning and approached the DOT for capital assistance. The federal government policy at the time was that financial assistance could only be given for the public (non-revenue) areas of the ATB. This would not be enough for such a major project as was envisaged. After negotiations between the city and the DOT, and a municipal plebiscite, the federal government agreed to purchase the city's investment in the Vancouver airport and assume full responsibility for its operation and maintenance. Transport paid $2.5 million for the land, buildings and equipment[458] and began plans to build a new terminal at the intersection of runways 12-30 and 08-26. Since 1929 the city had spent $1,239,365 on the airport, and the federal government $12,820,979[459] (almost all of which was from the BCATP program).

The new ATB cost $32 million and was opened on 10 September 1968. It had a design capacity of 3.5 million passengers per year. The old terminals on the south side were converted to other uses: the west terminal to be used for air cargo; the north terminal for general aviation until it was destroyed by fire in 1976.

Passenger loads continued to climb: 854,000 in 1962; 2,248,000 in 1968; 6,476,500 in 1979; and more than nine million in 1988.

Road access to Sea Island had long been an issue. There was only one bridge – the Moray Channel – to connect Sea Island to Vancouver via Lulu Island over the Oak Street bridge. To alleviate congestion DOT built two bridges: the Dinsmore Bridge in 1969, which gave access to Richmond; and in 1975, the Arthur Laing Bridge (originally called the Hudson Street bridge) to give direct access to the city of Vancouver.

In 1988 the ATB had 27 aircraft gates and 26 bridges. Services were offered by 26 airlines offering scheduled services to over 40 countries.

Four airport managers had served the community since 1931: William Templeton (1939-1950); William Inglis (1950-1976); Lorne Howell (1976-1987); and Frank O'Neill (1987-1992).

The Authority

In 1986 Graham Clarke, Past Chair of the Vancouver Board of Trade, oversaw a study to report on the potential privatization of the marine port and the airport. The report created discord, as some who read it agreed with its findings that both facilities

---

[458] $21.1 million in 2018 dollars, a bargain !!

[459] *Flying High.*

should be removed from federal government control, and others did not.[460]

Soon after the report was published TC began to put feelers into the local community that it would be interested in beginning discussions with a local group as to the possibility of privatizing the airport. In response the VIATAG was formed. It had as members Gordon Campbell (Mayor of Vancouver), Gil Blair (Mayor of Richmond), Lyle Knott (Lawyer), Chester Johnson (Chartered Accountant), Lucille Johnstone. CEO of Rivtow, John Watson (Professional Engineer), and others. It also had a close relationship with Frank O'Neill, then airport manager (and a federal public sector employee of TC). Frank was very much in favour of privatization, while many Transport Canada personnel were not convinced that privatization was the way to go.

VIATAG commissioned a feasibility study from one the major consulting groups, at a cost of several hundred thousand dollars, to see if the taking over of the airport was a reasonable proposition. VIATAG also engaged Bob Williams, from the Attorney General's Office of BC, to do a "reasonability" test – is this a "yes" or a "no"? His conclusion was that it was a stupid idea, can't be done.[461]

So Coopers & Lybrand were asked to give a second opinion. They wanted $250,000 to do the study. But by then VIATAG had run out of money. So it went to the Canadian banks, the US banks, and the Asian banks, and all said "no", we will not lend you any money. But Donald Potvin of the CIBC was a friend, and when VIATAG asked him he said "yes", CIBC will lend you $450,000. VIATAG said: "Under what conditions?". Potvin said: "we will loan you the money, and if you are able to form the airport authority then you will pay us back in one year, with interest at prime." So VIATAG said: "And what if we are not able to form the airport authority?". Potvin replied: "If you don't win, we don't

---

[460] With thanks to John Watson, PEng., for allowing me to interview him, 14 September 2018.

[461] Darcy Rezak, interview with the author, 12 November 2018.

need to be paid back." Corporate Social Responsibility at its best.[462]

Talks continued over the next two years with proposals being made that perhaps the Harbour Commission model would work for both the marine port and the airport. What would such a Commission/Board look like? How many members would it have? Who would those members be? Which organizations would be asked to nominate members? What would be the input from the local municipalities? What representation would the provincial and federal governments have?

Minister Pat Carney on the federal side and Minister Grace McCarthy on the provincial side both argued that there should be no governmental appointments to whatever form of board was eventually decided. They arrived at a recommendation that the new board should consist of non-elected representatives of the Cities of Vancouver and Richmond, along with the Greater Vancouver Regional District (now Metro Vancouver). Representatives from The Law Society of British Columbia, The Institute of Chartered Accountants of BC, The Association of Professional Engineers and Geoscientists of BC and the Vancouver Board of Trade, were also to be given a place at the table.

Discussions with both the federal and provincial governments continued and in July 1989 the federal Minister of Transport signed a Memorandum of Understanding to begin negotiations for the transfer of the airport to an AA. The airport would remain a federal asset, with air traffic control and safety and security under Transport Canada, but administration and economic planning would be handled by a local Board of Directors.

Eventually, in January 1990 the VIATAG incorporated a not-for-profit company and Letters Patent were issued for the formation of the Vancouver International Airport Authority (YVRAA).

The VIATAG then had to create a Board of Directors for the new YVRAA. It already had a core group, so it went about finding additional directors to make up the 12 directors required by the Bylaws (subsequent negotiations to reduce the exceptionally high

---

[462] Ibid.

rent to the federal government later resulted in the addition of two federal Government nominees to the Board).

The YVRAA Board then approached David Emerson. Emerson had been Deputy Minister of Finance for BC from 1984 to 1986, and then from 1986 to 1990 he was CEO of the Western Bank of Canada, which he had made a formidable competitor to the "big six" Canadian banks. In 1990 was named Deputy Minister to the Premier (Bill Vander Zalm) and then President of the British Columbia Trade Development Corporation. He was to prove an inspired choice.

Chester Johnson CA, was selected as Chair, and Lucille Johnstone as Vice Chair. Johnson was a bull in the woods. He didn't like to lose and just kept on driving until he got his way. He came with a vast amount of experience in the ways and life of BC. He had led Whonnock Industries, West Fraser Timber, B.C. Hydro, Western Pulp, and the Whistler Land Company. He had co-founded Casabello Wineries and Fibreco Export Inc. In the 1980's, Chester had led a dedicated board who started the transformation of the near bankrupt Whistler into a world-class, year-round resort by having the foresight and fortitude to plan and build a convention centre in Whistler.

YVRAA continued its close relationship with the federal government and asked Western Economic Diversification (WED) for funding to ensure that VIATAG would be in an adequate financial position when it signed a lease with TC.

There was also the issue of lands which had been contaminated due to air operations by the federal government over the years. Before the lease was signed there had to be an environmental assessment to establish a baseline. Any remediation of contaminated land that was identified prior to the signing of the lease would be the responsibility of the federal government. And land contaminated after the lease began would be the responsibility of the YVRAA. WED agreed to fund the environmental reviews necessary to establish the baseline.

As the meetings with TC continued with discussions as to the how and when of transfer, across the table from the YVRAA was Michael O'Brien, negotiator for TC. He had been the Chief of Staff for Flora MacDonald and was determined that the lease and the financial arrangements at time of hand-over were fair to both the YVRAA and to TC.

The local community also had concerns over the creation of the new AA. As several local groups expressed themselves: how do we ensure that a non-elected, private group administers the new airport in an appropriate manner? Who has control over the AA? What happens to any profit generated from airport operations? Who controls expenses?

David Emerson and Frank O'Neill kept the media wolves at bay. Through an extensive media campaign throughout 1990 and 1991 they gave countless interviews on radio and television, spoke at community events, and had articles written for the local newspapers explaining how the AA would operate, and how it would be different from, and also similar to, the existing TC operated airport. They spent a great deal of time explaining how TC had very little authority to actually accomplish anything at the airport. TC was responsible, accountable and answerable to Parliament. Anything that needed to be done at the airport had to be approved by Parliament and the Department of Finance.

In contrast, the new AA would be able to operate as a private sector corporation. It in and of itself would be able to develop strategic and tactical plans, make decisions, and govern itself. Any profits would be re-invested in the AA to finance capital expenditures. Safety and security oversight would remain as the purview of TC, but operations and governance would be in the hands of the AA.

In July 1992 the YVRAA assumed control and responsibility for air operations at the Vancouver airport.

The first Board consisted of some of the members of the VIATAG group and other newly appointed Directors. David Emerson was hired as the first CEO[463]. It was an inspired choice. He was a natural leader, not just a manager. One of the very first issues he had to face was the union. The previous labour contract had expired in 1991 and the union leaders[464] who came in from Ottawa were adamant that a strike was necessary. David had had

---

[463] Frank O'Neill had wanted the job, but was not chosen.

[464] Public Service Alliance of Canada - PSAC

some discussion with the local union leaders prior to the arrival of the PSAC folk and had come to an "understanding" with them. A strike was averted.

There was also a pent-up demand for "something" to be done about the ATB. Passenger volumes had increased so much that at times the ATB was bursting at the seams with passengers filling up every nook and cranny as they departed from and arrived at the ATB. When the overcrowding had been questioned in the past, TC had always replied: "we can't promote one airport over another because we control them all. They have to wait their turn for funding."

The new Board knew it was responsible, through the CEO, for air operations, but it also knew it needed to catch its breath before embarking on any new capital expenditure to enlarge the current terminal facilities with the addition of an International Terminal Building (ITB) and a second major east-west runway. The new board appointed a Capital Projects Committee to look after the Board's interests during design and construction. The Committee decided that a detailed project management process would be followed, and that before any capital project began a detailed, in-depth, Project Definition Report (PDR) document would be created. The PDR would define the requirement, define the direction and scope of the project, define a project timeline, establish a baseline budget and cash flow requirements, establish the economic feasibility of all major projects and act as the base document for its management, and define how success was to be measured. Not before all that was ready was the first construction project approved. It was to be six months before any announcement was made as to plans for expansion of the airport, the ITB and the North Runway.

From a financial point-of-view the YVR's banks favoured a "design/build" concept for any new construction. The YVRAA said "no". With a design/build we tell the builder and his designers what we need, and then we have to accept what they give us. If the builder/designer wants to cut corners, we have no say in the matter. But if we control the design, and we control the build, then we have far more say over what the final deliverable will look like.

There was a history to this. TC had not had a very good record of designing, building and delivering large construction projects, almost all related to how monies were spent in the public sector at that time. TC had to follow the fiscal policies of the federal government: projects had to be funded and the monies spent in a single fiscal year. Accrual accounting was a foreign concept to the Department of Finance. If Parliament gave TC $20 million to build a new ATB, that $20 million had to be spent in a single fiscal year. As a Project Manager at TC your job was to spend $20 million. Not a penny more, and, even more important, not a penny less. You got raked over the coals for spending too much because you exceeded the Deputy's spending envelope. But you got even more heck if you spent less, because next year's budget was based on what was spent this year. A "good" project manager was one who spent his budget. The outcome was almost irrelevant. Consequently, large construction projects were split into smaller parcels that could be completed in one year. This was an inefficient way of building stuff.

The YVRAA had no such restrictions. Accrual accounting and multi-year cash flows were the order of the day. If the budget was $20 million for a new ATB, and the money was spent in tranches over a period of years, then that was the way it was done. Just as in the private sector.

The awarding of work was also much different. In TC's day a Request for Proposal (RFP) would be issued and proponents would respond, usually with a two-volume proposal – a Technical Proposal, and a Financial Proposal in a separate, sealed envelope. The Technical Proposals of all bidders would be evaluated and points awarded for various, pre-defined items. Once all the bids had been evaluated the financial bids were opened. Bid award could be based on lowest price, "best value to the Crown" (i.e. lowest price per point), or maximum received points, with cost not a consideration. The YVRAA followed a modified "best value". The process started with a call for "expressions of interest) and three respondents were then invited to submit detailed proposals. A group of experienced engineers, architects and project professionals conducted an intensive interview and evaluation process. Only after that was a recommendation made for Management and Board approval. Consideration was given to the proponent's track record, senior people who would be assigned to the project, and the suggestions for improving the end result.

Most of the Public Works Canada (PWC) staff who had worked at the airport prior to transfer stayed on as employees of the VAA. This included the engineers and design staff. When they were working for Public Works, the engineers and design staff had had to go to PWC HQ in Ottawa for decisions and approvals. This was a time-consuming process that did not always end with a positive decision to proceed. It was cumbersome at best and demoralizing at worst. However, under the YVRAA the engineers could come to management with an idea or a proposal and get a decision almost right away. During the construction of the new ITB one engineer came to David Emerson with about 30 design changes. After explaining what he wanted to do, and why, Emerson told him to go ahead. The engineer said he could have a report on Emerson's desk within the week explaining the why and wherefore of his proposed design changes. Emerson told him not to bother – he already had enough information, and he was satisfied that the design changes were worthwhile. The whole exchange had taken less than 20 minutes. The staff now felt they were a valued part of the VAA, and could now do what they could not do before.

Governance was established as a policy from the outset. The Board was not a management Board. Its role was to set policy, create strategic plans, provide oversight, and guide and manage the CEO. It was the job of the CEO to manage the airport, to create operational plans, to oversee safety and security, and to report back to the Board.

Since 1992 the VAA has accomplished a great amount of construction, all of it on-time and in-budget. It has invested more than $3.536 billion in new construction since 1992 and has accomplished the following major items:

- terminal expansions
- a new North Runway
- runway, taxiway and apron renewals
- parking arcade and expanded parking lots
- monorail service to Richmond and Vancouver
- hotel on-site

- high-end outlets mall in the north-east corner of the airport property

It is almost impossible to imagine how all of this could have been accomplished if the airport had remained under the control of TC. Public sector constraints would not have allowed such a vast scale of development in such a short period of time.

The death of Robert Dziekanski at the airport on October 14, 2007 caused a massive review of how passengers and visitors were treated while on airport property and in the facility. The outcome of that review was a series of improvements announced on 7 December 2007:

- 24-hour customer care in the International Arrivals area and inside the Canada Border Services Agency (CBSA) Customs Hall;
- additional customer care training and tools;
- easily identifiable, terminal-wide access to translation services;
- 24-hour in-terminal medical response;
- messaging service from the CBSA Customs Hall to the public greeting area;
- larger, brighter signs with pictograms and multiple languages;
- hourly walk-throughs of the CBSA Customs Hall and 24-hour public safety patrols; and,
- in 2008, a redesign of the international passenger service and public greeting areas to provide a unified, full-service international welcome centre staffed 24 hours a day, seven days a week.

The NEXUS Air program was piloted at YVR and allows pre-screened passengers to avoid customs and immigration line-ups by using self-service kiosks. A NEXUS card can be used for automated border clearance into the United States. The program also allows for automated clearance into Canada from anywhere in the world, and access to priority pre-board screening lanes at airports in Canada, the United States, and some European countries. In 2007, the federal government announced the expansion of the program to additional Canadian airports and its combination with NEXUS Land and Marine into a single NEXUS trusted traveller program.

Perhaps Chester Johnson's proudest accomplishment was hectoring the Board into accepting a First Nations theme for the new ATB after Frank O'Neill, then Senior VP Operations of VIAA had proposed the theme to Chester. Frank then set up the Vancouver Airport Art Foundation, and negotiated individual works of art, in particular he negotiated with Bill and Martina Reid for the casting of the Jade Spirit of Haida Gwai. With Chester's strong support, Frank O'Neill's idea, initiative and project came to fruition. Frank also set up an exchange program with the Vancouver Art Gallery.

At the time the news media had a field day with reporting on the expense - $3 million for a statue!! What were these guys thinking? Have they gone mad with spending money? Today, the statue is worth many times that amount, and is one of the most photographed icons in BC. It also set the theme for the Airports award winning focus on Northwest First Nations art.

Figure 87: Vancouver Airport

Since transfer on 1 May 1992 the AA has spent more than $3.5 billion on capital investment in the airport, almost all of which has been spent in the Vancouver area. The AA contributed more than $211.3 million in 2017 to the local economy through salaries, taxes and local purchases. The airport began paying rent in 1992 and since then has contributed $1.4 billion to the federal treasury. It saw 25 million passengers in 2018.

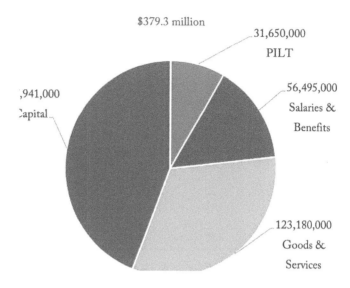

$379.3 million

31,650,000
PILT

56,495,000
Salaries &
Benefits

,941,000
Capital

123,180,000
Goods &
Services

Figure 88: Spending by the Authority in Vancouver in 2017.

Vancouver, British Columbia

Figure 89: Image courtesy of Google Earth Pro, 10 July 2017. The pin marks the location of the original BCATP aerodrome.

In 1930 there was an airharbour, owned by British Columbia Airways Ltd., "located on the southeastern extremity of Vancouver Island".[465] Before the establishment of Victoria Airport, service between Vancouver and Victoria was by seaplane.

In October 1937, the DND felt there was a need for a large military airport on southern Vancouver Island and favoured Sidney as the site for a civilian/military aerodrome. The DOT demurred at this suggestion since it believed that it had jurisdiction as to where civil airports were to be located. As we do best in Canada, a joint committee comprised of representatives from both the DND and the DOT was formed to select a site and to plan an airport agreeable to both.

After some extensive to-ing and fro-ing the committee selected a site at Patricia Bay since it had access to both a level piece of land relatively free of obstructions suitable for civilian and military operations, and easy access to water for seaplanes.

---

[465] Transport Canada, Pacific Region.

Construction began in the summer of 1939 and although the airport was ready for use in 1940 construction continued into 1941 to accommodate the necessary barracks, mess halls, HQs, and maintenance buildings required for the three forces of arms: the RCAF, the RAF and the RCN. There were three 5,000 foot (1 524 m) runways, in a modified BCATP triangle plan: 09-27; 02-20; and 08-26.[466]

The airport was the base for bomber reconnaissance and fighter units, and was home to two operational training units (OTU): No. 3 OTU (RCAF) and No. 32 OTU (RAF). No. 18 EFTS, operated by Boundary Bay Flying Training School Ltd., for the BCATP was also stationed there.

In December 1942 the DND gave permission to TCA to begin scheduled passenger service to Vancouver. Service began in January 1943 with two flights a day. By September 1946 TCA had three daily flights to Vancouver. Seattle was added in 1947 resulting in eight daily flights from Victoria.

DND transferred responsibility for the airport to DOT on 18 May 1948. A temporary license to operate the airport was issued on 18 January 1950, retroactive to 1948. A permanent license was issued to DOT on 8 September 1950.

By 1955 activity had increased to 77,000 aircraft movements annually. Principal users were Pacific Western Airlines, Fairey Aviation Ltd. of Canada, Victoria Flying Club, Vancouver Island Helicopters, and Pacific Aviation Services.

On 22 May 1959 the airport name was changed from Victoria (Patricia Bay) to Victoria International Airport.

In 1961 runway 08-26 was extended to 6,000 feet (1 829 m) and an ILS installed on runway 26 approach. In 1971 runway 09-27 (the old 08-26, renamed due to changes in the magnetic compass) was lengthened to 7,000 (2 134 m) to allow DC-8 operations.[467]

In 1964 DOT finally decided to build a terminal worthy of the name. The old "terminal" had been a WW2 hangar converted at the end of the war to accommodate passengers. The terminal was

---

[466] *History*, p. 248.

[467] Ibid.

enlarged in 1974 to handle the increased passenger traffic which by this time was approaching 500,000 passengers a year.

By 1988 passenger traffic had increased again, this time to 717,000 passengers a year. The terminal was bursting at its seams, but change had to wait until the Authority was put in place.

The Authority

Around 1990 Don Hancock, who was an Air Canada manager freshly retired in Victoria, called several people and told them that the airport transfer process was going forward. Under the transfer the airports would be turned over to local authorities, and would they be interested in helping him put together, through the Chamber of Commerce, a group of credible local people to begin discussions with TC and the government about the transfer of the Victoria airport to local control?

All of those approached thought it a great idea, that more of this kind of thing needed to get going in Canada, not just in airports but also in marine ports, because it made more sense to have local people in their own communities running these local strategic assets.

Andrew MacGillivray was one of the persons approached by Don Hancock, and he agreed to put together some names, call people, and beat the drum a bit to see who might be interested.[468] He assembled a group that included a lawyer (Alan Emery), an accountant (Andy Little), and a couple of retired aviation executives (including Jim Smith who was an airline association executive and who was particularly helpful), and another lawyer (Ian McPherson), who had been a senior executive with Air Canada. Another member of the group was Mark Scott who was very active in the business community and who had the Budget Rent a Car franchise at the airport, came onboard early. All these gentlemen were very helpful in finding the way around Transport Canada.

The Victoria Airport Planning Society (VAPS) managed to become recognized as a credible organization that could manage the process of negotiating a transfer of the Victoria airport to local

---

[468] Andrew MacGillivray, interview with the author, 18 December 2018

control. That transfer process took about ten years - an inordinate amount of time according to one member of the group.

At the time the VAPS formed, the Vancouver Authority was also well under way with its negotiations with TC and Chester Johnson from YVR came and spoke to VAPS and encouraged the group to go ahead, so the VAPS was early to the game relative to the other smaller airports.

At the beginning it was all volunteer work until such time as the VAPS was actually ready to convene a pro-forma Board. It approached the 13 municipalities in the area around the airport. Six of the 13 municipalities agreed that they would put forward names of nominees if asked. So the Board nominees ended up being:

- Government of Canada (2 positions);

- Government of British Columbia (1);

- City of Victoria (1);

- District of North Saanich (2);

- Town of Sidney (2);

- District of Central Saanich (1);

- District of Saanich (1);

- Capital Regional District of British Columbia (1);

- Greater Victoria Chamber of Commerce (1);

- The Board in its own right (3).

Once an actual pro-forma Board had formed to effect the transfer, it became incumbent upon the various nominees to put forward names for the members who would eventually form the operating Board.

The pro-forma Board had its first meeting in November 1995. It then spent 1996 and up to 31 March 1997 getting itself organized, with the pro-forma Board members getting to know each other and figuring out what it would do when it became the operating Board on the 1 April 1997 at transfer.

The Greater Victoria Chamber of Commerce gave the pro-forma Board offices to use, and it used its own resources to bootstrap the work until it became clear that the pro-forma Board was going to begin formal negotiations with TC for a transfer. At that time the pro-forma Board took an unsecured loan from what is now Coast Capital Credit Union.

The pro-forma Board thought it amazing for the Credit Union to give them an unsecured loan. But the members thought "they're [the Credit Union] supposedly focused on the local community, that's their mission", so in their opinion it was reasonable for the Credit Union to proceed to lend the money and in exchange end up as the Authority's banker if the pro-forma Board completed the transfer and could repay the loan, but there was no guarantee of that happening at the time. The Credit Union remained the Authority's main bank for quite a while, which really was quite extraordinary and the sole example of its kind in Canada, until it needed to borrow a substantial amount for the renovations at which point the Canadian Imperial Bank of Commerce (CIBC) became the Authority's lender and key banker.

From a human resources perspective it wasn't until it became obvious that the pro-forma Board was going to begin serious negotiations which would likely lead to transfer that the airport manager became quite a bit more interested in what the pro-forma Board was doing. Up to that point there had been somewhat limited interactions with the existing staff because negotiations with TC were the focus of everyone's energy, and the incumbent airport manager was "absolutely" convinced the airport would not transfer. But the HR issues of pensions and benefits and transfer of employees to the Airport Authority got put in front when TC said to the pro-forma Board "you're going to have to do this, and you're going to have to do that" and it was pretty clear that TC were going to support those employees with respect to employee benefits, and severances, and so on, as part of the process. That position on the part of TC gave the staff comfort that they were going to be supported no matter the outcome.

Negotiations went quite well. There was a clear will to get the transfer done on both sides, and by that time there was a broader mix of personalities in the pro-forma Board. There were a few members of the planning group who understood Ottawa much better than the other members because they had had quite a bit of experience in dealing with the public sector.

The whole issue of rent became semi-contentious with some of the pro-forma Board members saying the Authority should not pay any rent. But other pro-forma Board members took the position that as the Authority was being given a monopoly asset with cash flow it would be customary to pay some rent. That "discussion" went on for a long time after transfer with some Board members saying that Her Majesty should be pleased to have gotten rid of the airport, and others maintaining that it was a commercial enterprise and should bear an input cost for rent as a normal cost of doing business. Their point was that the airport was to be run more like a business than a government bureaucracy, with local management and governance and conventional accounting practices. Let TC provide the regulatory oversight, but the direction of the airport would be determined locally.

The contributions of some of the early characters like Jim Smith and Ian McPherson really made a difference to the creation of the Authority, even though they didn't end up on the either the pro-forma Board or the operating Board. Victoria is a repository for retired Canadians and a lot of the brightest and the best seem to land there. Consequently the VAPS ended up with enormous resources: people who knew Ottawa; who knew aviation; and who had been involved in everything from aircraft construction to airport management. The VAPS was really quite a strong group from the point-of-view of experience, expertise and intellect.

Once the pro-forma Board became an operating Board it then started to think about improving the facilities. That meant levying an AIF which it put in place, and putting priorities on what needed to be done. The Board decided to work on the departures area first, and after that to work on the arrivals area, and then to the runways, and aprons, and so forth. The Board also encouraged other airlines to come in, because at that time there were very few.

The Board had to establish a procedures manual, a book of the organizational structure, liaison between the CEO and the Chair. It did an evaluation of all the senior managers to see if they were appropriately qualified, and in the right slots, and once it became an operating Board it moved a few people around. The Board had to set up banking arrangements, choose an auditor, and come up with a logo. Most of the effort was in developing the organizational chart, who reported to whom, and what was their job. The Board examined all the job descriptions, and changed them as necessary.

Soon after transfer Linda Petch was retained as a facilitator for a strategic planning exercise, which, as one Board member recalled, was conducted over four full Saturdays of seven hours each.[469] Linda ran the strategic planning exercise. The Board found her to be very good and was pleased with the strategic plan developed over those four days. The Board members then went off to do their committee work and for the first year, if not two, with most members working on airport committee work almost every day. "We really had to turn things around. It was a mess."[470]

Another very important factor in the success of the Authority was that it acquired Richard Paquette as CEO. Richard was a particularly good, entrepreneurial and capable executive manager. He was there through the entire reconstruction phase which was very challenging. The airport manager incumbent at transfer had presented the Board with a budget of $60 million for the construction project to upgrade the terminal. The construction project consultant had said something pretty substantial could be done for about $15 million. The Board believed the consultant, hired Richard, and he proved that the lower number was the correct one.

The members of the Board take pride in what they accomplished for Victoria. The original terminal the Authority inherited was a small drab building with very few windows so when the opportunity to redo it arose the Board said "we're going to bring the incredible beauty of the surrounding environment into the new building by opening it up with high ceilings and lots of glass so that people can sit there and gaze out at Saltspring Island and the nearby mountains and appreciate the natural beauty of the West Coast when they are in the terminal. And if we can just do that we'll have done a pretty good job". And that's what they did.

---

[469] Graham Ross, interview with the author, 16 December 2018.

[470] Ibid.

The metal flowers outside were the idea of Linda Petch. Other Board members were not of the same opinion saying "Forget the public art. Let's just get this terminal rebuilt." But they now realize, looking back, that they were wrong about that.

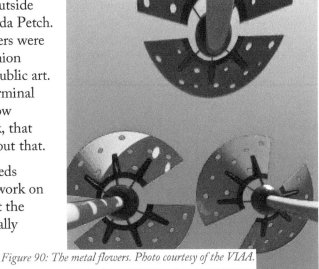

Linda Petch also needs recognition for her work on Board governance at the Authority. Linda really brought the Board forward in terms of more progressive views on governance, and in hindsight the Board now realizes that it needed that. At the time the Board thought it was maybe too much "touchy feely", but

Figure 90: The metal flowers. Photo courtesy of the VIAA.

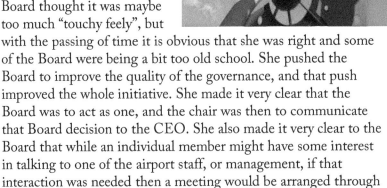

with the passing of time it is obvious that she was right and some of the Board were being a bit too old school. She pushed the Board to improve the quality of the governance, and that push improved the whole initiative. She made it very clear that the Board was to act as one, and the chair was then to communicate that Board decision to the CEO. She also made it very clear to the Board that while an individual member might have some interest in talking to one of the airport staff, or management, if that interaction was needed then a meeting would be arranged through the Chair talking to the CEO. Linda deserves a special accolade for her work on governance.

When Don Hancock called Andrew MacGillivray that day and asked if he would like to help take over a key local monopoly business Andrew thought "how many opportunities am I going to get to work with a monopoly business case?"[471] And this is no

---

[471] MacGillivray.

small-time monopoly here, the airport is arguably the key strategic business asset in the community. So he thought "it's going to be loads of fun if we can pull this off"[472] because he had never been in an environment like that. People in the community were not really seeing the business opportunity, with no one focusing on the economic generator/ monopoly aspect of it. People just saw the costs and potential liabilities. Now, after 20 years of the Authority operating the airport, "seasoned private business people would kill to get their hands on a toll positioned asset like that - where you're the sole owner of a key strategic asset. It's like a Rockefeller dream come true."[473]

But in the end it's always the people who make the difference. If

Figure 91: Victoria ATB. Photo courtesy of the VIAA.

you get the right mix of people and the right chemistry between them and you manage the inevitable conflicts well, then you can usually end up with a good outcome. As Andrew MacGillivray said "I think we ended up with a particularly good airport at YYJ. And Victoria deserves that. It's a great city and it deserves a great airport. I was fortunate to be able to help make that happen. I see my work at YYJ as my most important contribution to local public

---

[472] Ibid.

[473] Ibid.

service, as part of my giving back to a wonderful community that has been very good to me and my family over the years."[474]

Since assuming responsibility for the airport, the Victoria International Airport Authority has seen passenger traffic grow from 1.103 million in 1997 to 1.934 million a year in 2017. Revenues of $37.234 million were seen that same year. Also, since 1997 the Authority has invested more than $156.7 million in infrastructure in the airport, and has paid more than $20.1 million in rent to the federal government.

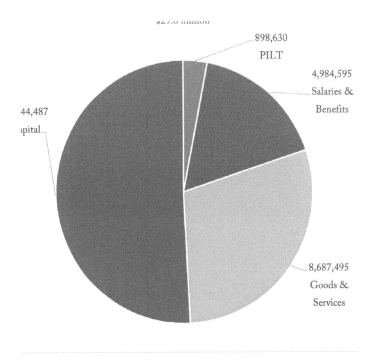

$27.6 million

898,630
PILT

4,984,595
Salaries &
Benefits

44,487
ıpital

8,687,495
Goods &
Services

---

[474] Ibid.

*Figure 93: Image courtesy of Google Earth Pro, 21 October 2017. The pin marks the
location of the original BCATP aerodrome.*

The first active airfield in Winnipeg was located at St. Charles, six
miles (10 km) west of the city. It had been built in 1919 by the
British Canadian Aircraft Company who had plans to construct an
aircraft factory. The plant was never built and eventually the
airport was abandoned.

Stevenson aerodrome was built by the Winnipeg Aeroplane Club
in 1928 on 160 acres (68 hectares) of prairie grassland leased from
the rural municipality of St. James, then a Winnipeg suburb. In
1929, under the federal government's light aeroplane clubs' scheme
of 1927, the club reorganized as the Winnipeg Flying Club and
entered in a 21-year lease to develop and run the airport for the
City of Winnipeg and the rural municipality of St. James. It was
decided to call the airport the Stevenson Aerodrome in tribute to
Capt. Fred J. Stevenson, a well-known WW1 RAF pilot and
Canadian bush pilot who had lost his life in a crash of a Western
Airways Fokker Universal at The Pas, Manitoba on 5 January
1928. It was only in 1959, at the request of the DOT, and with
the approval of the town councils of Winnipeg and St. James, that
the name was changed to Winnipeg International Airport so as to

407

be in accordance with meeting the naming conventions of the International Civil Aviation Organization (ICAO – headquartered in Montréal).

In 1929 the airport was designated as the eastern terminus of the western airmail route, and, in the following year when it became a Customs port of entry, federal and municipal funds enabled the installation of field lighting.

The first major scheduled airline was Western Canada Airways which in 1930 built a hangar and a maintenance facility, and made Winnipeg its headquarters. In 1931 Northwest Airlines was the first international airline to use the airport when it began service from Pembina, North Dakota, to Winnipeg.

Between 1930 and 1932 Canadian Airways flew the prairie section of the airmail from Winnipeg to Calgary, serving Regina, Moose Jaw, Medicine Hat, Saskatoon, North Battleford, and Edmonton.

The runways were sod and clay, the passenger terminal was a lean-to on the side of the hangar, and the snow was compacted, not cleared.

In 1934 the RCAF built a hangar for 112 Army Cooperation Squadron to house their five Gypsy Moths. The squadron eventually became the 402 (Fighter) Squadron flying in the Battle of Britain.

In May 1937 the City of Winnipeg and the rural municipality of St. James formed an Airport Commission to acquire lands and undertake the planning and operation of the airport. The Commission was approved by an Act of the provincial legislature on 25 February 1938. The Commission's first act was to construct various works to enable TCA to operate more effectively from the airport (TCA had began operations at the airport in 1937 after having chosen Winnipeg as its headquarters and training centre). A third runway was built, and the two existing runways were rebuilt with a hard surface.

By 1938 the airport had four civilian hangars, one military hangar, three hard-surfaced runways (two 3,000 feet (914 m) and one 3,200 feet (975 m)) and the airport had grown in size to 800 acres (324 hectares). Boundary lighting was in place, and a radio range station and weather forecasting facilities were in operation. Airport traffic control was installed in 1940.

On 1 April 1939 TCA began daily service for passengers, mail and cargo between Montréal, Toronto, Winnipeg, Lethbridge and Vancouver.

At the outbreak of WW2 the federal government took over Stevenson Field from the Commission for the duration and the DOT assumed responsibility for the civil airside.

Under the BCATP, Winnipeg became the focal point for training in the prairies. No. 2 Training Command established headquarters in downtown Winnipeg; No. 14 Elementary Flying Training School was set up with Tiger Moths; No. 5 Air Observer School set up operations with Ansons; and No. 3 Wireless Training School operated with Fleet Forts. In addition to the military operations at the airfield several civilian companies built aircraft and engine factories, repair and overhaul depots: MacDonald Brothers (bomber and trainer overhaul and repair) and Mid-West Aircraft (Hawker Hurricane aircraft and engine repair and overhaul) being two of the largest.

In 1946 the DND gave all its buildings and equipment to the DOT, and the Airport Commission refused to take back responsibility for the airport, despite the agreement of 25 October 1940. On 6 June 1964, after 18 years of negotiations, the DOT finally assumed control of all the land and buildings.

In the spring of 1947 DOT expropriated land for a new runway, 18-36, 6,200 feet (1 890 m) and commenced building another new runway, 13-31. Both were completed by August 1948 and ILS systems installed on the new runways that same year.

In March 1947 RCAF Station Winnipeg was formed, consisting of No. 111 Composite Flight, No. 402 (Auxiliary) Squadron, No. 11 Group of Northwest Command, and No. 14 Training Group.

The building and plant of Station Winnipeg were those inherited from wartime units and were grouped on the south side of Stevenson Field. At the outbreak of the Korean War, basic training units were moved from both coasts and concentrated in the prairie provinces. Winnipeg was chosen as the site for Observer Training. Navigator Training moved from Summerside, PEI to Winnipeg to cope with the flood of trainees from a dozen NATO countries.

The renewed military activities called for a great expansion of facilities: new hangars, repair and overhaul depots, instructional schools and facilities, mess halls, barracks, officers quarters, quarters for married personnel; and host of other buildings were constructed. By the time operations at Summerside were closed out, the No. 2 Air Observer School was the largest aircrew training depot in the RCAF.

A "modernized" civilian air terminal was opened on 15 December 1952 as an extension to the TCA hangar. With three parking positions for aircraft, it housed airline offices, ticket counters, baggage conveyor, and a waiting room. It remained in use until 1964.

By 1954 Winnipeg was the fourth busiest airport in Canada; headquarters for TCA; home to the largest NATO air training school, and No. 2 Air Navigation School; and supply point for the airlift to the construction of the Distant Early Warning (DEW) Line, a system of radars being built in Canada' far north.

A new runway, 07-25, was built in 1955, and in 1957 runway 13-31 was extended to 8,700 feet (2 562 m). In 1960 runway 18-36 was extended to 11,000 feet (2 353 m) to permits TCA's DC-8 flights to London, England.

Training Command of the integrated Canadian Armed Forces was formed at Station Winnipeg on 1 January 1966. Station Winnipeg was re-designated Canadian Forces Base (CFB) Winnipeg on 1 April 1966. Training Command was replaced by Canadian Forces Training System on 2 September 1975 and Air Command became operationally effective that same day, with headquarters at CFB Winnipeg.

The new air terminal opened on 17 January 1964. It had taken four years to build, at a cost of $18 million. The new terminal had 40 acres (16 hectares) of concrete apron, and, with the new passenger facilities, was a striking contrast to the cramped conditions of the old TCA hangar. The new terminal also had, like Montréal and Toronto, pre-clearance services to the United States offered by the U.S. Inspection Service.

Improvements over the years to the runways now gave Winnipeg International the following:

Runway 18-36   11,000 by 200 feet (2 353 by 61 m)

| Runway 13-31 | 8,700 by 200 feet (2 652 by 61 m) |
| Runway 07-25 | 7,000 by 200 feet (2 134 by 61 m) |

There were 12 civil aviation hangars and seven RCAF hangars.

TCA's facilities had also grown over the years. TCA, now Air Canada, opened a new cargo terminal immediately south of the passenger terminal. In 1975 it built a new engineering and maintenance complex on the west side of the airport. The cargo terminal expanded in 1982, and the maintenance complex was enlarged in 1983 with the addition of a second hangar.

There were now 34 major buildings on the 5,712 acre (1 741 hectares) site, with civil aviation concentrated on the east, and the military concentrated on the west. Four aerospace companies were in operation: Aero Recip Canada Ltd., Douglas Aero Engine, Bristol Aerospace, and Standard Aero Ltd.

Figure 94: Photo courtesy of the WIAA.

The Authority

By the late 1980's a group in Winnipeg saw that the creation of an airport authority was an issue that a local community might have a chance to discuss with TC. Consequently Otto Lang, Sandy Hopkins, Robert Gabor, and another couple of people recruited from the Provincial Department of Transport began discussions with local people including, many times, with the city about the kind of circumstances that would work for the airport and even eventually the makeup of the future airport authority. Because of these discussions organizations like the Chamber of Commerce, the surrounding municipalities and the city ended up nominating most members of the Board.

There are some interesting issues about the amount of rent the Authority keeps on paying.

Part of the reasoning behind the earliest endeavours to privatize was also that the individual airport could well decide that it was right to move ahead with a major investment, where their concerns only had to be whether they could handle the investment in the future, whereas if it was a federal thing, a federal decision as to a new ATB, that would come up as a huge federal commitment of dollars, which would be issues for the Minister of Finance and the Government, and where they stood in fiscal terms. It could often lead to a hold-up in the expenditure, whereas now it was a decision of the private sector. That in great part is why the AAs have been such a success.

In the long-term the AA was always satisfied that it could raise financing, particularly because of the right of the airport to impose fees related to the costs of the investments being made, and the need to cover those costs. Covering the costs was always easy because the airport is an "unregulated monopoly" with the unlimited ability to raise funds. In the short run the issue was to get some money to actually get the thing off the ground and to do the work that had to be done, and to convince people. So the organizing group went equally to the Province and to the city for financial support for that first year and a half of effort and was successful in getting the money it needed. The organizing group preferred the city and Province because then it was not putting itself as hostages into the hands of a bank.

There was some negative opinion, as there are always some who will voice a complaint or concern. The organizing group had some naysayers on the city council who were concerned that this was an attempt by the federal government to offload the cost of the airport onto the city. Some Provinces had that thought too when it came to the airports in their Province. But by-and-large people saw through that very quickly because people saw why the airports would have significant financial stability.

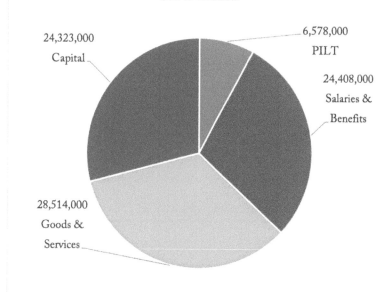

$83.8 million

6,578,000
PILT

24,408,000
Salaries &
Benefits

24,323,000
Capital

28,514,000
Goods &
Services

Winnipeg, Manitoba

Chapter 7: Policy development in a federal government department

TC is organized as most federal government departments are:

- a Minister of the Crown as the department head, who is responsible, answerable and accountable to Parliament for his or her department[475];

- a Deputy Minister[476] as the senior civil servant in the department, who takes political direction from an elected Minister of the Crown. Deputies are Order In Council appointments, recommended to the Governor General by the Prime Minister. Deputy Ministers serve "at pleasure"[477]. Since they usually last longer in their position than does the Minister, they quite often become the senior level "corporate memory" of the department[478]. A Deputy Minister has responsibility for a department's day-to-day operations, budget, and policy development. They must demonstrate sensitivity to the interests of their Minister and the Prime Minister;

- Associate Deputy Ministers are Deputy Ministers in waiting, often assigned to a specific project or initiative pending appointment to lead a department as Deputy;

- Assistant Deputy Ministers public servants occupying an "indeterminate"[479] position and have an operational function, usually carrying responsibility for a Branch which executes

---

[475] Eugene A. Forsey, *How Canadians Govern Themselves*, Library of Parliament, 1980

[476] Known as *Permanent Secretary* in England and *Departmental Secretary* in Australia.

[477] A legal term referring to undetermined length of service. A person serving "at pleasure" may be dismissed at any time, with or without cause.

[478] Gordon Osbaldeston, *Keeping Deputy Ministers Accountable*, McGraw-Hill Ryerson, 1989.

[479] In the Canadian federal public service an "indeterminate" position is a permanent job, i.e it has no determined end of employment since under the Canadian Charter of Rights and Freedoms no employee may be terminated for age. An ADM is the senior public servant in their Branch.

particular functions or administers particular budgets within a department.

- Reporting to an Assistant Deputy Minister are Directors General who are responsible for sectors within a Branch.

- Associate Deputy Ministers, Assistant Deputy Ministers and Directors General are civil servants hired by the Public Service Commission and are considered "indeterminate"[480] employees of the federal government.

TC has the responsibility for the effective and efficient oversight of transportation in Canada through the creation of appropriate policy, rules and regulations. Although this oversight is split into four major areas of responsibility: rail, roads, marine and air, the Department is organized slightly differently by functionality:

- Minister's Office;
- Executive Office;
- Regional offices for the Directors General of the Pacific, Prairie and Northern, Ontario, Québec, and Atlantic Regions;
- Corporate Services;
- Groups for Programs, Communications, Safety and Security, and Policy; and,
- Legal Services.

Aviation *policy* is the responsibility of the *Policy Group*, headed by an ADM, who has a DG for Air Policy, who in turn has a Director for National Airports and Air Navigation Services Policy.

Aviation *rules and regulations* come under the *Safety and Security Group*, headed by an ADM, who in turn has a DG Civil Aviation.

Stewardship of airports comes under the *Programs Group*, headed by an ADM, who in turn has a DG Air & Marine Programs, with a Director Authorities Stewardship.

Policy

In the Canadian federal government, *policy* may be defined as "a clear goal and/or direction. It comes from the considered selection

---

[480] i.e. they have no fixed term, or length of time, for which they are employed. Since the *Charter of Rights and Freedoms* came into being an "indeterminate" employee does not have to retire at age 65 and may continue to do their job until health or death intervenes.

of one choice among competing and compelling choices. Policy directs, but does not consist of, operational programs and details."[481]

If you have had no experience with how the federal government develops policy, it may seem a bit messy, as the excellent diagram on the next page shows (drawn by Glen Milne in 2001). Some have compared it to making sausage: you may like the finished product, but don't go and see how its done. The process does, after some time, begin to make a little bit of sense.[482]

Fundamentally, policy is created by a demand. Whether that demand comes from outside the government, or from within, the process is basically the same:

- A need is identified as a result of some issue;
- The issue is assigned to the appropriate department / agency;
- Research occurs to prepare background on the issue;
- Proposals are developed to respond to the issue (yes, no, maybe (depending on the political will and available political capital));
- Presentations are prepared and made to the senior management / Deputy Minister of the department affected;
- The Deputy approves the proposal;
- A Memorandum to Cabinet (MC) is prepared describing the issue and proposing a solution (with costs);
- Cabinet approves (or not) the MC;
- If the MC is approved, the Deputy is instructed by Cabinet to proceed and is given financial and human resources to implement the MC[483];
- It is at this point that "Policy" becomes "Action", for now the Deputy instructs the appropriate ADM to proceed, who tells the appropriate

---

[481] Glen Milne, *Making Policy: A Guide to the Federal Government's Policy Process*, self published, 2000.

[482] I first worked for the Canadian federal government in 1989 after spending 20 years in the private sector. For the first few years I would sometimes leave a meeting saying to myself: "What are these people thinking?" as we had gone through yet another series of proposals, and counter-proposals, and fact-finding exercises. It was mind-boggling at times.

[483] Cabinet does not always provide the resources to implement. If the MC addresses an issue considered by Cabinet to already be within the purview of the department, the Deputy will have to find money and people from within his/her existing spending envelope. However, refusal by Cabinet to fund would be a rare occurrence, since the Deputy would not put forward an MC if it was possible for it to be refused. It is not only politicians who have to husband political capital.

DG, who assigns it to a Director, who has a team that actually does the work.

So, policy may seem a little convoluted in its development, but it really does have some sanity about its creation.

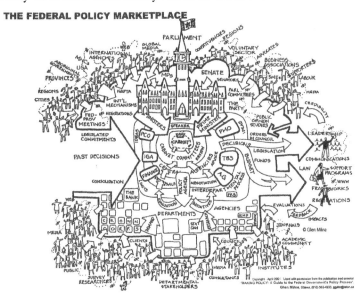

Figure 96: Copyright Glen Milne, 2001. Used with permission.

Chapter 8: Passenger volumes from devolution to now

There are 26 airports in the National Airports System (NAS)[484]. Approximately 90% of Canadian air passenger traffic is handled by 25 of those 26 airports. Twenty-one airports authorities manage 22 of the 26 airports. The airports are, from West to East:

Location	Airport Authority (Year of takeover from Transport Canada in brackets)	Passengers in 2017	Passengers at time of devolution
Victoria (YYJ)	Victoria Airport Authority (1997)	1,934,000	1,103,000
Vancouver (YVR)	Vancouver International Airport Authority (1992)	24,166,122	9,935,000
Prince George (YXS)	Prince George Airport Authority Inc. (2003)	499,125	
Kelowna (YLW)	City of Kelowna	1,893,470	Not an airport authority
Edmonton (YEG)	Edmonton Regional Airports Authority (1992)	7,807,384	1,500,000
Calgary (YYC)	Calgary Airport Authority (1992)	16,275,862	
Saskatoon (YXE)	Saskatoon Airport Authority (1999)	1,462,751	814,100
Regina (YQR)	Regina Airport Authority (1999)	1,219,311	
Winnipeg James	Winnipeg Airports	4,146,275	

---

[484] Montréal Mirabel (YMX) is a NAS airport but no longer has passenger flights. It is now used for cargo and as a base for aerospace companies.

Passenger Volumes

Location	Airport Authority (Year of takeover from Transport Canada in brackets)	Passengers in 2017	Passengers at time of devolution
Armstrong Richardson (YWG)	Authority Inc. (1996)		
Thunder Bay (YQT)	Thunder Bay International Airports Inc. (1997)	844,627	
London (YXU)	Greater London International Airports Authority (1998)	522,000	320,200
Toronto Pearson (YYZ)	Greater Toronto Airports Authority (1995)	45,440,557	
Ottawa Macdonald-Cartier (YOW)	Ottawa Macdonald-Cartier International Airport Authority (1997)	4,734,997	
Montréal-Pierre Elliott Trudeau (YUL)	Aéroports de Montréal (1992)	17,258,472	
Montréal Mirabel (YMX)	Aéroports de Montréal (1992 – ceased operation as a passenger terminal in 2004)	(2004)	
Québec City Jean Lesage (YQB)	Aéroport de Québec Inc. (2000)	1,670,880	
Fredericton (YFC)	Fredericton International Airport Authority (2001)	397,741	179,200
Greater Moncton (YQM)	Greater Moncton International Airport Authority Inc. (1997)	665,630	

Passenger Volumes

Location	Airport Authority (Year of takeover from Transport Canada in brackets)	Passengers in 2017	Passengers at time of devolution
Saint John (YSG)	Saint John Airport Inc. (1999)	263,719	
Charlottetown (YYG)	Charlottetown Airport Authority Inc. (1999)	370,688	187,300
Halifax Stanfield (YHZ)	Halifax International Airport Authority (2000)	3,966,228	2,981,000
Gander (YQX)	Gander International Airport Authority Inc. (2001)	239,200	465,252[485]
St. John's (YYT)	St. John's International Airport Authority (1998)	1,533,355	694,100
Yellowknife (YZF)	Government of the Northwest Territories	575,000 (2016)	Under Territorial control.
Iqaluit (YFB)	Government of the Nunavut Territory	130,000	Under Territorial control.
Erik Nielson Whitehorse International (YXY)	Government of the Yukon Territory	179,300	Under Territorial control.

---

[485] This number includes the number of passengers who landed after 9/11.

421

Chapter 9: Referenced Statistical Data: 1992 – 2017

Consolidated data for the period 1992 to 2018 (estimated data for 2018) for all airports in the NAS which have a Ground Lease showing the amounts paid in rent, the dollar investments made in the airports, and the rise in number of passengers:

Year	Lease Expense 000's	Captial Investment 000's	E&D Pax 000's
1992	24,698	32,149	25,780
1993	50,808	103,493	25,048
1994	49,993	143,511	25,990
1995	67,254	273,468	28,532
1996	84,281	225,025	33,650
1997	200,191	396,519	68,565
1998	198,570	440,358	71,004
1999	225,967	695,741	74,622
2000	245,847	1,011,258	79,529
2001	245,755	1,548,274	78,347
2002	254,390	1,578,755	74,416
2003	249,154	1,543,248	72,987
2004	275,772	1,253,812	82,772
2005	303,833	1,155,706	87,661
2006	283,336	1,108,830	93,827
2007	284,200	1,006,052	98,971
2008	273,848	1,218,440	101,605
2009	271,987	1,130,328	96,158
2010	245,158	832,282	101,129
2011	268,901	1,210,182	104,558
2012	285,926	1,740,786	108,630
2013	302,666	1,470,451	123,910
2014	317,744	1,471,810	129,869
2015	332,113	1,318,408	133,427
2016	351,000	1,300,000	140,893
2017	373,000	1,100,000	149,642
2018	400,000	1,200,000	160,000
	6,466,391	26,508,884	2,371,520

Chapter 10: Trans-Canada Airways - 1937

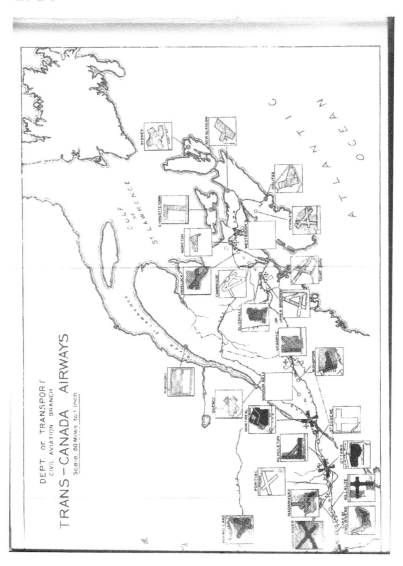

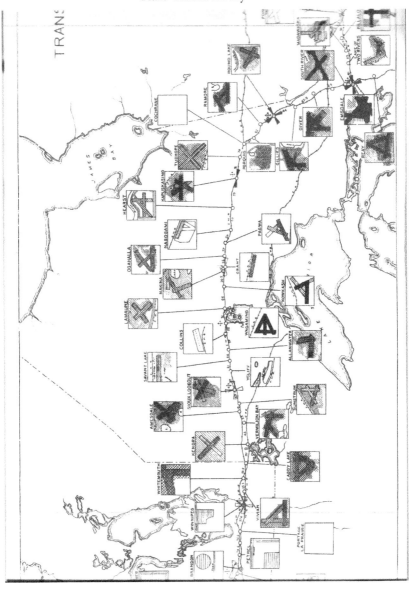

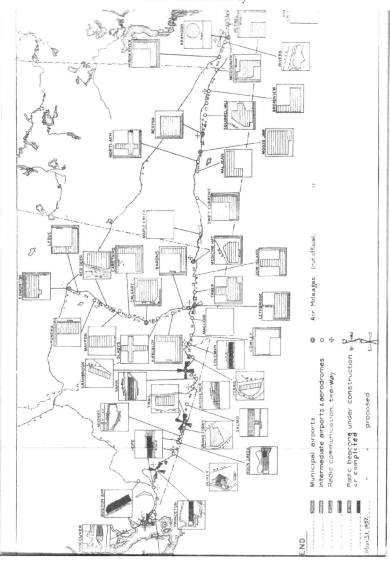

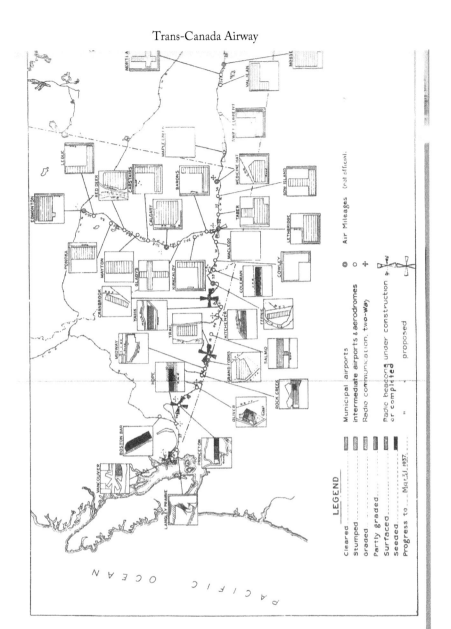

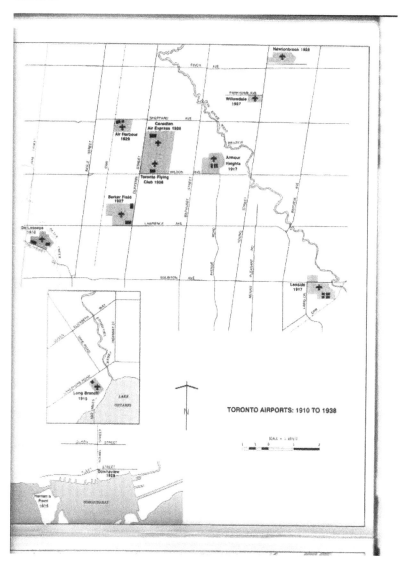

TORONTO AIRPORTS: 1910 TO 1938

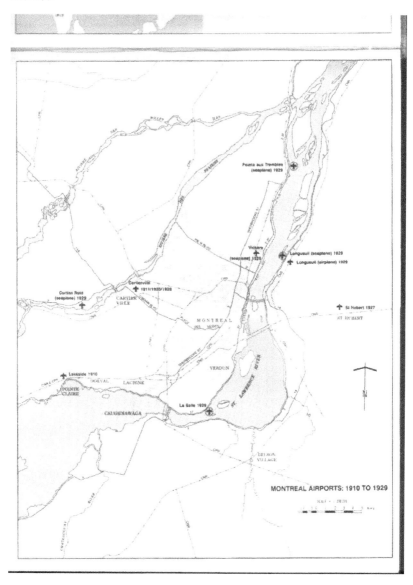

MONTREAL AIRPORTS: 1910 TO 1929

Sources

A Future Framework for the Management of Airports in Canada. Ottawa: Transport Canada, TP8353, April 8, 1987.

A History of the Airport. St. John's: St. John's International Airport.

Airport Activity Statistics. Ottawa: Statistics Canada, for the years 1968, 1971, 1975, 1996, 1998, 2000, 2002, 2004, 2006, 2008, 2010, 2012, 2014 and 2015.

Airport ASD. Ottawa: Treasury Board Secretariat, 1997.

Airport Divestiture Status Report. Ottawa: Transport Canada, undated

Airport Inquiry Commission. Ottawa: Information Canada, 1974.

Airport System Development. Washington: U.S. Government Printing Office, August 1984.

Airport Transfers: National Airport System. Ottawa: Auditor General of Canada, Chapter 10, October 2000.

Airports Act 1986. London: Her Majesty's Stationery Office, Statutes, Chapter 31, 1986.

Airports Authority Act 1975. London: Her Majesty's Stationery Office, Statutes, Chapter 78, 1975.

Army Air force units in Alaska (11th Air Force). http://www.armyairforces.com. Accessed 3 Sep 2018.

Brooks, Mary R. and Barry Prentice. *Airport Devolution: The Canadian Experience.* 2001.

Canada Flight Supplement. Effective 0901Z 19 July 2018 to 0901Z 13 September 2018.

Celebrating Success, Greater Toronto Airports Authority, 10 Year Anniversary, 1996-2006. Toronto: Greater Toronto Airports Authority, 2 December 2006.

Civil Aviation Infrastructure in the North. Ottawa: Auditor General of Canada, Report 6, Spring 2017.

Cohen, Stan. *The Forgotten War, Volume 1.* April 1990.

-----. *The Forgotten War, Volume 2.* March 2002.

Conference Board of Canada, *Impact Économique de l'Aéroport International Jean-Lesage de Québec*, June 2017.

Daniels, Ronald and Michael Trebilcock. *Choice of Policy Instrument in the Provision of Public Infrastructure*, in Infrastructure and Competitiveness (edited by Mintz), John Deutsch Institute, 1994.

Davis, Mark Douglas. *Changing Course: Commercializing Canadian Airport, Port and Rail Governance - 1975 to 2000*. PhD Thesis. Ottawa: Carleton University, 2016.

Deviaban, Stanley W. *US Army in WW2, Military Relations Between US & Canada*. Activities in Western Canada, Chapter VIII.

Dion, Joseph P. *Airports in Transition*. Ottawa: Transport Canada, 4 October 2002.

Doganis, Rigas. *A National Airport Plan*. London: Fabian Society, Fabian Tract 377, 1967.

Farquhar, Michael. *Airport Privatization – Magic Formula or Pandora's Box – The Canadian Experience*. 5th ACI Latin America / Caribbean Regional Conference, Santo Domingo, 12 July 1995.

-----. *Airport Privatization – The Canadian Model*. Vancouver, BC, Fall 1996.

-----. *Airport Privatization – The Canadian Model*. Munich, Germany, 19 July 1996.

-----. *The Airport Transfer Process – Challenges for Transport Canada and Lessons Learned – Personal Reflections*. The Canadian Institute, Toronto, ON, 2 June 1997.

-----. *An Executive Briefing on Partnership, Devolution and Power Sharing: Implications for Management*. Ottawa: Consulting and Audit Canada, 3 December 1992.

-----. *Changing Airport Structures: The Canadian Experience*. 1994 ACI-NA – 3rd Annual Regional Conference, 27 September 1994.

-----. *Community's Role in Promoting Aviation – the Structure of Airport Management Now and in the Future*. Saskatoon: Saskatchewan Aviation Council, 15 November 1991.

-----. *Financing Airport Transfers in Canada – A Progress Report.* Houston: Airport Operators Council International, , 3 October 1989.

-----. *The Future of Airports in the U.S. and Canada.* Vancouver: American Association of Airport Executives, Transport Canada Conference, 29 July 1991.

-----. *Infrastructure and Competitiveness.* Ottawa: 10th John Deutsch Round Table on Economic Policy, 3-4 June 1993.

-----. *Infrastructure in the Public and Private Sector.* Ottawa: Investment Canada, Seminar on Infrastructure and Competitiveness, 4 June 1993.

-----. *Local Airport Authorities.* Montréal: Air Transport Association of Canada, 17 November 1992.

-----. *Managing Smart During Lean Times. Local Airport Authorities – The Canadian Experience.* 1993 Airports Council International – North America – Economic Specialty Conference, 19 April 1993.

-----. *The Private Sector's Involvement in the Development, Funding and Operations of Airports and Terminals – The Canadian Approach.* New York: Institute for International Research, 12 July 1990

-----. *Privatization of Airports and Airport Operations – Airport Transfers – The Canadian Approach.* Washington: American Transportation Research Board, 23 January 1989.

-----. *Public – Private Partnering in Canada, An Overview of Transport Canada's Transfer of Infrastructure.* Toronto: Canadian Council, 25 November 1996.

-----. *Re-Inventing Government – Moving from Visions to Blueprint.* The Financial Post Conference, 15 November 1994.

-----. *Restructuring Strategies for the Public Sector – Airports Commercialization – The Canadian Approach to Restructuring Canada's Airport System.* Institute for International Research, 6 March 1995.

-----. *Speaking Notes for Talk to Deloitte & Touche Personnel.* 16 December 1993.

-----. *Talking Points for Initial Meeting with CAA.* TC, CAA Deliberations, 19 July 1996.

-----. *Transportation Privatization and Regulation – The Canadian Experience*. Kingston, Jamaica: 7th ACI Latin America / Caribbean Regional Conference, 29 January 1997.

Freedom to move: a framework for transportation reform. Transport Canada, Ottawa, 1985.

Future of Canadian Air Travel: Toll Booth or Spark Plug. Ottawa: Senate of Canada, June, 2012.

Future of the Toronto Island Airport: The Issues. Ottawa: Royal Commission of the Future of the Toronto Waterfront, Publication No. 7, May 1989.

Gill, Vijay. *The Devolution of Canadian Transportation Infrastructure and Services*. Montréal: CPCS Transcom Ltd, 15 May 2015.

Governance of Canadian Airports: Issues and Recommendations. Montréal: Institute for Governance of Private and Public Organizations, 2014.

Government of Canada Cuts Airport Rents, Transport Canada, News Release, No. H098/05, May 9, 2005.

InterVISTAS Consulting Inc, *The Economic Impact of the Edmonton Airports System*, 7 October 2010.

Langlois, David. *Interview: David Atkinson, 10 October 2018*.

-----. *Interview: Muir Barber, 9 January 2019*.

-----. *Interview: Robert Basque, 23 January 2019*.

-----. *Interview: Paul Benoit, 10 December 2018*.

-----. *Interview: Jim Blake, 18 September 2018*.

-----. *Interview: Jean-Jacques Bourgeault, 2 October 2018*.

-----. *Interview: Mary Brooks, 19 December 2018*.

-----, *Interview: Wayne Brownlee, 4 January 2019*.

-----. *Interview: Derek Burney, 13 December 2018*.

-----. *Interview: Nick Careen, 31 January 2019*.

-----. *Interview: Joyce Carter, 28 January 2019*.

-----. *Interview: Lino Celeste, 4 January 2019*.

-----. *Interview: Graham Clarke, 17 October 2018.*

-----. *Interview: John Cloutier, 23 October 2018.*

-----. *Interview: Skip Cormier, 3 January 2019.*

-----. *Interview: James Cowan, 20 December 2018, 28 January 2019.*

-----. *Interview: Bob Creamer, 2 January 2019.*

-----. *Interview: Mark Duncan, 26 November 2018.*

-----. *Interview: Doug Eyford, 1 October 2018.*

-----. *Interview: Michael Farquhar, 23 October 2018.*

-----. *Interview: Gaëtan Gagné, 11 December 2018, 7 February 2019.*

-----. *Interview: Gerry Gallant, 14 September 2018.*

-----. *Interview: Joanne Gallant, 17 September 2018.*

-----. *Interview: John Gibson, 18 September 2018.*

-----. *Interview: Ron Gilbertson, 19 September 2018.*

-----. *Interview: Daniel-Robert Gooch, 1 December 2018.*

-----. *Interview: John Hansen, 20 November 2018.*

-----. *Interview: Nancy Healy, 7 November 2018.*

-----. *Interview: Wilson Hoffe, 18 September 2018.*

-----. *Interview: David Innes, 18 September 2018.*

-----. *Interview: Richard Jasieniuk, 20 March 2019.*

-----. *Interview: Otto Lang, 12 December 2018.*

-----. *Interview: Rex LeDrew, 1 Oct 2018.*

-----. *Interview: Don Mazankowski, 19 November 2018.*

-----. *Interview: Tyler MacAfee, 11 December 2018.*

-----. *Interview: Wayne McAllister, 7 January 2019.*

-----. *Interview: Scott McFadden, 7 December 2018.*

-----. *Interview: Andrew McGillivray, 18 December 2018.*

-----. *Interview: Nick Mulder, 13 December 2018.*

-----. *Interview: Romano Pagliari, 12 December 2018.*

-----. *Interview: Wayne Pidskalny, 10 January 2019.*

-----. *Interview: Jacques Pigeon, 3 October 2018.*

-----. *Interview: Bill Restall, 10 October 2018.*

-----. *Interview: Darcy Rezak, 12 November 2018.*

-----. *Interview: Graham Ross, 16 December 2018.*

-----. *Interview: Michael Senzilet, 16 October 2018.*

-----. *Interview: Steve Shaw, 25 September 2018.*

-----. *Interview: Gerry St. Germain, 20 September 2018.*

-----. *Interview: Robert Stromberg, 3 January 2019.*

-----. *Interview: Mike Tretheway, 22 Nov 18, and 28 November 2018.*

-----. *Interview: Clint Ward, 15 November 2018.*

-----. *Interview: John Watson, 14 September 2018.*

-----. *Interview: Bill Whelan, 8 January 2019.*

Lasnier, Madeleine. *Aeroport International de Montréal / Montréal International Airport (Dorval)*, Department of Transport (Québec Region), September 1968.

MacKenzie, Alistair. *A CSCE National Historic Civil Engineering Project lays the groundwork for Canada's present air transportation infrastructure.* Canadian Civil Engineer, October 2001.

Matheson, Shirlee and Bill Watts. *A Western Welcome to the World – Calgary International Airport.* Encino, CA: Cherbo Publishing Group, Inc., 1997.

Matheson, Shirlee. *Interview: Garth Atkinson, 2 August 2016.*

-----. *Interview: Don Brownie, 21 March 2016.*

-----. *Interview: Ernie Caron, 4 August 2015.*

-----. *Interview: David Dover, 8 June 2015.*

-----. *Interview: Myrna Dubé, 29 February 2016.*

-----. *Interview: Roger Jarvis, 31 August 2015.*

-----. *Interview: Janet Kuzak, 18 November 2015.*

-----. *Interview: Eddie Laborde, 27 July 1995.*

-----. *Interview: Jack Leslie, 5 September 1995.*

-----. *Interview: Ken Lett, 16 December 2016.*

-----. *Interview: Dr. Michael Maher, PhD, 2 November 2015.*

-----. *Interview: Wayne McAllister, 7 January 2019.*

-----. *Interview: Gordon Pearce, 6 August 2015.*

-----. *Interview: Peter Wallis, 4 May 2016.*

-----. *Interview: Tom Walsh, 29 July 2015.*

-----. *Interview: Bob Welin, 2 July 2015.*

McGrath, T.M. *History of Canadian Airports.* Ottawa: Transport Canada, April 1984.

W.G. Morrison, *Dual-market airport operations and airport rent in Canada.* Laurier Centre for Economic Research and Policy Analysis, Wilfrid Laurier University, 2008.

NAV CANADA. Total aircraft movements by class of operation, 2017.

One Size Doesn't Fit All. Ottawa: Senate of Canada, April, 2013.

Overseeing the National Airports System. Ottawa: Auditor General of Canada, Chapter 2, February 2005.

Oversight of Civil Aviation. Ottawa: Auditor General of Canada, Chapter 5, Spring 2012.

Padova, Allison. *Airport Rent: Facts & Figures.* Ottawa: Parliamentary Information and Research Service, 23 July 2004.

-----. *Airport Governance Reform in Canada and Abroad.* Ottawa: Library of Parliament, PRB 07-12E, 5 September 2007.

Pearson Airport - Who's the pilot? Toronto: Globe & Mail, 16 January 2014.

Report of the Commission of Inquiry as to the Future of the Air Canada Overhaul Base at Winnipeg International Airport. Ottawa: Queen's Printer, March 3, 1966.

Report of the Standing Committee on Public Accounts on Chapter 10 of the October 2000 Report of the Auditor General of Canada (Airport Transfers: National Airports System). Ottawa: House of Commons, 21st Report, 37th Parliament, 1st Session, 2002.

Rideau Consultants Inc. *Fire Fighting Risk Management at the St. John's International Airport*, November 2014.

-----. *Risk Management Matrix*, St. John's International Airport Authority, 2007, 2014, 2019.

-----. *Performance Reviews of the Charlottetown Airport Authority*, 2004, 2009.

-----. *Performance Review of the Edmonton Regional Airports Authority*, 2017.

-----. *Performance Reviews of the Fredericton International Airport Authority*, 2006, 2011, 2016

-----. *Performance Reviews of the Gander International Airport Authority*, 2011, 2016.

-----. *Performance Reviews of the Greater London International Airport Authority*, 2003, 2008, 2013, 2018.

-----. *Performance Reviews of the Greater Moncton International Airport Authority*, 2003, 2013, 2018.

-----. *Performance Review of the Ottawa International Airport Authority*, 2017.

-----. *Performance Reviews of the Prince George International Airport Authority*, 2008, 2013, 2018.

-----. *Performance Reviews of the Regina International Airport Authority*, 2004, 2009, 2014, 2019.

-----. *Performance Reviews of the Saint John International Airport Authority*, 2004, 2009.

-----. *Performance Reviews of the Saskatoon International Airport Authority*, 2004, 2009, 2014, 2019.

-----. *Performance Reviews of the St. John's International Airport Authority*, 2003, 2008, 2013, 2018.

-----. *Performance Review of the Vancouver International Airport Authority*, 2013.

-----. *Performance Reviews of the Victoria International Airport Authority*, 2002, 2007, 2012, 2017.

-----. *Performance Review of the Winnipeg International Airport Authority*, 2016.

Sedgwick, J. Kent. *WW2 Aviation in Prince George*. College of New Caledonia Oral history Series, 2008.

LAA Lease Review Consultation Report. Ottawa: Transport Canada, 14 April 1999.

Pathways: Connecting Canada's Transportation System to the World. Ottawa: Transport Canada, 2015.

Public Accountability Principles for Canadian Airport Authorities. Ottawa: Transport Canada, 1995.

Transportation in Canada 2016. Ottawa: Transport Canada, TP No. 15357 E, 2017.

Transportation Research Board, *Considering and Evaluating Airport Privatization*, Airport Cooperative Research Program, Report 66, Washington, D.C., 2012.

Vision and Balance. Ottawa: Transport Canada, Report of the Canada Transportation Act Review Panel, June 2001.

Turner, T.R. *A Private Sector View of Airport Authorities*. Ottawa: Canadian Transportation Act Review Panel, 5 March 200

Index

444

450

453